Liberation Philosophy
From the Buddha to Omar Khayyam

Human Evolution from Myth-Making to Rational Thinking

Mostafa Vaziri
University of Innsbruck, Austria

Series in Philosophy

Copyright © 2019 Vernon Press, an imprint of Vernon Art and Science Inc, on behalf of the author.

All rights reserved. No part of this publication may be reproduced, stored in a retrieval system, or transmitted in any form or by any means, electronic, mechanical, photocopying, recording, or otherwise, without the prior permission of Vernon Art and Science Inc.

www.vernonpress.com

In the Americas:
Vernon Press
1000 N West Street,
Suite 1200, Wilmington,
Delaware 19801
United States

In the rest of the world:
Vernon Press
C/Sancti Espiritu 17,
Malaga, 29006
Spain

Series in Philosophy

Library of Congress Control Number: 2019936322

ISBN: 978-1-62273-719-2

Also available:

Hardback: 978-1-62273-531-0

Cover design by Vernon Press. Cover image by Sundar Basnet.

Product and company names mentioned in this work are the trademarks of their respective owners. While every care has been taken in preparing this work, neither the authors nor Vernon Art and Science Inc. may be held responsible for any loss or damage caused or alleged to be caused directly or indirectly by the information contained in it.

Every effort has been made to trace all copyright holders, but if any have been inadvertently overlooked the publisher will be pleased to include any necessary credits in any subsequent reprint or edition.

To the Nobel Laureate of 1901 Wilhelm Conrad Röntgen (1845–1923), a remarkably selfless and unassuming man whose discovery and invention of X-ray changed the course of health by saving a countless number of lives.

This modest book is written in his honor and remembrance.

Table of Contents

	Acknowledgements	*vii*
	Author's Remarks	*ix*
	Prologue	*xv*
	Part I. Biology: Panic	*1*
	Prelude - Human: Not a Fallen Angel	*3*
Chapter 1	A Tumultuous Human Evolution: The Leap and Lapse of the Mind	7
Chapter 2	The Cognitive and Biological Foundations of Religion: Terror Management	25
Chapter 3	The Instinctual Modules of Religion: Fear, Obedience, and Imitation	49
	Part II. Mythology: Taking Refuge	*65*
Chapter 4	Truth-Seeking and Myth-Making: Humans in Search of Reality	67
	Part III. Philosophy: Clarity	*101*
Chapter 5	The Indo-Greco-Roman Philosophies of Self-Rule: Nastikā Schools (Cārvāka, Ajīvikism, Jainism, Buddhism), Epicureanism, and Pyrrhonism	103
Chapter 6	Buddha's Self-Rule Philosophy: A Model for Ten "Mini-Nirvanas"	139
Chapter 7	Omar Khayyam's Model of Liberation: Construction, Pleasure and Nothingness	215
	Epilogue - Enlightenment Revisited: The Second Enlightenment	*257*

Bibliography 281

Index 299

Acknowledgements

Without my partner, Allison, whose inexhaustible focus on this manuscript cannot be measured, I don't truly know how I could have accomplished what I did. She remained ever-present to support me, and our conversations about the content of the book proved to be a leap in our own intellectual growth.

It is my pleasant duty to thank my friend and erudite colleague, Reinhard Margreiter. The ongoing dialogues I enjoyed with this unique professor, altruist, and genuine practicing philosopher was like having 'Epicurus' showing up in my life as a mentor. He read the entire manuscript, made wise suggestions, and constantly referred me to more sources. I am, as always, indebted to Michael Morony of UCLA, a highly critical thinker and a well-accomplished scholar, who despite his busy schedule read the final version of the manuscript. I am humbled by his supportive words.

I am grateful to other professionals who took the time to read and comment on parts of the book along the way: A brilliant colleague and prolific scholar, Marie-Luisa Frick, read multiple chapters of the book and provided constructive feedback. The chapter of the Buddha, as well as chapters 5 and 7, were read and critiqued by Stephen Batchelor, a world-renowned scholar of Buddhism. In his constructive critique, both compliments and criticism were equally uplifting. Mehdi Aminrazavi, a scholar of religion and philosophy and author of one of the best existing books on Omar Khayyam, read the chapter on Khayyam. His endorsement and helpful comments are highly appreciated.

My old-time friend in India, Raj, a reader and teacher of Sanskrit and Tibetan Buddhism, was gracious enough to read the entire Philosophy section. He sent me his handwritten pages of notes, offering additional insights regarding several key themes about the Buddha and the Cārvākas. It is a pleasure to thank another friend with a talented mind, Farhad Rostami, whose education and interests range from mechanical engineering to neuroscience. He read multiple chapters of the book and provided me his enthusiastic encouragement. My long-time and insightful friend, Shahrzad Esfarjani deserves lasting thanks for her engagement with and support of this research project. This brings me to mention my childhood friend, Oscar Feizi. Our dialogues involving conversations about the topics of this and other books have borne fruits difficult to describe in words. Last but not least, Uta Maley, an incredible friend in Innsbruck, has been nothing but an engine of energy and support for my research.

The free-lance editor, Ms. Margaret Puskar-Pasewics, is to be thanked for her editing of the first draft of the manuscript. The Acquisition editor of Vernon Press, Dr. Carolina Sanchez and Argiris Legatos, deserve gratitude for their enthusiasm and diligent guidance for bringing this project to light.

I am grateful to all the individuals mentioned here, as well as those who offered kind words and moral support but whose names are too numerous to mention here.

Author's Remarks

Among the many scientific milestones that have guided the evolution of human society, two of them stand tall and magnificent. The first came in 1953 when James Watson and Francis Crick discovered the molecular structure of double helix DNA, a revelation that changed the course of biological, medical and pharmacological research and the exploration of life. The discoveries revealed how genetic information is stored, how biological life is stabilized, and how genes mutate. This led to the mapping of the human genome some fifty years later, confirming the exact content of human genes, establishing which part of our DNA is responsible for what. Eventually, DNA research also led to the discovery of the genetic tree, elucidating the interrelationship of species and all living beings and revealing the interbreeding of modern humans with other hominids such as Neanderthal and Denisovans. Thus, DNA became a blueprint for unprecedented knowledge about the human past and our kinship with other primates. DNA also became the basis for a non-parochial and non-anthropocentric historical awareness. It overthrew the old understanding of humans as a wholly separate and divine creature in the animal kingdom. DNA was shown to be the common biological currency among *all* life, which belongs to humans as well as other beings.

The second milestone event was the orbiting of the earth in 1961 and 1962 when, for the first time as human beings escaped the bonds of gravity, Yuri Gagarin and John Glenn saw the earth from beyond. The view of the earth as a round planet floating unsupported in its orbit became yet another crucial crack in the old Christian cosmology that the earth was flat and unmoving. The public was shown how cosmic physics behaves, showing our own planet suspended in midair, an image which caused an irreversible paradigm shift. Even more radical was when the Hubble Telescope was launched in 1990, revealing to us billions and billions of stars, planets and galaxies that could not be observed with the naked eye – something unimaginable for our ancestors. This view of the Universe made Ptolemy's geocentricism seem a child-like astronomy, a remote past. It also altered the power of the argument of heliocentrism, as we had to accept viscerally that the sun and our solar system are but a miniscule sliver of the Milky Way, let alone the universe. The infinitesimal size of the earth and the inexhaustible size of the Universe render our previous and parochial myths of the earth as the center of the Universe nothing but a fragile sand castle. In the same way, a radical shift occurred in our self-absorbed and arrogant psychology when we learned about the existence of billions of distant galaxies, comets, suns and asteroids out there living for themselves. Our earth stands to be a trivial dot lost in the overwhelming juggernaut of existence.

These two paradigm shifts, from the subcellular to celestial, have compelled us to absorb such discoveries without resorting to ancestral cultural or religious beliefs. DNA and genetic discoveries challenged the mythical and religious belief that humans had appeared in the biological world as a distinct species created from the 'image of god', and instead proved that the human species is tightly connected to and is a product of biological evolution. And cosmological discoveries have taught us that our earth and humans are not the center of the universe. No matter whether mythical beliefs are interpreted literally or figuratively, it does not change the factual results of what we know today about cosmology and evolutionary biology. Thus, the facts about our life status on earth can be seen as liberating – liberating from the old myths and gossip-laden superstition. Knowing that the earth is round and that the laws of physics govern the earth and the planetary and interplanetary systems create an awareness that our earth and stars do not function just based on arbitrary magic or random acts of the gods. This orderly and universal knowledge in itself offers liberation from subjectivity and credulity.

More examples of such empirical liberation abound: For example, for centuries the old and outmoded understanding of deadly diseases such as diphtheria, tuberculosis and the stigmatizing condition of leprosy, among hundreds of other diseases, had been blamed on the devil or viewed as god's punishment (and some may still believe this in certain cultural traditions). People sacrificed animals to the gods in order to be granted mercy and cure. These depressing and hopeless conditions were eradicated by the isolation of the bacteria-causing agents of such deadly diseases. Doctors Emil von Behring, Robert Koch and Gerhard A. Hansen isolated the etiologies and developed the scientific basis for the treatment of these diseases, saving countless lives and prevented premature deaths. Such medical awareness was and still is simply an example of liberation from old parochial superstitions and beliefs.

It may be argued that liberation in the philosophical realm is not as precise as in the scientific realm and has no universal methodology. Liberation is indeed subjective, but can be universal as well, as in the case of agreeing on the principles of empirical sciences. The cognitive dissonance between the laws of nature and our subjective beliefs can drive us to sincerely seek clarity and liberation, particularly from our own failed opinions and the unsubstantiated proclamations of dogmatic sources. Liberation can find meaning when the deceptive, romantically-oriented mind is scrutinized and rewired, when the inner workings of cause and effect of our decisions and behaviors are put to the test insightfully, when the observation of the workings of nature itself becomes revelatory. The realization we often encounter is that the fetters within our closed-ended dogma and self-convincing ideas were acquired from our religious and traditional surroundings from childhood onward.

In order to live in the safety of our intelligence, everything we have believed, often at face value, and stored in our memory, needs to be reexamined and backed by sound reasoning and experiential proof. For every error, we make there is a consequence, so to speak. If we have perceived religion to be an emancipator of the human predicament, the price of the complete take-over of religion has come with it as well. In many instances, religion has become the captor rather than the liberator, preventing creative or alternative thinking. Meanwhile, those who thought to seek solace in public religion find themselves bewildered, either consciously or unconsciously antagonizing and even harassing other groups of the population who believe in other religions or may be secular or atheist thinkers. In this case, one is obliged to recognize what is harmful as well as what is beneficial in one's ongoing beliefs. It is analogous to medicine, in which we know very well the harm that is combined with the benefits of the medical enterprise. Many medicines can cause harmful side effects even though prescribed by caring doctors, inadvertently causing new problems for the patient. A hospital itself often becomes the source of new infections - the very place where vulnerable and desperate patients have gone to take refuge from illness. Thus, there are errors and failures even in the good things we believe to be helpful.

The philosophers of reason put forward compelling arguments in order to emancipate the human mind from the abyss of unknowing or misknowing. It was the psychiatrist-philosopher Karl Jasper (d. 1969) who proposed that a universally valid philosophy could even surpass science[1] in offering a glimpse of our true being, in order to debunk the indoctrinated interpretations and harmful beliefs that have entangled the human mind for thousands of years. The dangerous power of indoctrination, no matter in which culture or religion, compounded with the danger of modern racism and national-chauvinism, all have produced separation and hostilities among humans. Konrad Lorenz put it right when he said, "The thoroughly indoctrinated person does not notice that he has been deprived of a constituent feature of true humanity- the freedom to think."[2] The age of ignorance ("we didn't know"), dogmatism and imprudence can shift to an age of universal reasoning, dialogue and kindness, but only with awareness first, and by personal choice.

---

[1] See James O. Bennett, "Karl Jaspers and Scientific Philosophy," *Journal of the History of Philosophy* 31/3 (Jul., 1993), 437-453.
[2] Konrad Lorenz, *The Waning of Humaneness*, trans. Warren Kickert (Boston and Toronto: Little Brown and Co., 1987), 161.

***

In an age that dawned with space travel, we are now going back in time to meet our 'lost cousins' from the time we left Africa some 60,000 years ago. As we drifted around the globe, we developed distinct languages, skin color, religions and cultures. Despite the sharp differences that developed over the millennia of forgetfulness of our common origins, it behooves us to come closer to each other again and try to establish the common and appealing logic that we all honor. The fundamental separateness which needs to be bridged comes from the dogmatic interpretations of our common empirical reality and space. This crucial time will have to be the century of solutions, not just to find better techniques for making life more fortified and safer but also to rectify the dogmas and misunderstandings our ancestors created. Sound and universal thinking is a great "technology," so to speak, which can save us from the foolishness and superstitions of our narrow-minded ancestors. Instead of being fixated on our differences, there is a need to bridge our powerful commonalities.

Finding human liberation from conflict, hostility, and indoctrination essentially means pledging to a common and unbreachable universal logic, a universal dialogue whose content defends the wellbeing of everyone, not just one tribe or one nation. This does not necessarily mean leaving behind our traditions and customs. It is not even about education, putting more and more knowledge on top of a precarious dogmatic foundation. It is about becoming truly literate in our most vital century by learning, unlearning and relearning (to borrow the words of Alvin Toffler) the most innovative, mind-blowing and edifying findings. It is about reinventing ourselves by valuing all humanity, not just one's own group and belief system. The enlightened minds have always altered civilizations and have been able to help others. There is no end in sight when it comes to living an innovatively cogent and interesting life.

This book, with its forthright and daring premise, challenges and exposes many timeworn insidious beliefs by embarking on new levels of intercultural and rational conversations. In the course of writing this book, I realized firsthand that the content of 'liberation philosophy' is almost identical with the 'philosophy of self-reliance' or cultivation of pleasure by oneself as it was succinctly presented by the sharp thinkers and practitioners in the Indo-Greco-Roman-Iranian world. This interdisciplinary book is perhaps the first attempt to integrate the Indian, Greek and Iranian philosophical traditions, bringing them closer to each other by elucidating their common denominators. The substance of such philosophical traditions is about freedom from the captivity of superstition that developed over millennia of human development, as well as from one's own illusive certainties.

Author's Remarks

Liberation is perhaps when we take the first step to learn about the fascinating revelations of the sciences, to study philosophy, to build a stronger logic over emotions, to build a resilient body to resist hardship, to loosen the grip of the dogmas that have been preached to us from childhood, and to drop the ultimate 'truth' themes that have entangled us without having left room for cognitive fluidity and individual development. Personal transformation, philosophical therapy, and enlightenment deal with and safeguard these issues. Such rewiring of our brain, letting a new philosophy refashion our lives, is only possible if the first step is taken. The Persian poet, 'Attār (d. ca. 1220), appeases our anxieties and emboldens us to be the innovator of our own life through taking that first step, and then the path shall gradually appear by itself:

> If you are an authentic wayfarer, then prepare for a ferocious journey,
> Lose your attachments and annihilate your ego.
> Trust and take the first step,
> The chain of steps will then teach you how to tread the path.[3]

Mostafa Vaziri
Innsbruck, November 2018

---

[3] Fariddin 'Attār, *Mokhtār Nāmeh*, Section 18. Translation of the poem from the original Persian is by this author.

Prologue

The Contour of the Path Leading to Liberation Philosophy

Throughout the course of history, the intellectual campaigns of philosophers and maverick thinkers have offered fresh, inspiring, and liberating perspectives to replace religious beliefs and mindsets that had led to a misreading of reality. This book investigates that process of liberation of the mind, in addition to the biological and cognitive reasons behind the invention of myths and consuming beliefs that often trapped the trusting minds of the population. Through the lenses of biological, cognitive, and philosophical evolution, this book takes an unconventional look at that path of evolving thought, from natural freedom to mental entrapment, and back to freedom again. It asks the question: How did beings possessing a mind born with natural intelligence and freedom become beings with minds seized by mythical and superstitious thinking, thinking that would take them far from their vibrant and free original minds? And what solutions have been found over the centuries that offer liberation to the entrapped mind?

In order to trace the path of the necessity and the intervention of philosophy, it behooves us to backtrack to the time of 'pre-philosophy,' when human beings were doing what they needed to do to survive in the rawness of nature. In this book, first, we will take a look at the possible cognitive and behavioral effects of interbreeding among hominids such as Neanderthals and *Homo sapiens*. The genetic mix resulting from that evolutionary phase may have been a factor in critical cognitive changes that emerged in *Homo sapiens*. Chapter 2 then follows the continuing trajectory and consequences of that cognitive development as humans began to invent myths and create religions. Chapters 3 and 4 explore the biological roots of fear and the apparent need for truth-seeking, myth-making, and religion. In the final and pivotal part of this book, chapters 5, 6, 7 and the epilogue, some of the most powerful "liberation philosophies" are presented with their aim of offering a more natural and skillful outlook on the reality of life and how to overcome the fear and dogma laid in us from the past.

***

1. The Method and Goal of the Book

The narrative of the book engages with three major themes: the biology, mythology, and philosophy of human development. At first glance, the subject of biology does not seem to be directly correlated with philosophy. Here we have taken a detour to enter the gate of philosophy from the back door of the human past, a time of pre-philosophy, when humans were beginning to intellectually evolve, trying to construct the "facts" of reality using their new (in evolutionary terms) mental mechanisms.

a. Biology and Pre-philosophy

There was a time when philosophy never existed because it was not yet part of the human toolkit of survival. Philosophy eventually emerged out of curiosity and as a response to confusion and ancestral dogmatic errors. Needless to say, philosophy also developed as a means of exploring the deepest inspirations about life.

The relationship between philosophy and biology that we will focus on is the phase of existential chaos within the 'survivalist' or 'traumatized' brain until a time when deeper intellectual clarity gradually began to emerge. The traumatized brain comes from the havoc of the human evolutionary process, including competing with other hominids for survival but also interbreeding with them. This biological condition entailed the very slow formation of consciousness and perceptual thinking and ideas about the workings of nature. The emerging self-awareness of the brain of Homo sapiens became the source of anthropomorphized interpretations of nature.

The human brain also experienced millennia of different kinds of fear, ranging from object-based fear to non-object-based anxiety. Object-based fear was an expected reaction to natural challenges to survival such as predators and natural events like thunderstorms, earthquakes, floods, and droughts. Non-object-based fear was oriented towards the invisible force of nature like death or diseases or towards invented gods who seemed to run the world, sometimes bestowing their grace upon humans, other times unleashing their wrath. Humans operated under the influence of such object- and non-object-based fears, which led to the development of supernatural beliefs, myths, and religions as a way of soothing their fears.

Through the emergence of agriculturalist communities, certain peculiar characteristics of the human brain's tendencies became prevalent, including a religious response to fear, a sentimentalized anthropomorphizing of the world, and the development of fixed, written language that would preserve stories and information. These phenomena eventually become part of ordinary human consciousness in nearly all cultures. They resulted in the construction of our own human narratives of nature, including invented realities that we could understand. Gradually these neural pathways became the basis for fixed and conditioned religious thinking. Through the neural programming of fear, the pattern of development of cognitive habits and overpowering beliefs continued to repeat in emerging cultures. Along these lines, Epicurus was right when he pinpointed fear as being rooted in ignorance. And inversely, ignorance is rooted in fear.

The restrictive and often detrimental nature of counterintuitive and superstitious thinking eventually inspired the intervention of grounded and more didactic thinkers who challenged their own and laypeople's beliefs. The challenge was (and still is) whether learned beliefs, with their psychologically entrenched pathways in the brain, could be altered to interpret and experience the world the way it is, not the way one was conditioned or taught to understand it. Such preconditioned brain pathways are subjective and religiously-culturally adjusted.[1] These preconditioned and indoctrinated pathways are the result of the human propensity to follow, imitate and to be obedient. Fixity of habits and beliefs by and large became the rule for conformist individuals and communities, whereas plasticity and creativity seemed to be the exception – but still always possible.

Modern neuroscience and the study of neuroplasticity tells us that brain pathways are not permanently fixed at all – they can change and be rewired. There is the potential to change mental habits, whether from a lifetime or from centuries-old cultural and religious beliefs. That means the brain is prepared to change if the individual is consciously prepared to do the work of raising awareness. This is the change of consciousness by changing the brain pathways. To study and learn a new philosophy as well as unlearning the old mental habits and ancestral beliefs are all within the brain's power. Philosophers and maverick thinkers have been able to change their way of thinking, demonstrating the brain's plasticity. So even though the biology of the brain goes back to the genes, epigenetics, the fetal stage, childhood, adolescence, and the formation of many habits, behaviors, and beliefs while growing up in a group within a culture, the fixed behaviors due to human neuroplasticity can turn around at any age,[2] if not one hundred percent, then enough to change a person through thinking and deciding to act, without compromising psychological balance.

---

[1] The objective evaluation is when nature, the world, and natural laws are explored according to their laws and mechanism not the way we arbitrarily approximate them. One needs to step out of oneself in order to see things the way they are. Science investigates the parameters of the world the way they are not the way our consciousness is conditioned to understand them.

[2] Michael Merzenich, *Soft-Wired: How the New Science of Brain Plasticity Can Change Your Life*, 2nd ed. (San Francisco: Parnassus Publishing, 2013).

Negative-and-positive and irrational behaviors exist within a brain that is conditioned by its biology. Yet the neurobiologist and primatologist Robert Sapolsky in his noteworthy book *Behave: The Biology of Humans at Our Best and Worst*, also argues that though preconditioning seems final, the pressure and demand for flexibility usually takes place because of personal and societal reasoning based on self-interest and the ethical choices we constantly make. The brain and the back-and-forth behavior of "positive and negative" fits the paradigm that human can be both, or one or the other, and can shift sides. In other words, our realistic fluidity is the ability of cognition based on reason, not determinism.[3] Overcoming negative behavior through reflection and change is possible in a matter of seconds, days, or months. The counterargument for such optimism, however, demands a question: what if we do not have the biological freedom to do so?[4] In fact, the more important challenges are deeply rooted dogma, lack of awareness, and an unwillingness to change, as opposed to any biological determinism or chemical imbalances.

Perhaps the first step is to acknowledge that conditioned fear and anxiety continue to be passed down due to the nature of brain development, and beliefs and superstition continue to be passed down by means of religions and cultures. The alternative for the modern humans is to alter their conditioning and propensities through awareness, whether these forces in the brain are innate or culturally acquired. The cognitive challenge in rewiring one's own habits requires a steadfast dedication. The social challenge is to dare to withdraw from cultural or religious beliefs that restrict one's life and one's own development as a human being. It is an existential ambiguity, the conflict between the inner and the outer. Usually, the inner appeal is to maintain and perpetuate the pre-made beliefs of the dominant culture one grew up in, but the appeal can shift to a rational self with deeper clarity of the inner and outer.

A philosophical-psychological rewiring is thus only possible should the person set out to reinvent themselves, and when this happens, the previously entrapped mind may shift in order to enjoy new perspectives and to experience the evolution of oneself until the moment of death. Cultural or religious neural programming can shift through new associations, awareness of one's habits, and by analyzing and filtering incoming thoughts and words. The dogma can dissolve, and the irrational fear and anxiety may disappear. The central nervous

---

[3] See Robert Sapolsky, *Behave: The Biology of Humans at Our Best and Worst* (New York: Penguin Press, 2017).
[4] Steven Poole, "Behave by Robert Sapolsky Review – Why Do We Do What We Do?" Book Review of Robert Sapolsky, *Behave: The Biology of Humans at Our Best and Worst* in *The Guardian*, June 9, 2017.

system is designed to make new decisions and to be in control of itself every second if it chooses to do so; otherwise, the brain will simply follow the old pathways. The cultivation of pleasure instead of fear, following empirical logic instead of myth, and choosing well-being in the here and now instead of a sense of remorse and salvation after death, are actually choices that can be made by every individual. Genetic predisposition has no bearing on it. New biological-neural pathways of a healthy brain can always be created and recreated for the liberation of the old self into a broad-minded self by disowning inherited or undesired beliefs. Accordingly, part 1 of this book emphasizes the biology of religion and fear in order to better grasp how the human brain became conditioned and took refuge in self-invented myths and religions.

b. Taking Refuge in Mythology

Part 2 of the book is about the human propensity to seek truth and create myths during tumultuous periods of cultural evolution, particularly during the Neolithic period. The settlers of the earliest agriculturalist societies may have seemed to enjoy food surpluses with a permanent base not previously available to hunter-gatherer societies. But on a psychological level, it seems that hunter-gatherers did not suffer from the systematic slavery, inequality, genocide, and harsh religious hierarchies of agricultural societies. The centralized and at times quite brutal authoritarian rule, incarceration, religious persecution, and other urban anomalies were serious ordeals of the subsequent agrarian communities. The hunter-gatherers were instead agile, flexible, and free.

Thus, although through cooperation the Neolithic urban communities made marked achievements in the areas of architecture, invention of the wheel, writing, astronomy, and other impressive human ingenuities, they were at the same time subject to state-sponsored superstition that became increasingly harder to escape from. The act of mythologizing reality was systematized during the latter part of the Neolithic period when culture and writing became conduits of transferring myths to future generations. Truth-seeking was the impulse and myth-making the tool that was used to soothe, entertain and eventually lead the communities. The populations at large gradually became obedient followers of the messages and stories about created reality as social hierarchies developed and power structures emerged.

Chapter 4 discusses the basis for the human inclination to constantly seek truth, and how these "truths" took the form of myth. This led to the compilation of myths about the beginning of the world, natural disasters, the origin of human beings, life after death, and gods and heroes. The myths enjoyed the status of being "truth" and "sacred" as they evolved and be incorporated into emerging religions. Myths and religions intermingled and at times were indistinguishable, and some of the practices that emerged from them are shocking when seen with an objective eye. It was the mythical, religious mind that cultivated irrational practices and beliefs such as animal sacrifice for the gods – an irrational act of hurting an animal and also destroying a source of food. The language of the ancestral imagination was so convincing and deceptive that through this power of myths, even shedding human blood was practiced, for the sake of the gods.

Emotional fears compromised human intelligence and drowned humans in ignorance for a very long time. Reckless truth claims, hysteric fear, existential anxieties, and blind superstition ultimately triggered the rebellion of the earliest thinkers who introduced groundbreaking philosophies for life. It was about three millennia ago when for the first time, mythological and religious thinking was publicly confronted by an emerging naturalist philosophy. This critical phase was the first sign of maturity and audacity toward declaring human beings' preparedness to live in this emotionless and speechless world without resorting to irrational behaviors such as animal sacrifice. This kind of philosophy began to dethrone the mightiest indigenous gods in the early Indian, Hellenic, and Iranian worlds.

c. Philosophy and Clarity

Part 3 of the book presents several philosophical traditions, which in their own times stood up against the mind-numbing, millennia-old superstitions of their cultures. The basis of such philosophical thinking was perhaps much more straightforward than it sounded: it meant using one's nature-given logic to understand the logic of nature, rather than relying on ancestral myths and an unreliable imagination.

In bringing together several intellectual and spiritual movements, this section of the book dedicates four substantial chapters to what can be called "liberation philosophies." These chapters are about a number of schools and individual philosophers whose common goal was to emphatically combat human irrationality.

On the Indian subcontinent, the groundbreaking Nāstikā schools of philosophy, including the Cārvāka, Ājīvika, Jain, and Buddhist schools of thought, opened the gates for unprecedented public debate on the need to liberate the human mind from the fetters of religious superstitions. The Cārvākas' innovative and positivistic thinking denounced metaphysics and superstitions. They established the primacy of the body, its pleasure, and freedom. The Ājīvikas and Jains, in some ways similar to each other, promoted the importance of self-improvement through physical and mental abstinence. They also avoided religious rituals and indulgence in metaphysical beliefs.

Around the same time in the sixth century BCE, the person who would be called the Buddha also put forward stimulating arguments involving several existential levels. On an important level, as a key to understanding his nirvana, the Buddha proposed that all things inherently are empty of identity to a level that we do not even own our own self. Thus, humans are left with a transitory lifespan to enjoy the world in its suchness without indulging in greed, tension, and illusion. In order to elucidate the approach of the Buddha and to investigate the inter-Buddhist schools and sub-schools, in Chapter 6 a model of ten mini-nirvanas is presented. This anthropological approach to Buddhism encompasses multiple topics in the Buddhist philosophy of self-rule.

In the Hellenic and Roman worlds as well, from the fourth century BCE onward, liberation philosophy became a groundbreaking focus. For some centuries afterwards, this empirical philosophy was lost or buried under the weight of overwhelming cultural forces, but its rediscovery occurred during the European Renaissance. Arguably, the Renaissance, modernity, and the emergence of the Enlightenment resulted from the influence of emancipatory, forward-thinking ideas revived from Hellenic and Roman intellectuals. The trajectory of the complex sociological phenomena of the Renaissance and Enlightenment resulted from multiple intellectual streams that simultaneously pursued innovative and pioneering experimentation of all empirical ideas rather than waiting for god to take care of humanity. On the rational level, these Enlightenment thinkers followed the early seeds of thought that had been planted by atomist and skeptical thinkers such as Democritus, Epicurus, Pyrrho, and particularly the Roman poet-philosopher Lucretius. Many of these Greco-Roman philosophers' ideas were more consequential during and after the Renaissance as philosophers tried to step outside of old Christian beliefs. Both the Greco-Roman and Enlightenment intellectuals held that knowing the nature of things means freedom from cultural, religious, mythical and self-imposed dogmas. The purpose of knowing became liberation from ignorance, fear, and anxiety, which promoted the cultivation of pleasure in life.

In chapter 7, we see how Omar Khayyam, from the twelfth-century Persianate world, challenges us to arouse our critical faculties. By laying out the natural processes and the physics of existence in an eloquently literary and yet unrestricted language in his poems known as *Rubā'īyyāt* (quatrains), he offers us many didactic insights. The underpinning of Khayyam's revolutionary liberation philosophy was to categorically refute all human belief systems – not just the religious ones but literally all invented ones. In having done that, Khayyam is the first Persian poet to promote a non-anthropocentric understanding of the universal processes of nature, in which birth and death are determined, but joy is a choice we make. His poetical philosophy is divided and presented based on a five-spoked "wheel model," which allegorically represents existence in a constant state of motion and shifting. He reveals without any religious inhibition the unstoppable and all-encompassing natural-cosmic processes of *construction, becoming, nowness*, returning to *atoms*, and back to *nothingness*, which resembles the five spokes of a turning, churning wheel of construction and demolition. Liberation is the realization that the world is in a constant state of flux, that there is no fixed stage that is called the ultimate "truth." Khayyam masterfully depicts such natural movement in his clear and precise verses. He invites his audience to lead their precious lives in heedful joy before the juggernaut of existence swallows them back into demolition and nothingness.

Khayyam was a polymath who could be considered as the "father" of a missed renaissance in the East, not only because of his scientific achievements (non-Euclidean geometry, algebra, 1,000-year solar calendar, and astronomy) but also for his poeticized philosophy of nature and existential processes. Khayyam could not help but ridicule those who misread such clear-cut and observable chains of events and turned them into superstition and tautology. His ideas embraced atomism, realism, secularism, and humanism. No matter how the clergy and the religiously minded classes disparaged his empirical view of human life, like earlier liberation philosophers, Khayyam fully favored a calm, observant, and delightful life before one's chance at nowness ended.

***

As a whole, philosophical emancipation was an intellectual campaign to free the minds of those caught in their own corrosive and self-forged thinking as well as from the tyranny of thought from the religious states that had evolved over the ages. Some of these philosophers and their adherents on some level aimed for a return to natural thinking, dispossessing themselves of their own belongings and rejecting wealth. Instead, preaching free thinking, egalitarianism and simplicity of life, and advocating genuine happiness became their highest ideals. The naked or semi-naked wandering cultures of the Indian, Greek, and Iranian-Central Asian ascetics and philosophers were testimonies to how an austere life without property was linked with seeking to live freely, equally, and unflustered by existential anxiety. Their social opposition was an elaborate intellectual disputation against the overriding cognitive dissonance of living in a physical reality that is by nature rational and empirical while imagining and believing in things that have no real existence. Eradicating this anomaly in indoctrinated societies was, in their view, not a matter of differences of opinions between the philosophers and the priests; it became a fundamental and ferocious debate between the didactically inclined, those who sought to use their own logical mind for a natural living, and the non-didactically inclined populations, those who depended on the interpretations of others and on superstition and religion. Throughout this debate, the followers of such philosophies hoped to return the human mind closer to the natural processes and natural living of its original state.

2. Why Are These Old Philosophies Relevant Today?

It is certain that as much as human rational reasoning has come a long way since the Bronze Age, many today still subscribe to various forms of Bronze or Iron Age beliefs, finding psychological comfort in them. This psychologically dichotomous stance in our modern times has wrapped populations in the East and West in ambivalence, as we wonder about our species' penchant for subjectivity, and whether the rational language of philosophy has any meaning or even makes any sense.

Many ancestral or religious beliefs seem innocuous in theory, even though they are rooted in empirically ill-equipped ancestors who made irrational truth claims. It can be argued that a belief, even though irrational, helps the mind to maintain its continuity and therefore stability. But the issue is that the power of such irrational beliefs has stripped people of their own power of thought and self-direction, and the power of the institutions that enforce these beliefs have also often served to limit human creativity and autonomy.

In light of this, the methodology in this book is intended to challenge our imprudent dogmas as well as struggles and failings in the past, and grasp why liberation philosophers steadfastly opposed the traditional and often blindly revered gods, prophets, and avatars of their time. In light of this, the purpose of re-examining the arguments of the rebellious thinkers and philosophers is to determine whether their perspectives still resonate with our cognitive faculties and if they still offer a path out of the irrationality of the past.

Theodor Adorno supported the return of authentic philosophy, a philosophy whose time can never be riper than the present. He said, "Philosophy which once seemed outmoded is now alive because the moment of its realization has been missed."[5] The ingredients of these past and yet vibrant philosophies were enjoyed only by small minorities during their time, and in using the words of Adorno, were missed out on by the greater populations throughout the ages. Why missed out? Mass illiteracy, compounded by the oppressive monarchical-clerical tyranny and the restrictions and controls imposed by the greater powers,

---

[5] Theodor W. Adorno, *The Jargon of Authenticity* (*Jargon der Eigentlichkeit: Zur deutschen Ideologie*), trans. Knut Tarnowski and Federic Will (Evanston, IL: Northwestern University Press, 1973), vii.

resulted in limited awareness of such teachings. The relevance of these mind-shattering discourses in their transcultural context belongs to our age now, because they identify the common logic in our collective lives.

These philosophies from the past are archetypal and can be reconstituted, as the Epicurean philosophy was during the Enlightenment, based on the necessity of time and place – they are not to be upheld as beliefs. The power of these teachings is in their corrective approach towards Bronze and Iron Age truth claims as well as stagnant belief systems. The discourse of liberation philosophy, at least in this book, is intended to revitalize a cross-cultural, common philosophical language. It also aims to integrate a practical, prudently hedonistic, and rational way of thinking – an intellectual self-rule without being subject to an abject manipulation by our historically most dominant and even persuasive "alpha male" figures.

And finally, the connections between the topics in this narrative, from evolutionary biology to mythology and religion to philosophy and anthropology, may seem an arbitrary fusion. But in fact, these components of our human evolution are completely interwoven in reality, creating the fabric of our cognitive and social existence, and it is their separation that is arbitrary. The reunification of these topics creates an intellectual and interdisciplinary discourse for this generation, a time of bringing the wisdom of the past into the present while letting the mistakes of the past slowly fade away.

Part I.
Biology: Panic

Prelude -
Human: Not a Fallen Angel

The physical complexity of human evolution has been the subject of much research and investigation. The story of evolution was pieced together first through evidence from the fossil records, and ultimately has been furthered by genetic breakthroughs in DNA analysis. Even the fact that much of our body is constituted of primarily oxygen, carbon, hydrogen, nitrogen and other fine elements demonstrates how the stuff of our body, nature and cosmos are directly correlated. Such research faced metaphysical and religious difficulties, as it countered the old belief that humans were specially made by god, or were "fallen angels" from heaven, so to speak. But the narrative of science points to the fact that we are a high primate with great learning abilities, an "unfinished" product of nature. Through unremitting changes in our genes and environment, we evolved to become who we are today and will continue to evolve since change is the basis of evolution.

Besides physical evolution, we can also look at clues about the evolution of the human brain, and how cognition and thought patterns developed over eons. The changes ultimately resulted in the industrious ingenuities of humans all the way to the mind that conceived stories, myths, and religions. Factors such as genetic mixing through interbreeding with Neanderthals and Denisovans and potentially with other hominids may have been part of what led to the great diversity in the types of physical and mental characteristics of humans that we see today. Next to the macroevolution, the micro- or localized-evolution, as well as the role of culture particularly during the Neolithic period all, played roles in the rewiring of the brain for new tasks and activities. The diversity of human cognition is certainly a puzzle of evolution that may be linked to the distant past. Using other animals for comparison, one may say that certainly all dogs have different personalities, for example. Higher order primates show even more evidence of having diverse patterns of cognition. But despite their diversity, such animals show much more cognitive harmony than does the human species. It would be hard to refute that despite having one common human genome, human minds are incredibly complex and diverse.

Where did this complexity come from? How is it that the human mind and behavior can be both terribly violent and inspirationally altruistic? Or, both rational and irrationally dogmatic? We see such a range of dualistic behavior among humans: intuitive vs. counterintuitive, introvert vs. extrovert, rational vs. irrational, didactic vs. spiritual, and so on. In the following chapter, we will explore whether or not interbreeding, gene fusion, and biochemistry are contributing factors for the incredibly wide gaps in human cognitive function and ability. The range and magnitude of cognitive and behavioral differences could potentially have their basis in the remote genetic history of the species. Such cognitive diversity has led some humans to manage their existential fear-anxiety through mythical thinking, while other humans tapped into a mind that was more rational.

In other words, what brought us to the mind we have today? How much has the human mind *really* evolved? What prompted certain humans to invent religion and mythology, something non-recognizable in nature, a purely human construction? And why did so many humans believe such myths while there were those who did not?

Certainly, this distinction is not always definitive, because the attraction toward one set of ideas or another can depend on cultural factors, childhood upbringing, the wiring of the brain in a given culture, mental plasticity, as well as social choices. So, it is not a sociologically linear question. People are always prone to change based on external influences coupled with their internal tendencies and personal interest. The nature-nurture debate remains both in the realm of biology and sociology. The question of how human cognition has evolved to take us to the level of myth and belief and how our minds have evolved beyond such things remains.

In exploring these questions, we will take a general approach to human evolution that emphasizes two major points of departure. The first is the emergence of hominid bipedality, and the rise of Homo erectus 1.5 million years ago with its new abilities, namely tool-making, harnessing fire, to 100,000 years ago when Homo sapiens[1] acquired more complex thinking.[2] The second is over the succeeding millennia, when Homo sapiens interbred with Neanderthals and Denisovans (and potentially with other hominids), since such gene assimilation may have been a factor in brain development with unprecedented innovation and diverse mental tendencies, both virtuous and vicious.

---

[1] The designation of "Homo sapiens" was given to humans first by the Swedish botanist Karl von Linné (1707–1778). "Sapiens" or "wise" is because of the ability of humans to use their mind. See Ashley Montagu, *Man: His First Million Years* (Cleveland, OH: The World Publishing Co., 1957), 20. Joseph Campbell calls Homo sapiens "secular man," see Campbell, *The Masks of God: Primitive Mythology* (London: Secker & Warburg, 1960), 28.
[2] Frederick L. Coolidge and Thomas Wynn, *The Rise of Homo sapiens: The Evolution of Modern Thinking* (West Sussex: Wiley Blackwell, 2009), 5.

In addition, there was another critical juncture roughly 10,000 to 15,000 years ago. The Neanderthals and other competing hominids had by then been long extinct and Homo sapiens remained. The very gradual transition to agriculture began. Then, given the earliest agriculturalist communities, our ancestors began raising existential and metaphysical questions that demanded explanations suitable to their understanding. This behavior gradually gave rise to religion and bonded the tribe members together through a belief system. It is curious how the propensity and persistence in the belief of gods, hidden agents, miracles, magic, mysterious good-evil forces, and belief in another reality beyond this world arose in some societies more intensely than others, since everyone— whether hunter-gatherers or sedentary agriculturalists— was living in the same physical space and governed by the same laws of nature.

Even more curious is how within the same agrarian population who presumably had to share the same beliefs there were those who most probably remained skeptical. Eventually, there was a systematic resistance against superstitious beliefs, mythologies, and religions during the Iron Age when this opposition took a more outward shape. There seemed such contrasts in the workings of the human mind. Obscurity and clarity of thought, suffering and joy, ignorance and wisdom, tolerance and intolerance, and aggression and compassion, demonstrate the dominance of one behavior over another. Could these contrasts perhaps be the result of a combination of gene fusion, natural selection, division of labor, and much deeper issues in the function of the brain? We have alas more questions than answers. But what should be explicit in the next three chapters is that the forces of *biology* have influenced the unplanned or even haphazard cognition and behavior as witnessed in the course of history, seemingly not any predestined metaphysical source. The usage of biology, on one hand, is intended to convey a genetic predisposition as to why some people have a stronger inclination toward one behavior or another, and on the other to refer to using the mind and its rewiring through repetition and obedience. Biology also refers to the biology of fear that led humans to myth-making and resorting to supernatural powers or religion in order to appease their fear.

Chapter 1

A Tumultuous Human Evolution: The Leap and Lapse of the Mind

Human Evolution: What We Know

From the modern scientific viewpoint, humans are animals that evolved in nature and cannot be differentiated from the natural processes and the zoological world. Today, almost all the scientific evidence, including fossil records, genetic studies, and biological anthropology, points to human evolution from its lower form. This is demonstrated by the intermediate fossil record of Australopithecus, half ape-half human, and a dozen of other hominid species. Various intermediate fossils have pointed to the existence of proto-humans in the process of evolution. Some sort of hybrid fossil of Australopithecus and other *Homo* species, namely Homo naledi, almost human, was recovered in South Africa in 2013.[1] The disciplines of evolutionary biology, paleontology, and genetics take human origins back to 50 million years ago when the first mammals began to evolve. Eventually, primates separated from other mammals, and the human species further separated from their ape cousins about six million years ago. Based on the unearthed fossils, out of 350 different kinds of primates, the human species then evolved into different hominid species including the earliest hominids known as Lucy (Australopithecus), Turkana (Homo erectus), and tens of other categories and classes of hominids, all of which lived during the last 1.5 million years.

Neanderthals who migrated out of Africa a half million years ago shared a common ancestry with Homo sapiens. Our own species, Homo sapiens, whose fossil records go back roughly 100,00 to 250,000 years ago, migrated out of Africa between 80,000 to 60,000 years ago. Despite the challenges of emigration out of Africa, modern humans managed to survive and reproduce. Interestingly, Homo sapiens and Neanderthals met "again" in the Near East through Central Asia and the European continent and interbred roughly 25,000 to 40,000 years ago. Over time, the Neanderthals along with other hominid species seem to have disappeared while Homo sapiens survived as the only contender for control of the territories. Genetic studies reveal,

---

[1] See Jamie Shreeve, "Mystery Man," *National Geographic*, Oct. 2015, 30–57.

however, that Homo sapiens is the gene carrier of not only the mammalian past, the high primates, but the gene carrier of the extinct hominids such as the Neanderthal and Denisovan among others. Thus, even more reason to view humans as a by-product of evolutionary nature rather than being predestined by god or separated from the zoological world.

Bipedality Before Thinking

Based on the fossil evidence thus far, walking on two legs (bipedal) dates as far back as three million years ago. Physical changes such as an "S" shaped spine that supported the weight of the body, along with the altered shape of the pelvis and feet indicate a significant evolutionary alteration in hominid anatomy. The shift to bipedality may have occurred for different reasons, such as a drastic change of environment from forest to grassland, a volcanic cause of deforestation, or even flooding. The environmental change may have been the reason to keep straight and become bipedal by holding the heads outside of flood water. This provided free hands to carry tools even though the bipedality did not prevent four limbs from being used in walking or climbing.[2] Thus human colonization of the earth and the rise of civilizations were made possible by walking legs and grabbing hands.

The species could now migrate long distances on two strong and well-adapted feet. Bipedality and migration to distant lands also brought the species face to face with other hominid primates who had also migrated out of Africa, which became another source for further modifications. Bipedality was just the beginning of a new journey for future humans in having the means to explore and share other geographical regions often occupied by other groups and species.

Human bipedality also altered the character of human evolution due to the power of mobility and freeing up the hands for their work of tool-making and invention. Although such artisanal and cognitive skills did not cause alterations in physical DNA, the development of humans' cognitive ability to *teach others and pass on these new skills* effectively caused changes in "cultural DNA." This process of passing on what was invented would play an enormous role in the later processes of propagating myths, beliefs, and rituals.

Human primitive tribalism and territorial battles probably happened just like they did among other mammals, and primates, in particular, due to limited resources. Evolutionary capabilities emerged not as personal choices but as

---

[2] C. Owen Lovejoy, "Evolution of Human Walking," *Scientific American*, (Nov., 1988): 118-125, 118.

means of adaptation with the environment over a long evolutionary process. The adaptational capabilities included cooperative hunting techniques, adapting to life in the forest and in caves, having a gastrointestinal system suited to eat vegetables and meat, and keen eyesight and the power to kill in the world of predators. Other abilities were sharpened such as jumping, swimming, running and swinging. Thus, bipedality was not a choice but the force of natural selection as a consequence of adaptation.

***

Certainly, the theory of human evolution, as opposed to the creation theory, has been a blistering topic for the last 150 years between science-oriented and religiously-minded communities. The theory of creation is based exclusively on belief, whereas the theory of evolution is based on evidence and empirical reasoning in the biological domain. Even as a substantial theory, the exact details of human evolution and its diversity have been a matter of inferential evidence. The theory of the evolution of modern humans should be viewed in light of the two prevailing views of evolution. The first is the single origin theory, and the second is the multiregional (or microevolution) evolution theory which still awaits more evidence to be established with certainty.[3] As a whole, it can be assumed that fundamental evolution happened on the African continent with all of the earlier common ancestry. Humans began to migrate at several intervals. Each group colonized a region and gradually fashioned its own contained and localized microevolution. Microevolution and population diversity occurred in various regions of the world leading to all of the observable variability in humans' inherited characteristics.[4]

This human microevolution throughout scattered natural habitats around the world became evident in two major ways: drastic language differences and immense variations in physiognomy. Insular, clannish, and geographical isolation gave rise to variations in behavioral patterns, cultural traits, mythologies, and even certain genetic diseases. Thus, on one hand, Homo sapiens possessed genetic homogeneity and universality. On the other hand, vast differences in various populations still remain region-based in ways that are not species-related, especially over the last ten thousand years.[5]

---

[3] Marta Mirazón Lahr et al., "Towards a Theory of Modern Human Origins: Geography, Demography, and Diversity in Recent Human Evolution," *Year Book of Physical Anthropology* 41 (1998): 137–176, 138.
[4] Ibid., 137–176.
[5] Ibid., 169–170.

Interbreeding Between Humans and Other Hominids

The source of human differences will have to be assessed against several dynamics and influences. These include interbreeding with older hominid species, natural selection, mutations, genetic drift, and biological innovation of the newer populations.[6] The presence of Neanderthal and Denisovan genes in humans is probably one basis of influence, while other dynamics still remain for science to explore in order to understand cognitive differences and trends among human beings over the millennia.

Homo Neanderthalensis is a species of hominid that shared a common ancestor with Homo sapiens. Based on genetic evidence, Homo sapiens and Neanderthal shared a common ancestor some 600,000 to 800,000 years ago in Africa.[7] This commonality is confirmed through mitochondrial DNA, showing that the proto-Homo sapiens and Neanderthals stemmed from a common stock.[8] It is approximated that about a half million years ago these hominids went separate ways. As the fossil records show, Neanderthals migrated out of Africa and wandered into the Near East and the European continent. In contrast, the Homo sapiens branch remained in Africa for a much longer period of time.

The first Neanderthal fossils were found in 1856 in the Neander Valley in Germany, seven kilometers from Düsseldorf.[9] Evidence of the spread of Neanderthal out of Africa has since been found in the Near East, as far as Siberia, and in Central Asia[10] and Europe.[11]

These Neanderthal fossils give us an image of a well-adapted species that left Africa and settled in a different range of habitats. Their fate would change between 40,000 to 60,000 years ago with the arrival of a new species Homo sapiens who wandered out of Africa and into Asia and Europe and began

---

[6] Ibid., 170–171.

[7] David Reich et al., "Genetic History of an Archaic Hominin Group from Denisova Cave in Siberia," *Nature* 468 (23/30 Dec. 2010), 1053.

[8] Svante Pääbo, *Neanderthal Man: In Search of Lost Genomes* (New York: Basic Books, 2014), 185.

[9] Professors Johann Carl Fuhlrott and Hermann Schaaffhausen were the first to identify the bones of a newly discovered human species, which was given the name of the location where it was found, "Neanderthal" (*Tal* means "valley" in German – Neander Valley).

[10] Johannes Krause et al., "Neanderthal in Central Asia and Siberia," *Nature* 449 (Oct. 18, 2007), 902–904.

[11] The fossils of an earlier Homo sapiens, Cro-Magnon 5 feet 11 inches with brain capacity of 1,660 cc (somewhat larger than modern humans) was discovered in southern France in 1868 and 1872. See Montagu, *Man: His First Million Years*, 72–73.

encountering the Neanderthals.¹² Their close common ancestry must have resulted in a similar reproductive system which made possible the interbreeding between Neanderthal and Homo sapiens. In the 1990s, a 24,500-year-old skeleton of a child was unearthed in Portugal that morphologically demonstrated a potentially plausible interbreeding between the two hominid species as well as ongoing hybridization for thousands of years.¹³ Other discoveries of fossil evidence of interbreeding followed.¹⁴

Apart from paleontological studies and fossil evidence, genetics also provide further and more precise interbreeding evidence. The Max Planck Institute for Evolutionary Anthropology in Leipzig over the last several decades has pursued genetic research in order to find genetic proof to confirm this speculation of Homo sapiens-Neanderthal interbreeding. Finally, through the arduous work of Svante Pääbo and his team at the institute, it was finally established that modern humans outside of Africa are carriers of almost 1 to 2 (could vary to 4) percent of Neanderthal genes.¹⁵ Interestingly, it is known (and can be seen through popular modern DNA tests) that many humans *today* still carry the Neanderthal genes.¹⁶ This revolutionary fact again reveals to us that Homo sapiens are not a pure species. It also means Neanderthal genes have not died out and are still present in people today, having been passed on to Homo sapiens by means of mating.¹⁷ In other words, the Neanderthal species (perhaps among other hominid species) may not be considered "completely" an extinct species but has a genetic presence in

---

[12] Ian Tattersall and Jeffrey H. Schwartz, "Hominids and Hybrids: The Place of Neanderthals in Human Evolution," *Proceedings of the National Academy of Sciences, USA* 96 (June 1999): 7117–7119; see also Jill Rubalcaba and Peter Robertshaw, *Every Bone Tells a Story* (Watertown, MA: Charlesbridge, 2010), 72–73.

[13] Tattersall and Schwartz, "Hominids and Hybrids," 7117-19; see also Jill Rubalcaba and Peter Robertshaw, *Every Bone Tells a Story*, (Watertown, MA: Charlesbridge, 2010), 72-3.

[14] The discovery of a rare 55,000-year-old skull in Manot Cave of Galilee in Israel in 2008 suggests another hybrid of Neanderthal and Homo sapiens. The Cave was occupied by Neanderthals between 65,000 to 50,000 years ago. The location of this cave was a typical point lying between Africa and Europe where the interactions and mating between Homo sapiens and the Neanderthals could have taken place. See John Noble Wilford, "Skull Fossil Offers New Clues on Human Journey From Africa," *New York Times: Science*, Jan. 28, 2015.

[15] Pääbo, *Neanderthal Man*, 176, 194. See also Reich et al., "Genetic History of an Archaic Hominin Group from Denisova Cave in Siberia," 1056.

[16] See Pääbo, *Neanderthal Man*.

[17] Ibid., 188.

modern humans. The Neanderthal species was human, but merely a different version of the human species.[18]

The mating with the Neanderthals would have occurred between 40,000 to 60,000 years ago, which would not be without some biological and cognitive consequences. These consequences are yet to be assessed and researched, but some similarities between the Neanderthals and Homo sapiens have been discovered already. For example, Neanderthals were physically similar to modern humans who shared (or interborrowed) certain cultural practices and behaviors.[19] Certain parallels are burial rituals, making jewelry, and caring for the injured or the sick. There is evidence that since the Upper Paleolithic Era about 35,000 years ago, humans have observed the existence of certain religious burial ceremonies, ritual objects, and ancestor worship.[20] This may have been either a cross-influence or passed from the Neanderthals to modern humans. It seems that the Neanderthals made pigments to paint their faces and bodies, used feathers of certain birds for ceremonial purposes, developed local cuisines, and even used toothpicks.[21] The Neanderthals also produced tar for glue to attach handles to tools and weapons some 200,000 years ago.[22] On the language ability, the gene analysis suggests the same potential ability in the late Neanderthal.[23] This fact is important as far as Neanderthals were our older and immediate evolutionary cousin who through interbreeding passed on some of their already advanced genes to us, not vice versa. Even their adaptive immune system against certain viruses or diseases – Human Leukocyte Antigen or HLA complex is believed to be passed down to us.[24]

Thus, it can be acknowledged that Neanderthals were people too. Earlier paleontology may have gotten them wrong by pejoratively describing their

---

[18] Tattersall and Schwartz, "Hominids and Hybrids," 7117.
[19] Mirazón Lahr et al., "Towards a Theory of Modern Human Origin," 151.
[20] Matt Rossano, "The African Interregnum: The 'Where,' 'When,' and 'Why' of the Evolution of Religion," in E. Voland and W. Schiefenhövel (eds.), *The Biological Evolution of Religious Mind and Behavior* (Berlin, Heidelberg: Springer Verlag, 2009), 131–133.
[21] Jon Mooallem, "Neanderthals Were People, Too," *The New York Times Magazine*, Jan. 11, 2017.
[22] Nicholas St. Fleur, "Starting Fires to Unearth How Neanderthals Made Glue," *New York Times:* Science, Sept. 7, 2017, reporting from the journal *Scientific Report.*
[23] Johannes Krause et al., "The Derived FOXP2 Variant of Modern Humans Was Shared with Neanderthals," *Current Biology* 17 (Nov. 6, 2007): 1908–1912.
[24] Based on the findings of an international research group in Bonn University, Germany. See, https://www.uni-bonn.de/Press-releases/research-team-discovers-201cimmune-gene201d-in-neanderthals.

intelligence as low and depicting their appearance as "cavemen."[25] In fact, the Neanderthals developed large brains before Homo sapiens. There is the possibility that the transmission of some positive aspects of their cognitive qualities to modern humans may explain a progressive cognitive leap in Homo sapiens. For example, the emergence of Homo sapiens as modern humans with more advanced thinking and tool-making skills coincidentally took shape soon after the disappearance of the last Neanderthals during the last 25,000 years. This intellectual correlation is certainly a hypothesis, but perhaps a plausible one.

The genetic mixture that resulted from interbreeding may have contributed to qualities such as creativity and other higher-level cognitive functions, but on the other hand, could have caused certain changes in physiological and physical conditions. These changes include a propensity toward diabetes, high altitude intolerance, skeletal deformities, immune system disorder, and wisdom teeth in smaller jaws. Research suggests another hazardous genetic transfer from Neanderthal to modern humans: decreased fertility in males.[26]

Even a *lack* of Neanderthal genes gives clues to the effects of interbreeding: Modern Africans do not have Neanderthal genes since the Neanderthals migrated out of Africa over half million years ago. Recent studies have shown that these modern Africans without Neanderthal genes have a more effective immune system and response to infection. This immune advantage for Africans meant a stronger defense against acute infections. However, the downside for Africans without Neanderthal genes has been the increase of autoimmune diseases, such as lupus.[27] Thus it seems that the interbreeding of the ancient Homo sapiens of Europe with the Neanderthals resulted in Homo sapiens possessing a genetic immune response with a lesser degree of immune overreaction.

Another genetic discovery suggests an interbreeding of Homo sapiens with another archaic hominid, the Denisovans.[28] The Denisovan species, who lived

---

[25] Mooallem, "Neanderthals Were People, Too".
[26] Sriram Sankararaman et al., "The Genetic Landscape of Neanderthal Ancestry in Present-Day Humans," *Nature* 507 (March 20, 2014), 354.
[27] Sara Reardon, "Neanderthal DNA Affects Modern Ethnic Difference in Immune Response: Two Studies May Explain Why People of African Descent Respond More Strongly to Infection, and Are More Prone to Autoimmune Diseases," *Nature* (Oct. 20, 2016), first published as "Neanderthal and Infection," in *Scientific American*.
[28] Ewen Callaway, "Mystery Humans Spiced up Ancients' Sex Lives," *Nature* (Nov. 19, 2013), accessed Jan. 3, 2016. https://www.nature.com/news/mystery-humans-spiced-up-ancients-sex-lives-1.14196.

in Eurasia, shared a common ancestor with Neanderthals at some point.[29] Denisovans also carried archaic genes of earlier non-human, non-Neanderthal hominids as well as with Neanderthals who had passed on their genes to the modern humans in Eurasia.[30] The admixture of the Denisovan species near the Siberia-Chinese-Mongolia border with Asian Homo sapiens roughly 50,000 years ago reveals evidence of the genetic variance of Homo sapiens.[31] The genome contribution of Denisovan to the present-day Melanesians has been 4 to 6 percent, suggesting they may have been more widespread in Asia than previously thought.[32]

The claim of common ancestry with Denisovans is compatible with their gene flow from Neanderthals to modern humans. The variation in modern human genes and gene flow, particularly among Europeans and Asians, has to do with the diversity in the interbreeding with *at least* two archaic hominid populations, namely Neanderthal and Denisovans.[33] This common ancestry among the Denisovans, Neanderthals and modern humans means that at some point in the bottleneck of evolution, the three groups were separated and went into a genetic drift.[34] Besides all of the genetic evidence, it is fair to say logically that if all of the hominid species were able to interbreed, then their fertility mechanisms do actually come from a single lineage somewhere in the past.

Surprising genetic evidence has also surfaced which points to a mating between Neanderthal and Denisovan.[35] Genetic analysis of a 90,000-year-old bone from a female hominid revealed that her mother was a Neanderthal and her father a Denisovan, a previously unknown hybrid. Thus, with the

---

[29] See Katherine Harmon, "New DNA Analysis Shows Ancient Humans Interbred with Denisovans," *Scientific American*, Aug. 30, 2012, 1–4, accessed Jan. 3, 2016.
[30] Pääbo, *Neanderthal Man*, 242–251.
[31] Ibid., 235–250.
[32] Reich et al., "Genetic history of an Archaic Hominin Group from Denisova Cave in Siberia," 1056.
[33] Supplementary Information, "Map of Neanderthal Ancestry: Supporting Information," na. 15, 2014, 10, 90, DOI: 10.1038/Nature 12961. Inuit of Greenland and their tolerance of severe cold weather has a genetic reason: they share the same gene variant with Denisovans related to fat distribution and fat metabolism. See Steph Yin, "Cold Tolerance Among Inuit May Come from Extinct Human Relatives," *New York Times: Science*, Dec. 23, 2016.
[34] Reich et al., "Genetic History of an Archaic Hominin Group from Denisova Cave in Siberia," 1055, 1059.
[35] Carl Zimmer, "A Blended Family: Her Mother Was Neanderthal, Her Father Something Else Entirely," *New York Times: Science*, Aug. 22, 2018, the actual study was published in *Nature* magazine.

advancement of genetic studies, one can learn more about the generations of hybrids between the Neanderthal, Denisovan, Homo sapiens, as well as other human branches, and can lead us to wonder how such interbreeding may have ultimately influenced the cognitive development of Homo sapiens.

Thus, besides the physiological, genetic influences from interbreeding, there is also the question of the possible genetic influence on psychiatric conditions. As the genetic bases of certain or all disorders become fully known, it may be possible that the genetic roots of certain disorders could be traced back to the Homo sapiens branch, or the Neanderthal branch, and could point to the effects of interbreeding. The vast topic of psychiatric disorders is yet another open-ended human medical condition that requires deeper research in the distant genetic past and the genetic influences (even in the psychological realm) of interbreeding among archaic hominids – all of which may sway our studies of modern societies and their psychological tendencies. (In this connection, it is worthy to mention atavism, which is an occasional recurrence of an archaic ancestral genetic trait stored in DNA such as tails in humans, at times quite remote from the evolutionary past.)

A Neurological Leap

Apart from the physical and tangible changes in the human constitution over the years of evolution, the research also points to the development of higher functions of the brain. In order to understand how biology and evolution may have contributed to the human inclination to think, imagine, and even to construct myths and develop particular religious or philosophical predilections, it is important to look specifically at the path of development of the human brain.

From fossil records, it is clear that for a very long time, the size of the human brain has not changed. But perhaps its function has.[36] The size of the skull and brain of Homo sapiens has remained stable for the last 100,000 years, and yet at a juncture about 10,000–15,000 years ago, some important shifts occurred. The function of the brain drove psychological shifts, especially in those who settled in agricultural societies with social cooperation and new brain wiring. Greater intellectual resources began to emerge for advanced tool-making as well as music, art, abstract thinking, and much more. These

---

[36] Though different brain sizes in modern humans have been reported, it is perhaps more of an exception than the rule, or it is of a curious matter to be researched in the future. For example, the famous French writer Anatole France had a brain capacity of slightly over 1,000 cc. See Montagu, *Man: His First Million Years*, 58–59, 60, 66.

developments suggest a rather curious leap in sudden advancement.[37] Humans obviously evolved to more refined and sophisticated levels of cognitive function than other primates, and in the case of humans, it is significant to emphasize the *function* of the brain beyond an emphasis on morphology or the size of the brain. So what were some of these factors that influenced the development of human brain function?

One factor that may have had a substantial effect on human cognitive evolution, sending it in a different direction than other primates, was proposed by the anthropologist Richard Wrangham, who suggests that the power of controlled fire and consequently eating cooked food brought unprecedented benefits to human cognitive development. In his groundbreaking book *Catching Fire: How Cooking Made Us Human*, Wrangham has theorized that eating cooked food as opposed to raw food induced an enormous shift in human evolution because of new brain performance and changes in physiology and intellectual capacity.[38] Chewing raw meat and vegetables took much longer and took more energy while providing less energy than eating them cooked. After the advent of harnessing fire by Homo erectus, the Homo sapiens exploited fire for cooking. Thus, more physiological change occurred in a shorter time than in the long history of eating raw food, especially raw meat. In eating cooked food, humans chewed less, extracted immediate sugar and more calories for hungry neurons, and developed a quicker brain as the chewing jaws got smaller.[39] In the case of omnivorous humans, the energy to digest all of the uncooked food was conserved with cooking, and the cooked food provided the body and the sugar-consuming brain with a more efficient energy cycle. The evolution of the brain from Homo erectus to Homo heidelbergensis was due to improved dietary quality and cooking.[40] As a consequence of this dynamic course of events, the dramatic change in human physiology with more readily available energy for the brain enhanced the human brain, making it more and more

---

[37] V. S. Ramachandran, "Mirror Neurons and Imitation Learning as the Driving Force Behind 'the Great Leap Forward' in Human Evolution," *Edge* (2000), 1, www.edge.org/3rd_culture/ramachandran/ramachandran_p1.html.
[38] Richard Wrangham, *Catching Fire: How Cooking Made Us Human* (New York: Basic Books, 2009).
[39] See Carl Zimmer, "Unappetizing Experiment Explores Tools' Role in Humans' Bigger Brains," *New York Times: Science*, March 9, 2016.
[40] Wrangham, *Catching Fire*, 114.

efficient, with digestive organs becoming smaller over the course of evolutionary time.[41]

The connection between brain function and more readily available food energy can also be viewed against the background of the rise of agriculture in the last 10,000 years, and the availability of sugar-rich grain providing immediate calories for the brain. Genetics were playing a role at the same time: The arrival of Near Eastern farmers in Europe about 7,000 to 9,000 years ago not only brought agriculture to the continent, but it seems that also the DNA of those who arrived from the Near East affected the DNA of ancient European populations.[42] DNA analysis has shown that with the arrival of agriculture in Europe came various physical changes, all through mutation and natural selection.[43]

Thus, the effects of being able to cook food can be linked with having more energy for the brain, saving time in mastication, and increasing the efficiency of metabolism, all of which enhanced brain function and changed human destiny. For eons, the harnessing of fire by Homo erectus and its transfer to our human ancestor resulted in the discovery and savoring of cooking. Fire thus not only kept the body warm in the coldest temperatures and kept the predators away at night as Wrangham puts it, the discovery of fire also became part of human biology.[44]

But the question about the cognitive leap remains: what caused the human psychological revolution leading to innovative thinking, truth-seeking, myth-making, and other complex and debatable cognitive activities?

Social life in the Neolithic era brought with it unprecedented cooperation and craftsmanship that was passed down to later generations through the power of the human brain and the capacity of its imitating neurons. This cognitive leap points to the existence of mirror neurons, as proposed by Giacomo Rizzolatti and V. S. Ramachandran. The presence of cumulative mirror neurons in the primate world means learning occurred through imitation. In humans, their powerful mirror neurons showed readiness for

---

[41] Professor of journalism at University of California, Berkeley, Michael Pollan has written numerous interesting books on food among which is Pollan, *Cooked: A Natural History of Transformation* (New York: Penguin Press, 2013), 6–7, 56–57, 60 quoting R. Wrangham.
[42] Carl Zimmer, "DNA Deciphers Roots of Modern Europeans," *New York Times: Science*, June 10, 2015.
[43] Carl Zimmer, "Agriculture Linked to DNA Changes in Ancient Europe," *New York Times: Science*, Nov. 23, 2015.
[44] Pollan, *Cooked*, 110, quoting Wrangham.

higher cognitive function. The power of imitating others and performing repetitive actions are the work of the same set of neuronal activities – both when we see them and think of them. These neurons – known as mirror neurons according to research on human brain waves (EEG) – are seemingly responsible for a great leap forward in human evolution.[45] Such imitation seems to have had a neurological effect on two critical aspects of brain function: empathy and the sense of otherness or selflessness – in other words, seeing oneself in others and others in oneself. This development of the perception of self and relationships with the world arose through imitation and the work of mirror neurons.

The phenomenon of imitation made daily life more effortless with less critical thinking on a certain level, especially for a brain that has larger and other pressing tasks to attend to. Ramachandran encourages further enquiry into how this consequential change in human cognition happened in such a short time. The leap forward took a more concrete shape, but we are yet to confirm how much the mirror neurons were responsible for it.[46]

The theory of mirror neurons alone cannot fully explain the Neolithic cognitive leap forward in such a short time, because earlier Paleolithic populations with their artistic and tool-making skills also possessed mirror neurons. The Neolithic leap forward was a combination of using mirror neurons in agricultural societies, social cooperation, a division of labor, and grain as part of their diet, which provided a readily available sugar to be used by the brain for more precise function. In general, the agricultural revolution prompted a larger population because of the new mode of attaining food. Agriculture provided more time for some people in newly emerging, more sedentary population centers, particularly those people in new positions of power. It began to develop features of urban civilization – an unprecedented multitasking talent among human beings. The imitation of complex tasks during urban settlement made the leap forward more effective. Thus, the power of mirror neurons helped emerging civilizations to utilize these neurons as a tool of imitation and cumulatively, a "leap forward" with all of its pros and cons.

---

[45] Research was also carried out on monkeys. Giacomo Rizzolatti, Luciano Fadiga, Leonardo Fogassi, and Vittorio Gallese, "From Mirror Neurons to Imitation: Facts and Speculations," in *Imitative Mind: Development, Evolution and Brain Bases*, ed. Andrew N. Meltszoff and Wolfgang Prinz (Cambridge: Cambridge University Press, 2002), 247; see also Ramachandran, "Mirror Neurons and Imitation," 3.
[46] Ramachandran, "Mirror Neurons and Imitation," 5.

Let us turn to another important factor in the efficient functioning of the brain: the quality of a deep night's sleep. After millennia of living in the wilderness and sleeping in trees, humans probably began to sleep more deeply as they began to live in caves and build walls and roofs to protect themselves from predators. The well-protected humans, walls around them began to sleep more deeply as opposed to monkeys who constantly feared tree snakes and other night threats, noise from the wind, and potentially other competing primates.[47] It is due to poor sleep during the night that the primates such as chimps and bonobos constantly doze off during the day, just as sluggish and clumsy performance during the modern day has much to do with poor sleep.[48] Improved sleep hygiene for humans in urban settlements for the last 7,000 to 10,000 years provided another overall boost in brain function, daily performance and memory.

In sum, the agility of thinking was certainly easier for a well-rested, well-fed brain than for an exhausted, sleep-deprived, energy-deprived brain. In addition, observation and imitation of others through the work of mirror neurons probably contributed to an expanded range of human thought and awareness. Various interdisciplinary areas of research on additional potentially contributing factors such as minute shifts in physiology and body temperature, the impact of atmospheric pressure and climate change on the function of body and mind, and the role of micronutrients in slightly upgrading metabolic pathways are areas for further research that could bring us closer to deciphering the developmental stages of human cognitive evolution.

The Enigma of Cognitive Evolution: Reason and Lapse of Reason

Human evolution was driven by genetic and environmental factors, as we have seen. Evolution was based on survival in the face of competition for food, territory, mates, and avoiding predators in harsh and dangerous environments.

---

[47] According to Duke University researchers, bonobos and chimps build their sleeping platforms out of sticks and straws in order to make their sleep more comfortable. See Carl Zimmer, "Down From the Trees, Humans Finally Got a Decent Night's Sleep," *New York Times: Science*, Dec. 17, 2015.

[48] Limited research has been conducted about REM and non-REM in high primates in terms of traits and similarities. It is said that the ancestral primates slept eleven hours per day and only 1.3 hours in REM (almost 11 percent). We know that modern humans sleep less than ancestral primates and other primates, and about 22 percent of human sleep is in REM (Rapid Eye Movement), a deep and crucial phase of sleep. REM benefits the brain and improves memory. See www.researchgate.net/publication/45589599_Primate_Sleep_in_Phylogenetic_Perspective.

In other words, the survival of our early ancestors required domination over the physical challenges that they faced for millennia, just as all animal species have survived through adaptation or domination. In fact, human beings as hunter-gatherers perhaps saw not much difference between themselves and other animals; it was only in the Neolithic period that a rupture and modification in this attitude emerged.[49] Later human ancestors, in seeking superiority over nature, faced battles of domination over larger territories for hunting as well as dominion over the land through the harnessing of agriculture.

Gradually, however, as human societies began to emerge with more structure, there was a slow but steady transition to domination over each other. On one level, this meant domination over other human populations to control the labor needed to run an agricultural society. But the most dramatic evolving battle in the panorama of human evolution was the struggle for the *domination of the human mind*. Gradually, small groups of people began to exercise authority over larger groups of people, dominating how people thought by harnessing the human tendency of a survivalist herd-style of thinking. A "herd mentality" kept everyone together as a group, mentally speaking. As social power structures developed, the manipulation of this herd-like tendency resulted in a form of mental domestication very similar to the domestication of animals that accompanied the rise of agriculture.

The sedentary early city-state systems basically "domesticated" humans in their social structures and in some ways kept the hunter-gatherers out of their "civilized" systems. Subduing through domestication did not necessarily happen among hunter-gatherers since they lacked hierarchical and highly structured communities. While hunter-gatherer groups may have had group elders, they had no need to control large populations and seem to have been much more egalitarian.[50] Domestication of humans in the early agrarian societies was intended to produce "herds" who would uncritically follow common beliefs. The leap forward also brought with it anxieties, inequalities, slavery, genocide, discrimination, armies, tax-collector, empire, and cruelty, to the degree that using the word "progress" to describe civilization could be controversial.[51]

---

[49] This claim is from Jean-Denis Vigne of CNRS-Paris in a lecture, published Dec., 14, 2017 in Youtube: https://www.youtube.com/watch?v=5o1JZ5wo_Qs
[50] For a well-rounded and detailed discussion about the taboo of civilization versus the legacy of forgotten hunter-gatherers, see Scott, *Against the Grain*, especially 87–92.
[51] See John Lanchester, "The Case Against Civilization: Did Our Hunter-Gatherer Ancestors Have It Better," *The New Yorker*, Sept. 18, 2017. This article is based on the premise of Scott's *Against the Grain*.

The Paleolithic way of life of small bands of hunter-gatherers without land, without livestock, and without sociocultural bonding was slowly displaced by an agricultural, sedentary lifestyle that would not have survived in the face of nonconformity, lawlessness,[52] or independent thoughts and beliefs. Domestication of plants, animals,[53] and humans went hand in hand in order to keep the embryonic agriculturalist societies together. This human domestication was carried out through the formation of culture, common beliefs, and common codes of conduct and guidelines for conformity. In this domestication process, human behavior and the routine timetable for various activities for those who lived in the agricultural societies were codified and framed (even in the religious scriptures).[54]

We can imagine that through the process of beginning to live side by side in more crowded conditions in these emerging sedentary communities, the disparities in the psychic makeup of people would have become more apparent. Perhaps interpersonal and unavoidable frictions arose more easily and often, and these cognitive differences and variations in mental inclination hinted at future intellectual conflicts in the most urbanized communities. It also seems that the angst-ridden, fearful mindset became more common than the less fearful mind.

The foundation of mental domination was the part of domestication that came more directly from cognitive and social evolution. This process of mental domination corroborated existential fears and metaphysical

---

[52] James Gorman, "Prehistoric Massacre Hints at War Among Hunter-Gatherers," *New York Times*: Science, Jan. 20, 2016. In pre-Neolithic times, as evidenced in the tens of discovered skeletons near Lake Turkana in Kenya, reveal devastating wounds inflicted by arrows and spears on one another. The atrocious violence committed against a pregnant woman (with a fetal skeleton in her abdomen) and other defenseless victims as corroborated by the well-preserved skeletons demonstrate the mayhem of living in the wilderness.

[53] Before the domestication of other animals, humans had the longest experience with dogs during their days as hunter-gatherers. Dogs had proved useful as loyal friends, scavengers eating the left-over food, and guard animals warning against approaching danger. The human and dog bond goes back in time, perhaps between 15,000 to 30,000 years ago. See James Gorman, "The Big Search to Find Out Where Dogs Come From," *New York Times: Science*, Jan. 18, 2016. See also Marie-Pierre Horard-Herbin, Anne Tresset, and Jean-Denis Vigne, "Domestication and Uses of the Dog in Western Europe from the Paleolithic to the Iron Age," *Animal Frontiers*, 4/3 (2014): 23–31. Cats were domesticated much later during the agricultural and storing food period when barns and sheds were overrun by rodents.

[54] Scott, *Against the Grain*, 88–92.

curiosities about the world. Due to their own curiosity and supported by the impetus of domination, early "metaphysicians" and tribal leaders conceived stories that explained how earthly and celestial affairs were controlled and operated by mighty god-heroes as well as stories about creation and life and what comes after life. Of course, due to cognitive diversity, even within each tribe there were those who opposed or resisted such mythical fabrications, mental domination, and religious rituals or blood sacrifice for the hero-gods or kings, and remained in the shadow of their own communities.

The question is, why would large populations of people allow a small number of elites to dominate them, particularly through irrational stories about the supernatural? To answer this question is certainly more complex than simply assuming humans possess a herd mentality and blindly imitate. Kent Baily in his study of paleopsychology proposed that the true nature of human beings is undefined, and the perception of humans being one thing or another is elusive. The human inclination is to go back and forth – regression-progression. This primate tendency of herd-imitation became a characteristic in agriculturalist communities. Therefore, "animalness" and rational "humanness," Baily argues, have their place in social life as being rooted in both the evolutionary process and the drive of natural selection.[55] Regarding capricious human inclinations, Konrad Lorenz also believes that war, for example, is not in our nature but rather aggression is circumstantial and part of our animal instinct.[56] However, the oscillation of humans and choosing between animal-herd and thinking may be due to a survival strategy. Baily's point about our indefinable mental state may be considered valid in the general sense. Yet, the dilemma and the paradox are when those fixated in the herd behavior of the ancestral systems have difficulty understanding, respecting, and even coexisting with those who do not wish to imitate and follow the beliefs of others and would prefer to maintain their intellectual independence.

Conclusion

The complexity of human evolution and its cognitive trajectories will continue to be a great part of scientific research during this century. What is important to remember is the fact that the evolution of the human species is no longer an abstract theory – not only hominid fossil records but also the genetic analysis of humans and other apes demonstrate a common ancestry.

---

[55] Kent Baily, *Human Paleopsychology: Applications to Aggression and Pathological Processes* (Hillsdale, NJ: Lawrence Erlbaum Associates, Inc., 1987), 2–5.
[56] Lorenz, *The Waning of Humaneness*, 158.

DNA is a sort of evolutionary black box of genetic information about shared and common ancestors, information that has changed our perspective of natural history. Only mutations set us apart from other human species and high primates. This fact leads us to consider that humans evolved to be both an abrasive domineering primate with an alpha male leader, as well as a primate with a gentle, compassionate, altruistic side.

In the course of the evolutionary process, we humans have gone through many biological changes and environmental and societal adaptations. By becoming conscious of our own psychological evolution and knowing how much we have inherited and follow ancestral metaphysical ideas, myths, and beliefs in a herd-like manner, we can then reflect more deeply to resist and prevent human-human domination. The particular form of mental domination through so-called common beliefs and common identity is the most prevalent one.

The next chapter will provide some biological clues as to how counterintuitive thinking, as well as fear and mystery in the human mind, played a role in the formation of religion, thus limiting the mind from seeing clearly the fundamental laws that govern the natural world. The cognitive leap forward also brought with it a lapse.

Chapter 2

The Cognitive and Biological Foundations of Religion: Terror Management

From the time the brain of Homo sapiens became self-aware, existence has seemed challenging on multiple cognitive levels. The world's impersonal, speechless character and harsh natural events must have been the source of much anxiety for our ancestors. Confusion was entangled with the anxiety of existence.

Over time, the enigmatic world was given meaning by our earliest human ancestors. They anthropomorphized the world, explaining it using human speech that others could grasp and would then perhaps feel less anguished. Many such explanations gradually evolved to become myths and religions, stories that were told to appease fear, to satisfy the curiosity about the mysteries of life, and to provide some sort of meaningful direction for people to draw upon for living and dying.

Myth and religion and its written propagation played a role of keeping emotions, and even one's own thinking, at bay, almost like a form of defense against internal predators. Other animal species have defenses such as camouflage, long claws, clever mimicry, or sharp teeth. The human defense is the ability to make up stories against those inner demons of fear, hope and emotionality.[1]

The emotional reasons for the emergence of religion seem justifiable. But was there something else going on for our ancestors? Religion appears to be a basic need so fundamental to human existence that a biological explanation may help us to better understand the roots of mythology and religion, and today we know there is indeed a biological and cognitive component involved in the development of religious thinking. It is important to note that this chapter is not intended to take away the joy and support that many derive from religious thinking. Rather it is to explore the various causes that led to the diversion of the human mind, pulling it away from a life lived according to the natural biological

---

[1] Gregory M. Nixon, "Myth and Mind: The Origin of Human Consciousness in the Discovery of the Sacred," *Journal of Consciousness Exploration and Research*, 1/3 (2010), 24–25, 31, 38–39.

rules of physical existence and instead turning to a "hyper-mentalized" construction of reality created through the conceptualization of religion.

In earlier times, religion was given a place on a pedestal in societies and was never questioned, as it was thought to be the testimony of truth, an untouchable subject. But today, religion is being studied methodically in terms of the workings of the brain. Various empirical studies conclude that religion was an evolutionary invention, a cognitive tool for meeting psychological, emotional, social, and intellectual needs.[2] The supporting point here is that there is a biological basis for religion in which the frontal lobe, dopamine, and cognitive rewiring of the mind play their respective roles. It seems that fear and curiosity were the triggers of adaptive biology.

It is obvious, and yet important, to remember that religions are not part of the natural setting; they only exist in peoples' minds. The Cognitive Science of Religion (CSR) is a field of study that in the last two decades has tried to explain how the brain, by resorting to gods and other supernatural explanations, relieved itself of inner tension. Looking back, it may not have been completely an irrational process.[3] This theory of whether religion historically was a rational or irrational choice has been debated.[4]

CSR has been looking into how the human mind tends to locate "agents" for everything in nature and how childhood indoctrination turns the mind into a storytelling instrument. Out of repetition and conviction, conditioned minds easily claim the realness of their gods. The narrative of religion is often so engraved in the mind that it becomes difficult although not impossible to get it out of one's head. But because religions have no physical presence in nature, the whole premise of one religion can easily be overturned by the members of another group, whether through occupation of territory, the revolution of one sect against another, the replacement of the old religion by either a new one, or by choosing another set of beliefs. It has been made clear that all extinct and surviving religions, without exception, made spectacular claims without providing any hard material proof for the veracity of their religion. Perhaps due to this and other strategic factors, humans have been able to shift from one religion to another and consequently change the rewiring of their brains.

---

[2] Todd Tremlin, *Minds and Gods: The Cognitive Foundations of Religion* (New York: Oxford University Press, 2006), 197–198.
[3] Joshua C. Thurow, "Does Cognitive Science Show Belief in God to be Irrational? The Epistemic Consequences of the Cognitive Science of Religion," *International Journal for Philosophy of Religion*, 74/1 (2013), 77–98.
[4] Hans Van Eyghen, "Religious Belief is Not Natural. Why Cognitive Science of Religion Does Not Show That Religious Belief is Rational," *Studia Humana* 4/4 (2016), 34–44.

As for our archaic ancestors, answers to the many riddles of nature were unknown. In their fear and creativity, they produced metaphysical scenarios which stressed and gullible people often believed. Fear also subjugated them to the earthly and celestial authorities for mercy. In becoming obedient and faithful, it has been mostly a matter of following one's impulse of fear, emotional state, cultural imprinting and social-cognitive strategies.

The analysis that follows examines the inevitability of the rise of religion in the context of evolutionary biology, as a biological response to the general human need for mental and emotional stability. It also assesses factors in the rise of religion without assuming that such factors were absolute. It is important to bear in mind that all past cultures were finite and transitory, therefore their rationality and irrationality were relative to one another and the needs of their time. There is no absolute form of religion and culture. Thus, the non-absoluteness of past and present religions and cultures reminds us to claim things only to a certain limit and to leave the rest to the next generation who can build on others' research with more perspective.

1. The Enigma of Human Cognition and "Hidden" Agents

To understand ourselves and our religiously-minded ancestors, we need to grasp a tenet central to cognitive science: before understanding *what* we think, we must understand *how* we think. How we think owes its biological processes (brain rewiring) to the past workings of the brains of our ancestors. Over the course of biological and cultural evolution, humans have cultivated "cognitive modules." The presence of these modules in the brain is the basis for a child in any culture to be able to learn and adapt to an environment of religious beliefs and dogma – the same is true for learning a native tongue, for example. These cognitive modules, whether they are sets of imaginary-religious ideas or practical ideas that have been used as tools to counter the pressure of survival, have persisted to our time.[5]

The intricate operations of the brain, particularly in the frontal cortex, result in skills, refined thinking, and ultimately the development of the habits and beliefs of culture and religion.[6] The reason behind the cognitive modules is physiological, but how these modules can be used and adjusted may be the work of personal intention and intellectual faculties. In other words, the

---

[5] Tremlin, *Minds and Gods*, 7, 15, 57.
[6] Maria Montessori calls this "spiritual territory," and she has a drawing of a toddler-age child sitting on the floor with two antennae picking up all the "waves' around her – language, religion, culture, and much more.

growth and continuity of culture and religion have been the work of brain modules rather than the result of pure sociological causes. Sociological causes are primarily the result of how our brain has been trained to think, behave, and react. So, the implication here is that the sociological influences come later, after the cognitive modules have been established during childhood.

Due to childhood learning and the formation of cognitive modules, there is the human tendency to protect one's belief, especially when it is supported and believed by others around them. Thus, when a particular belief is in place, it is hard to discredit it because there is rarely a tendency to think one's theory is false, and in fact, contradictory evidence is often ignored.[7]

The concept of agency plays a critical role in the development of religious thinking. The term *agent* in cognitive science is used to describe a non-detectable entity in causal reality. Agents are not objects but are features such as noise, wind, ambiguous information, hidden relations, and formless phenomena that are not easily detectable by the mind but which mental interpretation links with causal reality. Queries in the cognitive science of religion are aimed at what compelled our ancestors to think of gods, ghosts, and other invisible agents. Neurocognitive science has a significant interest in understanding the inner workings of the brain and how and why it conceives of invisible agents as the basis of religion and religious thinking.

This is why it is important in this context to again consider *how* we think, not just *what* we think. From the moment of self-awareness and tool-making, humans began to think in a "tool-making" mindset: everything in the world is a "tool" and therefore must have a "maker." At that point, it certainly never occurred to them that in the natural world and in the cosmos there are processes and laws of transformation via the natural mechanisms of change or that things are not created or made by an agent at every turn. The formation of all things is, in fact, the result of processes. But from the inexperienced anthropocentric and tool-making perspective of our human ancestors, things and events could not have come into existence simply by themselves without a specific agent. From this perspective, animals, forests, the rain, thunder, earthquakes, and all aspects in the theater of existence must have had a maker and operator. The notion of *process* was unknown to them. This agent mindset continued in different forms over time and was certainly not limited just to our prehistoric ancestors. It reached fruition in the nineteenth century with the famous "watchmaker" claim of the British theologian William Paley (1743–1805), when he put forward the proposal that the intricate creation of nature,

---

[7] Frey, "Cognitive Foundations of Religiosity," 232.

adaptation, and fitness cannot happen by itself; there must be a "watchmaker"[8] behind it all. Paley's clever analogy of a watchmaker was inspired by an aboriginal who found a watch and having never seen one before, curiously asked about its function, who made it, and why. Thus, Paley's overarching thought that there must be a watchmaker/creator[9] somewhere, sometime.

Paley's "watchmaker" and similarly anthropocentric notions of a creator were referring to a god or gods who patiently designed stars, galaxies, mountains, oceans, bacteria, frogs, vultures, trees, and all of the other 250 million species on earth for a particular purpose.[10] This clever argument in regards to the theory of creation certainly continues to be claimed by religious followers who believe in an intentional design by a creator rather than a pure mechanism of *process* of change and evolution through the laws of nature that move the species forward and are irreversible.[11]

And so, although it may sound simplistic, the anthropomorphism of gods along with the idea that everything has an agent has been fundamentally based on humans' tool-making mindset. This was palatable and familiar to the inner workings of the minds of our ancestors within their cognitive environment. It was a successful strategy used by the human mind as a template to conceptualize supernatural prototypes and gods.

Ulrich Frey provides insight into the cognitive foundations of religiosity. Frey explains that it is easier for the mind to make correlations among patterns of events by the "hidden agents" operating the world, calling them "illusionary correlations."[12] In regards to such perceived agencies and plans,

---

[8] The "watchmaker" metaphor goes back to the theologian and philosopher, Samuel Clarke (1675-1729). See "Samuel Clarke," https://plato.stanford.edu/entries/clarke/. Samuel Clarke had tried to prove the existence of god by the mathematical methods, using Newtonian mathematics – "it was said that no one had doubted God's existence until he had tried to prove it." See Anthony Pagden, *The Enlightenment and Why It Still Matters* (Oxford: Oxford University Press, 2015), 105.

[9] In response to the religious concept of the "watchmaker," the evolutionary biologist Richard Dawkins was prompted to write his book, *The Blind Watchmaker: Why the Evidence of Evolution Reveals a Universe Without Design* (1987; New York: W. W. Norton and Company, 2015).

[10] Paley (a creationist) ironically inspired Charles Darwin to adopt the scientific terms "adaptation" and "fitness." See Wolfgang Achtner, "The Evolution of Evolutionary Theories of Religion," in E. Voland and W. Schiefenhövel (eds.) *The Biological Evolution of Religious Mind and Behavior* (Berlin, Heidelberg: Springer Verlag 2009), 264.

[11] See Lorenz, *The Waning of Humaneness*, 35, 53.

[12] Ulrich Frey, "Cognitive Foundations of Religiosity," in Voland and Schiefenhövel (eds.), *The Biological Evolution of Religious Mind and Behavior*, 231–232.

Frey asserts, it is a causal error to imagine such correlations, whereas in fact there are no patterns to be found other than what is knowable so far. In pre-scientific times and even in non-literate traditional communities of today, people maintain their knowledge of the world by correlating external stimuli- in the case of religion, correlating gods as the active agents- with their internal cognitive interpretation of them.

Frey provides additional insight into the cognitive foundations of religiosity. He describes three intuitive forms of traditional knowledge stemming from the beliefs that there are always actors and certain intention behind the events and movements in the familiar world. These relate to 1) the awareness and existence of living beings ("folks-biology"), 2) the motion of physical objects ("folks-physics"), and 3) the mental states of other people and their interpretation as well as the analysis of the inner worlds of others ("folks-psychology"). For example, the movement of the moon and sun, or objects falling to the ground, are believed to be possible only by the intention of an *actor;* they cannot just happen on their own.[13] In the same mindset, the earth was believed to be flat and it was certainly impossible to imagine it round and floating in space without anything to hold it up. This type of "physics" persisted for a long time due to a rigid anthropocentric interpretation of reality, combined with the need to relate everything to the visible physical reality, where things do not "float" unsupported, for example, so the earth must have something holding it up.

For our archaic ancestors to come up with the idea of external agents or invisible actors, they needed to depend on the workings of their brain in the most intelligent way they could. They used cognitive tools to conceptualize the world and its events. The cognitive science of religion has tried to identify and understand the mechanisms of the highest abstract mental tools.

One such mental tool, which is responsible for many beliefs and behavior and the designation of imaginary agencies, is called Agency Detective Device (ADD). It works in combination with another mental tool called the Theory of Mind Mechanism (ToMM).[14] In his study *Minds and Gods*, Todd Tremlin proposes a series of interesting insights on how the Theory of Mind Mechanism, the appearance of gods in human culture, and the brain, are all interrelated in the creation of religion. In order to make sense out of the movements, phenomena, and gestures of the world, humans imposed (or rather superimposed) their *own* minds on gods as invisible agents who created the world and went on to operate

---

[13] Ibid., 229–230; see also, Tremlin, *Minds and Gods*, 66–68.
[14] Tremlin, *Minds and Gods*, 76–79, 80.

it. These gods (invisible agents) were perceived to have minds, feelings, anger, and intentions resembling those that human beings possess. Thus, religion became the way that humans thought of gods.[15] It was as though knowing the minds of others (and by extension, the minds of the gods) became a means to read the underlying reasons for the existence of nature and its events. Humans made nature and natural processes, like the interactions of gasses, elements, moisture, pressure, the making and unmaking as the working of gods. The primary difference between gods and humans was only that the gods knew more than humans.[16]

Archaic ancestors were under psychological pressure and needed to see the non-visible actions of nature and the sky as the *actors* or agents of the world, and this resulted in the creation of a cognitive bias and eventually a cognitive habit. It was a yearning to anthropocentrically perceive the world in a way that would fit the everyday experience of the informal mind. Thus, the best the human ancestors could do was make the world explainable to themselves, and these explanations gradually became the basis of the evolution of religion.

Many remarkable, ferocious and dramatic things have been attributed to gods, ranging from creating a beautiful world to inflicting punishment, triggering natural disasters, giving incurable illnesses to people, and neglecting mentally ill people. In fact, god was itself seen as the source of mental illness in the "cursed" people. These religious beliefs certainly have a neurocognitive underpinning in the belief that there is always an agent behind all events of life.[17] What is interesting is that these invisible agents possess human tendencies, particularly the tendency to reward friends and punish enemies. This cognitive predisposition for conceiving intentional agents behind unexplained natural events also paved the way for more complex religious and esoteric beliefs. These agents ranged from supernatural bodies and ghosts to ancestors, fairy entities, and gods.[18] The same mindset of agency invented angels and demons too which made religion a reality in human cultures.

---

[15] Ibid., 80, 81–83, 86–87.
[16] Ibid., 99, 102, 104, 186.
[17] Martin Brüne, "On Shared Psychological Mechanisms of Religiousness and Delusional Beliefs," in Voland and Schiefenhövel, *The Biological Evolution of Religious Mind and Behavior*, 217, 218, 226. A recent report reveals that a large percentage of schizophrenic patients attributed their illness to being either a test or punishment by God.
[18] Rebekah A. Richert and Erin I. Smith, "Cognitive Foundations in the Development of a Religious Mind," in Voland and Schiefenhövel, *The Biological Evolution of Religious Mind and Behavior*, 181–182, 187, 192.

Monotheism over the last three thousand years has anthropomorphically depicted a god involved in an ongoing battle against evil. It was in the formative period of monotheism that god took a strong and harsh stance against sinners who followed the bad god (the devil) by inflicting severe punishment on them. In the ferocious battles of this god, as it is claimed in the monotheistic scriptures, god revolts against and even destroys the natural world of his own creation by sending floods, earthquakes, and volcanoes. This was signaling to humans who the mighty god is and what he is capable of doing. The nature of god, in the evolution of monotheism, remains the same. He still punishes and shall punish (at the end of time) those who are in breach of his covenants.

The commonality of cognition in perceiving gods, and the similarities among many traditions found around the world, is an indication of the commonality of the inner workings of the mind,[19] and consequently the commonality of human cognition and biology. On the broader and pyramidal level, typical human psychology and cognition determines the culture of religion, biology determines psychology, and biology itself is determined by natural selection. By this successive progression, it can be concluded that conceptions of religions and beliefs in gods emerge out of a biological impetus. The emergence of religion is because of the activities of the brain rather than theological reasons. It is rather a "pancultural phenomenon" which must have a common biological basis.[20]

Religion is thus a learned biological strategy to tackle emotional turbulence, fear, mental frailty, and other psychological vulnerabilities or emotional needs. Although the neurological links between emotions, cognition, and religious concepts have been argued in the context of neurotheology, the ideal existential state or enhanced-fitness can only be reached through the mechanism of our neurobiology.[21] The neurobiological mechanism decides the ideal options, and for our ancestors, the conception of the supernatural and religion was perhaps their best option. So, it can be said that despite religions' unrealistic claims, they were (are) the mental tools needed by some to reach their ideal state, without completely compromising their entire cognitive faculties.

The implementation of a cognitive strategy is based on past adaptation and memory. In this case, religion is taught and remembered as being useful. This cognitive modularity is called computational modularity by evolutionary psychologists, referring to recalled knowledge operating at both universal and

---

[19] Tremlin, *Minds and Gods*, 75, 87.
[20] Ibid., 128, 132, 145–146, 157–159.
[21] Ibid., 124–126.

local adaptation levels. In this way, the continuity of religion is justified cognitively, even though the computation contains irrational knowledge.[22]

This strategic behavior related to irrational knowledge is not fixed; it can be altered should the individual choose to pursue an alternative rational knowledge outside the group. A new cognitive initiative, stepping out of the old mode of ancestral-religious thinking, would require a new system of creative, non-modular planning and organizing. Thus, the strategy of adaptation on the individual level can involve combinations of familiar and new beliefs and practices, such as the use of old cultural channels along with newly conceived intellectual options. An individual may choose to pursue both the programmed modular (religious) and the new non-modular (creative thinking) systems. At times, one may even use one system to prove or discredit the other to oneself. Even though this cognitive quarrel is complex and exhausting, it is more sophisticated due to acknowledging the existence of a counterargument. The key thing in this modern quarrel is to maintain an open and dynamic intellect, rather than stagnation from not pursuing anything outside of one's monolithic dogma.[23] Given the global dialogues on religions and debates about science and religion in our era, using logic and logical justifications to prove one's religious beliefs and their imbedded cognitive habits produces greater dialogues than just resorting to plain and bare illogic.

2. Biochemical-Biocultural Factors in Religious Thinking

Some fascinating work has been done in the realm of biology that offers an intriguing biochemical perspective on how religion works in the mind. For example, it seems that intrinsically higher levels of dopamine can increase the intensity of religious experiences and induce an even stronger belief in god.

In neurotheology,[24] the strength of religious superstition and high levels of dopamine are correlated. Even the link between Obsessive Compulsive

---

[22] Peter Carruthers and Andrew Chamberlain (eds.), *Evolution and the Human Mind: Modularity, Language and Meta-cognition* (Cambridge: Cambridge University Press, 2000), Introduction, 8, 10.

[23] Ibid., see especially chapter 8 by David Papineau.

[24] Although controversial, the premises of sociobiology and neurotheology argue that the social and religious mind have a biological origin more than a sociological or theological origin. Their paradigms offer some usable arguments. See Rüdiger Vaas "Gods, Gains, and Genes on the Natural Origin of Religiosity by Means of Bio-cultural Selection," in Voland and Schiefenhövel, *The Biological Evolution of Religious Mind and Behavior*, 25–26, 28.

Disorder (OCD) and religiosity has been debated.[25] The role of high dopamine levels not only in OCD but also in schizophrenic, bipolar, and epileptic cases suggest certain imagined religious experiences in these individuals. And the reverse is also evident: Harris and McNamara's studies explain that patients with Parkinson's Disease, particularly "left-onset" cases (right hemispheric impairment) with reduced dopamine production, have less tendency to religiousness compared to their healthy-age-match control counterparts.[26] Without dopamine, the prefrontal cortex function is either diminished or becomes dysfunctional, a circumstance where social skills, planning, judgments, and even religiosity can be selectively impacted and shrunken.[27]

While we may not be able to draw a universal conclusion that people with high levels of dopamine are more religious or more superstitious than those with normal or reduced dopamine levels, it is an area worthy of attention. But this single piece of physiological information does not necessarily produce sufficient evidence for how the masses of people throughout history have espoused or instrumentalized religion for better adaptability in nature. Definitely, the combination of biological (on the level of the brain) and non-biological (namely, cultural and sociological) factors have caused religion to persist, no matter which god was put in charge each time.

This being said, Todd Tremlin states that science has been accused of stripping away the mystery, delight, and hopes that make life worth living by replacing these marvelous aspects with cold facts and calculations.[28] This is a well-taken criticism: no cold scientific facts should rip spiritual experiences apart, especially as long as people need these spiritual experiences to maintain their mental stability and health. This criticism against science, however, is true only if such spiritual experiences are personal, and do not involve public proselytizing, are not used as tools of domination, and do not distort history such as organized religion.

But the moment spirituality steps out of the personal domain involving the private relationship between a person and a deity, it becomes a public affair and therefore is subject to scrutiny, especially if the claims have a missionizing aspect to them. Thus, science takes an interest in the roots and rise of *public* religious thinking but without disturbing the multitude of

---

[25] Ibid., 30–34.
[26] Erica Harris and Patrick McNamara, "Neurologic Constraints on Evolutionary Theories of Religion," in Voland and Schiefenhövel, *The Biological Evolution of Religious Mind and Behavior*, 205, 208, 209, 212.
[27] Ibid., 208.
[28] Tremlin, *Minds and Gods*, 199.

personal emotional-spiritual experiences of individuals. People are entitled to maintain their views even though irrational as long as their rational views are integrated into the public interest in politics, society, and even with rational scientific approaches, such as modern medicine, germ theory, genetics, evolution, geology and modern physics.

The question arises as to why, if humans invented religion in order to feel security and comfort, would they create imaginary deities that they would have to fear and obey? The immediate answer could be the biological need of a "comfort level" with needing/wanting an alpha figure to obey and fear. However, not all religions have generated fearful deities, such as a large number of Native Americans, aboriginals, and Druids, whose deities were not the angry, wrathful type. Interestingly all of these groups were hunter-gatherers and not agriculturalists. Thus to answer this question, the approach will have to shift from solely a biological answer towards cultural psychology as a bedrock for the development of culture of religion and religiosity. A proposition has been made by Rüdiger Vaas that the rise of religion may follow three plausible biological and cultural hypotheses: 1. Religion is the direct product of biological evolution and is adaptive; 2. Religion is a by-product of traits that are biological in nature and are adaptive; 3. Religion is exclusively a cultural by-product.

Vaas's makes an additional proposition regarding why people believe in god, obey theologians or authorities, and believe without questioning, drawing upon three possible scenarios: 1. social imprinting from parents and groups; 2. personal experience, such as marveling at nature and reading the scriptures; 3. rational hermeneutical studies and philosophical debates. As valid as these reasons may be for individuals, Vaas says that the fact remains that even in arguing the positive utility of religion, none of these prove the existence of god or any other supernatural forces.[29] This is the central dilemma. No metaphysical claims in religion can be proven, yet massive numbers believe in them. Why? Let us briefly bring childhood and social imprinting into the discussion.

Religion Is a Childhood-Historical Encoding, Not a Delusion

Religious believers in every culture did not necessarily choose their faith freely nor have they necessarily scrutinized why they believe what they believe. Religion is given to them by their parents and their sociocultural surroundings. The bio-cognitive wiring in the brain picks up religion just like it picks up a native mother language – the religious themes take formative shape in the mind

---

[29] Vaas, "Gods, Gains, and Genes On the Natural Origin of Religiosity," 37, 39, 40–42.

and in the social attitude. In fact, children themselves seem to show a certain developmental predisposition to absorb the theistic faith of their parents.

The beginning of religious cognitive behavior starts from childhood. In general, children from an early age are cognitively prepared to believe in gods or other non-human supernatural beings behind unexplained events.[30] This tells us something about the conventionality of the human mind's expectation that there is always an agent, as discussed before, that there is "someone" behind every event. The propensity of personifying everything in the world is a strategy of a quick, pre-packed understanding of reality without much reflection – a child-like approach.

Children absorb their parents' religion to continue their mental and social survival in a common culture. Children naturally memorize, imitate, and follow parents blindly in the beginning. In adolescent years and beyond, the general tendency can go in the direction of people valuing religion over reflecting about the purpose of their life and the meaning behind it. Thus, religion has remained as a substitute for and defense against emerging confusion, against thinking too much and too often. Religion can be a comfortable standby mode of being and operating. Parents often attempt to raise children in the safety of religious thinking rather than what is perceived to be wild and directionless thinking.

The impact of belief in god and religious thinking, no matter which god or religion, creates an imprinting in cognition during childhood that is hard for many to unlearn. Those who can unlearn have been able to dismantle the wiring of the old and familiar cognitive modules to creative modules and new reasoning. The very fact of this dismantlement and new cognitive wiring, as many secular and atheists have done, is itself a clue to how the old learning can be unlearned – the religious people are therefore capable of unlearning without being framed as "delusional."

The term "delusion" may be problematic and not reasonable to use for religious people as some modern authors have.[31] The condition and diagnosis of delusion has its own set of clinical criteria and verification, which is beyond the scope of our discussion here. It can be said that religious people are not delusional per se, but that clinically delusional people may have a great affinity toward fantastical and supernatural-religious ideas.

---

[30] Rebekah A. Richert and Erin I. Smith, "Cognitive Foundations in the Development of a Religious Mind," in Voland and Schiefenhövel, *The Biological Evolution of Religious Mind and Behavior*, 183–85, 187.
[31] See Richard Dawkins, *The God Delusion* (London: Bantam Press, 2006).

However, the condition of "delusion" is associated with someone who believes that they are themselves an agent of the supernatural whose influence could change all aspects of their life and other people's lives, as claim many self-designated messianic preachers and thinkers, although perhaps charlatans. This self-deceptive condition is potentially more prevalent among religious people who have the ability to deceive others.[32] That is also to say, when a religious person allows religious beliefs to assume control of their entire personality by silencing all other motivations, a neurosis is potentially in the making – and when the collective mind of a group allows such attitude, it is then an epidemic neurosis.[33]

3. Religion as an Adaptive Survival Strategy

The path that led to religion was a human survival strategy on a level unknown to other animals. Having developed higher cognitive powers, such as self-awareness and reflection, human beings were not content with only eating, sleeping, reproducing, living, and dying like other animals. With the development of the frontal cortex of the brain, they found the ability to think, ruminate, wonder, and worry. The frontal lobe of the brain prioritized survival on at least two fundamental and complex levels: physical and psychological. The physical level required the combination of food, shelter, security, and comfort in the face of all natural and biological challenges. The psychological level was more intricate. The frontal lobe fabricated stories about the world not based on any external reality in nature; it was simply a "placebo" narrative of the disquiet mind as a means to psychologically survive the questions of the nature of existence. The adaptation of the strategy of religion for those whose minds strived for fitness seemed reasonable. Mental fitness in an evolutionary sense has a more complex pattern than the physical adaptation. Fitness-enhancing is an evolutionary impulse with a goal of balance and improvement.

Some have proposed that religion is the work of natural selection as part of a terror-management theory.[34] It has also been argued that religion provides certain biological kinship – an ecologically suitable behavior of selecting and

---

[32] Brüne, "On Shared Psychological Mechanisms of Religiousness," 222, 225.
[33] For the definitions of neurosis and epidemic neurosis see Lorenz, *The Waning of Humaneness*, 164.
[34] Detlef Fetchenhauer, "Evolutionary Perspective on Religion – What They Can and What They Cannot Explain (Yet)," in Voland and Schiefenhövel, *The Biological Evolution of Religious Mind and Behavior*, 279–80.

supporting kin within a group.³⁵ It is also important to remember that "altruism, compassion, empathy, love, conscience and the sense of justice – all of these things that hold society together, the things that allow our species to think so highly of itself, can now confidently be said to have a firm genetic basis."³⁶ So, it is not necessarily that religion provides virtue, trust, and morality, but that such qualities are in the set of behaviors that make survival and cooperation, (or even a higher quality of life) in the natural world possible.³⁷

It is worth pondering whether religion has been a useful tool to explain the awe of the world, to manage terror and fear even of death, to create hope (whether true or false), and to manage emotions. It can be said that religion deals with a trajectory of issues. The fear of death, hope of eternal return and rebirth, meaning-making, and access to some secret knowledge of existence seem to be enough reasons for the rise of religious thinking.³⁸ The human species has always experienced intensified emotions that are either repressed, sublimated, or expressed. Religion simply had more emotional utility than plain sensible thinking. Religious enthusiasm can often be used as coping mechanisms, as many people still do to cope with pain, guilt, and death.³⁹ V. Frankl suggests that the door of religion remains open "for drawing upon the spiritual resources" and finding an anchor with a feeling of security found nowhere else.⁴⁰ Perhaps religion still has the same exhilarating, emotionally utilitarian function today. Eckart Voland points out that the spontaneous affinity toward religion simply does not arise through intellectual and rational analysis; otherwise, the entire premise of faith would have to be rationally dismissed.⁴¹

It is easy then to see how the adoption of religion generally follows three stages that meet people's mental and emotional needs:

---

[35] See Bernard Crespi, "The Kin Selection of Religion," in *Oxford Handbook of the Evolution of Religion*, ed. J. M. Liddle and T. Shackleford (in press). Also see online: www.oxfordhandbooks.com/view/10.1093/oxfordhb/9780199397747.001.0001/oxfordhb-9780199397747-e-9.
[36] Tremlin, *Minds and Gods*, 35 quoting Robert Wright.
[37] Ibid., 35.
[38] Gregory M. Nixon, "Myth and Mind: The Origin of Human Consciousness in the Discovery of the Sacred," *Journal of Consciousness Exploration and Research*, 1/3 (2010), 10, 19, 25, 27, 37.
[39] Frankl, *The Will to Meaning*, ix, 72.
[40] Ibid., 140, 144.
[41] Eckart Voland, "Evaluating the Evolutionary Status of Religiosity and Religiousness," in Voland and Schiefenhövel, *The Biological Evolution of Religious Mind and Behavior*, 9, 10, 12.

1. The invisible actor, god, or avatar is designated to supplicate to, for appeasing one's fear and to elicit the gratifying emotion of feeling protected.

2. This invisible actor, due to human loyalty, decided to share his secret and the truth of creation with his chosen people, and the believer then experiences the good feeling of belonging to a group.

3. Believing in this actor means earning approval and blessing in all life events, being able to request favors from time to time, and being able to be reclaimed after death.

These three aspects of religion gradually became ingrained and universal in much of humanity's social conduct. In this way, believing in gods is not just pious thinking, or contemplation about the afterlife. Instead, it has had to do with adaptive and "computational utility," sometimes in the most profound and mysterious ways, offering techniques to negotiate one's inner conflict and needs by reaching out to the ultimate outer authority. The mystery of believing in gods resides in the implicit, unconscious plane, but such a belief system is used for explicit and conscious reasoning, for practical purposes, for moods, worries, and real-life issues.[42] Although religion may still be considered an emotional or unconscious strategy for many people to rescue their psychic and emotional stability, at other times religious thinking overshadows the rational mind. Thus, religious compulsions override deeper rational considerations and easily lead a person to become an enthusiastic devotee of a religious institution.[43]

There is one other aspect of biology to be taken into consideration regarding religious behavior, and that is our unmistakable primate behavior. Human behavior emulates the primate behavior model of fear and subjugation to higher command. In ethology, as Jay R. Feierman notes, two primate behaviors have been observed. Type I behavior is the act of submission due to fear, anxiety, and self-protection, the "make-oneself-lower-or-smaller-or-more-vulnerable" behavior. Otherwise, anger and the punishment from a more powerful member of the group may ensue. In the human case, Type I

---

[42] Tremlin, *Minds and Gods*, 179–181, 185–186.
[43] It is about how the religion/divine and spirituality can capture the mind and form thoughts and emotions. See David A. Kessler, *Capture: Unraveling the Mystery of Mental Suffering* (New York: Harper Collins, 2016), chapters 6 and 7.

behavior takes the form of supplication and lowering oneself to appease religious authorities and the gods.[44]

Type II behavior is a fear-reducing and favor-demanding primate behavior that involves pleasing the dominant figure or the alpha male. In this corollary for humans, it is the chanting, praying, rituals, and animal sacrifices done in order to appeal to god for fear-reducing purposes as well favor-demanding. This behavior is not phylogenetically adaptive nor is it the work of natural selection; it has simply evolved with the fluidity of adaptation.[45] Generally speaking, humans have fear, but a more expressive fear is vis-à-vis the higher authorities. In the case of religion, the greatest fear has been of gods and the priests or the kings. Type I and II behaviors, lowering themselves and asking to receive protection for their life, are complex adaptational behavior of the high primates. The role of an alpha male in its different manifestations has played the role of a superior entity who provides protection and shows mercy to the obedient ones as seen in all human societies. Desmond Morris in his well-written and well-argued book, *The Human Zoo*, has linked human biology to culture by describing the role of the alpha male, the dominant males and super-leaders of the tribe being replaced by a super- and single-god, an all-seeing and all-controlling god who manages at times larger size of the tribes. The evolutionary process of religion through centuries has been to bring the tribe together in precarious conditions with the help of male protectors or super gods who cannot be around to answer questions but will punish and reciprocate violence with violence and demand subservience.[46]

4. The Logic and Strategy of Religion in Evolutionary Biology

The strategy of religion as a form of mental survival comes head to head with logic and rational thinking, especially when arguing physical and metaphysical claims. It can be said that the laws of reasoning are part of the laws of evolution and adaptation. So, if life, or biology, is the law-giver, then humans are both the followers and the implementers of the logical laws of biology. By following the laws of evolution, the species is rewarded by moving forward. Any species that violate such laws would wane and go extinct. As William Cooper argues, there is no doubt that evolution itself is not the law

---

[44] Jay R. Feierman, "How Some Major Components of Religion Could Have Evolved by Natural Selection?" in Voland and Schiefenhövel, *The Biological Evolution of Religious Mind and Behavior*, 56.
[45] Ibid., 57–58, 64.
[46] Desmond Morris, *The Human Zoo* (1969; London: Vintage, 1994), 7–9, 9–14, 15.

but is the enforcer and law-giver, and its laws are unchangeable;[47] abandoning its laws would be fatal to the process of natural selection and moving forward. And yet, religion offers ideas that supersede and are outside of the laws of biology, and hence the laws of nature.

The very existence of religion seems to be an anomaly to evolutionary theory, says Detlef Fetchenhauer. Evolutionary epistemologists have proposed that animals, humans included, are always expected to perceive their environment in a valid manner, but the irrationality of religion would seem to contradict a "valid" perception of the environment. Even though humans perceive their environment in a valid manner, the margin of fallacy in humans is higher than in other animals due to manipulation and deception through sophisticated mental imagination and linguistic expression.

Biology is not a gamble but is founded upon logic. As Cooper suggests, logic itself was primordial and the platform of evolution. Logic "as a body of principles, has always existed and always will ... and adaptation took place because the laws of pure logic are independently correct."[48] The challenging issue here is to seek a proper definition for the term and the function of "logic." In religion, the faithful follow probabilistic logic, a logic that suits the needs and performance of the mind in a particular generation and circumstance. So, this logic is not a durable, constant, or objective logic. To support the non-absoluteness of religious logic requires extending it to the general nature of logic. Although pure logic exists outside of relativistic biology, some have argued this logic may not be constant. This means logic itself may be unfolding and non-absolute in its core.

The challenge rests in the unfolding nature of logic which cannot be used as the backbone of any "truth" representing an absolute entity. Ethologist and Nobel Laureate Konrad Lorenz challenged Kantian logic by concluding that logic or pure reason should not be treated as though it was in a central stillness, fixed and absolute. The peak of human thinking itself is not absolute nor does it have *a priori* validity; even mathematics follows the laws of biological relativity.[49] In other words, not only is biology a dynamically open system which does not permanently hover around any absolute and static logic, but also humans as logicians still lack a great deal of experiential and empirical input to suppose a more comprehensive non-anthropocentric and nonlinear logic.

---

[47] William S. Cooper, The *Evolution of Reason: Logic as the Branch of Biology* (Cambridge: Cambridge University Press, 2001), 2–3.
[48] Ibid., 178–179, 191–192.
[49] Ibid., 2–3, 16.

This being said, the higher order of biological life follows logic and natural selection, but when it comes to human thinking and emotive aspects, this logic becomes fussy and unclear. This means religious beliefs cannot be assessed or measured against a logical system such as deductive logic, which is used in mathematics and scientific methods. The application of religious logic may be considered as chance theory, more like flipping a coin than precise deductive logic. Religious logic is a utilitarian logic with a non-thinking trust in one's counterintuitive perception, and trust in religious authorities. "Trust" is the work of transient probabilistic thinking, not durable logic. Thus, religion does not follow any logic, but it is a probabilistic calculation by people in a given generation and culture.

The predominant fact about religious "logic" is that average believers in god tend not to change their religious trust until the end of their life, simply because to their estimation religion has offered less risk than non-religion. Such people cannot get rid of their faith, nor can they substitute it with something "less." Emerging out of the psychological habits of generations, the metaphor of "god" has found such a deep seat in the brain that its negation feels like a frightening emotional impossibility, an unsuitable logic, or a bad probability. In other words, a shift from "god logic" to "no god logic" may not easily happen. Even though the psyche of the thinker is presented with the rational basis for such a shift, it is not a given that religious or counterintuitive logic can be overturned by an empirical, deductive logic. However, conditional social and cultural logic are sets of logic which function according to circumstances. These sets can be both deductive and inductive but are continuously in flux and at times are replaced by new sets of social logic.

The logical biological strategies of an animal's survival and defense, such as camouflage, shells, sharp claws, horns, etc., provide for defense, survival, and maintenance of security. If those horns or sharp claws turn out to be useless, they become extra things that inhibit the animal in its normal function. At this point, the logic of natural selection will cause it to wane. If we take this logic of biology and apply it to the choice of religion, it serves as a cognitive protection like a shell, for as long as humans need it to survive. Religion could plausibly be seen as a defense strategy that follows an inner logic by appeasing human anxiety and the fearful mind, even when the *content* of religion does not match the logic of the natural world and its function. The paradox of this relationship between logic and illogic lies in the contrast between what is necessary and useful and allows humans to adapt and stay fit (biologically logical) and what is not necessary and damages their wellbeing (biologically illogical). The middle and subjective ground is when the illogic of religion helps a death-fearing or god-fearing person, for example, to stay biologically (psychologically) fit.

But if the remedy of religion gradually becomes more and more oppressive, illogical, and hyperbolic through acts such as ordering the killing of non-believers, or attributing disease and healing only to god, or conducting harmful religious rituals, then certain aspects of religious logic become destructive. These damaging aspects inhibit the development of humans in an evolutionary sense, particularly in the face of scientific understanding, such as the reasons for diseases and healing, which are better understood and cannot be attributed to gods. In these cases, religious logic may easily be replaced by alternative logic or "updated" remedies for one's fear and anxiety. The pointlessness of religious logic can be seen clearly with the Aztecs, who believed that the sun rose due to the results of sacrifice and needed to be fed human blood every day in order to make it rise. Only if they stopped sacrificing would they see whether or not the sun still rose, but this was out of the scope of the Aztecs' cognitive biases.[50] In another example, before the arrival of the Inca, the powerful Chimu civilization in Peru killed hundreds of children between the age of five and fourteen and sacrificed animals as part of religious mass rituals.[51] Such lapses of reason, at least through our modern lens, in the context of religious thinking are countless throughout history.

Correspondingly, how personally and deeply a scientific belief is held can also be an example of lapsed reason that has become another "religion." For example, the belief in Ptolemy's geocentric model and the movements of heavenly bodies around the earth was replaced with the Copernican heliocentric model. But as we know, some scientists had a very hard time letting go of their theories, even in the face of evidence. The contrast between errors in science and religion is that science is unfolding and self-corrective, whereas religion and religious logic may be resistant to self-correct because its legitimacy depends on its absoluteness, even if it is wrong. Errors occur either in the absence of knowledge or as a consequence of computational errors. Both cases of human error can be corrected if lapses and slips can be detected, and feedback is taken into consideration. As to why humans continue their errors and remain insensitive to empirical evidence in the case

---

[50] Brüne, "On Shared Psychological Mechanisms of Religiousness and Delusional Beliefs," 221.
[51] The archaeologists discovered a mass grave of about 140 children who were believed to be killed as part of religious ritual. International news agencies reported it on April 28, 2018.

of religion is perhaps due to fear and emotive cognitive propensities, which lead them to rely on probabilistic and risk calculation.[52]

How do humans bridge this distance between logic and illogic, between causal reality and illusory beliefs?[53] How do they live with this cognitive dissonance? The short answer is the importance of a sense of belonging to a community, and the cleverness of strategy. Since external circumstances were in a constant state of flux and transformation, our ancestors had to adapt to their environment with beliefs that corresponded to their needs (even if illogical) in order to survive better. If a religious tradition was time-location-bound, it would tend to expire and be replaced by a newer one when there was no further use for the original. This behavior in human evolution is called "strategy."[54] Our ancestors' choices were limited, and the populations chose a model of logic that would operate on its own pillar as a survival strategy,[55] even though this strategy may have stood in breach of deductive logic and sound intuition. Religion, a strategy of psychological survival, has produced an abundance of counterintuitive ideas through lapses of logic. Against this backdrop, the "logic of decision" is the choice of the most reasonable course of action from a set of available courses of action.

In putting Blaise Pascal's probabilistic strategic decision-making in perspective, Fetchenhauer writes that in the past many people believed in their respective gods even though they were not sure if such gods existed. Indeed, it was easier and less costly to side with religion just in case if gods really existed. So, Blaise Pascal's strategy was an archetypal strategy that many humans intuitively have also followed.[56]

In simpler Pascalian words, to believe in god and follow religion may be innocuous, and might even bear many rewards in this and the next world. No matter how naïve the content of the religion, the strategy of survival ranks first and takes precedence over any pure reason. In the same vein, the proposals of hell and heaven given by the priests, although unprovable, acted as a

---

[52] For more technical discussions on computational errors, see James Reason, *Human Error* (1990; New York: Cambridge University Press, 2003).

[53] It is interesting to relay the story of a medical doctor in a Varanasi hospital, India, with whom I met and spoke as a colleague some years back about the water-borne disease as the result of drinking the water of the Ganges River. He personally believed the Ganges was holy and would never make people sick, even as he treated dozens of people with water-borne illnesses.

[54] Cooper, Th*e Evolution of Reason*, 5, 7.

[55] Ibid., 8–9, 21, 28.

[56] Fetchenhauer, "Evolutionary Perspectives on Religion," 289.

psychological tool for encouragement and deterrence, since the risk of not believing in such things could be risky: "What if they are right?" Thus, with a pragmatic approach, imagination is transformed into belief out of a sheer strategy for survival from the wrath of gods.

The effect of religion and religious belief on human personality and sociocultural dynamics is immeasurable. The real issue is how much free-thinking people have experienced in spite of having firmly believed in one religion or another. The last theme to consider in the treatment of religion is how absolute and flexible it actually is and how different cultures evolved with their open and closed religions.

***

Open and Closed Gods

As we explore the evolution of human thought from pre-philosophy to liberation philosophy, it behooves us to also consider that perhaps some religions are more limiting to philosophical thought than others. Henri Bergson (d. 1941) in *The Two Sources of Morality and Religion* discussed morality and religion as natural products of human psychological evolution. In his discussion, Bergson specifically referred to the danger of maintaining a static morality as opposed to a dynamic one. He believed that as a consequence of the dissonance between a static and dynamic morality, two types of societies could arise: a closed society which possesses codified laws compelling humans to mechanistically conform, and an open society with free creativity in art, philosophy and mysticism.[57] Through this bifurcation in human decision-making about morality closed and open religions evolved, each one highly influencing the nature of individuals and societies. Closedness and openness of morality thus became an important psychological material in concretizing closed and open religions. In the course of history, even closed and open gods emerged.

---

[57] See Henri Bergson, *The Two Sources of Morality and Religion* (Notre Dame: University of Notre Dame Press, 1977). See also "Henri Bergson," https://www.britannica.com/biography/Henri-Bergson#ref202567, accessed October 28, 2018.

In brief, an "open" religion connotes being non-essentialist,[58] non-ethnocentric, non-theological, open to all, non-authoritarian, non-centralized, probably polytheistic, tolerant, and may have contained more than one interpretation. A "closedness" religion, in contrast, is theological, tribe-based, strict, centralized, authoritarian, probably monotheistic, often intolerant of others. It perceives itself as absolute.

The open or closed nature of gods and the corresponding religious culture formed due to intricate dynamics coming from people, the size and the landscape of geography, central or decentralized city-states, the power of myths, and the vulnerability or the temperament of the population. As myths were gradually assimilated and adopted by different religions, stories were given divine or superhuman status, and thus were revered as unchangeable. This attitude created mild to severe degrees of intolerance., The attitude of intolerance had to do with the "closed" religions which were viewed as absolute and ultimate. Conversely, an attitude of tolerance appeared, with some religions in various parts of the world being open to evolution and further interpretations.

One may also ask whether having adopted a *deist* belief or a *theist* makes a difference in a religion's perspective and tolerance of others. Deistic religions adopt the notion of one or more gods in the universe, but such gods do not necessarily intervene in the daily affairs of the phenomenal and dynamic world. This deistic approach allows other religions and forms of spirituality to develop alongside of it. Theistic religions, on the other hand, hold that god is the creator and the ruler of the universe who also governs the world and the personal lives of each generation in every culture. And yet, theism is the narrative of a god who is both involved in and aloof from the world of humans: he is so close that he keeps accounts of people's good and bad deeds and promises rewards and punishments, yet is so aloof that he simply cannot attend to every wish that humans make. This reasoning provides an irrational outlet for the rational question of how an apparently all-powerful god cannot manage to make things right on earth and for all humans.

We can say that the narrative of each religion historically evolved around the attitudes of either "open" or "closed," "tolerant" or "intolerant," "deist" or "theist." Perhaps some of the ancient Greek religions, for example, developed

---

[58] See Torsten Hylen, *"Closed and Open Concepts of Religion: The Problem of Essentialism in Teaching about Religion,"* in *Textbook Gods – Genre, Text and Teaching Religious Studies*, ed. Bengt-Ove Andreassen and James R. Lewis (Sheffield: Equinox Publishing, 2014), 16–42.

open religions that allowed philosophers and critics (although not without friction) to live side-by-side. India's various religions of the past and today are generally representative of open religions, somewhat tolerant of one another.

The Abrahamic creeds Judaism, Christianity, and Islam, in contrast, represent closed religions with fixed narratives reflected in their scriptures. The Abrahamic religions present archaic myths as actual historical episodes in their sacred scriptures and epitomize the claim of the mighty, living, and invisible god. This inflexible stance caused polarization of the faithful with their own strong theological positions against the "gentiles," "pagans," or "heretics" who remained unblessed and unfavorable in the eyes of god. Jan Assmann points out that a propensity to violence is not exclusively an Islamic phenomenon, but it is inherently a problem with all the truth-claiming monotheistic religions, especially when the rhetoric of tension draws a sharp line between a believer and non-believer. The distinction between a "believer" and "non-believer" reduces the cognitive space to maneuver flexibility for the practitioner.[59] These Abrahamic religions, each with their exclusivist attitudes and closed qualities, historically constructed an absolutist interpretation of reality, and at times caused irreconcilable confrontations between their theologians and critical mystic-philosophers of their own and other religions.

Conclusion

The earliest innovators of religious ideas conceived of themes and rituals, from simple worship all the way to peculiar practices vis-à-vis invisible and supernatural agents who operate and control life here and now, as well as life after death. This desire for an independent reality outside of this world had its basis in biological adaptation and psychological survival in the face of a cold and unresponsive natural world. In certain ways, religion may have been a response to the monotony of "secular" life.[60] The mechanical, unresponsive and impersonal nature of the world, however, did not lend credence to the idea of a belief in god. The nature of reality was left wide open for interpretation, leaving people vulnerable to cognitive deception, and as a result, hundreds and thousands of beliefs and stories were invented.

The curious blind spot in human history is how a number of clever humans conceived of so many non-verifiable and non-visible religious ideas and managed to convince large crowds of their and future generations to believe

---

[59] Jan Assmann, *Totale Religion: Ursprünge und Formen puritanischer Verschärfung* (Wien: Picus Verlag, 2016), see the first four sections of part one of the book.
[60] Montagu, *Man: His First Million Years*, 181.

these counterintuitive stories and parables. But if people are evolutionarily hardwired with a propensity toward religious thinking, perhaps that leads to being convinced by such religious imaginations and counterintuitive beliefs.

Pascal Boyer in *The Naturalness of Religious Ideas: Cognitive Theory of Religion* (1994)[61] defends the naturalness of religious thinking despite the variations in religious representation and skewing of previous generations' representations. "Naturalness," as Boyer explains, means self-evident, being human in this world. It also entails the non-observable and extra-natural agencies and processes in most human cultures. In making the case for religion, he asserts that there is stable and systematic continuity and even predictability within the cultural transmission of the meaning and truth claims.[62] In other words, there is an agency of biology and mind, a *reason* for the ongoing recurrences of religion in human societies.[63]

However, given the diversity in cognitive function and human intelligence, in the context of critical philosophy or free thought, people have criticized themselves and have either rejected religious thought or never entertained religious thoughts to begin with. Boyer's theory is hence criticized for its linearity, that all humans operate based on evolutionary hardwiring. People are not trapped by religion, in any absolute way, and are free to imagine and invent new ideas, be they religious or non-religious.[64]

The importance of the religious imagination lies in its evolutionary utility during critical times when archaic humans used it as a shield from their fears and to provide explanations about the unknowable. Today some critical thinkers consider such imaginations simplistic and their necessity far-fetched. However, fear with all of its trajectories is the basis for many irrational behaviors including blind imitation and herd-like obedience, as we see in the culture of popular religion.

---

[61] Pascal Boyer, *The Naturalness of Religious Ideas: Cognitive Theory of Religion* (Berkeley, Los Angeles: University of California Press, 1994).
[62] Ibid., chapters 8 and 9.
[63] Ibid., 4–7. However, historically speaking, larger populations of communities have tended to take refuge in religions more than smaller minorities. This is perhaps a reason why empires with a religious veneer have held greater longevity in history.
[64] Niels Henrik Gregersen, "The Naturalness of Religious Imagination and the Idea of Revelation," *Ars Dispuntandi* 3 (2003), 1–27.

Chapter 3

The Instinctual Modules of Religion: Fear, Obedience, and Imitation

After having recognized how religion emerged as a bio-cognitive by-product, we can now look in more depth at three prominent mental routes responsible for the choice of religion over no religion. Against this background three strong tendencies loom large: 1. Fear, both existential and of higher authorities, 2. Obedience, a kind of subjugation to the gods and religious establishments, and 3. Imitation of parents and communal practices and beliefs. Before being able to deal with the "philosophy of existence," earlier humans had to figure out how to keep their *biology* of fear at bay in order to make that existence more manageable.

The human species, like all other species, has been forced to follow one of three evolutionary loops: *adapt, change,* or go *extinct*. These processes forced humans to constantly make new decisions: to migrate, shelter themselves from the external elements, adapt to food and climate changes, and win over competition. But the handling of cognitive matters was far more taxing on the human psychological system than the physical ones. The paradoxical shift in brain function had brought with it talents unprecedented in previous hominid species, but at the same time the new brain function generated a hyper-reflective tendency, with anxiety, mental crisis, and even a propensity toward spatially imaginative ideas by perceiving things that never existed in reality. With the development of the frontal lobe, the overwhelming capacity to reflect led to serious perplexities – such as wondering why we exist in the world, what is the meaning of this existence, and who are the operators of the world – which resulted in anxious thoughts.[1] The detriment of hyper-reflection and anguish could have easily brought humans to the verge of their collapse by falling into depression or committing suicide. But such extinction did not happen. Instead, adaptation and change won out. However, adaptation

---

[1] In the brain, although various cortical regions together with the midbrain and brainstem through interactions participate in responses to fear, the *amygdala* is primarily responsible for fear and the nearby nucleus of the *stria terminalis* for anxiety. See Ralph Adolphs, "The Biology of Fear," *Current Biology* 23/2 (Jan. 21, 2013), 82–83, 88.

was not without severe psychological consequences, which seemed to usher in new crises, as we will see.

Fear

It is said that fear is the first emotion of the fetus.[2] It is also said that "the oldest and strongest emotion of mankind is fear, and the oldest and strongest kind of fear is fear of the unknown."[3] Fear continues to revisit humankind in different stages of life. There have been times that even one's own thoughts and freedom have been feared.[4] The cognitive response to a triggering instantaneous event is usually excitation and expression of emotion[5] in the short term. In the long term however, sublimation of *fear* can turn into an ambiguous state of *anxiety*. Thus, fear can become a psychological construct without being precisely discoverable.[6] Because the complexity of fear-anxiety often has no particular object to fear, the impulse can generally stem from being trapped in one's own thoughts. The propensity of too much thinking turns into an obsessive tendency, at times towards obscure things. Among many, latent fear turns into irrational anxiety. Fear causes emotions and excitation of the brain that can cause the disturbance of the logical faculty. Simply said, "what is not understood generates fear."[7]

In the course of cognitive development, generally speaking, Homo sapiens faced two dominant fear phenomena. The first was a trajectory of object-based fears and anxieties stemming from the physical elements such as thunder, earthquakes, floods, and other spectacularly scary natural events. There was also the fear of predators as well as human enemies– all physical objects. The second set of fears, it can be assumed from the perspective of our current mindset and the history of human psychology, was triggered by things

---

[2] Joseph Campbell, *The Power of Myth* (New York: Anchor Books, 1991), 59.
[3] It is the saying of the American Novelist H. P. Lovecraft. H. P. Lovecraft Quotes. BrainyQuote.com, BrainyMedia Inc, 2018. https://www.brainyquote.com/quotes/h_p_lovecraft_676245, accessed November 28, 2018.
[4] Erich Fromm, *The Sane Society* (1956; London: Routledge & Kegan Paul, 1976), 34.
[5] Almost 20 percent of the population suffers from an anxiety disorder in any given year. See Adolphs, "The Biology of Fear," 89. The propensity for anxiety among human ancestors probably ranged from real panic to phobia, stress, thoughts, memories, premature death, fear of predators, inability to cope with life circumstances, and all the ways to misinterpret and personalize natural disasters.
[6] Adolphs, "The Biology of Fear," 79.
[7] Eckart Voland, "Evaluating the Evolutionary Status of Religiosity and Religiousness," in E. Voland, W. Schiefenhövel (eds.), *The Biological Evolution of Religious Mind and Behavior*, Berlin Heidelberg: Springer-Verlag, 2009, 13-14.

which were *not* material or object-based, such as a fear of the mysterious forces of nature, including death, and the imagined actors behind natural disasters as well as similar illusory and unexplained fears.

Historically and evolutionarily, object-based fear was a common daily experience, compelling the brain to qualify and try to allay unpleasant and impenetrable occurrences. Trying to understand the world around with its millions of stars in the dark night sky, observing the shifting seasons, and experiencing terrifying events have always been awe-inspiring. Such events were obscurely mysterious phenomena to our ancestors. Fear-inducing phenomena were natural events like the daily sunset and the corresponding fear of predators with the coming of night, thunder, earthquakes, volcanoes, eclipses of the sun (which must have seemed like Armageddon), and massive floods. Other existential fears were diseases, high fever, sudden death, child mortality, maternal mortality during birth, fear of one's own death, and other obscure personal anxieties. All of these occurrences were painful and unexplainable.

The phenomenon of fear of non-physical objects emerged due to the rise of *self-awareness* in humans, something perhaps distinct in the animal kingdom. The change in morphology and function of the frontal cortex in the brain made self-awareness such a strong characteristic that the human being became a hyper-reflective animal. Out of this evolutionary change in self-awareness, simultaneously a greater intelligence and daunting angst were produced. Vague concepts such as one's life circumstances and destiny, full of uncertainty, loomed as one such source of subliminal fear. Over time, objectless fear grew emotionally serious.

Searching for solutions became more and more urgent in order to fend off these anxieties, especially when humans faced their own powerlessness in nature. Rather than be paralyzed by fear, our human ancestors employed creative mental strategies for appeasing these existential fears. It was panic in response to terrifying situations of nature as well as the fear of imagined objects or situations that brought about magic and superstitious rituals.[8] For example, the rise of early shamanism, perhaps the oldest spiritual practice, was not to necessarily change the outer reality but to alter reality in one's own perspective.[9] Groups made fires, chanted, and perhaps danced, all of which would result in formless mental energy. In this way, the response to fear was to change the

---

[8] Walter Burkert, *Creation of the Sacred: Tracks of Biology in Early Religions* (Cambridge: Harvard University Press, 1998), 46–47.
[9] See Richard Leviton, "Through the Shaman's Door," *Yoga Journal*, July–Aug., 1992, 52–55, 102.

mental configuration. The priest and medicine man were one and the same thing who sought in healing the soul and the body by elevating the spirit to distant realms through the medium of dance and drum beating.[10] Around these and similar themes, elaborate stories, beliefs, and ceremonies were constructed.

The gradual formation of groups with social hierarchy produced more shamans and priests who performed such rituals to change perspective, create formless mental energy, and appease fear. The alteration of reality through this mental configuration gradually evolved into a dependence on belief and rituals, and eventually, systematic religious thinking. Thus the rise of religion, with no external form or materiality in nature itself, became an inner phenomenon that changed human perception for dealing with many disturbing emotional matters, fear in particular. Religions in actuality did not promise anything perceptibly deliverable; it was inner cognition that converted the fear into hope.

The development of priest-dominant societies who organized such rituals made communities dependent on priests for the fear-reducing rituals. Gradually, authoritarian rule was founded and the effect of religion shifted through the priests' terrifying threats of punishment by mysterious forces of nature and gods. Religion *itself* sometimes became a source of fear, supplanting the original fears of nature and existence. Complex feudal city-states orders additionally created more fear that made voicing one's opinion a distant memory.[11]

It is important to remember of course that religion did not originally create fear in humans; religion was created *because* of fear. Religion was a mechanism to cope and respond to fear in the most powerful cognitive fashion, but it then became a source of collective thinking and control.

Priests and rulers capitalized on the element of fear in solidifying their domination, perhaps as early as the Neolithic period. The 'theology of fear' became a historical condition between the theocratic rulers and the ruled. Gods became entities to whom humans prayed and appealed in order to handle emotional and psychological quandaries. Meanwhile, in sociocultural evolution, fear became a commodity for the ruling class to maximize religious lies so that

---

[10] Wade Davis, *Shadows in the Sun: Travels to Landscapes of Spirit and Desire* (New York: Broadway Books, 1999), 144, 146, 148, 150.

[11] Beginning about 3,000 years ago, the longing for ascetic and monk-like life, various Indian teachers by dispossessing themselves from property, land, live stocks dwelled from place to place half- or fully-naked. Their search of natural and mental equilibrium was perhaps an impetus to leave behind their own agriculturalist communities for a better life of "hunter-gatherer' in a true sense.

they could exploit emotionally fragile and fearful people. The ruling class also shared the same fears, as they were trapped in their own fears. These rulers were subject to the same religious "laws" and fears of the gods, but they were also the manipulators and controllers of the religion and the people. The more gullible the groups, the greater the scope of manipulation under the umbrella of religion for the sake of managing the fear. The fear-manipulating ruling class possibly defrauded themselves as much as the weak.

Fear, thus, remained a singular influential dynamic in the development of religions as they were adopted and adapted by humans. Can we say then that religion was perhaps the result of the earliest human experiences of Post-Traumatic Stress Disorder? The forces of fear in the psyche remained so dominant that the irrationalities contained in beliefs were often ignored or even sublimated. As the members of a community committed to the same beliefs, their irrationalities were given even stronger immunity from criticism from within, and consequently the prospect of living in fear and irrationality within the walls of a common culture remained the only option. Fear was institutionalized and enveloped through the medium of religion.

Obedience

Obedience in the human context generally stands in opposition to self-rule or autonomous thinking, thus fear and obedience usually develop together. The psychological discrepancy of why people choose obedience over self-rule is partly biological (innate in primate life, as discussed earlier), and partly a cognitive-cultural calculation. This is to say, if fear is the punishment, obedience must then produce a reward. As Tim Friend has colorfully noted, the millions of species on this planet are for the most part concerned with the same four things: 'sex,' 'real estate,' 'who's the boss?' and 'what's for dinner?'[12] This fundamental question of "Who's the boss?" leads to the issues of obedience and power structure within a species, and the blueprint of the power structure in the high primates must have influenced humans in the manifestation of obedience in human society, including religious obedience.

Obedience seems to have been the foundation of human history partly due to our biology. In viewing humans as social animals, there is always a "boss." Thomas Bouchard describes three questions that humans had to ask in regards to obeying the highest and most legitimate authority, from ground-level realities to greater terrestrial and even celestial levels: "Who is in charge?" "What does he/she want?" and "What do I do?" The answers to these questions in a religious

---

[12] Quoted in Tremlin, *Minds and Gods*, 25–26.

context are: "God is in charge." "He wants obedience." And "You must believe in him and carry out the wishes of god's representatives." Human-constructed tribal gods became the target of obedience, often for emotional and cognitive survival. The strength of the urge to obey and the power of the fundamental question of 'who's in charge?' is striking and baffling, especially considering cases when obedience is intolerably oppressive, and yet many endure their abject predicament either by adaptive-addictive habit or by force, rather than disobeying and finding liberation.

Obedience is an accord between the domineering and the dominated. Since it is a characteristic of high primates to follow a male leader, the alpha male, humans also, in the course of history and even on an everyday level have shown an unequivocal propensity to follow a (typically) male leader, taking the role of chief of a clan, a king, a warlord, a prophet, a priest, or even a political and military leader in different times. Fear and obedience, in a certain sense, explain how humans have justified relinquishing all their responsibilities and giving it over to the leader; through the relinquishment of self-responsibility and being obedient followers, they anticipate less personal fear.

Being inferior to and obedient to other humans are as much social choices as religious ones. The strangest acts of obedience in ancient times were rooted in fear. Genital mutilation such as castration or circumcision has a complex psychological background in ancient traditions as a form of ransom and a means of being saved, on the assumption of being inferior vis-à-vis the superior force. To accept genital mutilation has to do with certain anxieties for better chances of survival, a rather desperate objective.[13] Accepting the position of *inferior* and giving in to being obedient is a strategy of survival and minimizing threats. Obedience to god and acceptance of an inferior or subservient rank in human perception is the most important maneuver; in fact, this inferior attitude to god has made the whole difference in appeasing fear.[14] People who show submission to god (and accept their inferiority) are operating under the assumption that therefore god will not attack them without cause. The action of fear and its reaction of obedience in curtailing trepidation has had to do with making life safer through believing in religion.[15]

It is however puzzling, considering the immense thinking capacity of the human mind, that we obey people (or invisible gods) without thinking. Why

---

[13] Burkert, *Creation of the Sacred*, 47. The author states that when the hunter traps his prey without the possibility of escaping, prey bites or cuts one's own testicles as a means of surrender and obedience.
[14] Ibid., 80.
[15] Ibid., 31.

should we, or what happens if we do not? It may be that a great deal of human behavior is rooted in blind obedience without analysis. The experiment of blind obedience to authority conducted by Stanley Milgram at Yale University in 1962 showed the complexity and dangers of obedience by average and decent people. In this experiment of social psychology, it was revealed that average people followed orders of their superiors without any critical objections, even though they knew following such orders required inflicting pain and suffering on other fellow human beings. The experiment showed that each and every person had the freedom to choose disobedience for the good of their own conscience and well-being of others, but the majority did not.[16] In the mechanism of blind obedience without objection, the phenomenon of compassion was blocked, even though unintentionally, which made the suffering of others likely. The core of this experiment was to expose the dark side of obedience, when blindness and irrationality are accompanied by a casual following of orders and norms without critical evaluation of their damage, and this must certainly play a role in people's blind obedience to the dictates of a religion.

In the religious context obedience is identified with virtue, and disobedience obviously associated with sin; at times, the definition of a "good person" has been one who does not possess one's own thoughts, is subdued and anesthetized, or brainwashed rather than having thoughts of being free.[17] This type of obedience has historically benefited the religious ruling classes who have used threats, promises of rewards, other manipulative language, or sheer force to maintain their positions. It has been this frail human condition that has often called for disobedience for the sake of freedom.[18] As Erich Fromm puts it, disobedience for the sake of freedom is out of reason and is not directed *against* something, but *for* something – it is to bring light to darkness, it is waking up, and daring to know.[19] Fromm also points to the priestly way of anesthetizing people by controlling their thoughts and brainwashing them to the point where they can kill ruthlessly out of faith – a way of sustaining prehistoric savage thinking.[20]

---

[16] The concept of "Obedience to Authority" was coined by Stanley Milgram in his controversial book *Obedience to Authority: An Experimental View* in 1974. Since then Hannah Arendt and Erich Fromm have written on the subject.
[17] Fromm, *The Sane Society*, 35.
[18] Erich Fromm, *On Disobedience and Other Essays* (London: Routledge & Kegan Paul, 1984).
[19] Ibid., 33, 34.
[20] Ibid., 28–29.

Obedience to god is so important to the structure of a religion that there are myriads of stories that teach the dangers of disobedience. In the Judeo-Christian-Islamic religion, this is symbolized by the anecdote of Adam and Eve in the Book of Genesis, who received the divine consequence of being thrown out of Paradise into the carnal world because they disobeyed God's orders, or "for having swallowed an apple."[21] This ancient story carries a message of serious consequences that will ensue as a result of any defiance, including self-reflecting or self-deciding. Adam and Eve were thus made responsible for the "original defiance," interpreted by Saint Augustine as "original sin."

As Stephen Greenblatt expounds, Augustine had to justify the original mistake that took place in Paradise, stating that god is not responsible for the innate defect of the Creation: it was Adam and Eve who had to fall from grace. This meant that disobedience was *not* part of the original design, and thus all human kind are sinful when they participate in disobedience.[22] Obedience to the divine remains primal, and any longing for freedom without being given divine permission would be subject to earthly pain, as Adam and Eve discovered. Perhaps Adam even represents the first defiance against god or religion, someone longing for existential freedom. Therefore, Adam and Eve's story can be read as freedom from god's "golden cage" of Paradise, so to speak.

Blind and dogmatic obedience represses rationality, as it did for Augustine in his treatment of dialectical human reality. Augustine's interpretation implied that nakedness, sensual lust, and making love was nothing but disobedience. Copulation was certainly not part of god's plan in and out of Paradise; it was out of defiance to god that sensual love caused pregnancy, followed by the increase of human progeny. Out of this pre-Augustinian rationale, Jesus had to be born from a virgin, a non-sexual occurrence, since in Heaven there was never any temptation of sexuality or the means of procreation. According to Augustinian thinking, one should remain obedient to god, and couples should not enter into pleasurable sex. In his "obedient" mind, he did not want to acknowledge nor deal with the basis for sexual intercourse, pregnancy and bearing children and continuing the foundation of the human race.

---

[21] Anthony Pagden, *The Enlightenment and Why It Still Matters* (Oxford: Oxford University Press, 2015), 91.
[22] See Stephen Greenblatt, "How St. Augustine Invented Sex: He Rescued Adam and Eve from Obscurity, Devised the Doctrine of Original Sin – and the Rest Is Sexual History," *The New Yorker: Annals of Culture*, June 19, 2017. See also Stephen Greenblatt, *The Rise and Fall of Adam and Eve* (New York and London: W. W. Norton and Company, 2017).

Imitation and Obedience

Imitation and obedience in human life possess a two-fold paradoxical disposition: the push for *continuity-stability* on one hand and *stagnation* on the other. Religions and religious beliefs have persisted because of the imitation of generations, out of obedience to previous generations, due to the behavioral imitation characteristics of mammalian-primate life. The puzzle of imitation-obedience, in the case of the human species, is that the individuals sometimes behave contrary to their own interests, and instead act in the interest of a group, a loftier purpose, or loftier authority, and influenced by genes as well as by one's own personality – a trajectory of herd-altruism prompted by the "selfish gene" for survival of its kind.[23] Imitation is nevertheless part of a survival pattern, and thus usually results in continuity.

The study of imitation offers its own set of scientific inquiries about the origins of the human mind.[24] The capacity of imitation, a mechanism from brain to behavior, is an indication of coding "self and other" in the brain. The imitation of others seems to demonstrate the same neuronal activities by the mirror neurons of the actor and imitator, as discussed in chapter 1. This phenomenon is theorized as a great leap forward in human evolution.[25] By coining the term *meme* (imitating behavior), Richard Dawkins intended to clarify that evolution can take place by the replication of genes on one level, and the replication of behaviors and their cultural transmission on another level without interfering with our brain biology.[26] This means, in the course of evolution of culture our anatomy and the core brain biology remained stable, but our behavior was modified. During this time our universal brain was rewired in a particular culture in order to both replicate behaviors and upgrade them to more socially complex level.

---

[23] Thomas J. Bouchard, Jr., "Authoritarianism, Religiousness, and Conservatism: Is "Obedience to Authority" the Explanation for Their Clustering, Universality and Evolution?" in Voland and Schiefenhövel, *The Biological Evolution of Religious Mind and Behavior*, 174, 175, 176, 177. For a broader biological definition of "selfish gene," see Richard Dawkins, *The Selfish Gene* (Oxford: Oxford University Press, 1987).
[24] Wolfgang Prinz and Andrew N. Meltzoff, "An Introduction to the Imitative Mind and Brain," *The Imitative Mind: Development, Evolution, and Brain Bases*, ed. Andrew N. Meltzoff and Wolfgang Prinz (Cambridge: Cambridge University Press, 2002), 1.
[25] Giacomo Rizzolatti, Luciano Fadiga, Leonardo Fogassi, and Vittorio Gallese, "From Mirror Neurons to Imitation: Facts and Speculations," in Meltszoff and Prinz, *The Imitative Mind*, 247; see also Ramachandran, "Mirror Neurons and Imitation," 3.
[26] See Dawkins, *The Selfish Gene*.

In the realm of human development, imitation has its invaluable side, since obviously the imitation of adults by children is what facilitates the acquisition of language and other learned human skills. Jean Piaget, the child psychologist, speaks of sporadic and systematic imitation of movement as well as higher forms of imitation, such as representational or deferred imitation often interiorized from childhood onward as coordination and the absorption of mental images. Symbols and meanings slowly take shape.[27] Yet in the case of adult human psychology, once these human skills are mastered, imitation out of blind obedience leads to stagnation and degeneracy, which is detrimental to one's nature-given freedom and creativity during adulthood.

When living as a member of a larger community, the phenomenon of blind imitation of others without scrutiny of content is common. This is because imitation and obedience are nearly effortless tasks, easy to carry out, and they make it easier to avoid confrontation with the majority. Thus, imitating ancestral religions within the permitted boundaries, even following the strange beliefs of one's culture, does not seem unusual or odd. Even the oddest belief is in fact safeguarded because everyone else believes in it too, and it becomes a non-self-deciding ingredient guarded by the collective culture. Culture is made rather contagious by propagating ideas and beliefs.[28] Imitation is therefore a convenient, non-reflective way to handle one's environment. Imitative behavior also has its time-saving advantages: simply do what others have already mastered, such as certain behaviors, skills, tasks, knowledge, etc, rather than have to figure it out all over again. Yet when it comes to the critical matters of the human life story that determines one's destiny, freedom, intellectual integrity, and a deeper understanding of existence, more creative thinking is required, not just a duplication of other people's thoughts.

Nobel Laureate Daniel Kahneman argues that there are two dominant systems of thinking in humans: fast and slow, or Systems One and Two. System One, "fast thinking," which does not require analytical assessment and new judgments, is imitative thinking, a cognitively lazy and familiar way of rapidly responding to a situation. This rapid system of thinking comes from the memory of language, cultures, and images of ready-made responses from others without a deeper cognitive check of reality. This system of thinking can be clever, practical, and skillful, and yet can also be blind. Without any effort, one's ideas can be turned into beliefs of certainty, a type of pseudo-certainty that Kahneman refers to as

---

[27] Jean Piaget, *Play, Dreams and Imitation in Childhood* (1951; Oxon: Routledge, 2007).
[28] Tremlin, *Minds and Gods*, 149–150.

the "illusion of certainty."[29] This is typically an imitative mind, partly a survival apparatus, and partly self-convincing redundancies of claims made by others without a reality check in the background, referred to as "useful fictions."[30] Religion falls in this category of thinking. Humanity in general bases its adult life on this system of fast-imitative thinking.

System Two, however, is "slow thinking," when one uses critical and creative thinking, a process undertaken recurrently by a small minority. It is a system of thinking that overcomes impulses, resists cognitive illusions, is suspicious of feelings alone, controls anger, examines facts, and makes better choices.[31] System Two thinkers constantly use System One for practical purposes, whereas the persistent System One thinkers often fail or are oblivious to using System Two more consistently. Kahneman points out that System One invents a story or a fictitious reality and tries to convince System Two thinkers to believe it, while in the meantime are unwilling to investigate it.[32] System One thinkers and followers are endangered and can themselves become dangerous through manipulation and brainwashing by the deceivers.

Perhaps if the Aztecs, as "practitioners" of System One thinking with redundant and imitative beliefs under the "illusion of certainty," instead of following the imitative belief of shedding human blood in order for the sun to rise every day had used System Two, thinking with some insightful contemplation, the results of their society would have been radically different. Many human lives could have been spared. They could have also been less vulnerable to the conquistadores, questioning rather than thinking the conquistadores were gods. This in mind, one could actually say that the history of South America could have turned radically different.

The calculus of imitation and obedience often times bears a greater conformity, utility and is less frightening, more reassuring. Due to mental tension, the propensity of fear focuses the mind on finding order, security, and a group of like-minded people to follow. Fear of god, fear of psychological alienation, and ironically fear of freedom, have always paved the way for a less anxious life of imitation and obedience. Religions and cultures perpetuate because of these factors, no matter what the components of a particular religion and culture are, even if completely illogical or absurd.

---

[29] Daniel Kahneman, *Thinking, Fast and Slow* (New York: Farrar, Straus and Giroux, 2011), 5.
[30] Ibid., 23.
[31] Ibid., see Part 1: Two Systems and Part 3: Overconfidence, especially the chapters on "the Illusion of Understanding" and "the Illusion of Validity."
[32] Ibid., chapters, 17, 19, and 20.

So, imitation and obedience play essential roles in maintaining culture and religion. In fact, imitation and obedience within a religio-cultural context have been survival tools, without which one would have had to constantly refer to critical thinking or new computations for new solutions, a rather exhausting possibility along with the danger of becoming a social outcast. The inclination toward imitation has seemingly brought a certain ease and consistency to human life. But the discomfort of blind imitation has caused inner tension between one's own "split mind": on the one side, one seeks conformity, consistency, and security; on the other, one searches for freedom, seeking an exhilarating dynamic mind with a stance against all the binding conventionalities. Sometimes, both of these tendencies overlap or subtly compete against each other, a sort of an inner tension and discord while one constantly measures oneself against the forces of the psyche and life circumstances and strategizes accordingly.

As our human ancestors became aware of and wondered about death, that death seemed to be a loss of connection with reality where one becomes unreal and therefore joins nothingness, a certain sense of *meaning* had to be created. But meaning often stood higher than freedom. A life lived with "meaning" by following a god and imitating one's parental culture seems to be more gratifying than living a free life but (seemingly) empty of meaning. As Keiji Nishitani extrapolates, there was a time when ego came to save humans and prevented nihility and the laws of nature from degrading human life, even though all things in the world symbolized nihility and death.[33] By inventing stories, the nothingness of life changed to something, to meaningful living. The stories sometimes promised a glorious return to life, an eternal homecoming. This myth-making scenario turned the existential anxiety of nothingness into purposeful living. Telling each other thousands of untruths (which felt true) helped to curb emptiness and boredom. It was this paradoxical performance that led on one hand to finding structure through obedience to the messages in these stories, and on the other to living with the derailment of one's own dynamic and evolutionary mind – living in self-deception for the sake of feeling good.

Both Daniel Dennett and Richard Dawkins in addressing the question of "purpose" have emphasized two types of purposes for survival: "arche-purpose" which is nakedly instinctive and serves existential survival. The other is "neo-purpose" which the individuals build upon the arche-purpose to satisfy their "why" question. The 'why' question for the appearance of the universe and its

---

[33] Keiji, Nishitani, *Religion and Nothingness*, trans. Jan van Bragt (Berkeley: University of California Press, 1983), xxxiii, 7, 11, 47, 85, 88, 93, 230.

direction has no definitive answer. It does not seem any non-human animal would be engaged with the "platonic" debate of "arche-purpose" let alone "neo-purpose"; this question is instead an emanation of the human being's tool-maker mindset, a mind that cannot even comprehend where its own competency of making tools comes from (borrowing Dennett's idea).

People fabricated a meaning for life by making myths about the hidden dimensions and intentions of the world. In these myths, humans were promised to have a higher place than this world. Many similar thoughts were replicated and followed for millennia. The exaggerations reached their peak at a time when rational thinkers and naturalist philosophers could no longer condone such astonishingly dramatic and fictitious accounts of reality and were arguing against their fabricators and imitators. It became clear to them that these fictitious stories clashed with the reality of complex life and the integrity of human mind. Despite this, the fictitious, religious interpretations of the reality of life continued to satisfy some audiences, while the rational interpretations satisfied others. It is said there are times when the mind of the myth-maker perceives things that the intellectuals fail to perceive.[34] At the same time, the mind of the intellectual perceives the immeasurable power of nature and the infinity of life which cannot and does not remember all the personal, culture-based, religion-based stories, even though "meaningful" in their own way. This is when the intellectual sees things that the myth-maker and unseeing imitator has failed to see.

Fear was the key premise of generating religions, making up stories, erecting gods to worship, and creating an indisputable system of obedience. Imitating the traditions of their ancestors kept people captive to themselves. The hyperbolic attitude of religious obedience however remained so anticlimactic that it prompted the maverick Prometheus, a Titan and a friend of humanity and enemy of the god Zeus, to say, bringing a tremor to the priests and the followers of Zeus[35]: "I would rather be chained to this rock than be the obedient servant of the gods."[36]

Conclusion

The quintessence of myths out of which religions emerged has in some ways been useful for many frightened people throughout history. Hundreds of religions have formed around the globe to accommodate communities in

---

[34] Ibid., 239.
[35] Campbell, *The Masks of God*, 281.
[36] See Fromm, *On Disobedience*, 1.

dealing with their psychological fears and hopes, to give meaning to their lives, and even offer the promise of an afterlife, whether a life in heaven or a virtuous reincarnation. Religion has also fulfilled a social component, connecting people on a wider scale – an adaptative (or perhaps maladaptive[37]) human behavior passed on through culture.[38] It has given a sense of community, a broad and biologically-psychologically-linked kinship social cooperation,[39] a feel-good sense of a place in which to share space with like-minded people.

However, religion, perhaps involuntarily due to fear, was embarked upon to offer a path not for actually understanding the world and themselves, but to do precisely the opposite – to obscure the world with anthropocentric fictional tales, comfortably leaning on it through faith for thousands of years. Many conventional or mythical "truths" under the flag of religion deal with the same archetypal fear of the unknowable. Parochial cognitive faculties of human ancestors produced sketchy approximations of life and reality, something that suited their truth-seeking efforts and psychological requirements of their days, but blocked them from a rational understanding of the world and themselves and each other. Self-analysis and empirical investigation of the world have had less value in various religious traditions than a surrender to own emotional construction of reality, to the tenets of faith and to the calls of higher authorities. Imitation-obedience has generally been easier for the human brain. In some sense as James C. Scott puts it, "the spread of sedentism transformed Homo sapiens into far more of a herd animal than previously."[40] And cultures, as Daniel Quinn mentions, became large "prisons" that no one, whether rich or poor, could escape.[41] The brain was separated from nature due to its laziness and irrational anxieties.

---

[37] Richard Dawkins argues religion and religious ideas are maladaptive especially when they are passed on to children who cannot make their own decision. See R. Dawkins, *The God Delusion* (London: Bantam, 2006).

[38] See Peter J. Richerson and Lesley Newson, "Is Religion Adaptive? Yes, No, Neutral, But Mostly, We Don't Know," in *The Evolution of Religion: Studies, Theories, & Critiques*, ed. Joseph Bulbulia, Richard Sosis, Erica Harris, Russell Genet, and Karen Wyman (Santa Monica, CA: Collins Foundation Press, 2008), 61–66. They argue against Dawkins's analysis of maladaptive notion of religion, considering it too simplistic.

[39] See Bernard Crespi, "The Kin Selection of Religion," in *Oxford Handbook of the Evolution of Religion*, ed. J. M. Liddle and T. Shackleford (in press), 15–16.

[40] Scott, *Against the Grain*, 83.

[41] Daniel Quinn, *Ishmael: An Adventure of the Mind and Spirit* (New York: Bantam Turner, 1992), 252. The conflict of human's instinct with the demands of culture has been a theme visited by various thinkers. See Konrad Lorenz, *The Waning of Humaneness*, trans. Warren

And so, despite religion's utility for certain people, critical philosophers and thinkers have been arguing that fear and religious thinking distort reality. This process of reality distortion was encompassed in the powerful process of myth-making.

Kickert (Boston and Toronto: Little Brown and Co., 1987), 129. Lorenz specifically refers to Kant and Schiller. Freud also addressed this conflict thoroughly.

Part II.
Mythology: Taking Refuge

Chapter 4

Truth-Seeking and Myth-Making: Humans in Search of Reality

The war of seventy-two tribes was based on absurd pretexts, pay no heed.
As they all failed to unveil reality, each then took the path of making a myth.

—Hafiz

Prelude

We often think of the humans of antiquity and their beliefs as being separate from us, ancient, and irrelevant, quaint and fascinating. And yet today we are the direct descendants of their mythical heritage. The beliefs of today have flowed directly from those earlier minds and imaginations, no matter how modern and advanced we may think ourselves to be. Seeing this process through a new lens of awareness is like having X-ray vision; we can see how myths, and the religions that sprang from them, not only exerted control in the past but *continue* to control much of human thought and society.

In this chapter, we will explore how myths arose out of a truth-seeking impulse. Truth-seeking is the human propensity to constantly search for an ultimate explanation of things, a lasting truth. This uniquely human tendency emerged with the expansion of brain function and self-awareness over time. Seeking truth may seem to be a worthy undertaking, but in ancient times, given the low level of knowledge and lack of scientific information, the impulse toward truth-seeking was so strong that it resulted in 'creating' truths in which the boundaries of logic were breached and thus truth-seeking led to myth-making. 'Truths' emerged as myths that eventually became the foundations of religious scriptures and practices. As romantic as these myths may seem, in fact myths in many preliterate cultures possessed insidious despotic aspects that dominated societies, locked people in for the sake of homogeneity, and punished defectors in ways we are usually quite unaware of. Furthermore, the myths and religions exploited the human imagination with the idea of miracles to explain the events of nature and human reality. The framing of imaginative ideas as absolute knowledge ultimately became a treacherous enterprise, leading people to believe in mythical realities, something from which modern humans must draw lessons today.

The two inclinations of *truth-seeking* and *myth-making* were primarily responsible for shaping the cultural and religious beliefs of the latter part of the Neolithic period, particularly during the Bronze and Iron Ages in various parts of the world. On the universal level, truth-seeking and myth-making projected the curiosity and imagination of the human psyche. But on the local level, each story took on its own flavor, with innovative allegorical metaphors that engaged the geographical landscape and the needs of its population. The culture of storytelling gradually integrated such myths into the broader cultural and religious consciousness of the masses at large. Framing an amorphic reality into morphic narratives satisfied the cognitive and emotional curiosity of preliterate communities. The visualization of the plots about life events, heroes, creation, or even afterlife induced emotional uplift and even transcendental elation, experiences that have given many in the past (and the present) a strong and appealing sense of meaning and mental direction (a kind of basic logotherapy, "a will to meaning" or "existential psychiatry" as developed by Viktor Frankl [d. 1997]).[1]

Myths by themselves inherently may have aesthetic and allegorical beauty and can be quite captivating. Even though these myths have certain literary value for us today, for our ancestors they ultimately concealed more than they revealed about the reality of existence. Our interest here lies in exploring how the pursuit of explanations and truth as a psychological solution to existential confusion resulted in human populations sacrificing their own judicious empirical thinking. Imaginative stories were given a sacred and perennial status. This imprudence, of course was not without cognitive cost, and much later was met with strong opposition by logicians and naturalist thinkers-philosophers whose goal was the liberation of minds from fictitious, mythical constructions.

With the development of writing, these imaginative narratives told as stories were embellished, systematized, and eventually recorded. Many such myths labeled as "truths" began to develop their own grammar, which became the foundation of cognitive encapsulation, neural programming, and ultimately a deep belief system. Myth-making and mythology was thus an existential response by the mind that required a form of language to vocalize the myths[2] and eventually be able to write them down. The human drive to know the unknowable – such as the "creation" and direction of the world and how

---

[1] See Viktor Frankl, *The Will to Meaning: Foundations and Applications of Logotherapy* (New York: Meridian, 1988), 1–7, 15, 20.

[2] Gregory M. Nixon, "Myth and Mind: The Origin of Human Consciousness in the Discovery of the Sacred," *Journal of Consciousness Exploration and Research*, 1/3 (2010), 37.

humans, the stars, and sky emerged, even to know the enigma of immortality – was a desperate search, a quest for closure instead of open-endedness.

The hunter-gatherers certainly must have had superstitious beliefs, but the drive for truth-seeking and myth-making was eventually systematized when populations transitioned from open nature to culture, or from orality to literacy. In the course of cultural evolution in agriculturalist communities, a small minority of truth-seekers and myth-makers went on to irreversibly influence larger populations, not only for one generation but consecutive generations. The mundane world was turned into something exciting and theatrically spectacular through storytelling. The motivating promise of immortality in a better world in the context of myth-religion also provided certain incentive to follow leaders; it only took people to *believe* it, nothing more. The ruling oligarchs of city-states drove this process. This was not the work of farmers, slaves, or ordinary residents, but instead was the work of Mesopotamian kings and Egyptian pharaohs, for example. Thus, while the hunter-gatherer's mind would probably have the same desire to "know" the unknowable, and likely fabricated stories to justify existence, their myths and truths were never written down. The egalitarian and nomadic system of the hunter-gatherers passed on myths in an oral fashion, instead of using them as means of dominating their fellow companions as occurred in hierarchical, agriculturalist and more literate systems. Hunter-gatherers with their natural-biodegradable materials of life, along with their oral transmission simply vanished from the historical and archaeological records.[3]

The goal of this chapter is to explore with a new perspective examples of myth-based "truths" that turned into the pillars of religions. The myths incorporated in the Abrahamic and other scriptures became "truths" in ancient times, some of which continue to be strongly believed in our day. The focus here is to illuminate the tendency to make truth claims through the lens of myth, which was the only tool available to our human ancestors – but which we need to be aware of, or risk still being bound by today. By seeing these myths more clearly, we can see how they obstructed the path towards a clear, unencumbered view of the world and ourselves.

The Compulsion of Truth-Seeking

Truth-seeking, as a whole, is the desire to have a unified explanation of reality. There seems to be an obsession with seeking truth about absurd and even unknowable things. Truth-seeking may be purely human; such an impulse does

---

[3] Scott, *Against the Grain*, 13.

not necessarily serve the objectives of the animal world. Animals, seemingly, have a greater sense of acceptance of the state of reality than humans. As Erich Fromm has put it, the difference between a non-thinking animal and a thinking human being is that an animal *is lived* through the forces of nature and a human being *must live* through the forces of cognition. It is almost like life passes through an animal, but humans create life or engineer life. The animal lives in "harmony" with nature, whereas human life has been disrupted by a sense of truth, imagination, and reason, all of which has created a dichotomy between their animal side and their existence, a dichotomy that has left humans without knowledge of themselves.[4] It also left humans without the knowledge of the natural world, its inception and its direction.

Apart from truth-seeking being a way of dealing with existential matters, curiosity about the supernatural (unexplainable natural phenomena) became an urge of the mind, a self-captivating practice to please or distract the fearing mind. The Bronze and Iron Ages were a high point of a "compulsive behavior" to engage with metaphysical themes. Various ancient cultures went on to invent myths about the constant battle of gods and forces of nature. Myths also led to the astrological belief that the dwelling forces, stars, and gods in the heavens implicated and impacted the human soul in the battle – a sort of making sense of everyday life.[5]

The growing link between truth-seeking and myth-making paved the way for the imaginative enthusiasts to improvise idiosyncratic hypothetical answers to various unknowable topics, such as the source of the beginning of the world and the first human life, the condition and location of the human soul after death, and the idea of an immortal return to a better world. The compulsion to ask clever metaphysical questions and provide clever answers gradually became programmed into "ordinary" everyday human behavior. This behavior picked up momentum during the latter part of the Neolithic period: for every supernatural question there was an answer or a story.

With repeated tellings of these stories over time and generations, the masses at large began to believe the stories and answers given to address the unknowable inquiries. These explanations gradually became part of the inner environment of the mind and its beliefs. When this happens, such beliefs are no longer easy to challenge. As a psychiatrist and evolutionist thinker, Anderson Thomson explains, it is through the attachments to one's ideas and

---

[4] Fromm, *The Sane Society*, 22–24, 60.
[5] David Ulansey, "The Mithraic Mysteries," *Scientific American* 261/6, Dec. 1989, 130–135.

experiences that beliefs are concretized and the difficulty rests in these attachments from which the beliefs cannot be set free.[6]

This classical picture of a conditioned and self-convinced mind refers to "tough-minded" people (borrowing a term from William James) who claim to know the truth of things without realizing that the premise for their metaphysical and unverifiable knowledge is simply a story, a *belief*, not proof. Besides William James and other modern thinkers realizing the pitfalls of this mindset, long ago the Buddha also argued that an obsessed mind is implicated in itself. He put forward that what one feels, one perceives; what one perceives, one reasons about. What one reasons about, one is obsessed with, and is assailed by it.[7]

The human tendency to attach to beliefs seems to trap the mind in itself, and in fact in his book *Capture*, David Kessler describes a theory of mental "capture" that involves three shifts in the human mind: a narrowing of attention, a perceived lack of control, and a change in emotional state.[8] In brief, it is argued that habits and beliefs that have "captured" an individual's mind exert power over the individual, influencing their behavior, dominating their consciousness, and dictating their attitudes. The results of this type of "capture" feel familiar to the environment of the mind, and this familiarity then becomes a hassle-free habit and even a need.[9]

It seems that truth-seeking and believing in myths became a source of such mental "capture" for multitudes of human beings. Humans in general may have shifted from one truth to another over time, but they have maintained their addiction to living with some sort of confirmation, belief, or truth. For example, when shifting from one religious belief to another, new converts often develop another "capture", or set of obsessive beliefs, towards their new religion. This means such converts cannot disengage their mind from the tenets of the new belief system.[10] This is historically true and is often repeated

---

[6] J. Anderson Thomson, Clare Aukofer, and Richard Dawkins (Foreword), *Why We Believe in God(s): A Concise Guide to the Science of Faith* (Charlottesville: Pitchstone Publishing, 2011).

[7] David J. Kalupahana, *Ethics in Early Buddhism* (Honolulu: University of Hawaii Press, 1995), 40; see also David J. Kalupahana, *A History of Buddhist Philosophy: Continuities and Discontinuities* (Honolulu: University of Hawaii Press, 1992), 32.

[8] Kessler, *Capture*, 7.

[9] Ibid., 7–9.

[10] Ibid., 257–262.

in human behavior: "we find stability and self-awareness by exchanging one capture for another."[11]

The tendency of the mind is to ensnare itself by its own stories, under the guise of seeking and knowing the truth. Such neurological "capture" is a result of a neural sensitization and brain wiring. This has consequences ranging from suffering, to being inspired, to being dependent on how the mind is oriented and where it takes the person. Whatever one is "captured" by may produce a stronger and localized focus and create a purpose and a change in perception, or can cause affliction, addiction, or even damaging emotional states. In his recent book, Michael Pollan researches how a captured, ego-fear-ridden, depressed and a defaulted area of the mind can be shifted or transformed through the effects of experiences ranging from psychedelic drugs to transcendental meditation.[12]

As a consequence, the truth-seeking and the eventual myth-making process of human ancestors and the propagation to the later generations inhibited populations who then reverted to the ready-made beliefs originating from the ancestors. One's belief in the tribal "truth" competed with other tribal "truths"[13] on one hand and blinded the believers of one truth to all other versions of truths on the other. In the absence of any deeper science of things, this trend led to inflated stories through tagging them as perennial and the truth.

Any criticism directed against these behaviors or challenging these ancient truths within well-accommodated cultures seemed antithetical because people tend to make a virtue out of their staunch belief, simply out of personal and social necessity.[14] Defending "truth" against "untruth" in the course of history has sadly caused much bloodshed. Often the crowd of believers, simply by outnumbering their opponents, established what was truth and what was untruth.

---

[11] Ibid., 7, 223–224.

[12] Michael Pollan, *How to Change Your Mind: What the New Science of Psychedelics Teaches Us About Consciousness, Dying, Addiction, Depression and Transcendence* (New York: Penguin Press, 2018).

[13] Even beyond religion, this process continues today: It is easy to see how the tribalism of the past has become the nationalism of the present. National myths (narratives) serve exactly the same role in bestowing national identity as religious myths bestowed tribal identity.

[14] *Aus der Not eine Tugend machen.* This relevant German proverb means: "to make a virtue out of necessity" or "to make a virtue out of one's own desperate condition."

Origins of Personalized Truths-Myths

Psychoanalytical theories about the emanation of myths abound. We know that ancestral myths in many cultures have been conceived both while in trance and in a sober state. Myths may concern celestial or earthly matters, animals, humans, the occult or physical world, fantasy or real, sacred or profane. Brilliant and provocative ideas range from arguing the role of the subconscious to the role of the collective unconscious. Understandably, with human self-awareness the clash between the *personal* wish to connect warmly with the world while cold and *impersonal* Nature led humans to develop an obsession with explanations about existence and natural events.

The foundations of myths have universal similarities. Esteemed researchers such as Carl Jung (d. 1961), Joseph Campbell (d. 1987), and Mircea Eliade (d. 1986) expound on this idea of universal similarities. They present myths as being relative to each other among diverse global cultures stemming from the same human desire to tell fundamental stories in their own figurative language.

For Jung, myths arose from unconscious archetypes, and the content of myths can be said to belong to those who produced them as well as to those who accepted them because such myths have made a difference in their lives.[15] In the same line as Jung, Joseph Campbell's depiction of universal and archetypal mythology ("monomyth") is represented in *The Hero with a Thousand Faces* (1949), and *The Masks of God: Primitive Mythology* (1960). Campbell describes the same story in multiple myths of the universal hero who makes extraordinary returns from a journey, each time with more power and knowledge. The longing of the second or eternal return to the world in a religious context is the perpetuation of the myth from the earlier version of the return of the hero and savior to the world.[16]

Eliade has his own distinctive and sentimental outlook on the emergence of myth in human history. Eliade in certain ways reverses the process proposed by Campbell and Jung, claiming first the persistence of certain primordial truths out of which myths were then conceived. Eliade proposes that the reason some myths were made "sacred" in religions was due to an intrinsic or absolute truth in each of them. It was this "sacred" sense that accelerated the process of making the myths into "truths." In other words, myths became sacred in Eliade's conception because of the existence of truth from the

---

[15] Robert A. Segal, "Jung on Myth," in *Teaching Jung*, ed. Kelly Bulkeley and Clodagh Weldon (New York: Oxford University Press, 2011), 75–76.
[16] For broader discussions, see Joseph Campbell, *The Hero with a Thousand Faces* (Princeton: Princeton University Press, 1968) and *The Masks of God*.

primordial times.[17] But what Eliade and similar thinkers have handled with disdain are the questions at the root of philosophical arguments and conflicts in human history: what is truth, or whose truth is it? Is there a universal criterion or is it simply an individual approach to knowing truth, especially when the content of this truth stems from a myth? The relativistic personal or tribal religious claims of truth leave us not only the same question about what is concretely meant by truth, but also remind us that bringing in a personal belief cannot be counted as the basis for truth. Truth and myth can thus overlap in the mind without conscious awareness.

According to the extremely influential physiologist-psychologist-philosopher William James (d. 1910), many myth-truths have personal and practical value only in the individual's life. He believed that the utility of a mystical or religious experience make it true just for the person. James's pragmatism[18] takes interest in the personal truth and variety of religious experiences.[19] The personal experiences remain personal. Any universal truth or experience, however, must pass the test of empiricism and be verified in terms of making sense. James's seemingly paradoxical position gives the individual the "free will to believe"[20] in whatever works for one's life; meanwhile the individual and the community must live harmoniously within the limits of practical logic.

James was interested in resolving the dispute between the personal and universal meaning of life through exploration of the pragmatic application of truth, sound mind, and pluralism.[21] James's pragmatism allows myths to operate and create meaning for those individuals who prefer a myth over logical thinking, but he warns against allowing personal experiences to compromise the sanity of a pluralistic coexistence with others, especially speaking to preserving the privileges of those who do not share the same experiences drawn from the myths or religious sources. Konrad Lorenz describes this differently by quoting Viennese physicist, Herbert Pietschmann. According to Pietschmann, there are two avenues of thought: one leads to a *correct* conclusion and the other to a *true* experience. *Correct,* in this context may allude to something like

---

[17] For a detailed work of Eliade about myths and dreams, see Mircea Eliade, *Myths, Dreams and Mysteries: The Encounter Between Contemporary Faiths and Archaic Realities* (New York: Harper & Row, 1961).

[18] William James, *Pragmatism: A New Name for Some Old Ways of Thinking* (1907). Reprinted by Floatingpress.com, 2010

[19] William James, *The Varieties of Religious Experience: A Study in Human Nature* (1902). Reprinted by Seven Treasures Publication, 2009.

[20] The title of William James' lecture and essay was "The Will to Believe," in 1897.

[21] https://plato.stanford.edu/entries/james/, accessed May 3, 2018.

mathematics for measuring the smaller and measurable things in the world, whereas *true* is an experience within our emotions, which may remain unverified forever.[22] In other words, for as long as humans remain attached to the non-quantifiable and unknowable, or unconscious reasoning, experiences in principle shall equate with supernatural or extranatural.[23] This unconscious reasoning under the banner of truth cannot allow a person to claim to know or objectify the whole world. The *perception* of truth, however, is an emanation of feelings and a personal experience.

Belief in myths often resulted in the rejection of other explanations about the world, an intellectual tragedy not to be underestimated. The loss of individual cognitive freedom began when myth and religion were intertwined and institutionalized in the Bronze and Iron Ages. Thus, individuals came under the rule of institutions while also losing their own intellectual self-rule.

Myths and beliefs evolved into public religions with rituals that often brought their believers into confrontation with non-believers. Through the wars of conquest, conquerors took the "right" to dominate the vanquished, and often imposed their religions and myths. The power of the idea of "sacred" (the term often used by Eliade) gave license to the conquering armies, or even the majority of a society, to treat the "pagans" or "heretics" or "outcasts" viciously. The juggernaut of mythological beliefs in religions provided empires and their ruling classes psychological authority over others. Those who were conquered learned to adapt to new myths and religions.

The Marriage Between Myth and Religion

Oftentimes the border between myth and religion is blurry, perhaps because both stem from the same counterintuitive sources of cognition. The interconnection between myth and religion has been argued differently by two twentieth-century German philosophers, Hermann Cohen (d. 1918) and Ernst Cassirer (d. 1945), as compared and analyzed by Reinhard Margreiter. In distinguishing the difference between myth and religion, Cohn believed that the success of Judaism arose from bringing myth out of its primitive state and turning it into a religion of ethical reason (Religion der Vernunft).[24] Cohen further declared that with the development of monotheism and its brands of

---

[22] Lorenz, *The Waning of Humaneness*, 75–76, here Lorenz also quotes Erwin Chargaff.
[23] Ibid., 77, 81, 113.
[24] Reinhard Margreiter, "Mythos versus Religion?: Über eine Denkfigur bei Cohen und Cassirer," *Philosophisches Jahrbuch* (Freiburg, München: Verlag Karl Alber 2003), 132.

ethic and sin, myth came to an end and religion began to take over.[25] On the other hand, Cassirer took a different position, stating that myth is a systematic prerequisite and the basis for religion. Cassirer regarded myth and religion as competing for different claims on different levels, despite having the same "genetic" roots through archaic language.[26] Thus, myths and religious truths were often an intertwined act of storytelling about the beginning of time, creation, heroes, battles, and miraculous events. In this context of religion, myths were propagated and underwent many transitions and adaptations in the process.

The marriage between myth and religion was strengthened through elaborate linguistic metaphors and grammars. In the long run, it was as if languages competed for greater allegories and more accessible metaphors, changing at a faster pace than the religions themselves.[27] The power of a new religious language evolved in a two-step process: first inventing a "sacred" language, and second, transmitting myths in the framework of religion.

1. The Sacred Language of Myths

Of course, it was through writing that in earlier societies, organized politics, science, jurisprudence, religion, theology, and dogmatism and sophisticated mode of communications were established.[28] Written language not only influenced the content of human thought, consciousness, and action but also caused a leap forward in the cultures with literacy and written language as opposed to those cultures just working with oral and unsystematic transmission.[29]

In making truths and myths believable, the language of the sacred was conceived. Life and the repetition of day and night were taken out of their "meaninglessness". Natural events, themselves fundamentally wordless, were described using dazzling human vernacular. Through visionary images and the use of metaphorical language, as G. M. Nixon explains, the attempt was to make the world a livable and "sacred" space which would connect individuals to the world in a more emotional way.[30]

---

[25] Ibid., 132.
[26] Ibid., 135-136.
[27] See Nicholas Ostler, *Passwords to Paradise: How Languages Have Re-invented World Religions* (New York: Bloomsbury Press, 2016).
[28] See Jack Goody, *The Logic of Writing and the Organization of Society* (New York: Cambridge University Press, 1986).
[29] Walter J. Ong, *Orality and Literacy* (Oxon: Routledge, 2012). See especially the introduction, chapters 4 and 6.
[30] Nixon, "Myth and Mind," 8–11, 21–22, 31, 34, 38.

The common denominator between religion and sacred language has been communication through symbolic metaphors. Such metaphors are supposed to hint at a symbolic "truth" while at the same time keeping themes fluid and subject to newer interpretations. Hans Blumenberg (d. 1996), in his *Paradigm for a Metaphorology* (*Paradigmen zu einer Metaphorologie*), examines this power of metaphors. Metaphors may inhibit clarity of thought - or perhaps they make deeper philosophical thinking accessible which conceptual judgments cannot express due to rigidity of thought and language.[31] The two stances are paradoxical. Metaphors, in other words, could lead us to errors as much as they could present a well-rounded panoramic outlook on life that conventional language is unable to express. This being said, our goal here is to come closer to understanding the cognitive lenses through which human ancestors perceived reality and life and which led to the development of religion and its powerful language of control. And if fear or subjugation was the prime basis for inventing metaphors, then the knowledge offered through religion and religious language gives its followers a figurative image of life.

The language of myth had much to do with this connection of individuals to the world. The proposal of the metaphor of "god" alone made an enormous difference in connecting average folks to the world, offering a paternal or a maternal chaperone who looked after everyone and was personally involved in people's lives. So, through the mediation of language and myth-making, the cold, speechless, and impersonal environment of Nature became a personal home, with a personal god or hero overseeing minor and major human affairs.

The linguistic aspect of the truth-myth pursuit played a significant role in bringing unity within communities. The words and stories of ancestors were repeated and passed on. Transmitting the thoughts and ideas of previous generations occurred both orally and in written form, and was a means for creating bonds with the past and one another.[32] Supported by the power of language, the social roles of myth and eventually religion were used to create community, piecing together certain rules of conduct and providing the clan with a common lineage identity. However, this unity created the limits of insider-outsider borders that often led to punishing, at times quite

---

[31] For details see, Hans Blumenberg, *Paradigms for a Metaphorology*, trans. Robert Savage (Ithaca, NY: Cornell University Press, 2010). The first German edition was published in 1960.
[32] Craig T. Palmer, Ryan M. Ellsworth, and Lyle B. Steadman, "Talk and Tradition: Why the Least Interesting Components of Religion May Be the Most Evolutionarily Important," in Voland and Schiefenhövel, *The Biological Evolution of Religious Mind and Behavior*, 105–116.

ferociously, the *defectors* of the tribe or religion.³³ (The closest human counterparts, the higher order primates, have the same social order that dictates loyal behaviors by the members of the pack; otherwise, dire consequences could ensue for the defectors, particularly for the "adulterous" females.) The bonds created through the common language of myth for humans produced a more enclosed atmosphere that encouraged living together rather than easily shifting sides and abandoning the clan. Putting myths inside a religious framework strengthened the social fabric while addressing existential riddles, not just for one generation but for all posterity through the power of written language.

Dynamic oral traditions gradually evolved into static and unalterable written texts.³⁴ Putting mythical stories and religious "truths" in writing gave fixity to the stories and beliefs, with the use of sacred and embellished language creating a sort of immortal knowledge for posterity. When it came to bonding the members of the clan through the metaphorical power of language, it made a stronger difference when the myths that were presented to the crowd came from written sources rather than oral, especially in more literate communities.

Thus, the allegorical narratives were believed to be inviolable actualities which must remain immortal. Static words representing symbols were framed as truths and as a result, beliefs were intensified. Gradually, written language also became a means of spreading dogmatism and even lies under the banner of truth, for generations to come.

In the myths which were adopted by religions, particularly in the Abrahamic religions, gods have often been the authors of world "history" and were the deciders of its destiny. Such myths were given a greater boost through the invention of religion with the notion of *revelation*, in which god spoke directly with a select few human beings, providing greater validation and superiority over previously anonymous authors. In the written language used for legends and religious scriptures, sometimes god is the narrator and speaks as the first person singular ("I") while at other times god is referred to in a third person singular ("He") even all in the same narrative (see for example the syntax in

---

³³ Self-awareness and language have obviously made humans unique among primates, while still possessing strong primate qualities. The tendency to exhibit primates' clannish bondage has remained. The closest human counterparts, the higher order primates, have the same social order dictating loyal behavior for the members of the pack; otherwise dire consequences could ensue for the defectors.

³⁴ See Marilyn R. Waldman, "Primitive Mind/Modern Mind: New Approaches to an Old Problem Applied to Islam," in *Approaches to Islam in Religious Studies*, ed. Richard C. Martin (Tucson: University of Arizona Press, 1985), 91–105.

Truth-Seeking and Myth-Making

the Koran). In the transition from the Bronze Age to the Iron Age, among the Semitic tribes, god is the narrator and eventually the author of human and global stories. In fact, in the godly revelations in the Semitic tradition, god recites the stories (histories) of the past generations, about those who sided with god and with the tribe, and those who persisted as foes. The idea of a revelation from god thus gave the status of world history greater legitimacy and transformed mythical narratives into uncompromising language for religions that communicated absolute truth and even world history.

With the overlap between myth and religion, people began identifying themselves by the myths that they believed in. As the culture of revelation and direct intervention by god developed, god's role increased, narrating the story of life in his own divine language through those receiving the revelation. The average fallible man and woman were left out of the process, instead being simply passive receivers. The contents of these revelations through the agency of prophecy and priesthood were then propagated during the Iron Age and onward.

2. How Myths Flowed Through Time

Myth-making stems from "the human desire to bring the universe into some sort of manageable form through the play of the imagination."[35] Ancient myths were not seen as untrue even though we know today they were for the most part imaginative stories; on the contrary, they were trusted as the interpretations of reality that permeated people's lives. Through the performance of rites and rituals that developed around various aspects of the myths, as well the evolving dynamic of divine rulers with god's revelation, religions developed. And we know that such myth-religions had a highly functional application for people of that time, providing comfort and assurance in the face of frightening and unexplainable natural phenomena.

So we might be tempted to assume that since the scientific era provides empirical explanations for natural phenomena, our modern view of life and religion is myth-free. But in fact it is not.[36] It has become problematic that myths

---

[35] Montagu, *Man: His First Million Years*, 191.
[36] There are also modern fabricated myths: the idea that people only use 10 percent of their brain power, that playing Mozart to infants boosts their intelligence, that only depressed people commit suicide, that psychiatric wards may receive more patients during a full moon, and many more myth-based themes that people repeat to others by using scientific jargon. See Scott O. Lilienfeld, Steven Jay Lynn, John Ruscio, and Barry L. Beyerstein, *50 Great Myths of Popular Psychology: Shattering Widespread Misconception about Human Behavior* (Chichester: Wiley Blackwell, 2010).

in the context of religion continue to persist today, in a time of rational thinking and understanding about how the natural world works. Followers continue to make assertions based on the irrational mythical claims of the archaic ancestors.

How can such a need for myth persist through time? We can more deeply appreciate the depth and power of the psychological interlinking of myth and religion by looking at some examples of the truth-seeking/myth-making/religion-forming process and the resulting myths, from antiquity to now. The goal is not a comprehensive study of comparative mythology, but is to look at a few example myths with a new perspective of awareness of their role and effects on the mind. It is also to provide interesting examples of regional cross-influences among some myths in the Near East and Mediterranean regions, since the myths, gods, and heroes of ancient traditions became so intertwined over the course of several millennia of interactions that it is difficult to disentangle them from each other, and consequently from the human psyche. We will explore how myths resulted in strange religious practices like sacrifices, rituals, spells, and organized worship. It reveals the roots of irrationality, transitioning from simple stories to complex religious beliefs and rituals, that would eventually be addressed by philosophers who saw greater value in a rational approach to life instead. Understanding these myths is important in the larger perspective to realize how entrenched mythical thinking was in one form or another, and how prevalent it still is today.

Creation Myths

Creation myths explaining how the world came to be and how it was be divided among peoples are among the earliest systematized stories that took the status of sacred truths and became popularized through religious beliefs.

Some interesting examples are the overlapping stories from the Iranian tradition, such as the legendary Iranian literature the *Shahnameh* of Firdousi (d. 1020) which is itself based on other ancient myths – all once upon a time believed to be true. In the *Shahnameh*'s creation story, Fereydoun is the immortal descendant of Jamshid (Avestan Yima) who bore three sons. The earth was divided into three territories among these three sons for them to rule and spread their race and civilization.

In the meanwhile, Fereydoun's immortality was annulled by Ahriman, the Zoroastrian evil-god, and Fereydoun's beloved younger son Iraj (to whom the territory of Iran and India was bestowed) was killed by his two brothers.[37] This story of the three sons of Fereydoun resonates with the biblical story of Noah's three sons Shem, Hem, and Japheth who, according to the myth, were respectively given the Near East, Africa, and Europe to spread their races. (This mythology became so strongly integrated into the cultural consciousness that the names of the sons of Noah were used centuries later by linguists to label the language families from those regions accordingly: the Hamitic languages in Africa and the Semitic languages in the Near East.[38])

In another regional myth of the Zoroastrian-Iranian tradition, the god Ahura Mazda created the world and then created Keyumars as the first human being, the first king who introduced codes of conduct and spread his progeny on earth. This myth, like so many others, clearly distinguishes between those who sided with the tribe and those who sided with the enemy. In this connection, the serpent king Zahak conquers Iran but was eventually defeated by Fereydoun and chained to Mount Damavand. In this myth, the victory of the "righteous" king over a "wicked" king under the influence of the devil Ahriman is a typical story of a tribe complimenting and congratulating itself with all kinds of divine virtues while demonizing the enemy.

The Indian Vedic tradition meanwhile produced its own detailed and intricate creation story of how water, fire, thunder, and other components of nature came into existence through the power of specific deities. The Brahmanical tradition establishes a beginning for this existing world. The Vedic self-born god Brahma (not the Upanishadic Brahman), also called Prajapati (*praja* in Sanskrit means "offspring") is the god who put the world into action. Not long after creating the world, Brahma withdrew and left his creation to the superhuman-god Viṣnu and his various consecutive incarnations, such as Ram and Krishna, considered to be invigorating and wise gods who helped to preserve and perpetuate Brahma's creation.[39] The

---

[37] See Ahmad Tafażżolī, "FERĒDŪN: Iranian Mythic Hero," *Encyclopedia Iranica*, Dec. 15, 1999, accessed Dec. 23, 2016.

[38] The term "Semitic" based on the name of Shem or Sam, Noah's son was adopted for the linguistic purposes in 1781 by the historian and orientalist, A. L. von Schlözer, a member of the Göttingen School of History.

[39] Many mythological epics of the Brahmanical tradition are recounted in numerous Puranas (exegetical literature, or popular Vedic anthologies) as well as the four Vedic texts. The *Mahabharata* (the Great Bharat or Great India, or the Great Story of India) is another sacred source for mythical stories of kings and saints. Mahabharata as a legendary book of the Indian world which like the Old and New Testaments is often understood literally, not metaphorically. Thus, the effort of a genre of modern archaeologists is to look for the real

god Shiva completed the picture by serving as the god of destruction, thus establishing a pantheon representing the cycle of existence: creation, preservation, destruction.

These written myths that separated tribe and enemy or described how the creation came into existence and is sustained fundamentally served to keep each tribe proud of its inception and evolution by claiming the mightiest gods to be on their side.

Greek Mythological Pantheons

The stories of the Greek pantheon, with the gods' roles and interactions with mortals, permeated all aspects of Greek life and were so compelling that even today they are a great source of entertainment for children and movie-goers. But for the ancient Greeks, their gods and stories provided real panacea for confusion and fear, whether of death (Hades) or of the ocean (Poseidon) or of thunder (Zeus). We would think that anyone who believes in Zeus today lives in a nonsensical fantasy, but to the ancient Hellenized people he was real, the supreme and mighty god, the king god of justice who used lightning as a weapon to destroy his enemies. It must have been the incredible epic language that made the gods' might so convincing and brought a sense of comfort to the worshippers during frightening thunder storms or other overwhelming natural events. The collective nature of the human fear of phenomena of the sky is evident from the fact that other mythologies also had gods analogous to Zeus, such as the Nordic god Thor and the Vedic god Indra.

We can see how the people's gods manifested and attended their concerns and needs. The Greek god Apollo, for example, worshipped among the Hellenic populations in Southern Europe and Western and Central Asia, was a multifaceted god. He was the god of the sun, a warrior, the slayer of pythons, protector from evil, and winner of battles, who later became a wise god, the patron of music, art, healing, and inward contemplation. Apollo-worship met a range of followers' psychological needs, and this was the role of gods, mythology, and religion on a large scale. Gods' gender roles flip-flopped, sometimes male and at other times female, because one god or the other was blamed for having lost the power to control natural disasters, win battles, or even fulfill the wishes of their worshippers.

---

sites and artifacts in order to try to prove the veracity or at least find some historical connection of the stories reflected in Mahabharata or even in the Bible.

Thus Apollo, Zeus, and dozens of other Greek gods, as well as analogous pantheons in other cultures around the world, formed myth-religions that once upon a time provided compelling and authoritative belief systems for a significant era of human cultural evolution.

Biblical-Koranic Stories and Influences from Mesopotamian-Egyptian Myths

To appreciate the integrative power of mythology, we can look at the connections between the creation stories in Mesopotamian legends and the stories of Adam and Eve and the Garden of Eden in the Book of Genesis. The Garden of Eden was probably near the Tigris and Euphrates Rivers in Mesopotamia and is described in the myths as the place of creation of human life. The "human" genealogical construction beginning with Adam and Eve in the Garden of Eden in Mesopotamia was the start of a mythology of humans in Paradise coexisting with god, with those outside still being of the savage animal kingdom. The Adam and Eve myth of the Garden of Eden symbolizes, as James C. Scott put it, humans leaving the hunter-gatherer life, a natural and free lifestyle, and as a punishment from god, shifting from living with god to a life of toil in the sedentary agriculturalist system in Mesopotamia.[40]

This expulsion from heaven is a metaphor that disguises the story of a small tribe living near the Euphrates and Tigris Rivers as it made the sometimes-painful transition from being a hunter-gatherer group to an agriculturalist society. They lived with animals, sharing pathogens which caused cross-infection and epidemics.[41] This could have easily been viewed as god's punishment, kicking Adam and his progenies out of the heaven into this misery of agriculture, so to speak.

Being the first human, Adam and his descendants through tribal myth were identified as the "Chosen People," leaving out other human beings, especially those who lived outside the tribe and outside of the geography of the Garden of Eden, which represented an organized and opulent agriculturalist society.[42]

---

[40] Scott, *Against the Grain*, 10, 72.
[41] Ibid., 8–9, 83–84.
[42] The story of savagery is reflected in the scriptures when two powerful sons of Adam and Eve, Abel and Cain, the second generation of humans. The two sons planned to kill each other. Curiously this violence could not be prevented by god, as humans had been abandoned and yet at the same time held responsible for their acts of good and evil. Through the lens of anthropology, the story of the two sons seems to originate with a Hittite myth which was then transferred into the Semitic, Greek and Roman sources. See Walter Burkert, *The Orientalizing Revolution: Near Easter Influence on Greek Culture*

Although kicked out of heaven, they viewed themselves as "humans," and those who were still wanderers, outsiders, and hunter-gatherers were seen as "savages," almost non-human. Gradually, the state-based religions kept non-state scattered populations as non-domesticated humans.[43] In this geographical connection, it is pertinent and fascinating to note that not only Adam[44] and Eve but also Noah and Abraham were all from Mesopotamia, and the myths of creation and massive floods became intertwined, passed on, and fully incorporated into the psyches of the Judeo-Christian-Islamic people.

Given these creation myths, none of the communities could have imagined that someday we humans through science of genetics could trace our human ancestors back to Africa, in the distant and unrecorded past.

a. God's Retribution and Miracles

The anthropomorphic conceptualization of god has given rise to various myths in which humans are usually the objects of god's superior maneuvering, whether he is doling out rewards or punishments. The punishment by god was often used to explain natural disasters, and the disaster of a flood was a powerful lingering myth in the Mesopotamian region for centuries, from the ancient Babylonian texts, to the Hebrew Book of Genesis, and including the Koran (7:64, 10:73, 11:37, 43–44, 25:37, 29:14).

The biblical story of Noah's flood describes a global flood annihilating the entire natural setting, in which rain fell for 40 days and 40 nights (Genesis 7:17), and the resulting floodwaters covered the earth for 150 days, in which all living beings drowned (7:11–24). This particular punishment from god was said to target the depravities committed by humans, and therefore erase from the world the animals, insects, trees, and all other living creatures. (An interesting choice, considering that they were not involved in the human depravities and sins.) The world was later rebuilt with the return of animals and people because god ordered a pair of each sentient being to be taken onto the ark built by Noah (following instructions from god) so that in the

---

in the Early Archaic Age, trans. Margaret E. Pinder and Walter Burkert (Cambridge: Harvard University Press, 1992), 111–112.

[43] Scott, *Against the Grain,* 12, 16–17.

[44] In a later Persian and Sri Lankan Muslim legend, Adam is believed to have fallen from Heaven on a mountain peak in the Sri Lankan island where he had left his footprint, a place known as Adam's Peak, although the footprint, as the legends of the island report is the Buddha's. See Mostafa Vaziri, *Buddhism in Iran: An Anthropological Approach to Traces and Influences* (New York and London: Palgrave Macmillan, 2012), 68–69.

Truth-Seeking and Myth-Making

new world order they could reproduce again, this time from a sanctified ethnic line, and within a renovated natural setting with the hope they would not sin another time. It was an attempt to "start fresh" with creation.

The fantastical and earlier aspects of this myth-making legend of flood have precedent in the same region in ancient times. As Eric Cline explains, in all the flood myths the storyline is the same; only the name of the hero changes.[45] Cuneiform tablets dating back to seventh century BCE provide a parallel pre-Noah legend, in which the flood was sent by the gods because these gods felt their peace was disturbed by the noisy humans.[46] The legend tells the story of the king Ziusudra being ordered by god to build an ark since the flood was imminent. A modified story was later attributed to Atrahasis, and then to Utnapishtim. Another hero associated with the flood is the half mortal/half immortal warrior-king Gilgamesh who listens to the story of the survivor of the flood, Utnapishtim. Utnapishtim tells Gilgamesh that a god came to him in a dream and ordered him to build a ship and fill it with his kin and family, as well as all the field animals.

Presumably it is from the latest version of the Utnapishtim-Gilgamesh legend that the biblical version of the flood narrative in the same region, with minor changes, was drawn. Differences included the size of the ark, the number of days and nights it rained, and the divine reason for the flood.[47] Interestingly, the number of gods changed in the stories. Noah's story had only one angry god, but the Mesopotamian story involved lots of irritated gods. Moreover, connecting the story with Gilgamesh's quest for immortality perhaps explains Noah's very old age, which was alleged to be 950 years old,[48] at least according to the Koran (29:14; see also 54:11, 69:11).

The actual flood after all may have a historical foundation. Many banks of rivers, particularly the Euphrates and Tigris, flooded often. Thus, a massive flood in the Mesopotamian region could have in actuality happened, and humans afterwards mythologized and allegorized it. The allegory relates an act of divine intervention and retribution against the sinners, a belief that has been upheld in the Abrahamic religions even until today.

Another side of Gilgamesh's legend carries an undertone of human solitude and mortality. The legend alluded to the problem of separation between god

---

[45] Eric H. Cline: *From Eden to Exile: Unraveling Mysteries of the Bible* (Washington DC: National Geographic Society, 2007), 22–24, 26, 31.
[46] Ibid., 22–23.
[47] Burkert, *The Orientalizing Revolution*, 89.
[48] Many biblical prophets are believed to have lived a long life up to 800–900 years.

and human, immortality and mortality, innocence and corruption. The symbolism of the snake stealing the medicinal flower of immortality from Gilgamesh in the story is also strikingly similar to Adam and Eve losing immortality in the Garden of Eden when they are tricked by the serpent. (In the Koran the serpent is replaced with Satan who mimics the same snake-beast). The immortality of Gilgamesh was an existential quest, typical of the human psyche. Gilgamesh was disappointed in his quest for immortality (the yearning for immortal life has been an age-old desire) he came to accept mortality as the fact of existence.[49]

In the spirit of a hero and his miracles, the biblical tradition tells of Moses[50] parting of the Red Sea as proof of the magical power given to him by the god of the Israelites. The Egyptian enemies and their gods lacked such powers (in the Book of Exodus, 13:17–14:29; also, mentioned in the Koran, 26:60–67) and so Moses, a non-military man with god on his side, defeated the army of the pharaoh. It was through the episode of Exodus, as Jan Assmann argues in his latest book, that a new religion of faith and revelation was invented.[51] The message is that god and heroes always defeat the villains, and those who manage to escape the wrath of god in this world will ultimately be punished at the end of time. Not only good wins against evil but also to say 'my tribe wins', a hopeful message repeated in many myths.

The story of David and Goliath gives the same message. David, a young shepherd boy, hit Goliath with a rock from a slingshot and then threw Goliath, an experienced giant fighter, on the ground and killed him (in fact beheaded him). This one-on-one battle and the defeat of Goliath despite his colossal size represented the victory of those who side with god against those who are faithless and disloyal to god's command. In both Judaism (Book of Samuel, 17:23) and Islam (Arabicized name of Goliath in the Koran is "Jalut," 2:247–

---

[49] Elenita Garcia, "Immortality Lost: Existential Themes in Gilgamesh and Other Hero Epics," *Philosophia: International Journal of Philosophy*, 31/2 (2002). https://philpapers.org/rec/GARILE.

[50] Another set of intertwined myths involves stories relating to the biblical character Moses. In the legend Moses was born without anyone knowing who his father and mother were. After his birth, he was put in a basket and forsaken in the river. After being rescued on the shore of the river, he was taken to the Egyptian palace where he grew up to be a prince and ultimately a leader of the Israelites. Interestingly, the story resembles the myth of a Mesopotamian prince, King Sargon, whose legend involved a virgin priestess mother who gave birth to him, put him in a basket, and released him in the river. See Burkert, *Creation of the Sacred*, 72.

[51] Jan Assmann, *the Invention of Religion: Faith and Covenant in the Book of Exodus* (Princeton: Princeton University press, 2018).

52), the story of David and Goliath has been utilized as a psychological and military symbol of god's victory over non-believers. In the early days of Islam and Islamic Shi'ite legends, Ali, the young cousin of Mohammad, appeared like the young and courageous David, fighting the mightiest titleholders in a battle of truth against falsehood.[52] The Abrahamic story of David and Goliath signifies an allegory of a fight with full faith in god without fear, a battle which can be won in the same way that David as an underdog won it for the Israelites, or Ali for the faithful Muslims. Both reinforce the importance of belief in a godly hero of the religion.

The myths of the earliest civilizations in the Near East thus personalized and anthropomorphized the events and natural forces shaping their lives, whether floods, tribal wars, fertility or drought, victory or defeat. The idea of god was seemingly used as the proxy explanation for all such events in life.

b. Death and Immortality in Underworld Myths: The Influence of the 'Egyptian Book of the Dead'

Legends about the underworld are an enormously important area of mythology and religion that has preoccupied people for millennia, stemming from the ancient and primal fear of death. The *Egyptian Book of the Dead*[53] from 4,000 years ago demonstrates the compelling need for humans to generate explanations about death and after-death, and shows how imaginative these explanations were. It is the first testimony that outlines the stages and themes of funerary rituals and maps out the passages of the

---

[52] The Shi'a legends attribute the same heroic scenario of young David to young Ali, the first Shi'a Imam, and the cousin of Mohammad, who fought and killed the enemies at the very young age. Ali in his teenage years is recounted to even have beheaded "Amr, the giant and undefeatable warrior – a reminiscent of David and Goliath legend. It is a typical symbol of victory of those who side themselves with god and the tribe members over the demonized outsiders and pagan.

[53] The premise of this underworld narrative deals with the fundamental notion of reward and punishment by divine judges after death. Its earliest forms appeared on the tombs of royalty, but the full text from over 3,200 years ago was recovered in *The Papyrus of Ani*. Ani was a wealthy deceased man who could afford to have such a spiritual work, and ordered it for his journey of death and afterwards. The first set of documents of similar nature was translated by the German Egyptologist, Richard Lepsius in 1842, until the full discovery and acquisition of the *Papyrus of Ani* by E. A. Wallis Budge in 1888. The main core of the document describes the existence of an afterlife, one of the earliest systematizations of primitive notions of reincarnation, resurrection, and immortal life after death. Eternal life after death was a privilege that the pharaohs, as the virtuous progenies of gods, would naturally be entitled to.

individualized soul after death. It explains that after death, the dead undergoes cross-examination by divine judges using weighing scales. The judges put the person's good deeds on one side and bad ones on the other. After many such stages and cross-examinations, the virtuous may enter a realm where they can enjoy eternal life, offering one of the earliest historical versions of "heaven." In contrast to the destiny of the virtuous, the sinner would suffer and be devoured by wild beasts, a preliminary conceptualization of "hell." Even Moses' Ten Commandments are arguably said to be based on the do's and don't's presented in the earlier prototype *Egyptian Book of the Dead* (or the *Book of Going Forth by Day*)[54] or from the earlier Code of Hammurabi in Mesopotamia, or perhaps extracted from both sources.

Through their conception of the underworld and reincarnation, the Egyptians of the Bronze Age found a radical solution to existential anxiety and fear of death.[55] It was the invention of an afterlife that would be even greater than life in the present world. The solution was safe passage through the "undesirable" corridor of death. This helped the mind accept death instead of running away from it in fear. Ancient Egypt with its so-called "cult of the dead" was a systematic beginning of burying the dead properly and hoping for a return to life, this time eternally. The narrative of eternal life after death may have come from the imagination, but it was revered and believed and evolved into a religion in ancient Egypt.

This cult of the dead was once a central belief in Thebe to the south of the Nile and flourished in the Valley of the Kings. Since the dead pharaohs needed an undisturbed journey to the afterlife, the royal tombs had to be buried in secret places where people could not disturb the pharaohs by making noise when paying homage to the tombs. The tombs were glamorously decorated and filled with valuable objects, furniture, and wealth for the underworld. With all that was placed in their tombs, the dead were equipped for life in the

---

[54] Two sources, at least to my knowledge, have made the necessary connections between the Egyptian ancient legends, foremost, the *Book of the Dead*, and the Old Testament. See John H. Taylor (ed.), *Ancient Egyptian Book of the Dead: Journey Through the Afterlife* (Cambridge: Harvard University Press 2013); see also Ahmed Osman, *Moses and Akhenaten: The Secret History of Egypt at the Time of Exodus* (1990; Rochester, VA: Bear and Co., 2002). For the refutation of Ten Commandments and its influences from the *Egyptian Book of the Dead*, see H. E. Hadrian Mâr Élijah Bar Israël, *The Twelve Commandments and the Egyptian Book of the Dead* (Nazarani Foundation, 2013). In the conclusion, the author points out that the Ten Commandments have more in common with the Code of Hammurabi which is older than the *Egyptian Book of the Dead*.

[55] A nearly similar reincarnation cult was developed in the Indian and later Tibetan world (*Tibetan Book of the Dead*).

underworld; pharaohs would overcome death, defeat evil, and come back to save those who had followed them. The god of the afterlife would then bestow eternal life on these pharaohs. This longing for resurrection, coming back to life after death, emerged as an intense human desire due to the fear of the unknown of death, as is evident by how ubiquitous the idea of resurrection is in so many myths and religions even today.

The professional myth-makers in early urban societies such as the Egyptian delta, with their highly sought-after supply of stories, attracted the enthusiasm of the crowd and created a demand for their psychological commodity. It is hard to know which one was greater, the supply of the stories or demand from the people. The business of myth-making flourished and became lucrative for the powerful. Understanding this is important for penetrating in the inner workings of how the human mind made up myths then accepted them as truths that became beliefs.

c. Changes in Theism

In ancient Egypt, three gods were prominent: *Ra* the sun-god, the creator of the world; *Thar*, the god of the underworld, the afterlife, and a guide to eternity; and *Ammon*, the powerful and mysterious hidden god. Perhaps it was not coincidence that in Greek theism, a set of three god-brothers, Zeus, Poseidon, and Hades, managed the tasks of the physical world and the hidden world.

The waning of the Egyptian religious cult with its three gods resulted in a slow mythological evolution in the Near East. Eventually the mythology of multiple gods was displaced, and the diverse gods were brought under the umbrella of one single god (as instructed by a number of prophets) during the Iron Age.[56] Polytheism became questionable, particularly in the Near East. Abraham's one god replaced the Mesopotamian pantheon; in Iran and Central Asia, Zoroaster introduced the one god Ahura Mazda; and even in Western India, the site of pantheistic Hinduism, the Upanishadic yogis focused on their supreme single god Brahman. Interestingly, the authors of the Old Testament anachronistically regarded all the previous Mesopotamian gods as representing the same god just with different names, as if that was what they meant all along.[57]

---

[56] For more detailed information of the evolutionary character of the Near Eastern God, see Karen Armstrong, *A History of God: The 4,000-Year Quest of Judaism, Christianity and Islam* (New York: Ballantine Books, 1993).

[57] See "Yahweh," *New World Encyclopedia*, accessed Dec. 17, 2016, www.newworldencyclopedia.org/entry/Yahweh.

The Mesopotamian pantheon including Ishtar, Marduk, Enlil, and many others, had been quite elaborate and extensive, with a fluid boundary at times between gods and mortals. But with the advent of the concept of one single god, the power of mortal or semi-mortal gods gradually lost popularity, as opposed to the immortal might of one eternal god. In the Book of Genesis, Yahweh became the only legitimate god who evolved or perhaps survived out of the previous gods of the Mesopotamian traditions. In monotheism, the tasks of creation, managing the world, and the afterlife were all embodied in one god capable of all of these marvels, not just one arena. The Abrahamic religion prided itself on monotheism, focusing on the immortality of god, possession of the absolute truth, law giving, and rightful prophecy as well as the promise of the coming of a savior to end injustice and human misery.

In at least one instance, the Book of Genesis speaks of an anthropomorphic god who sounds different from the mighty and invisible god. It speaks of Jacob wrestling with god from night to daybreak in order to be blessed before he let god get away, at which time god told Jacob, "from now on your name is Israel." (Genesis 32: 22–32). The anthropomorphized god seems to be more of a protohuman than god.

More examples of theism and religious cross-influences abound: the allegory of Jesus being the "Son of God" in Christianity was not unique nor original. It is possible that this narrative of Jesus was either influenced by or borrowed from the earlier Egyptian legend of Ramses being the son of Ammon. It is possible that various pre-existing Jesus-like heroes and saviors, for example from Greek civilization (ie, Dionysus), were worked into what became the figure of Jesus.

It is, however, more probable that Jesus and the Iranian deity Mithra (also known as the Roman god Mithras) shared a common mythological root. The Roman myth tells of a human-god named Mithra born without a known father[58] on the winter solstice.[59] Jesus's birthday is, as we know, claimed to be December 25, strikingly near the winter solstice and birthdate of Mithra. It is likely that the top Roman generals, with their Mediterranean Mithraistic heritage, may have

---

[58] From the pictorial representations, Mithra is born/emerging from a rock.
[59] See Tim Callahan, "The Triumph of Christianity," *Skeptic*, 8/4 (2001), 82–6. Similarities between Mithraism and Christianity are summarized as the following: virgin birth, twelve followers, killing and resurrection, miracles, birthdate on December 25, morality, mankind's savior, known as the Light of the world. See The *Circle of Ancient Iranian Studies* (CAIS) (School of Oriental and African Studies – SOAS London): www.caissoas.com/CAIS/Religions/iranian/Mithraism/mithraism_and_christianity.htm, accessed Dec. 29, 2016.

been responsible for this intriguing overlap of myths and dates which served to provide a sort of support for the new Christian mythology.

Another similar cross-influence can be seen in the Manichaeism and Islamic depictions of the story of Jesus and his crucifixion. The Koran speaks of Jesus as a great apostle of god, in the same vein as Noah, Abraham, and Moses. The story of Jesus' crucifixion echoes the unique Manichaean account in telling a "non-Judaized, non-Christianized" account of Jesus and his life. The Manichaean sources told the story of Jesus's crucifixion more imaginatively than their Christian counterparts, whom, from Mani's point of view, were Judaized Christians. The expanded Manichaean version of the story describes how another person's body was crucified in Jesus's place, while Jesus ascended intact to Heaven. This version of the story was recaptured and echoed in the Koran (4: 157–8).[60] The newer versions of a previous story such as that of Jesus by the Muslims served to correct and at the same time authenticate the premise of the story. The Koranic version, however, is asserted to be original in comparison to the Christian (or even Jewish) literature.

Thus, the emergence of Christianity, as so often happens with religions, was inspired by earlier mythical stories. The similarities we have explored as well as many others are not mere coincidence, but involve the incorporation of previous legendary stories, each time in a more current adaptation with new and different characters, but often following the same mythological plot. The incorporation of older myths lent credibility and authenticity to new myths as the myths began to be accepted as truth by followers. Each new religion in history stands on the shoulders of previous myths and religions, each one exemplifying the power of collective human imagination, and the relinquishment of a natural, rational understanding of how the world works.

d. Myths Involving Meteorite Worship

Another unique source of myths within religion is the role of meteorite stones. These extraterrestrial stones coming to earth have often triggered new myths about celestial and divine messages for terrestrial people that were then perceived as truths.

One such story is embedded in the Islamic tradition of the pilgrimage to Mecca, called the *Hajj*. The *Hajj* involves visiting *Ka'aba*, a cubical structure

---

[60] See N. C. Lieu, *Manichaeism in the Later Roman Empire and Medieval China* (Tübrigen: J.C.B. Mohr, 1992), 53. See also Vaziri, *Buddhism in Iran*, 38; see also the third chapter of the same book, titled: Mānī, "the Buddha of Light."

around which a pilgrim must circumambulate.[61] *Ka'aba* is believed by the Muslims to have been built by Adam out of mud and stone to simulate the "House of God" in Paradise. Nestled in a nook of the east corner of *Ka'aba* are the fragments of the original Black Stone, The stone is said to pre-date the creation of the world, having come down from the abode of god. The myth says that after *Ka'aba* was destroyed in Noah's flood, it had to be rebuilt.[62] The angel Gabriel then gave the Black Stone to Ishmael, Abraham's son, while they were searching for stones to rebuild.[63] The Hajj pilgrimage requires reverence for this Black Stone, even with a tradition of kissing it. But this story and ritual, interestingly, have no Koranic basis; it simply stems from the compilation of one tradition after another in Islamic ceremonial rites and rituals. Furthermore, the reverence of the Black Stone in Mecca dates back before Mohammad's prophecy.

The Black Stone representation in Mecca can be correlated with and is reminiscent of earlier worship of meteorite stones common in other traditions and cults.[64] In the Bible, the story of Jacob involves veneration of the "meteorite" holy stone upon which he laid his head and fell asleep: while sleeping on the stone he had a profound dream that led to his building a temple, a "House of God." The temple was built around the very stone upon which he had laid his head (Book of Genesis 28:19, 35:15).

In Greco-Roman traditions, it was believed these fallen stones were from the god Jupiter from the sacred heavens.[65] Meteorite worshippers of all kinds raised the previous cult of "earthly stone worshipping" to a new level of "divine stone

---

[61] The circumambulation must take place with shaved head and must wear a monastic sleeveless unsewn robe - interestingly and noticeably paralleling the Buddhist ritual performance. See Vaziri, *Buddhism in Iran*, 95.

[62] The view that Mecca was the original holy city of Islam is challenged by Dan Gibson in his controversial book, *Quranic Geography* (2011). He uses archaeological and textual references to argue the original city was Petra (now in Jordan), and after the destruction of *Ka'aba* in the first Muslim civil war, the Black Stone and the pilgrimage site was moved to its present location in Mecca.

[63] For an alternative interpretation of *Ka'aba*'s legend, see M. Vaziri, *Buddhism in Iran*, 91–5. *Ka'aba* may have potentially been a Buddhist stupa (lying near the Red Sea) with the adherers shaving their heads, wearing monastic robe and performing the act of circumambulation around the structure; all of which were transferred most probably from Buddhism and incorporated into the process of Hajj in Islam.

[64] Tor Andrae, *Mohammed: The Man and His Faith*, trans. Theophil Menzel (1936; Mineola: Dover Publications, 2000), 14.

[65] See Oliver C. Farringto, "The Worship and Folk-Lore of Meteorites," *Journal of American Folklore* 13/50 (July–Sept. 1900), 199–208.

worshipping." To human ancestors living in isolated geographies of the past, the rarity of stones falling from the sky imparted such stones with immense mythological significance as gestures from outer space and thus from the gods.

e. Angels and Myths

Angels often play a very important part in many myths in numerous traditions. Their role has often been to keep humans connected to god, a theme that has preoccupied humans from the ancient times onward. Looking at some of the stories of angels in mythology can again serve to remind us how strongly the human mind is drawn to inventing and imagining ways to explain reality or finding ways to defend itself against the vagaries of the world. Like the strong beliefs in the stories and characters of mythology, the belief in angels has often resulted in humans abdicating their own sense of responsibility and control over their own lives and thoughts.

Invisible, winged, and able to fly, angels were believed to live a mystified life between heaven and earth, between spirit and body, and between god and humans. In the biblical tradition, angels are identified as the "sons of god," perhaps resembling god, believed to pre-date the creation of humans (Job 38: 7). The angels are communicators, defenders of the truth, and messengers from god, offering and issuing stern warnings against falsehoods and paganism as well as words of comfort and encouragement to those who "see" them.

The Judeo-Christian and Islamic traditions share nearly parallel stories and beliefs about angels, and all of these angels represent and deliver the commands of god to humans. These angels have remained hidden from the sight of most ordinary humans, except for the prophets who pass on the commands from the angels. For example, the angel responsible for the end of time is Archangel Isrāfīl in Islam, known as Raphael in the Judeo-Christian tradition. In the Islamic belief system, Isrāfīl will blow a trumpet from Jerusalem to announce the day of judgment,[66] while other literature points to Mecca where the call of the end of time shall take place for the return of the messiah (Mahdi) and the day of judgment.[67] A number of important immortal angels in Islam have been assigned tasks by the creator god. Some of these angels have already performed their duties while others are still on active duty; the rest will have to wait until doomsday, the day of judgment.

---

[66] See www.britannica.com/topic/Israfil, accessed Apr. 26, 2018.
[67] See Mohammad Baqir Majlisi, *Bihar ul-Anwar*, vol. XIII (Tehran: Dar ul-Kutub al-Islamieh, n.d.), 1066–1239.

In Islam, other angels are appointed to carry out specific tasks, such the two angels, Nakir and Munkir, who affirm or negate the Islamic faith of the dead in the grave. The angel of death is Izrā'īl, and the angels who record the good and bad deeds are Kirāmān Kātibin. Among others, the most creeping angel is Shaitān (Satan), the fallen angel who actively and perpetually corrupts the human mind and heart.

Another category of angels is believed to have inhabited the earth before the arrival of humans; they are the hidden creatures, the Jinns or genies. Considered to be between human and angel, at times they are equated with the devil.

The psycho-emotional impact of these angelic stories on the populations at large has been real, even without angels ever having been seen. The impact on social behavior on one hand and the control of the human mind on the other have bolstered deeper beliefs in the hidden power of god(s) in daily life. Perhaps this is because angels seem smaller, more "human," and easier for people to relate to than larger-than-life mythical gods who live in the skies. For this reason, people often take great comfort in feeling they have a "guardian angel" who is looking out for them, is on their side, and helping protect them against the bad forces of the world.

f. Religious Sacrifice and Rituals for Gods

The belief in angels may have been harmless in general, or perhaps even beneficial for believers who feel they have that 'guardian angel' watching out for them. But mythologies often lead to religions with rituals that involve belief systems with irrational and shocking acts of worship. Walter Burkert's research provides a detailed description of religious rites designed to please and appease the gods of the myths and religions, from archaic times to the Bronze Age and through the early Iron Age in the Near East. This extensive range of religious rites and practices included such things as: making statues of gods and offering them valuable food items such as milk, honey, and oil, lighting candles to gods, priests appearing as representations or manifestations of gods, chanting hymns and retelling myths, putting mud and ashes on the body, conducting fire rituals to keep evil spirits away, performing in festivals in special uniforms, entertaining gods in banquets, inducing ecstasy and divination, shedding blood of animals and humans, purifying oneself with blood, and finally ,making rules for sexual union as sacred marriage.[68] Many

---

[68] Walter Burkert, *Greek Religion*, trans. John Raffan (Cambridge, MA: Harvard University Press), 1985, 54–118. See also Burkert, *The Orientalizing Revolution*, 41–127.

Truth-Seeking and Myth-Making

such rituals were modified and transferred in the religions of the Iron Age, and some even continue to the present day.

The practice of sacrifice is a particularly important ritual to examine with the new eyes of awareness regarding the power of myth and irrationality. In some traditions, animals were respected highly in the mythology and were worshiped as gods themselves, but more often animals were sacrificed regularly to the gods and after the sacrifice would be eaten.[69] Zeus, Poseidon, Apollo, and Artemis were all offered animal sacrifices,[70] and the practice was common among the Jews and Muslims as well as many others.

The sacrifice ritual was also an ancient Mesopotamian tradition for satisfying demonic carnivores, a sort of hybrid reason for animal sacrifice intended to appease the healing gods to cure an illness (mental or physical) and to offer blood to the demons.[71] An unconscious intention behind sacrificing animals, as Burkert points out, may have been for people to observe the bleeding animal suffering as a means of relieving their own anxieties and healing their illness (ironically to have the "pleasure" of not being sacrificed oneself).

Even today, animal sacrifice continues to be commonly practiced. In Hindu traditions in places such as Nepal and India, animal sacrifices are ritualized in order to gain favor with the goddess Durga: those who have little money sacrifice a chicken; those with a little more money sacrifice a goat; the wealthy sacrifice a buffalo. And in the Islamic tradition today, a sheep is sacrificed upon completion of the Hajj pilgrimage, offered to the god of Abraham.

The original goal behind such sacrifices seems to have been to keep the gods happy, paying homage to them, hopefully preventing the gods' anger which could cause storms, disasters, failure of crops, battles, and diseases, etc. It does raise an important (and perhaps unanswerable) question revealing the irrationality of these practices: if people believed that the gods created the earth and everything on it, why would they then believe that *killing* those creatures that the gods themselves had created would make the gods happy? And the fact that in today's empirical world, people continue to sacrifice animals to a god emphasizes to the extreme psychological power of myth and religion. Even more critically, this extends beyond animals: one could say that the killing infidels or apostates under the banner of religion and purity is done for the sake of making god happy.

---

[69] Burkert, *Greek Religion*, 64.
[70] Ibid., 65.
[71] Burkert, *The Orientalizing Revolution*, 73–75.

The fear of an angry god led to the psychology of animal sacrifice in Abrahamic and other religions, often having to do with an unconscious human panic leading to even more extreme types of sacrifice. In ancient times, Jews, West Semites, and Phoenicians would burn whole animals, and even humans, making holocausts ("whole burning") on the altars of the temples to the gods. In Jerusalem, lambs were burned daily in the temple, and even children were burned and offered to gods in Carthage.[72] In the Old Testament story, god asked Abraham to sacrifice his own son Isaac (or Ishmael, in the Islamic tradition) and Abraham was ready to do it, for the sake of god's wish. But god stopped him and sent a sheep to sacrifice instead.

Thus, myth is so psychologically powerful that it would lead people to even sacrifice a child. By becoming aware of the evolutionary irrationality of these acts that humans were performing, such as killing the children of their species or destroying sources of food, we can begin to see the intensity of the controlling narrative of myth and religion. While child sacrifice obviously no longer happens in modern times, the Christian theme of god sacrificing his son Jesus on the cross still provides subliminal support for the irrational act of child sacrifice on a symbolic mythological level. This idea is obviously still taken quite seriously by Christian believers: even god sacrificed his only son.

***

Social Side Effects and the Dangerous Power of Myths

The above examples show us that in the last 3,000 to 4,000 years, the truth-seeking and myth-making compulsions of our archaic ancestors resulted in psychological dependency on these self-made myths. On one hand, myth-making was a sort of rudimentary and uncomplicated method of "psychotherapy," conceivably a useful tool in difficult times. Intricate myths about creation, the afterlife, and immortality were intended to offer alternative stories to an abrupt and meaningless existential end and served as cognitive solutions to appease anxiety about death. But believing in many of these ancient myths that were camouflaged as truth, also known as the words of god, has resulted in grim social, cultural, and intellectual consequences.

People always want to claim a myth as original and "their own." There is usually little awareness or acknowledgment of any preexisting myths that might have served as the original framework. Practitioners were probably quite unaware of the sorts of cross-influences explored in this chapter that we

---

[72] Burkert, *Greek Religion*, 63.

can see in historical hindsight. A myth thus has a personal and tribal component that serves to strengthen the sense of identity and belonging to the group. Such strong identification with a myth also minimizes the impetus for a personal quest for understanding. In other words, the encompassing reach of cultural/religious myths dulls the natural desire for self-rule, or thinking and deciding for oneself.

Following the path of ancestors as outlined by a specific set of myths meant remaining loyal to the principles of the covenant conceived by the tribe and its god. What stands out in the paradigm of most mythical narratives is that it is often about one tribe, such as the Israelites as being the Chosen People, or certain Muslim prayer ("thanks to god that I'm a Muslim,") or the Christian dogma that everyone is going to hell except for those of us who know Jesus. So, the mythical-religious narratives are not about all of humanity, since the rest of humanity would have to include non-tribal members. As Ashley Montagu rightfully puts it: "The myth-makers usually elect *themselves* as the chosen people or as the first and originally created people."[73] So myths, like religion, served to divide humans from each other ultimately, even while binding together people of a group or tribe. (It is easy to see how the tribalism of the past has become the nationalism of the present, and that cultural/national myths/narratives serve exactly the same divisive role as religious myths.)

We can also see the contradictions and limitations in mythology as a basis for a moral society, while bonding people together at the exclusion of others. For example, the slaves of Israel toiled in Egypt, and their liberation became the goal of their god, the god of Abraham. At the same time, it has been asserted the Egyptian laborers, many of whom were also slaves, moved some 4,883,000 tons of stones just to build a pyramid.[74] In the religious narrative that developed around the Israelite slaves being liberated in Egypt, the liberation of the native Egyptian slaves who suffered the same injustices and cruelties of the same pharaoh did not seem to warrant the same level of god's concern as did the Israelite slaves, and were in fact not mentioned in the myth at all.

The practice of enslavement of others, as a matter of fact, remained unchallenged and permissible by the theology, even practiced by Christian

---

[73] Montagu, *Man: His First Million Years*, 191.
[74] Morris, *The Human Zoo*, 9.

and Islamic benefactors until very recently.[75] In other words, the freeing of slaves was not a humanistic endeavor, but was only focused on freeing those of the "chosen tribe" in the mythology. God's shadow remained in the background of slavery by not abolishing it altogether. Shedding the blood of a non-tribe-member was often allowed or even encouraged by god, but not the blood of a tribe-member. "Thou shall not kill" is a valid rule, but tends to be taken more seriously among the tribe members, such as Israelites not killing the Israelites. Thou shall not kill those who follow god's laws. But those who subversively disobey (impure people/disbelievers), as portrayed in the Pentateuch's book three, Leviticus, and in Deuteronomy, did not enjoy the same protection under the commandment. In these books, god in fact orders the killing and dispossessing of the neighboring population and land.

The same is true for the members of *Umma*, the 'tribe' of faithful Muslims, in the face of people without the faith, outside the Islamic-Abrahamic tradition (*kāfir*). The practice of killing outsiders in certain religious traditions may be deeply rooted in the biological-tribal disposition for maintaining the primacy of family and kin. In fact, it still happens on a psychological level, rejecting or mistrusting people who are not in their 'tribe' (be it the tribe of religion or country).

Sometimes the essence of a myth was to convince tribe members to be patient and loyal. In the narratives of certain myths, it is promised that the patient believers will be rewarded, and the selfish deserters would suffer. The substance of reward is to practice *patience* and *loyalty* to the religion without question. These two virtues would turn defeats into victories, despair into bliss, and mortality into immortality. But they also send the message of 'do not question'.

For example, in the Old Testament and the Koran, the story of Job (Ayub) is an archetypal example of patience and loyalty in the face of suffering. It is presented as a test from god, to assess Job's endurance and ability to overcome evil and materiality. This way god would grant his obedient servant eternal

---

[75] Slave-taking was certainly practiced among Christian missionaries and colonizers for centuries. It was never abolished under the Islamic tenets, as Muslim patrons continued to own slaves throughout their history. In fact, the homeland of Islam, Arabia (Saudi) under the Wahhabis was one of the last countries in the world to abolish slavery in 1962, not willingly but under international (British) pressure (Mauritania was the last country, in 1981 and 2007 again). As much as the Christian particularly the Portuguese and Americans maintained the slave-trade, certain British Christian missionaries tried to abolish slavery.

freedom and bliss.⁷⁶ This psychological strategy may have helped those who were suffering and had few choices in their lives, reassuring them that they would ultimately be rewarded. But meanwhile this promise of patience kept populations waiting, like sheep, without any impetus to seek their own personal solutions. As a result, instead of being taught how to look at suffering as a natural process to be managed with the mind, religion weakened the self-awareness of people to think for themselves. It was perhaps a strategy to have the tribe members to be bound to the tribal code of conduct with an oath of allegiance and obedience without critical questioning.

Myths were designed to meet the requirements of the tribe's covenant, even at the cost of intellectual denial and lapse of reason. Blind obedience toward myths and ancestral truths seemed to weaken self-rule and personal inspirations. Myths should not be seen merely as romantic, innocuous symbols of cultural, religious, and literary beauty. Instead, the propagation of such core beliefs often suppressed the philosophical and empirical ingenuity of generations, meanwhile the beliefs created dangerous misunderstandings. We would like to think our beliefs are our own but in fact they are based on someone else's account of reality not ours. It is extremely difficult to extricate the mind of a believer from such accounts and stories. It is like a fish trying to think about the water in which it swims.⁷⁷

Conclusion

The beauty and literary value of some of the ancient myths should be counterbalanced against the damage they have done in perpetuating a false understanding of reality, while also alienating those outside of the tribal group. By giving the myth-making process of premodern human ancestors an intellectual, historical, and even an idealistic twist, as Joseph Campbell did, we are left with savoring the very same literature that has kept the human family detrimentally divided for so long. Let us make no mistake, Campbell's contribution to the scholarly field of comparative mythology is unparalleled. What Campbell and even Mircea Eliade have often loathed discussing in their

---

⁷⁶ See Oliver Leaman, "Hiob und das Leid: Ursprung des Bösen, Leiden Gottes und Überwindung des Bösen im talmudischen und kabalistischen Judentum," in *Diskurs der Weltreligionen: Ursprung und Überwindung des Bösen und des Leidens in den Weltreligionen*, ed. Peter Koslovski (München: Wilhelm Fink Verlag, 2001), 103–128. The story of the suffering of Job is a subject that the Jewish philosopher, Maimonides (d. 1204) undertook in order to disentangle it from psychological and philosophical ambiguities.

⁷⁷ This analogy was used by Daniel Quinn in *Ishmael* to represent the power of the cultural background in which we all swim.

writings is the danger of the transference of myth into religion, and the resulting "xenophobic" or even "persecutory" tone against the outcasts and "non-believers." Campbell however did not remain totally aloof from the "primitive credulity" of religion. He finally had to utter these words about the danger of myth and religion: "Communities that once were comfortable in the consciousness of their own mythologically guaranteed godliness find, abruptly, that they are devils in the eyes of their neighbors."[78]

Through mythical stories, wide rifts developed between a theological interpretation and a factual approach to history. Such dissonance continues to visit us frequently in modern times. It is important to remember that while we tend to think of myths as things of the past, there are millions today who continue to live under the thrall of ancient mythologies. Few people still believe in the world of Apollo and Zeus, but hundreds of millions of people give offerings to Shiva every day, accept literally the story of Adam and Eve, devoutly pray to Jesus who rose from the dead, and passionately throw stones at the devil while on pilgrimage in Mecca. Thus, this is not a dry and distant treatment of the human mind of the past, but instead it is a highly relevant topic for millions of people around the world who continue to believe in myths of religion, and who let such stories guide their lives and influence their beliefs about the world and others.

Myths captured the imaginations of so many believers to the degree that natural and historical processes seemed essentially to be frozen in time. A clear split occurred that separated humans from their unconditioned mind. Religion and myth isolated humans from the natural biological defenselessness inherent in aging, death, and decay. Through the work of the brain, religion and myth ironically tended to alter awareness of this vulnerable biology and isolated the mind-brain from the rest of the organic world. Needless to say, the solution has always rested in awareness.

Thawing out the mind of the myth-makers, myth-maintainers, and myth-followers is a task that natural philosophy with its critical thinkers has undertaken, attempting to encourage vibrant, empirical and judicious thinking about reality.

---

[78] Campbell, *The Masks of God*, 18, 23.

Part III.
Philosophy: Clarity

Chapter 5

The Indo-Greco-Roman Philosophies of Self-Rule: Nastikā Schools (Çārvāka, Ajīvikism, Jainism, Buddhism), Epicureanism, and Pyrrhonism

As we have seen, the Bronze Age (3300–1200 BCE) was a period of rudimentary metaphysical beliefs. The worship of the supernatural, anthropomorphization of nature and gods, veneration of ancestors and celestial entities, and the worship of animate and inanimate objects, and sacrificial rituals were all among the traditions of this period. The mayhem caused by these superstitious beliefs and behaviors was destined to be addressed somehow, sooner or later.

The shift began to appear after the beginning of the Iron Age (ca. 1200 to 550/700 BCE), when reformers surfaced, ushering in a period now known as the Axial Age,[1] including Pythagoras, the Buddha, Confucius, and others. Natural philosophy and coherent philosophical thinking began to emerge to confront and replace myths and mythical thinking. And thus, about three thousand years ago, many Bronze and Iron Age beliefs were radically challenged by minority thinkers and reformers. Even though at first such thinkers were fringe groups, the astonishing shift in thinking spurred by these reformers signified a transition from believing in god(s) to focusing on the liberation of the self. They invited people to give up false hope in favor of contemplating their own role in their destiny and happiness. During the Axial Age, a number of these rebellious philosophers appeared in the Indian subcontinent as well as in the Helleno-Roman world, making consequential impacts in the intellectual life of those regions and beyond.

---

[1] *Achsenzeit*, a term coined by psychiatrist-philosopher Karl Jaspers, refers to the time period between the eighth and third centuries BCE, although the root theory of Axial Age goes back to the late-eighteenth-century Orientalist Abraham Hyacinthe Anquetil-Duperron (1731–1805). See Jan Assmann, "Transkulturelle Theorien – am Beispiel von Jaspers' Achsenzeit-Konzept," in *Theorietheorie. Wider die Theoriemüdigkeit in den Geisteswissenschaften*, ed. Mario Grizelj, Oliver Jahraus (Hg.) (München 2011), 263.

1. The Indian Philosophies[2] of Self-Rule

The ancient religions of the region had been steeped in established rituals for centuries, such as animal sacrifice for the gods, ceremonies performed only by priests, and dogmatic beliefs such as karma and reincarnation. The earliest written records of dissent against superstition in the Indian subcontinent reveal that a transformation began to take place around the eighth century BCE in northwest India. The ancient theism of the time, with its fixed ontological construction, ritualism, and non-egalitarian caste system, called for a philosophical rebellion, while the existing social structures based on rigid religious hierarchies with vast ownership of land and livestock, called for a new outlook on the values of spiritual austerity, detachment from wealth, and compassionate egalitarianism.

Animal sacrifice became an early target of reform. The earliest opponents of animal sacrifice were yogis whose revolutionary philosophical and spiritual ideas were gradually recorded under the title of the *Upanishads*. The Upanishadic yogic approach targeted polytheism and reincarnation as well. "God" is not mentioned in the Upanishads, but Brahman is, representing the ultimate principle of "expansion," not necessarily god per se (much the same way that Tao is mentioned in *Tao Te Ching*). Such early attempts countered entrenched religious and polytheistic beliefs, starting with the misleading beliefs about animal sacrifice, and reintroduced new debates about the self and ideas of illusive and genuine reality. In the Upanishads, Brahman became the ultimate and permanent Reality of everything, which all entities carry within them and eventually return to. This was a philosophical breakthrough that paved the way for bolder and more sophisticated concepts.

These groups of thinkers rejected the authority and rigid ritualism of the sacred religious texts, the Vedas. Gradually these groups became known as the nastikā schools of philosophy. *Nastikā* comes from the Sanskrit *astikā* ("is") with *n-*, a negating Sanskrit prefix. Thus *n-astikā* means "is not," and is referring to the *refutation* of the Vedas and gods. As a result, members of the nastikā schools became known as heretics. For example, the Buddhists and Jains were accused of heresy [*nastikā*] by the Brahmanical priests. The conformist astikā schools, in contrast, accepted the authority of the Vedas.

---

[2] It would be improper for any students of Indian philosophy not to acknowledge and pay homage to the classical and monumental work of Surendranath Dasgupta, the five-volume *A History of Indian Philosophy* (1921–1952). Nevertheless, due to the highly technical and sanskritized premise of his coverage and analysis, such work will have to be left out since it is beyond the goal of this modest chapter.

The emergence of the nastikā movement can be marked as the beginning of classical nontheism or nontheocentrism and the move toward detribalization, with an accompanying deconstruction of hierarchical religious authority.

Four nastikā schools emerged, in this order: Çārvāka, Ājīvika, Jainism, and Buddhism. These schools dismantled the beliefs in sacred scriptures and gods, sacrificial rites, and other highly regarded external practices. They also challenged oligarchic ownership of land and livestock and took steps to rid themselves of personal possessions. The founders and proponents of these schools, by living their philosophies, showed practical ways for those who wished to attain liberty and happiness and restore a natural and autonomous mode of existence, without belief in the supernatural. Their philosophies also abolished violence against one another and against animals, acts which had previously been carried out in the name of religion or tribe.

The interactions among the founders and the earliest thinkers of these schools, or at least their knowledge of each other, is indicated by interborrowing and their shared approach of relying on oneself and not gods. Legends claim that the young Buddha met and exchanged dialogues with Mahāvira, the older patriarch of the Jain school. Similarly, Mahāvira interacted with Gośāla, the patriarch of the Ājīvika school. The Jain and Ājīvika schools competed and yet also became tightly entangled with each other.[3] In fact, Gośāla of the Ājīvika emerged as the most steadfast rival of the Buddha.[4] The rivalry may have been the way they addressed their messages to different crowds and followers. Given their intense exchange of ideas, it is fair to presume that the Buddha stood on the shoulders of his predecessors and developed many of his arguments on the basis of their teachings.

The nastikā opposition movement emboldened more thinkers to defy repressive modes of psychological penance and lifestyle. They made a number of straightforward yet shocking (at the time) claims: that there is no other world than the existing world, nor another self other than the body; that consciousness and the body are connected; and that upon the collapse of the

---

[3] Gośāla is claimed to have attained Jain-hood two years before Mahāvira, A. L. Basham, *History and Doctrines of the Ājīvikas: A Vanished Indian Religion* (1951; Delhi: Motilal Banarsidass, 2009), 31 and 50.
[4] Ibid., 55.

body, the consciousness would collapse as well. The four nontheistic[5] schools of nastikā were clear that there is no soul that survives after death. Along with this notion, the idea of the return of another self to another world through reincarnation was rejected. Scriptures, heaven and hell, priests, rules, and prohibitions as the basis of belief were all seen as ideas invented by human forerunners, and not based on reality. These philosophical movements were a revolt in defense of the individual mind, speaking for those who were caught in the religious gridlock of their generation.

Each of these schools developed its own unique set of ideas and practices to separate themselves from the entrenched religious and culturally assembled beliefs of their day. The proponents of the Cārvāka school were the first group to openly attack and reject existing superstitions of the time as a way of putting an end to religious fear and inhibition. In order to appreciate the teachings of subsequent naturalist maverick philosophers, let us first scrutinize the key tenets of Cārvāka, one of the earliest systematic doctrines to lay the foundation of nontheism, self-rule, and liberation philosophy.

Cārvāka: Rebelling Against God, Seeking Pleasure in Life

The existence of a pre-Cārvāka materialist school going back to the eighth century BCE has been suggested, although not fully established.[6] What is historically known about the Cārvākas generally comes from secondhand non-Cārvāka sources, their critics who attempted to discredit them.[7] Some of these comments come from Jain and Buddhist polemical sources (although Persian and Arabic sources refer in passing to this Indian materialist school as

---

[5] (Although the ancient pre-Buddhist *Samkhya* school of thought, a dualist materialist-yogic movement, was perhaps the first to reject the existence of gods, they never challenged the legitimacy of the Vedas. Therefore, they are not considered part of the nastikā movement.)

[6] Ramkrishna Bhattacharya, "Development of Materialism in India: The Pre-Cārvākas and the Cārvākas," *Esercizi Filosofici* 8 (2013), 1, 3. Though the origin of the Cārvākas is unknown, the first classical work about them, from the eighth century, was *The Lion of Annihilation of All Principles* by Jayarāśi Bhatta. See Deepak Sarma, *Classical Indian Philosophy* (New York: Columbia University Press, 2011), 3.

[7] Debiprasad Chattopadhyaya indicates that the Jain and Buddhist sources are the main sources of knowledge about the Cārvākas, but Chattopadhyaya does not necessarily consider the Cārvākas to be followers of *Lokāyata*. See Debiprasad Chattopadhyaya, *Lokāyata: A Study in Ancient Indian Materialism* (New Delhi: People's Publishing, 1959), xxiii. See also Günter Zehm, *War Platon in Asien?: Adnoten zur Globalisierung des Geistes* (Schnellroda: Anthaios, 2008), 64.

well.)[8] Otherwise their writings, apart from some fragments, are lost to us. But even the marginal commentaries about them still reveal a great deal about their radical ideals.

The etymology of the name Çārvāka is uncertain. "sweet talk" (Çāru "sweet" and vāka "speech") as one of the translations of the term may refer to their optimistic view and speech about life. Emerging as one of the earliest nastikā or non-religious and materialist[9] schools in India, the Çārvāka school was a pragmatic philosophy believed to have been brought to prominence by the popular Ajita Kesakambali, a senior contemporary of the Buddha and Mahāvira. Moreover, Çārvāka as a materialist school has been associated with the Lokāyata system of philosophy,[10] Lokā-yata meaning "common to people" in Sanskrit, or "people's philosophy."

The Çārvākas promoted simple and easy to understand concepts for people, including the nonexistence of any independent reality other than this world, the primacy of self and the body (as opposed to god), the cultivation of pleasure, the reduction of pain, the enjoyment of scents, food, and clothes. They held that no penance or unnecessary asceticism are needed to live a fulfilled life.[11] They preached no god, no heaven or hell, no sin, no soul, no reincarnation, no savior. They claimed that the world is as we see it, not as others interpret it.[12] The individual became the epicenter and source of one's own understanding, not scriptures or priests. From an ontological perspective, the Çārvākas believed in the laws of cause and effect and a rational universe.[13]

---

[8] Ramkrishna Bhattacharya, *Studies on the Çārvāka/Lokāyata* (London: Anthem Press, 2011), see chapters 2 and 22. There are three Perso-Arabic sources about Çārvāka/Lokāyata materialism: 1. Al-Biruni's *India*, 2. Shahristānī's *al-Milal wal Nihal* (*Ārā' Ahl al-Hind*), and 3. Abu'l Fadl-i Allāmi's *Ā'in-i Ākhari*. In Shahristānī's *al-Milal wal Nihal*, there are references to the Indian sects, the Dualist [Samkhya], and Materialist or *Dhahriya* [*Lokāyata*], but no specific reference to the Çārvāka school per se. See the twelfth-century heresiographer, Abdulkarim Shahristānī's *al-Milal wal Nihal* (*Tozih al-Milal*), trans. Seyed M. R. Jalali Naini, vol. II (1387; Tehran, 2008), 417.

[9] Bhattacharya, "Development of Materialism in India," 4.

[10] For a detailed study of *Lokāyata* (700 pages from a Marxist perspective) and a critical chapter on early Buddhism (chapter 7), see Chattopadhyaya, *Lokāyata*. (Debiprasad Chattopadhyaya was a student of the prominent Sanskritist and philosopher Surendranath Dasgupta.)

[11] Sarma, *Classical Indian Philosophy*, 10–12.

[12] Bhattacharya, *Studies on the Çārvāka/Lokāyata*, 63, 91.

[13] Bhattacharya, "Development of Materialism in India," 8. The Çārvākas' earliest predecessors may have believed in some sort of accidentalism of the world.

Thus, the central philosophy aimed to enjoy life today, without accepting gods or the prohibitions of religion in exchange for the promise of tomorrow. All other philosophical details of their school focused on living freely and happily and perceiving reality based on what it presents to one's sensory faculties, not allowing the authority of the priests and scriptures to defraud one's understanding.

The Çārvākas saw death as final, renouncing the idea of an otherworldly or eternal self and relinquishing all religious mysteries. They rejected what was believed at the time about the existence of a soul that would survive death and all forms of unverifiable speculation about the reality of an afterlife.[14] The Çārvāka concept of death as it is reflected is in the Buddhist *Ten Suttas:* "Both the fools and the wise are annihilated and destroyed after death and the dissolution of their bodies. Nothing exists after death." "The remains of the dead can be seen up to the cemetery where bare bones lie greying like the color of pigeons."[15] Once the body turns into ashes, it is asked, "How can it ever return again?"[16] Similarly, this quatrain is attributed to the Çārvākas:

> While life is yours, live joyously;
> None can escape death's searching eye,
> When once this frame of ours they burn,
> How shall it ever return?[17]

Instead, the Çārvākas believed in consciousness as an epiphenomenon produced by the four unchanging elements. The elements join the mind and body together as an interconnected entity; the mind works as long as the whole body and its interconnected elements function.[18] Consciousness is nothing mysterious. It is similar to a bubble in the water or a rainbow – it appears and disappears without having gone through many bodies and rebirths.[19] Consciousness and its nature is produced from the kinetics and

---

[14] Bhupender Heera, *Uniqueness of Çārvāka Philosophy in Traditional Indian Thought* (Delhi: Decent Books, 2011), 8, 26, 38, 41–42. See also "Lokayata/Carvaka – Indian Materialism," *Internet Encyclopedia of Philosophy,* accessed Jan. 11, 2017.
[15] Bhattacharya, *Studies on the Çārvāka/Lokāyata,* 28, 37.
[16] Ibid., 201, quoting Brhaspati.
[17] Heera, *Uniqueness of Çārvāka Philosophy,* 43. The content of this quatrain is reminiscent of Omar Khayyam's philosophy in his quatrains, see Chapter 7.
[18] Sarma, *Classical Indian Philosophy,* 4, 5; see also Bhattacharya, *Studies on the Çārvāka/Lokāyata,* 141, 170.
[19] Bhattacharya, "Development of Materialism in India," 5.

configuration of the four elements similar to how the stimulating fermentation of wine stems from its elements; there is simply no rebirth.[20]

The Cārvāka philosopher Ajita believed that upon dissolution, the four elements of the body go back to earth, water, fire, and air, and mental faculties are released into space. He also taught that due to the absence of an otherworldly being, there is no next world, and he endorsed hedonism by rejecting religious duties. These concepts were passed on to the later Cārvākas.[21] These later Cārvākas developed the informal idea of four permanent elements in motion, or "atomism," in fact had a well-established earlier Indian philosophical precedent, namely the earliest philosophical systems of Nyaya-Vaisesika,[22] (sixth to second centuries BCE). It may be that this earlier atomism was passed on to Jainism and Buddhism,[23] perhaps even reaching and influencing the Hellenic Atomists such as Leucippus, Democritus and Epicurus who also believed the world and its objects are made of four elements.[24]

The Cārvāka's epistemology[25] was simple and straightforward: using the eyes, ears, nose, and other fine sensory systems, one can perceive and appreciate the world. Direct perception and experience of the objects is the only means of cognition. Jargon, testimonies of others, analogies, and religious texts and interpretations were considered invalid, irrelevant to one's personal experiences. Gods could not exist because, the Cārvākas argued, they are not perceptible by the senses. On the same epistemological grounds, they refuted the substantiality of the soul, immortality, reincarnation, ultimate reality, heaven, hell, and a separate existence in an afterlife as

---

[20] Ibid., 7; Heera, *Uniqueness of Cārvāka*, 2, 36–37.
[21] Bhattacharya, *Studies on the Cārvāka/Lokāyata*, 37, 49, 62, 91.
[22] See Chattopadhyaya *Lokāyata*, xv.
[23] The Buddha spoke of four elements. See *Majjhima Nikaya*: Mahahatthipadopama Sutta (MN 28). See Nāgārjuna, *Mūlamadhyamakakārikā*, 140, 147-8.
[24] See Ferdinand Tablan, *Early Philosophical Atomism: Indian and Greek* (2012), Online PDF. www.academia.edu/9514956/Early_Philosophical_Atomism_Indian_and_Greek, accessed Jan. 15, 2017. See also Heera, *Uniqueness of Cārvāka*, 1; Thomas McEvilley, *The Shape of Ancient Thought: Comparative Studies in Greek and Indian Philosophies* (New York: Allworth Press, 2002), 321.
[25] For a technical discussion of pramāna according to the Cārvāka school, see Pradeep P. Gokhale, "The Cārvāka Theory of Pramānas: A Restatement," *Philosophy East and West* 43/4 (Oct. 1993): 675–682.

asserted by religious thinkers. All these religious positions were believed to be contrary to and to clash with one's rational experiences.[26]

To challenge the ongoing dogma and unwarranted beliefs, the rational campaign took a more intricate intellectual turn. For the Cārvākas, inference or deductive supposition, especially verbal testimony,[27] was subject to doubt and mistakes and could be even be considered a leap into the dark, from the known to the unknown.[28] For example, inferences about heaven and hell, or having awareness after death, were not acceptable because no one had ever perceived such circumstances. The early Cārvākas partially accepted inference.[29] Inference was only accepted if it was compatible with some previous sense experience, but it was still considered secondary knowledge as opposed to the primary knowledge of sense perception.[30] Cārvāka thinkers had thus distilled their epistemological understanding of the world down to one set of criteria, ignoring speculative attempts to add to or subtract from what the sense organs perceive.

The Cārvākas clearly rejected any kind of metaphysical inferences: "Inferences that seek to prove a Self, God, an omniscient being, the other world, and so on, are not considered valid by those who know the real nature of things."[31] Thus on the issue of sensory perception and unfounded inference, they maintained a position that the later Jains and Buddhists would also adopt. This rejection of accumulated metaphysical knowledge may have been an effort to avoid capitulating to the words of scriptures, gurus, and all other sources of unfounded claims.

Presumably, the Cārvākas' emphasis on sense perception as the only means of knowledge was intended to come down hard on religious-metaphysical claims rather than to be irrational about daily affairs. The Buddhists also used the possibility of worldly inference or deductive reasoning as a way to view things that the sense organs failed to detect. Such inferences would provide the thinker with additional tools for extrapolation, interpretation, supposition, deduction, reduction, and syllogism and give permission for logical reasoning outside the

---

[26] Ram Adhar Mall, *Indische Philosophie – Vom Denkweg zum Lebensweg: Eine interkulturelle Perspektive* (Freiburg: Alber, 2012), 218; Bhattacharya, *Studies on the Cārvāka/Lokāyata*, 57, 87; Heera, *Uniqueness of Cārvāka*, 18, 29–31, 36, 51, 60, 69, 73.
[27] Bhattacharya, "Development of Materialism in India," 1.
[28] Heera, *Uniqueness of Cārvāka*, 58–59.
[29] Bhattacharya, "Development of Materialism in India," 6, 8.
[30] Bhattacharya, *Studies on the Cārvāka/Lokāyata*, 57–59, 62, 140–141.
[31] Ibid., 92.

sensory organs.³² Thus, for the Çārvākas and the Buddhists, tools such as deductive reasoning had a worldly application, not a metaphysical one.

Such a radical position on rejection of metaphysical inference had to do with their empirical-individualist approach – using one's own personal judgments rather than giving in to herd-like tribalism by blindly following the teachings of a guru or sacred texts. It was also to reject any kind of absolute knowledge in dealing with fluid life circumstances or taking an absolute position in philosophical thinking; instead, everyone could exercise their freedom by formulating ideas and opinions from their own perspective.

The Çārvākas were quite clear about the impersonal universe being indifferent to human questions of "the purpose of life" and the downfall of the body by death.³³ It was through their rejection of religious-metaphysical systems that they made their even bolder pronouncements, rejecting the authority of the Vedas as well as ridiculing priestly worship, sacrifice rituals, and the credulity of the masses.³⁴

Even religious morality was considered as nothing short of fraud. The Çārvākas believed that concepts such as "sin" and "virtue" had been invented in order to frighten people, exploiting the religious sentiment of the masses.³⁵ The Çārvākas also did not shy away from ridiculing the Brahmanical sacrifice of animals or preparing food for the gods or the dead. They questioned how men of experience and wisdom could engage in sacrifices involving high expenditures and physical efforts, as it was cleverly a source of financial gain for the priests.³⁶ The priestly work which the Çārvākas called 'livelihood' and which involved exploitation of the masses, was antithetical to Çārvākas's system: "Hence it is only a means of livelihood that Brahmins have established here. All these ceremonies for the dead, there is no other fruit anywhere."³⁷ The animal sacrifice by the priests met harsh criticism by the Çārvākas questioning the logic of such a ceremony. If the slaughtered animal

---

[32] See Dharmakīrti, the seventh-century Buddhist philosopher who was trained at Nālandā University in Bihar and is famous for his work on Buddhist logic and epistemology, or pramāna. See also Chapter 6. For further reading, see Tom J. F. Tillemans, *Scripture, Logic, Language: Essays on Dharmakirti and his Tibetan Successors* (Boston: Wisdom Publications, 1999).
[33] Heera, *Uniqueness of Çārvāka*, 30.
[34] Mall, *Indische Philosophie*, 292–293.
[35] Heera, *Uniqueness of Çārvāka*, 92.
[36] Sarma, *Classical Indian Philosophy*, 6.
[37] Bhattacharya, *Studies on the Çārvāka/Lokāyata*, 91–92. See also Mall, *Indische Philosophie*, 219; Sarma, *Classical Indian Philosophy*, 10.

in the Jyotistoma[38] [Vedic sacrifice] ritual shall go to heaven, the Çārvākas asked: "why then does not the sacrificer forthwith offer his own father?"[39] These and other provocative statements were aimed at encouraging people to drop religious inhibitions and express their rational views more frequently and loudly. For the Çārvākas it was nothing but foolery and a lapse in sanity when people refused to think for themselves and instead depended on the gods to avenge wrongdoings.[40]

An important element of Çārvāka philosophy, which will come up in some of the other philosophies we will explore later, was the concept of hedonism. The Çārvākas represented the hedonism of their time, focusing on a satisfaction of the senses (*kāma* meaning "pleasure") by avoiding painful circumstances. For example, they refused to subscribe to the dietary precepts of the Brahmins, declaring that not taking tasteful food because it has been forbidden "defrauds the stomach."[41]

In the Çārvāka view, there could be nothing more supreme than earthly existence, which is proven by the sensory experience, and liberation is nothing but the final dissolution of the body.[42] The proponents of the Çārvāka way of life left their materialistic-hedonistic impact by offering this pragmatic outlook on life: "While life remains, let a man live happily; nothing is beyond death. When once the body becomes ashes, how can it ever return again?"[43] The pleasure of living here and now in this material world was a value strongly held by the Çārvākas, and we notice it being fully expounded upon later by the Buddha. The Çārvākas' philosophy of liberation and experiencing joy in life, in fact, became the central teaching of the Buddha himself. But because Buddhism evolved as an ascetic and monastic tradition, the Buddha's original hedonism was muted and even derailed.

Similarly, Çārvāka hedonism was criticized on the grounds of immorality by the Brahmanical tradition and by a later monastic-based Buddhist and Jain definition of morality. Ajita's preaching of hedonism raised ethical considerations and criticism, particularly by the Jains. But since no personal

---

[38] *Jyotistoma* means "a praise of light." Performed every spring, the victims sacrificed are dedicated to Agni ("Fire"). See H. W. Bodewitz, *The Jyotiṣṭoma Ritual: Jaiminīya Brāhmaṇa* I, (Leiden: E. J. Brill, 1990), 1–11.
[39] Bhattacharya, *Studies on the Çārvāka/Lokāyata*, 9; Heera, *Uniqueness of Çārvāka*, 74.
[40] Heera, *Uniqueness of Çārvāka*, 42.
[41] Ibid., 39, 50.
[42] Sarma, *Classical Indian Philosophy*, 6.
[43] Bhattacharya, *Studies on the Çārvāka/Lokāyata*, 91.

fault could be found with Ajita himself, who lived an austere life, his students were accused of heedless pleasure instead. The critics' viewpoint resulted in a narrow resentment of the Çārvākas and the urge to polemicize and deny acknowledgment of their wider worldviews.[44]

Despite this rejection, the Çārvākas paved the road for other radical and nastikā thinkers, agnostics, and critics of domineering and anxiety-ridden religious politics. They represented an optimism that depicted the world as a source of joy and liberty, and a place where animals and humans alike are designed to live in the present because of the shortness and precarious nature of life. The Çārvākas established a rational, pragmatic, and pleasure-seeking philosophy that encouraged people to use every opportunity to cultivate the highest pleasure of living in impermanent conditions, without any fear of religious consequences formulated by priests.

Treated as outcasts by the rulers of the social order who considered only themselves as "moral," the Çārvākas were accused of breaching the highest moral values achieved by religious people. But by rejecting the Vedas, gods, priestly culture, a soul, and an afterlife, the maverick Çārvākas emboldened people to think for themselves, a groundbreaking idea 2,500 years ago. The cycle of fear and religious domination was cracked open for future critique and evaluation. Thus, the momentum towards an era of self-rule was set into motion, which was taken up by two more pre-Buddhist groups, Ājīvikas and Jain.

Ājīvikas: The Acceptance of Reality and Liberation

The mandate of independent thinking was passed down to the Ājīvikas, as well as to the Jains, both of whom developed but each in a different style, in the sixth century BCE. The Ājīvikas enjoyed strong political patronage and popularity during the third century BCE in the Mauryan period.[45] The Ājīvika and Jain schools maintained much in common with each other,[46] but the Ājīvika school disappeared some six hundred years ago, in the fourteenth century, while the Jain school has survived in the Indian subcontinent to this day. This continuity

---

[44] Ibid., 30–31, 123–124.
[45] The founder of the Mauryan dynasty, Chandragupta, converted to Jainism and was ordained as a monk. (Chandragupta's grandson Asoka converted to Buddhism.) The theme of a king abandoning palace life to become a monk was common to the stories of both Mahāvira (the patriarch of Jainism) and the Buddha.
[46] See Piotr Balcerowicz, *Early Asceticism in India: Ājīvikism and Jainism* (Abingdon, Oxon and New York: Routledge, 2016), Introduction, 5–6.

has provided the Jains with a better basis for defending their claims of originality. Nevertheless, the Ājīvikas' philosophy should be viewed in a historical context for their influence on both Jainism and Buddhism.

Makkali Gośāla, (a contemporary of Mahāvira of the Jain school) brought earlier Ājīvika teachings[47] out of their obscurity and systematized what would become known as the Ājīvika school. Gośāla appeared naked in public as a symbol of naturalism and the rejection of possessions. He denied the existence of gods or a permanent soul and future life. He declared the idea that karma accumulates through the sins and sufferings of previous lives to be baseless, and denied that deeds of penance or virtuous acts can determine future karma.[48] From these beliefs, one can see how the name *Ā-jīva* could mean "for-life," "for-livelihood" arose.[49]

Ājīvika could also mean "liberated from the fetter of karma," connected to the belief that human efforts can do nothing to determine the future, including religious acts from animal sacrifice to personal piety. No one can stop the actions of nature such as the movements of the planets, the rising and setting of the sun, the growing of bones in humans, the aging process, and death, as all this is beyond human will. The universe itself is the sole agent of change in all phenomena. Thus, Gosala believed in cosmic and biological determinism. For the Ājīvikas, the origin and the direction of the world was considered unknown but determined.

Their philosophy combined this determinism with atomism. Along with the four uncreated elements of fire, earth, air, and water, the Ājīvikas added three *less* tangible and perceptible components: joy, sorrow, and life. With this pragmatic logic, the Ājīvikas avoided plunging themselves into too much speculation about what could not be changed; instead, they moved on to deal with the little that could be managed and useful in human life.

Arthur L. Basham's pioneering study (1951) of the Ājīvikas, which was further researched and expanded by Piotr Balcerowicz (2016), brings to light the thorough philosophical approach of this enigmatic school of thought. According to the Ājīvika description of the order of reality, within the universe, nothing is produced and nothing is destroyed. Physical existence is a setting for the nullification of all dynamic transactions in it, actions, and

---

[47] Ibid., 9.
[48] Basham, *History and Doctrines of the Ājīvikas*, 3, 224–225, 258–259, 263.
[49] It is even possible that the name Ājīvika was given to this group by their opponents in later years. Ibid., 103.

reactions, or the formation and demise of all objects – some sort of "nothingness" or non-addition. In the same vein, when one speaks of timelessness in the universe, there is only the "moment," and in fact, there is "no time at all" to be lost.[50]

The Ājīvikas contended that the destinies of human beings, with the haphazard conditions of grief and happiness, are not under their own control, nor do these conditions come through the agency of gods – they simply come as they do. This required accepting the predisposed, innate abilities and talents that people possess. No human birth and no new construction can cause any fundamental change in the sameness of the universal process.

By the same token, the Ājīvikas believed that human birth and death in the world have no effect on larger universal processes.[51] The randomness of human destiny and each person's experiences are based on chance more than anything else, whether they end up "humpbacked, a dwarf, one-eyed, diseased, grieved, or happy." These conditions all seem to be emanating from the random activities of the surface of the world, which itself rests upon an underlying changelessness and determined state. This reasoning of the Ājīvikas dismisses the notion of predestined "karma" as a separate and otherworldly phenomenon. By rejecting karma, they believed that personalities and life circumstances are responsible for people's grief and happiness. The concept of karma, the Ājīvikas argued, is a baseless excuse to negate the underlying reality of the cosmic process, which is free from accumulating sins and suffering caused by so-called karma in previous lives.[52]

The Ājīvikas' approach to pain and pleasure was that both of these feelings come to human life on different levels and from different circumstances – which they saw as reasons to cultivate detachment from both, pain and pleasure.[53] An identical equanimous position regarding detachment from pain and pleasure was held by the Buddha (and expanded by the Madhyamika and Yogācara schools). This even-handed relationship with the nature of life led to a degree of abstinence from what causes too much pain or too much pleasure on any level. The goal of the Ājīvikas' aloofness and renunciation was to lead a life without going through too much fluctuation, whether good or bad. It meant avoiding personalization of natural processes and keeping sight of the recurring cycle of birth and death (*samsara*). The goal

---

[50] Ibid., 227, 236–237.
[51] Ibid., 230–232.
[52] Ibid., 224, 232, 235.
[53] McEvilley, *The Shape of Ancient Thought*, 602.

was to destroy false perceptions about their own birth and death. To the Ājīvikas, birth and death constituted an impersonal and unstoppable universal process. To the universe, humans were sheer numbers.

Through asceticism, avoidance, detachment, and meditating on the erroneous nature of the mind, the Ājīvikas focused on purging the displeasure produced by the anxiety-ridden mind and its ceaseless thinking. If the mind became unbearable and incompatible with the natural life, its suffering would have to be dealt with sooner rather than later. Some Ājīvikas even resorted to taking their own lives by starvation, a practice later carried out by the early Jains.[54] (Similar types of suicide were practiced by a number of Greek vegetarian and ascetic philosophers, such as Diogenes, who died by voluntarily stopping his breath.[55] The Stoic philosophers also sought dignified suicide as a last resort when the power of reason fails and suffering becomes dominant.)

Perhaps in an effort to improve on the Ājīvika conception of exit – some form of mental or physical "suicide" or voluntary death as a means to end the suffering – the Buddha introduced the experience of nirvana followed by a natural death, and the final exit from the cycle of existence, *parinirvana* (the dissolution of the body, and therefore the mind, forever). The nirvana of the Buddha and the teachings of the Ājīvikas reflected one another by referring to the determinism of birth and death, the propensity of the mind to be deluded, the reality of suffering, the emptiness of things including the soul, and karma, which cannot be stored anywhere. Karma is like an extinguished fire.[56]

Despite the rejection of karma by the Ājīvikas, philosophically the concept of karma remained fluid and variable in various sectarian literature including the Buddhist literature. Nevertheless, the early proponents of Ajīvikism, generally speaking, tried to remove themselves from mysterious metaphysical speculations by accentuating the unchanging laws of cause and effect in the universe.

Another aspect of the Ājīvikas, as mentioned earlier in relation to Makkali Gośāla, was their practice of public nakedness, which may have been rooted in[57] an earlier attitude toward the naturalness of the body. It may have

---

[54] Basham, *History and Doctrines of the Ājīvikas*, 4; McEvilley, *The Shape of Ancient Thought*, 443, 602.
[55] McEvilley, *The Shape of Ancient Thought*, 443.
[56] David Kalupahana, "Consciousness," *Buddhist Psychology, Encyclopedia of Buddhism Extract* (Dehiwala, Sri Lanka: Ministry of Buddhasasana, Department of Buddhist Affairs, 1995), 76–77.
[57] Basham, *History and Doctrines of the Ājīvikas*, 108–109.

influenced the early Jains, as exemplified in South India by a giant statue of Bahubhati, an ancient Jain patriarch standing naked, and it is believed that when Mahāvira (the founder of Jainism) and other Jains later practiced public nakedness, they were imitating Gośāla. The nakedness of Indian sages, known to the Greeks as *Gymnosophists* (naked sages), may have indirectly influenced some of the Greek sages who also appeared naked in public.[58] The practice may even have influenced the Buddhists, though in pictorial representations the Buddha and Buddhists appear partially clothed or half-naked.

The Ājīvikas manifested their philosophical beliefs through the practices of chanting, dancing, fasting, *ahimsa* (non-killing), and taking alms (although not accepting food from pregnant women, nursing mothers, or during drought). They were vegetarian and refused to eat fish or meat, drink wine, or eat any food that had flies around it. Whether they practiced celibacy is not certain.[59] These ascetic practices promoted living in simplicity and throwing the mind and body into the wilderness of naturalness without being entangled by the conventions of the culture and the morality of religion.

Their reputation reached the authors of Chinese and Japanese Buddhist texts, and even found their place in the Indian *Pancātantra* in which certain characters were Jaina and Ājīvika. During the Buddhist time of Asoka, the Ājīvikas continued to receive support even as the Buddhists and Jains continued their harsh criticism of the Ājīvikas as heretics.[60] But because of the loss of the Ājīvikas' literature and the consequent waning of their teachings, along with their rejection by the later Jains and Buddhists, their most powerful ideals have been veiled in the history of philosophy. Although their doctrines formally died out, many of their strong teachings stayed behind and were integrated into various schools which followed.

Jain: Nonviolence and Ethics Without God

In the Jain school of thought, a *tirthankara* or "master" was one who provides possibilities for seekers to "cross the river of birth and destiny."[61] Mahāvira, or

---

[58] Diogenes of Sinope lived and appeared naked in public. Although Pyrrho and Democritus did not appear naked, Laertius claimed they met and came under the influence of certain Indian Gymnosophists. See in a bilingual Greek and English edition, Diogenes Laertius, *Lives of Eminent Philosophers*, trans. R. D. Hicks (London: William Heinemann and New York: G. P. Putnam's Sons, 1925), IX, 445, 475.

[59] Basham, *History and Doctrines of the Ājīvikas*, 112, 117, 118, 120, 123, 126.

[60] Ibid., 112, 118, 121, 161, 167, 184–185.

[61] M. S. Abhinandan, *A Journey Through Jainism* (Delhi: Indialog Publications, 2005), 12.

"Great Hero," was considered one such master and is credited with the systematization of Jainism, although in fact, the Jain approach was an ongoing tradition of unconventional teachings. It had existed long before the time of Mahāvira, who is recorded to be its twenty-fourth teacher [Tirthankara]. Mahāvira is said to have succeeded Rishābha, an ancient master of nonviolence, and Parshwānath (around 750 BCE), and was a senior contemporary of the Buddha.

The nontheism of the Çārvākas and Ājīvikas was upheld and practiced by the Jains (and soon after, by the Buddhists). The Jains, like the Çārvākas and Ājīvikas, established their own unique way of viewing life and the world in order to attain liberation from the mind's negligent misreading of reality. By holding no belief in a creator and instead concentrating on the eternalness of time and the universe,[62] the Jains focused on the primacy of self and aimed to conquer the wrong views and temptations that continuously emerge in one's mind. The name "Jain" is derived from the verb *ji* meaning "to conquer" (*jina* or "conqueror" in Sanskrit) – a suitable noun for those practitioners who have been able to conquer their impulsive and excited mind.

The Jains' focal practice was to uproot and reverse the factors that cause the harmful acts which torment the mind. The five vows that Mahāvira made after his enlightenment were to be observed by all Jains: not to lie, not to hurt, not to steal, not to be greedy, and to maintain celibacy. The central tenet of non-killing (*ahīmsa*) for the Jains became a symbol of not harming the natural universe. Although there is always change in the universe, these processes of the rise to existence followed by its fall and demise are part of the non-changing and endlessness of the materiality of the world. This rise-and-fall occurs through the interaction of the nonliving and living things. Material or atoms are believed to be nonliving (*ajīva*) and continuous in time, and when they bind with the eternally living (*jīva*), it causes the soul or consciousness to arise. With this "dualism" of matter and mind along with agnosticism, Jain has been seen as an old dualist school from the pre-Vedic times that reemerged to challenge the dogmatism and polytheism of Brahmanism.[63]

---

[62] G. Ralph Strohl, Paul Dundas, and Umakant Premanand Shah, "Jainism," *Encyclopaedia Britannica*, www.britannica.com/topic/Jainism , accessed Jan. 15, 2016.
[63] See Heinrich Zimmer (edited and completed by Joseph Campbell), *Philosophies of India* (Princeton: Princeton University Press, 1969), 185, 219, 242. See also Kailasha Chandra Jain and M. A. Jaipur, "Antiquity of Jainism," www.fas.harvard.edu/~pluralsm/affiliates/jainism/article/main.htm, accessed Jan. 15, 2017.

Thus, the Jains aimed to liberate the pure mind from the impurity of corporeal behaviors and tendencies. Jainism blended self-restraint with a naturalistic attitude based on action,[64] not just withdrawal of the mind. The accumulation of good, nonviolent, and virtuous acts provided the means to refine the mind.[65]

On the psychodynamic level, the Jain guideline for evaluating oneself against the dynamic world is summarized in the *Seven* Truths (as opposed to Buddha's *Four* Noble Truths). The seven truths are a combination of material and ethical approaches to understanding; it is interesting to note that there is no god mentioned in the seven truths.

1. *Soul* is a body of matter which has infinite knowledge of things – a kind of "black box" of the body and the universe.

2. *Matter* is something invisible to the naked eye but ubiquitous all over the universe, especially the "good and bad matter," known as *karmic matter,* which keeps the universe in a ceaseless unfolding of events.

3. *Influx* is the input of the soul in manipulating the bad karmic matter and converting it into good – a lively mechanism of cause and effect.

4. *Bondage* is an attachment to karmic matter which varies in nature and intensity. The bond begins with birth and takes its dynamic course through human behavior. Its negative aspects can obscure awareness and liberation.

5. *Stoppage* of one's karma is accomplished through knowledge and through overcoming the bad karmic matter that moves in action, thought, and speech. Stopping the bad karma requires following the five vows as mentioned above. During this phase, other vows per se are important, including renunciation of possessions, awareness of impermanency, forgiveness and overcoming anger, and bearing discomfort, fatigue, and pain.

6. *Shedding* of karma is by strict observance and undoing previous deeds and conditions through beneficial deeds.

---

[64] David J. Kalupahana, *A History of Buddhist Philosophy: Continuities and Discontinuities* (1992; Delhi: Motilal Banarsidass, 1994), 15–16.
[65] See "Jainism," *Encyclopaedia Britannica,* accessed Jan. 15, 2017.

7. *Self-realization* means regaining the mind's true and uncontaminated nature. This is possible by the inner and outer correction of actions, speech, and thought. Silence, inaction, and mental peace are the methods and goals of the practice.[66]

On an epistemological level, the Jains maintained a strong non-absolutist view of the world. This had an important impact: by continuing the movement away from religious absolutism, it ultimately helped to pave the way for the emergence of the Buddha's non-absolutism. The Jainist opposition to holding a singular absolute view is illustrated by the widely used parable of blind men touching different parts of an elephant and each characterizing the elephant differently based on which part of the elephant they were touching. (The same parable was transferred into Buddha's discourse [*Udāna*], as well as among later thinkers in the Islamic world such as al-Ghazzāli [in *Ihyā ul-'ulūm*][67] and Rumi [in an allegory used in his *Masnavi*].) The point of the story is that each blind man described his "truth" of only the part of the elephant he touched, without having "seen" the whole truth of the whole elephant. No man could claim to know the absolute truth of the elephant. This non-absolutism of Jainism was relativistic in avoiding contradictions and circumventing limited conclusions about the larger context of life and the universe, which we are "blind" to and yet tend to describe according to our understanding.

The rise of the Jains along with the nontheistic Çārvāka and Ājīvika schools challenged the conventional religiosity of Brahmanism. These three schools all advocated self-correction by self-reliance rather than reliance on gods and scriptures. Mahāvira's traditional, unadventurous approach was that only through good deeds and positive karmic particles would the mind be cleansed and brought back to its natural purity.

Interestingly, the biographies of Mahāvira and the Buddha possess similar elements: both are said to have come from a princely life before adopting ascetic practices to free themselves from convention and to conquer their misled mind. However, Mahāvira would have the work starting from below and moving up to the mind, whereas the Buddha taught the inverse – not through self-mortification,[68] but through taming the mind first, then promoting good deeds as a consequence.

---

[66] Abhinandan, *A Journey Through Jainism*, 48–53, 56–64.
[67] See Vaziri, *Buddhism in Iran*, 57.
[68] See *Majjhima Nikaya*: Devadaha Sutta (MN 101).

The Indo-Greco-Roman Philosophies of Self-Rule

In brief, these nastikā schools promoted similar approaches to adjusting the mind toward self-rule, and in later centuries they began to enter larger arenas of society and politics, receive political patronage, and attract a great number of followers. These Axial Age intellectual revolutions helped to overturn old, fear-based religious ideas, offering instead liberation and a way to find one's own happiness in life.

Before we delve deeply into the dialectics of the most influential nastikā school, Buddhism, in the succeeding chapter, let us first look at Greco-Roman thought along the same lines of philosophical thinking.

2. The Greco-Roman Search for the Philosophy of Liberation and Happiness

With the advent of new ideas and philosophies in the Axial Age, the thick skin of time-worn religious beliefs continued to shed. Much as the India-based nastikā movements rejected Bronze Age religion and theism, a similar nontheistic movement appeared systematically among pre-Socratic Greek philosophical thinkers beginning around the fifth century BCE. A century later, Plato declared that nontheism was a harmful shift, but despite that, the idea of nontheism survived and was promoted by Democritus, Epicurus, and many who followed. These Greco-Roman thinkers, like their Indian counterparts, confronted the religious dogma of their day and developed certain philosophical similarities, and perhaps even shared cross-influences. The atomism and empiricism of the Çārvākas and Ājīvikas influenced other emerging Indian materialist and nontheist thinkers, but also, as suggested by Thomas McEvilley, probably influenced the Greek atomist nontheist thinkers such as Leucippus, Democritus, Epicurus, and Lucretius through their Persian counterparts.[69] The earlier studies of George P. Conger also found sporadic cross-influences between Indian and Hellenic philosophers, particularly in pre-Socratic philosophies.[70]

The parallels between the Ājīvika outlook and the atomism of Democritus are of this interest. Democritus, a pre-Socratic philosopher of 5th century BCE, believed that the mind is comprised of fine atoms and is produced spontaneously similar to everything else, not planned.[71] He held a set of specific ideas that sound very similar to the Ājīvika: 1. elemental substances are unchanging, undying, and no more of such substances can come into

---

[69] McEvilley, *The Shape of Ancient Thought*, 121–122, 126, 142, 318–320, 333.
[70] See George P. Conger, "Did India Influence Early Greek Philosophies?" *Philosophy East and West* 2/2 (July 1952): 102–128.
[71] McEvilley, *The Shape of Ancient Thought*, 320, 331.

existence; 2. the qualities of things are revealed when the sense organs come into contact with the elements; 3. the soul or consciousness is a material thing; and 4. all changes are illusory.

McEvilley also deftly draws similar parallels between the Çārvāka worldview and the Hellenic atomism of Democritus and Epicurus: 1. the world is made out of four essential elements; 2. all objects are made out of four elements and no more; 3. consciousness is temporarily produced as the by-product of the four elements; 4. no residue of a person will be left after life.[72] The followers of Epicurean principles finalized that the mind is a temporary by-product of interactions among the four elements, and death represented the collapse of this condition.[73]

Democritus

Diogenes Laertius of the third century CE, probably himself an Epicurean or Pyrrhonist, provided an account of Greek philosophers and their opinions, including Democritus, in his *Lives of Eminent Philosophers*. Laertius devoted (in its current published form) ten pages in Book IX, chapter 7, to the biography and ideas of Democritus. He said the wise Democritus may have been the student of certain Magians from Iran and Chaldeans from the Near East. He explained that Democritus's philosophy was based on the principle that everything in the universe – the sun and the moon as well as everything else in nature – is made out of atoms and space. The atoms are unlimited in number and size. The qualities of things exist merely by conventional definitions and relative to one another. Things come into being due to necessity and go out of existence in tranquility.[74]

The twelfth-century Eastern Iranian writer al-Shahristānī, in his heresiography *al-Milal wal Nihal*, provides a short account of Democritus as a unique philosopher of his time. He claimed that Democritus spoke of the four elements existing from primordial times which make up impermanent structures – from the primitive, elemental level to the complex sensorial level and eventually to the planetary level.[75] He went on to say that Democritus believed human emotionality is the main obstacle to controlling the self: it blocks knowledge and the faculty of pure rationality, which should not be manipulated for the sake of personal inclinations. Democritus believed that

---

[72] Ibid., 318, 320.
[73] Ibid., 320.
[74] Laertius, *Lives of Eminent Philosophers*, IX, 442, 453–456, 442–463.
[75] Shahristānī, *al-Milal wal Nihal*, 168–169.

human sentimental faculties are imaginary, but free will is real, and knowledge alone cures people.[76]

It is likely that some of these nontheistic revelations did indeed arise after contact with the Indo-Iranian world, since Democritus, using his wealth in a quest for knowledge, is believed to have traveled to Egypt, Ethiopia, Iran, and India.[77] Being the student of Leucippus, it is of interest to know how deep Democritus learned his atomism from his teacher, and whether he furthered his research among the Indian philosophers. It is not recorded whether Democritus interacted with wider communities of the materialist and atomist thinkers of India, but the parallels in thinking are striking. As a nontheist and atomist thinker, Democritus resembled his Indian counterparts, who also favored a philosophy of happiness. He thought "the right-minded man is he who is not grieved by what he has not but does enjoy what he has."[78] His wisdom of true happiness could have very well been influenced by the atomism and philosophy of pleasure of the Çārvākas as well.

Democritus and Pyrrho of Elis shared the common belief that human reality consists of outer conventions instead of inner essences, and that this hinders attaining true happiness. Humans follow conventions already decided for them rather than experiencing the essence of their own existence based on their inclinations, talents, and profound thinking. Pyrrho, similarly to Democritus, sought *ataraxia*, the peace of mind made possible by a psychological state that is unaffected by the fleeting nature of phenomena – all phenomena. Pyrrho's famous verse, "As leaves on the trees, such are the lives of men."[79] points to the precariousness of life without an exclusive or exceptional place for humans. It was the influential Democritus who paved the way for Epicurus' atomism and philosophy of tranquility.

Epicurus

Epicurus, the iconic figure of the Hellenic "school of true happiness" whose major written works were lost, also seems to have shared a worldview

---

[76] Ibid., 200–201.
[77] On the way to Taxila, an important ancient Buddhist center, now in ruins not far from Pakistan's capital, Democritus is said to have met some Buddhists. See McEvilley, *The Shape of Ancient Thought*, 332.
[78] Ibid., 332.
[79] Ibid., 452. (Interestingly, Rumi composed a similar verse describing leaves as humanity, whose death is only falling of the leaves, whereas the true life of the tree is hidden in the fleeting reality.)

identical to that of the Çārvākas. He considered religion to be false and a fraud perpetuated by a class of priests for their own benefit. He advocated demystifying superstition, eliminating baseless causes for fearing gods, promoting knowledge by observation (like the sensory perception advocated by the Çārvākas), and experiencing the world without committing to conceptual and interpretational errors.

As he did with Democritus, Laertius discusses Epicurus's life, letters, and philosophy at some length. Al-Shahristānī also writes that Epicurus taught that all objects are made of material stuff, and recurrent reappearances of things can occur because there is a void where the material reconfigures.[80] Epicurus held that all things are impermanent; there is no retribution in an afterlife; suffering is a result of one's own actions, not a consequence of rebirth (comparable to karma); humans and animals follow the same material laws; pleasure is the product of a pleasurable mind; and wickedness is the product of a wicked mind.[81] Pain and pleasure are states of feeling that one can choose or avoid, and we are pained in the absence of pleasure: thus, for Epicurus, the natural choice of pleasure was the highest good to cultivate.[82] Of course, not all pleasure is good; it is necessary to evaluate whether a pleasure brings good or trouble.[83]

The Epicurean development of the philosophy of atomism as originally founded by Leucippus and followed by Democritus pursued a naturalist-rational foundation to rid oneself from the fear and pain that were exploited by religions in general. Epicurus rejected any fear of the supernatural that relates to us: "Topple the gods from their thrones … for our life has not now any place for irrational belief and groundless imagining, if we are to live happily."[84] His philosophy also was intended to justify the essentialist world view by making life seem real, its freedom real, and its pleasure possible and genuine.

In view of that, at the age of thirty-two in the garden of his house outside of Athens, Epicurus began a school open to everyone, including women and slaves. The purpose of this egalitarian garden-academy was to expand on his philosophy of addressing the substantiality of the mind and the world by advising his audience to live prudently while cultivating pleasure as the

---

[80] Shahristānī, *al-Milal wal Nihal*, 178.
[81] Ibid., 179.
[82] Laertius, *Lives of Eminent Philosophers*, X, 565, 603, 651, 655.
[83] Ibid., X, 655.
[84] McEvilley, *The Shape of Ancient Thought*, 333, 334, 611–612.

highest good.⁸⁵ His school was called "The Garden," a designation that was replicated in a trajectory of literature and mystical approaches by the later Persian thinkers and poets.⁸⁶

Epicurus's philosophy of pleasure (*hédoné* in Greek) was later criticized, just as the Çārvākas' philosophy had been, as being reckless hedonism without ethical considerations. His philosophy became mislabeled as sensual hedonism, equating his use of *hédoné* with the goddess of sensual pleasure in Greek and Roman mythologies. Thus, Epicurus was subsequently by the religious and moralist foes stereotyped and discredited as a lavish pleasure-seeker, and this reputation has followed him through the ages.

But in fact, it is an undeserved and misguided reputation: Epicurus emphatically alluded to *nonsensual* pleasure. He didn't deny that the body experiences pleasure in motion and in resting (kinetic), but also spoke at length about the pleasure of the *mind* (static) when in a state of delight. Epicurus saw mental pleasure as more lasting and greater than physical pleasure. He considered bringing bread and water to hungry lips to be the highest possible pleasure and necessary for health, but the pleasure of the body cannot be accumulated and does not last for many days.⁸⁷ The way Epicurus died testifies to his valuing of mental pleasure over physical: he is reported in a letter to have suffered and died from a kidney stone. When in severe pain in the last moments of his life, he got into a lukewarm bath and asked for undiluted wine. He then asked his friends to hold on to the truth of the doctrine, and he breathed his last. His admonition to his friends meant that even at the time of death, the clarity of mind should not lack mental enjoyment.⁸⁸

To Epicurus, pleasure also meant prudence and sober reasoning – virtues he considered more precious than philosophy – and pleasure without wise prudence was not pleasure. By pleasure, he meant the absence of mental

---

[85] Stephen Greenblatt, *The Swerve: How the World Became Modern* (New York: W. W. Norton, 2011), 73–80.

[86] The metaphor of a garden, whether or not in imitation of Epicurus, was subsequently used by various Persian thinkers and poets, particularly Abdullah Ansari (d. 1089), being in the "Garden of the Divine" (*Bāgh-e Elāhī*). See A. G. Ravan Farhadi, *Abdullāh Ansārī of Herāt (1006–1089 CE): An Early Sufi Master* (Surrey: Curzon Press, 1996), 132. The metaphor of "being in the garden" in Ansari's thought meant "having an insight or knowledge into things." In addition, Sa'di (d. 1292) was a Persian poet who also adopted the Epicurean concept of "Garden." Sa'di called his two books of wisdom *Bustān* (The Garden) and *Gulistān* (Flower Garden).

[87] Laertius, *Lives of Eminent Philosophers*, X, 657–659, 667.

[88] Ibid., X, 543–545, 671.

pain.⁸⁹ The Epicurean references actually point to the opposite of reckless hedonism, with Epicurus' austere diet of bread and water.⁹⁰ In contrast, even eating cheese would have been a luxury, let alone meat and wine. In referring to time in contemplation as well, Epicurus must have meant the inner pleasure of equanimity, not an outward sensual pleasure. And when there was sensual or physical pleasure, according to Epicurus, it would have to be prudently evaluated for its harm and benefits to oneself and others. Caring for one's physical health and mental tranquility in an Epicurean sense means dropping the fear of things which are to come, and abandoning the need of things which are lacking –health means simply making time to entertain things that bring happiness and tranquility to one's life.⁹¹

For attaining deeper contentment, Epicurus emphasized the power of friendship and described spending precious moments with true friends as being the wealth of one's life. With friends, one feels safeguarded against the random events of life, and with friends, one can engage in reasoning things out; otherwise, life would be wastefully spent on absurdities and distractions.

In one instance, Epicurus taught something important about fear being rooted in ignorance and pleasure being grounded in knowledge. According to Laertius, Epicurus related, fear would entangle people if they didn't know the nature of the world. What legends tell us is nothing but belief whereas the study of nature is sheer pleasures.⁹² Knowledge of nature and reality thus liberates one from illusion and enables one to live within the framework of expected events. It was out of this conviction that Lucretius wrote about Epicurus' ideas in his *Nature of Things*, in order to bring the empirical reality of things out of the darkness and to repel fear rooted in the mythical understanding of the world.

The purpose of pleasure (*ataraxia*, or freedom from anxiety), according to Epicurus, is to maintain a state of profound release from all forms of short- or long-term anxiety. Tensions in life are raised from different sources, internal and external. Internal tension is the work of a relentless mind. External tensions come from keeping up with societal and religious expectations. *Ataraxia* means turning a jittery mind toward its natural tranquility.⁹³ *Ataraxia* of the mind is analogous to the natural tranquility of water: after it is agitated,

---

[89] Ibid., X, 657, 661–663, 667.
[90] Ibid., X, 539, 541. For the biography of Epicurus and his philosophy, see 529–677.
[91] Ibid., X, 649, 651, 653, 655.
[92] Ibid., X, 667.
[93] Adrian Kuzminski, *Pyrrhonism: How the Ancient Greeks Reinvented Buddhism* (Lanham, MD: Lexington Books, 2008), ix, 43.

the ripples (tension) should gradually abate and the water return to its quiet nature. Any upsetting impediments to the true tranquility of the mind have to be abandoned and removed. Epicurus, like the Cārvākas, believed that even the highest level of sacred knowledge would have to be relinquished if it prevented attaining tranquility and joy of mind.

Thus, the approach to maintaining peace of mind for Democritus, Epicurus, Pyrrho, and their Indian nastikā counterparts focused on developing a psychological understanding of the nature of life through contemplation, tranquility, and the joy of being. Wealth and other elements of a good life played a secondary role in relation to the equanimous focus that emerges with the joy of knowing.

Pyrrhonism: Skepticism and Happiness

In exploring the similarities between the nastikā movements and Hellenic philosophy, Pyrrho of Elis of the third to fourth century BCE fits in this debate in two respects. First, in recent scholarship, he is compared with the Buddha as having similar skepticism about metaphysical knowledge. Second, like the Buddha, he was a strong proponent of a liberated happiness over the accumulation of "useless" knowledge.

The comparison also shows the development of ideas that parallel those of the Buddha and Nāgārjuna. Friedrich Nietzsche may have been the first to refer to Pyrrho as the "Greek Buddhist."[94] His inference may have been based on the study of the Pyrrhonian school of skepticism, a school specially developed by second-century philosopher-physician Sextus Empiricus. Pyrrhonian skeptics held that relinquishing all judgments and beliefs by living undogmatically would result in a quiet mind or *ataraxia*. This and the idea of experiencing the world based on the instantaneous appearances of things (phenomenological experience) is greater than the interpretation of a third party based on speculations (non-rational *phantasia*). This makes up Pyrrho's philosophy of sound thinking for the sake of sound living, which is fully

---

94 In naming Pyrrho as "einen *griechischen Buddhisten*," see Nietzsche: *Nachlass 1887–1889*, 264 [*Nachlass 1887–1889* (1999) DTV/Walter de Gruyter, München/New York], quoted in the doctoral dissertation of Marie-Luisa Frick, University of Innsbruck, Austria. I am grateful to Professor Frick for the courtesy of sending me this quote.

expanded by Sextus in his *Outlines of Pyrrhonism*.[95] It must be remembered that Pyrrho (similar to the Buddha) never wrote anything down, possibly fearing his own misreading of reality and misinterpretation of others.

Traveling with other philosophers alongside Alexander's military expeditions to Iran, Central Asia, and India, as Pyrrho is reported to have done, may have resulted in encounters with Buddhist and other adepts in those regions, much as other Hellenic thinkers including Democritus and Pythagoras had probably gone to India before.[96, 97] In Book IX, chapter two, of his *Lives of Eminent Philosophers*, Laertius provides an account of Pyrrho's meetings with Magians and Indian Gymnosophists (naked sages) – a meeting which led Pyrrho to adopt a noble philosophy.[98] These encounters may have led Pyrrho to unconsciously import Buddhist ideas into Hellenic circles. Pyrrho, in fact, was the first to spread the notion of immeasurability and even the impossibility of truly knowing whether things "are" or "are not" because of constant change, the strong skepticism about absolute knowledge that Buddhist thinkers adopted.[99]

A brief scrutiny of the similarities between the critical and psychological views of Pyrrho and the Buddha is revealing. In his 2008 book, *Pyrrhonism: How the Ancient Greeks Reinvented Buddhism*, Adrian Kuzminski vigorously discussed Everard Flintoff's thesis of "Pyrrho and India" from Flintoff's 1980 article. Flintoff mentions that Pyrrho met Magians from Iran, and monks possibly from Jain and Buddhist orders.[100]

This topic was revisited by Christopher Beckwith, in *Greek Buddha: Pyrrho's Encounter with Early Buddhism in Central Asia* (2015), this time with more historical depth. Beckwith presents a controversial yet well-documented assertion that the historical Buddha (Śakamuni or Sanskritized Śakyamuni) was a Scythian (Central Asian Saka) sage, a view which, needless to say, has

---

[95] See Sextus Empiricus, *Outlines of Pyrrhonism*, trans. Benson Mates (New York and Oxford: Oxford University Press, 1996), www.sciacchitano.it/pensatori%20epistemici/scettici/outlines%20of%20pyrronism.pdf. After the translation of Sextus Empiricus into Latin and later other languages beginning in the sixteenth century, it started having a wide readership and gaining fresher interpretations of Pyrrhonism and Skepticism in European philosophical thinking.
[96] Kuzminski, *Pyrrhonism*, 37, 44.
[97] Ibid., 46. Shahristānī's *al-Milal wal Nihal*, 466, 471–472, mentions that students of Pythagoras went to India spreading Pythagorean teachings.
[98] Laertius, *Lives of Eminent Philosophers*, IX, 475.
[99] See Batchelor, *After Buddhism*, 254–255.
[100] See Everard Flintoff, "Pyrrho and India," *Phronesis* 25/1 (1980): 88–108.

not gone without challenge.¹⁰¹ These possible meetings, in addition to the similarities between early Pyrrhonism and early Buddhism, provide modern thinkers a counter-argument against the earlier claims that the roots of Pyrrho's philosophical and spiritual learning were fundamentally Greek.¹⁰²

Connected with Flintoff's thesis, Kuzminski demonstrated similarities in the way Pyrrho and the Buddhists (especially the Madhyamika school, although this school was officially founded by Nāgārjuna in the third century CE) defied absolutism of knowledge. The non-absolutism of the Buddha and his refusal to frame reality in words pointed to his skepticism about whether it would ever be possible to know reality as it is, was, and will be in its totality. Pyrrho also held such a view. Pyrrho is argued by Kuzminski to have *reinvented* Buddhism in the Hellenic world, not merely transmitted it.¹⁰³

The defiance of both the Buddha and Pyrrho against scholastic knowledge is evident. The Buddha left no writing behind so that his words would not be misinterpreted or locked into fixed concepts. Pyrrho, as mentioned earlier, also left no writing behind¹⁰⁴ owing to his hatred of dialectics and of virtuosic display, a self-indulgence that was at the time considered part of philosophy.¹⁰⁵ In fact, the similarity between Pyrrhonian (or even Greek) skepticism¹⁰⁶ and Indian skepticism has strong relevance in recent studies.

The general tendency of the Hellenic philosophers was to win arguments over others' ideas, or refute the beliefs of their adversaries in favor of newer beliefs, or to search for the "truth." But for Pyrrho, as for Democritus and Epicurus, the purpose of philosophy was to achieve tranquility of the mind (*ataraxia*), not to defeat others in debate – a goal equally emphasized and advanced by the Buddha in his concept of nirvana.¹⁰⁷ Both philosophers tried to solve the problem of the grief-stricken mind, and focused on easing the aching and anguished mind.¹⁰⁸

---

¹⁰¹ See Stephen Batchelor, "Greek Buddha: Pyrrho's Encounter with Early Buddhism in Central Asia by Christopher I. Beckwith," book review article in *Contemporary Buddhism* 17/1 (2016): 195-215.

¹⁰² Christopher I. Beckwith, *Greek Buddha: Pyrrho's Encounter with Early Buddhism in Central Asia* (Princeton, NJ: Princeton University Press, 2015), see the Prologue.

¹⁰³Kuzminski, *Pyrrhonism*, 5. See also Beckwith, *Greek Buddha*, 20.

¹⁰⁴ Laertius, *Lives of Eminent Philosophers*, IX, 513, 517.

¹⁰⁵ From Nietzsche's book, *The Will to Power*, quoted in Kuzminski, *Pyrrhonism*, 15.

¹⁰⁶ Laertius, *Lives of Eminent Philosophers*, IX. 483; the philosophy of skepticism is discussed in the latter part of the chapter about Pyrrho.

¹⁰⁷ Kuzminski, *Pyrrhonism*, 43, 47; see also Beckwith, *Greek Buddha*, 16, 18.

¹⁰⁸ Kuzminski, *Pyrrhonism*, 37, 42.

The methodical goal of these philosophies was to train oneself for independent, modest, and quiet thinking without depending on the extraordinary speculations of others. Their philosophies aimed at living happily in the world without giving in to the drastic fluctuations of one's emotions. From Pyrrho's and the Buddha's points of view, the assembling of massive quantities of metaphysical speculations combined with various inflexible doctrines would only become fetters and a source of dogmatic attachment rather than a means of liberation. It is thus not surprising that the Buddha advised his followers that his teachings on the Dharma were like a raft: once used to reach the other shore, the raft had no more use and must be abandoned and not carried over the head.

The Buddha and Pyrrho were both interested in discussing the apparent, visible things which could be experienced by the sensory system and mental faculties, whereas many others were still interested in discussing the non-apparent things of the world. The Buddha and Pyrrho called into question two categories that scholastic thinkers and their followers speculatively claimed knowledge about: the nature of nonapparent things, and whether apparent things are permanent and have fixed natures. In the Buddhist (predominantly Madhyamika) context one can never be sure of nonapparent things; even all apparent things such as the "self" are doomed to change as their apparent character becomes degraded and gradually nonapparent. Pyrrho, like the Buddha, took the middle road, an undifferentiated position of assertion and nonassertion, neither accepting nor rejecting anything.[109]

Thus, the Buddhist and Pyrrhonian worldview is reluctant to express fixed ideas, particularly on topics seemingly absolute in nature on one hand and yet "useless" in producing true happiness in life on the other. For example, one's view on whether the world was created or has existed eternally suggests a fixed belief, yet at the same time, holding either such belief does little to produce happiness and tranquility in one's life. Belief in gods was viewed by the skeptics and naturalist philosophers as irrelevant to human life. The rejection of gods was meant to emancipate ordinary people.[110] In the practical sense, the main goal of knowledge was to produce nirvana or *ataraxia* – true happiness and harmony in daily life without a sharp duality between suffering and happiness. If any knowledge is ineffective in removing mental tensions and ignorance, then this "knowledge" is nothing but an ingrained dogmatic belief, a set of words to remember, adhere to, and repeat – in other words, a rather fixed societal convention. The *ataraxia* of Pyrrho had the same

---

[109] Ibid., 52, 55–56, 83, 114.
[110] McEvilley, *The Shape of Ancient Thought*, 619.

function as the nirvana of the Buddha, which was meant to rid people of the anxious mind and ingrained belief systems. Thus, it meant liberating the mind from all kinds of fetters, even unnecessary knowledge. Thus, despite leaving no writing behind, their teachings inspired future thinkers to adopt a non-absolutist and non-metaphysical approach.

Lucretius: Mind Is Matter, Humans Are Not Unique, and Joy Is Real

Some 2070 years ago, Titus Lucretius Carus, a Roman poet, atomist, and dedicated follower of the Epicurean school, composed a series of poems entitled *The Nature of Things* (*De rerum natura*). These poems epitomized the Epicurean philosophical ideals. Lucretius carried on the Epicurean tradition, and then his succinct ideas were passed down all the way to modern times, having a great impact on modern thinkers, particularly in the Enlightenment period. For a while during the medieval period, his work was lost until it was rediscovered by a Renaissance-era book-hunter, Poggio Bracciolini, in 1417. The incredible impact and legacy of Lucretius' collection of poems in the formative Renaissance period in the Western hemisphere has been covered in an engaging and exhilarating narrative, *The Swerve: How the World Became Modern* by Stephen Greenblatt (2011). The overwhelmingly positive reception of Lucretius' didactical poems, which brought back the earlier ideas of atomism-pleasure of Democritus and Epicurus (and even subliminally the ancient nastikā schools of philosophy), is not surprising because the literati craved liberation after a long history of religious oppression.

Lucretius' 7400-line work was a poetic treatise that denied the existence of magic and the supernatural in the workings of nature. Instead, the processes of nature reveal themselves based on recurrent and familiar patterns. Lucretius succinctly proposed that no *atoma* (bodies which cannot be divided) can be created and none can be destroyed, that nature, body, and soul are purely material, and that their dissolution is a reconfiguration of the atoms into something else. This dissolution and reconfiguration is not the privilege of the gods but is the mechanism of nature's give and take.[111] Lucretius provides a myriad of imageries of atoms, the field of energy, thermodynamics, and the behavior of atoms and other particles from the smallest to the largest in his Book II of *The Nature of Things*. Lucretius' writings are "theories", but they are theories about the natural world and how it seems to work on a level that is not based on god or belief.

---

[111] Lucretius, *The Nature of Things*, trans. A. E. Stallings (London: Penguin Classics, 2007), introduction, vii–xv. Book II, 38.

Since the goal of being in this world is pleasure, according to Lucretius, pleasure is the shaking of loose atoms to bring them to their balanced and proper places.[112] The dread of death must be discarded. Death as the end is liberation; hell is nowhere to be seen.[113] Lucretius believed in no return to previous stages of construction or existence – the new and creative construction is the rule for the dancing atoms of the universe. Lucretius described death as liberation in order to point to the finitude of joy and of all beautiful life experiences. If an infinite search for joyful living is painful, death is liberation and a glorious goodbye to life.

As an astute atomist, Lucretius describes the mind as a physical phenomenon just like the physical body, only with finer and smoother and more numerous particles vibrating much faster and more easily than the thicker and rougher particles of the body.[114] In Book III, he goes on to compose verses about the disarray of the body's elements and the exact same thing happening to the mind – the body-mind goes through an Eternal Death by joining those people who had died months, years, and centuries earlier.[115] In asserting that there is no soul, and that the body and mind are physical entities that eventually die, his thought-provoking poems speak for themselves. The mind or spirit can also be healed or sickened by medicine just as the body can – further evidence that the living mind is physical and mortal.[116] Thus, not only is the mind an epiphenomenon of the physical body, but it is itself made out of atoms that are subject to the same processes of aging, and then it fades as does a flame or the scent of perfume. The following verses clarify:

> in Death, indeed, the mind… wanders astray ....
> At other times, the mind is carried off into a deep
> Coma, and sinks down into a never-ending sleep;
> The eyes rolled back, the head nodding, it cannot hear the sound
> Of voices, cannot recognize the people gathered round.[117]

Lucretius explicitly counters many of the claims of religion about things such as souls, death, and reincarnation. He categorically rejects the metaphysical

---

[112] Ibid., II, 64–65.
[113] Ibid., II, 37; III, 72–73, 78.
[114] Ibid., III, 76–78.
[115] Ibid., III, 105. Omar Khayyam composed a quatrain with exactly the same content: see Chapter 7.
[116] Ibid., III, 87.
[117] Ibid., III, 85.

claim that the soul is separate from the body and is immune to the event of death. He says there is no such thing as reincarnation or the resurrection of souls. He expresses in the manner of a parody that, if minds are immortal, they should convene somewhere, mate and make babies, and enter bodies from outer space. If there was such a thing as reincarnation of souls, this would mean the deeds of one human who had already died would be counted against another innocent baby who is just born without any memory or thought of its previous life. Furthermore, Lucretius maintains that in a violent death, whether drowned, frozen, killed by a beast, or decapitated by earthquake, the body and mind will not be separated, one destroyed but another spared. No part of the body stays alive to mourn its own death. In death, everything is destroyed and all cognitive faculties are lost. The mind loses contact with the outside world, with children and family, and by this demise, Nature absorbs us and all our arguments.[118] No return or eternal life is possible, except in scenarios invented by the senses.

Lucretius' masterful language not only demythologizes the false hope of eternal life and permanency of the soul, but also encourages people to relax and allow the natural processes to beautify life the way they always do. The phenomenon of death shows us it is nothing to be feared. It is a peaceful sleep without anxieties or uncertainties, no need to despise oneself, or wishfully think of joining all the previous generations (ancestors or religious figures) who died before us.[119] He invites his readers to know the nature of the mind and the nature of things: the mind dies like the body. All illusions shall also die, rather than surviving without the body – the mind does not work that way.

Lucretius provides numerous examples to demonstrate that the mind and sensory system can interfere with a sound understanding of things. The illusions of the sensory system deceive the mind, making it perceive things in ways that are not their true nature, like seeing a village in the distance as a dull spot without details. Meanwhile, the mind cannot perceive particles that the wind blows to our right and left. Either the mind misses many images in nature, or optical illusions show us distorted images of them. This is problematic when we only maintain in the mind images that we wish to occur. We like to pin down certain patterns in our mind for these images, but our "conclusions" are only the web of delusions of the mind.[120] Using these examples, Lucretius describes the anomaly of the mind: it is unable to detect

---

[118] Ibid., III, 76, 91, 98–99.
[119] Ibid., III, 102–105.
[120] Ibid., IV, 109–131.

real things and yet enjoys illusions and images that have no reality, such as immortality of the soul and images of a pseudo-real afterlife.

Advising us to untie the knot of the mind from the bonds of religion, Lucretius takes us from Book IV to Book V. There, he boldly refutes the concept of an anthropocentric universe. He deems the world is not for and about humans. If it really were designed for humans, it has turned out to be deeply flawed. It contains ferocious beasts, thorns, deserts, violent storms, heat, frosts, diseases, flood, harshness, terror-stricken nights, dying in storms at sea – all quite unfriendly to humans. If the world were designed for humans, human babies would not be so helpless and vulnerable to predators.[121] Lucretius vilifies anthropocentrism in his writings. That is another illusion that Lucretius would like to deconstruct, in order to liberate the human mind and enable it to live and die humbly, like all other earthly and heavenly bodies.

In challenging the beliefs of the credulous, Lucretius approaches from another angle to say that the earth and celestial bodies may seem to be holy and godly, but in fact, they are not divine at all. Their days are also numbered – even the shrines and statues of gods crumble. Nature is the graveyard of species and it grows them anew; then the new becomes old again right before our eyes. Therefore, the belief in godly creation should be abandoned.[122] The earth, moon, sun, and odd creatures are not alien objects; they are atoms in different configurations tightly coming together and ultimately disintegrating again. Only three things are eternal and resist the winds of time: matter, emptiness, and space. Atoms find room to dance in the space in which bodies are made and unmade, again and again; allegorically this is neither birth nor death.[123] This is why Lucretius sees death as "nothing to us." It is the dance of atoms in space and there is never "death," only the reconfiguration of things.

The poem's triumphs in bringing out Epicurean atomistic deliberations about the material world and human liberation. Lucretius' philosophical creativity ventured into ideas about rationalism, atomism, nontheism, free will, and happiness. The universality of his philosophy can hardly be challenged. Lucretius provides a wide range of themes that were and still are undeniably defiant against religious and supernatural beliefs. Greenblatt lays out a noteworthy list of these themes among which are: there is no creator, the atoms are in constant motion, the universe is not made for humans,

---

[121] Ibid., V, 153–155, 179.
[122] Ibid., V, 150–51, 152–153, 155, 156–157.
[123] Ibid., V, 157–159, 161–162, 165.

humans are not unique, after death the soul dies and there is no afterlife, the real goal of humans is to cultivate pleasure, and understanding the nature of things is a profound realization.[124]

The reemergence of the book of Lucretius, *The Nature of Things*, with its radical themes, caused a sociocultural shake-up in the highly religious Europe of the Middle Ages. According to Greenblatt, in the 15th century, the post-medieval European quest for true happiness without god prompted Lorenzo Valla to write *On Pleasure* in defense of the Lucretian-Epicurean philosophy of joy and the naturalness of things. Valla further based his discourse of materialism on the Epicurean principles that nothing remains of a human being after death. As the lion, wolf, dog, and other living beings eat, drink, sleep, give birth, feed their offspring, and then die, so does the human being. Differences between people such as possessing more material things than others do not eliminate humans' fundamental alikeness. Thus, pleasure is and must be the ultimate good that one cultivates.[125]

Of course, the propagation of this and other Epicurean ideas did not go unnoticed by the Church, which received the ideas as heresy and with predictable hostility. Censorship led high-ranking priests in the early sixteenth century to ban the reading of Lucretius' poems in schools in some parts of the continent.[126] It took five centuries for the far-reaching effects of Lucretius' liberation philosophy to become evident. Despite the antagonism of the Christian establishment, the atomism of Lucretius and his intellectual mentor Epicurus seems to have influenced a great number of Renaissance and Enlightenment thinkers. Isaac Newton declared himself an atomist, attempting, like many other Christian thinkers, to reconcile divinity with the world of solid indivisible particles (*atoma*) that keep making and unmaking new things and bodies.[127] This vision paved the way for an exploration of the theory of materialism and evolution, and even the origin of the human species. It underlined new revelations for the thinkers and scholars of the following centuries. Even the politician Thomas Jefferson possessed several copies of Lucretius' book. Inspired by Epicurean philosophy, Jefferson inserted the phrase "Life, Liberty and the pursuit of Happiness" into the American Declaration of Independence.[128]

---

[124] Greenblatt, *The Swerve*, 182–202.
[125] Ibid., 222–225.
[126] Ibid., 226.
[127] Ibid., 261.
[128] Ibid., 263.

Lucretius recognized that the joy of life comes from only living once and using the opportunity to savor the beauty of life. In the beginning of Book II of *The Nature of Things*, he provides an account of how straightforward it can be to become aware or even forget of one's own privilege and happiness in day-to-day life. Pleasure in life is to be free from all misfortunes as well as free from feasts and luxuries. One merely needs the "bare minimum to keep suffering at bay."[129] Lucretius, like Epicurus, understood the pleasure of living to mean the absence of trouble and pain – a simple and yet a significant state of awareness that requires constant reminders and practice.

Conclusion

These Indo-Greco-Roman philosophies opened the gates of debate on how to free the mind. They aimed to free communities trapped in dogmatic cultures and the obsolete ways of religious thinking inherited from our human ancestors. As a result, the cognitive tools of social and cultural systems that developed during the Bronze Age and the early Iron Age were radically challenged and displaced.

Over the centuries, the Upanishadic yogis challenged many preexisting religious beliefs and practices. The Çārvākas proposed that individuals take charge of their own salvation and happiness. The Ājīvikas made it clear that the predetermined laws of nature and the cosmos cannot be altered because of our wishes and prayers. Jains provided the human mind, paralyzed by religion, with an innovative remedy: liberation through one's own virtuous and nonviolent actions. The Buddha, as we shall see in the following chapter, provided another groundbreaking method for understanding the human mind and its deeper use and ultimate liberation.

A similar intention of liberating the human mind took shape among the Hellenic nontheistic thinkers such as Democritus, Epicurus, Pyrrho, and those who followed. Although of course there are some differences among them, the principles common to the Indian and Hellenic schools of naturalism, empiricism, and skepticism are summarized by McEvilley as 1. the importance of sense experience, 2. rejection of the esoteric, 3. objectivity, 4. order and regularity – an order that cannot be changed by belief, magic, sacrifice or prayer, 5. renouncing supernatural power, and 6. embracing the biological nature of human beings rather than being a divine entity.[130] Two

---

[129] Lucretius, *The Nature of Things*, 36–37.
[130] McEvilley, *The Shape of Ancient Thought*, 325.

other commonalities can be added that Lucretius points out: the world is not made for humans, and death should not be thought of as something special.

The quintessential philosophy of self-rule and true pleasure claimed that one's happiness should *not* be decided by others, and one should not allow oneself to be the intellectual prey of self-righteous scholastic and cultural authorities. But the philosophies that the Çārvāka, Buddhist, Pyrrhonian, Epicurean, and Lucretian movements put forward were not intended to bring about a superficial happiness. Having more sophisticated objectives in mind, their philosophies took shape during difficult times when human populations were living under brutal regimes controlled by a few feudal, military, and religious authorities. These liberation philosophies were formed when the unquestioned obedience of the people was the rule. However, the content of these philosophies was not a call for a social revolution per se. It was meant for the transformation of the human attitude toward oneself and to finding respect for one's own capacities. It was intended to provide a perspective of choice by exercising free will rather than giving in to a communally preplanned destiny.

Despite the assumption of some scholars that each culture produces a set of thinkers with a thinking mechanism that is distinctly its own, the common denominators in philosophical thinking patterns are greater than the dissimilarities. The desire for true happiness and pleasure in life is already rooted in the universal human psyche. The search for and attainment of happiness has engaged humans of different cultures in many labyrinths of psychology and experimentation. Although some may have gotten lost along the way, the dormant intelligence of joy, detachment, and tranquility has always remained a potential choice. The words for pleasure and tranquility, whether *kām(a)* काम in Sanskrit, *kām* کام in classical Persian, or the Hellenistic Greek *hédoné* (pleasure) and *ataraxia* (tranquility), all stem from the very same consciousness, representing the ultimate psychological and philosophical yearning to explore individual freedom and peacefulness in nature.

Chapter 6

Buddha's Self-Rule Philosophy: A Model for Ten "Mini-Nirvanas"

Against the backdrop of thousands of existing monographs and manuscripts on Buddhist topics, from abstruse philosophical ideas to spiritual instructions for devotees and the lay public, it may seem that there is little new to say. Nevertheless, this chapter with its synthesis and reformulation of essential ideas is a new attempt to bring the core themes of the Buddha's teachings (Dharma) from various schools of Buddhism into a fresh, methodically organized light. In a way, the narrative of this chapter is an anthropological approach to reassembling the major themes of Buddhism, in spite of Buddhism's inner diversions. It is also incorporating certain subspecialties of Buddhist discourse into one single and accessible narrative. But on a broader scale, this concise model of nirvana primarily aims to bring the Buddha, a protagonist and one of the first teachers of liberation philosophy, closer to the ideals of our modern times and to enhance the conversation about liberation philosophy and self-rule from the Buddhist perspective.

The goal here is to elucidate Buddhist philosophy in the context of the power of reasoning in modern, secular language without sectarian or religious baggage. The model of liberation of the self that the Buddha envisioned, offering freedom from mental and cultural entanglements, was not personalized or dogmatic, but rather was a methodic approach that had to work for other people.[1] It seems that the rational approach of the Buddha and other Buddhist dialecticians over the last 2,500 years has been remarkably applicable, and continues today.

In the first part of this chapter, we begin with the Buddha's rebellion against the scriptural and ritualistic ceremonies of his time with his intention of introducing a philosophy *outside* of the scriptures and Brahmanical theology of the day, focusing on the primacy of the individual instead of terrestrial and celestial gods. We'll follow the historical circumstances as the Buddha's teachings themselves were corrupted by followers, becoming a scholastic scriptural tradition, ultimately deifying and worshipping the Buddha himself.

---

[1] Batchelor, *After Buddhism*, 62.

The second half of the chapter aims to salvage the core of his philosophy of self-awakening, known as nirvana. In the course of history, Buddhist literature and commentaries have been accumulating on top of one another; the ideal of nirvana became more complicated with the emergence of different schools and masters with different instructions, such as Theravada, Mahayana, Zen, and Tantric Schools of Buddhism. The schisms that arose in Buddhism were a matter of historical evolution that, similar to other philosophical schools, pushed Buddhism in different directions. Thus, the adepts of each school held different interpretations of the Buddha's message based on the demands of their era and their personal inclinations and understanding. One downside of such schisms is that the followers of each school tend to then remain loyal to the fixity of their own school's scholastic texts, and teachings become fragmented.

In this chapter, however, we seek to discover the rational-secular components that we in modern times need from Buddhist philosophy, beyond what the religiously-bounded interpretations can provide. We can encapsulate the conceptual power of nirvana by relying on texts, traditions, and consistency of the Buddha's discourses without framing these discussions within a particular Buddhist scholastic school, or focusing on the person of the Buddha or a particular Buddhist adept. It is an integrative attempt to provide ten essential conduits to attaining nirvana, a model of ten "mini-nirvanas", that arise from taking an overarching non-dogmatic approach to Buddhism.

Rebellion for the Sake of Liberation

As discussed in the previous chapter, the nāstika movement in India defied the authority of the Vedic scriptures and priests, rituals, animal sacrifices, gods and earthly vicars, and self-subjugating acts under the banner of religiosity or spirituality. By the 6th c. BCE, audacious Çārvāka school thinkers had been opposing the Vedic Brahmanical clerical tradition and its stultifying ritualism for some time, and the Ājīvika and Jain schools continued these efforts. The school of Buddhism also had its roots in this heretical or nāstika[2] (nonconformist) movement.

Siddhartha Gautama, who later became known as the Buddha, "the awakened one," emerged as another nonconformist critical thinker around the sixth century BCE. Unlike the Brahmanical ascetics of the day, the Buddha did not preach the denial of physical self or advocate seclusion or ascetic

---

[2] *Astikā* refers to the acceptance of the Vedas, as opposed to *Nastikā* which refers to the rejection of the Vedas.

cognitive suicide. On the contrary, he believed that liberation in this short life is within reach.

The Buddha's stance in challenging abstract beliefs was thus similar to other contemporaneous nāstika, agnostic, and *lokāyāta* (worldly or materialist) groups, and equally as fraught with rebellion against the mainstream. In contrast to the highly dogmatic and mythically oriented Brahmanical religion surrounding him, after his awakening the Buddha held that there is no independent reality other than the empirical reality perceived by the senses here and now. His teaching was that the present living self is the only self that exists and continues to change until death. He opposed the notion of "ultimate self" (atman) which had been claimed in various religious texts of his time.

The message of the Buddha was to eliminate dependence on the gods and supernatural forces and abandon the "truth-seeking" activities that had been framed in fixed, sacred, religious words. On a practical level, this meant that the Buddha spoke out against animal sacrifices, priestly rituals, and mythical beliefs, claiming that such practices are not helpful for one's life. The rebellion of the Buddha has to be viewed against the long history of the masses taking refuge in the supernatural, and relinquishing many of their own essential pursuits and emotive accountabilities. But the Buddha's clear words put the matter into contrasting perspective: "Seek no other refuge but yourself." In this case, "rely on yourself" connoted not relying on gods and beliefs. A belief system under a clerical hierarchy had suspended the masses from taking charge of their own destiny. Needless to say, this was perceived as an enormous threat against the powerful religious forces of the time. The Brahmanical leaders faced the task of dealing with the doctrinal challenge presented by the Buddha and his teachings, and tried dealing with this rebellious thinker during his time and after his death in creative ways.

First, the nervous religious authorities attempted to co-op Buddha's existence, portraying him as actually supporting the work of the gods by bringing the Buddha under the Brahmanical umbrella. At least one of the popular medieval Vedic anthologies praising gods and heroes, the *Purānas*, refers to the historical Buddha as the ninth reincarnation of the Hindu god Viṣnu, whose purpose was to delude the demons and bring people back to

Brahmanism.³ Having thus claimed divine reincarnation for the Buddha, this attempt carried praise for Viṣṇu, rather than the person of the Buddha. Viṣṇu's reincarnation was called *Buddha*, but his presence, in this story, was only significant for helping the gods in their wars against demons, the kind of demons who manipulated or degraded the Vedic sacrifices. Thus, the fact that Buddha preached sacrificial ceremonies again was turned around to give Buddha a Vedic element, since it was said that Buddha helped the gods win the battle against the demons who were using Vedic sacrifice to their own advantage. This gave Buddha-worship a Brahmanical dimension so that mainstream Hindu opinions about the Buddha were positively and definitely Vedic.

When syncretism didn't work, direct opposition against the Buddha surfaced. The classic attack was by the *advaita vedantist* (non-dualist Vedanta) thinker, Adi Shankara (d. 820). Shankara, among other medieval critics of Buddhism, said the Buddha was a "great deceiver" or "seducer," meaning the Buddha was malicious enough to deliberately confuse his followers by telling different things to the Hinayanists (Theravada), the Mahayanists, and other Buddhist sects. Thus, the label of "seducer"[4] in medieval times represented the cultural and religious attitude toward the Buddha's philosophical rebellion against the establishment in the Indian religious culture.

Some modern Indian scholars even think that the Buddha remained a Hindu but was a reformer of that religion, and was inspired by the Vedic and Upanishadic thoughts to restate the so-called Indo-Aryan ideals.[5] In softening the sharp position of the Buddha against the ancient scriptures and rituals, various modern Hindu authors have insinuated that what the Buddha had tried to achieve was actually not outside of the Vedic and Brahmanical ideals.[6] This claim, however, ignores the historical fact that Buddha's Dharma did not thrive in India nor within the Vedic tradition, due to the Buddha's rejection of

---

[3] See Shree Madh Bhagvad Maha Purāna, part 1, chapter 3, stanza 24; see also, Lal Mani Joshi, *Brahmanism, Buddhism, and Hinduism: An Essay on Their Origins and Interactions* (Kandy, Sri Lanka: Buddhist Publication Society, The Wheel Publication No. 150/151), 5, 22. First published in 1970, references refer to the 2008 online edition, https://what-buddha-said.net/library/Wheels/wh150.pdf.
[4] Joshi, *Brahmanism, Buddhism, and Hinduism*, 11.
[5] Ibid., 7–8.
[6] Ibid., see the first part of the essay which speaks of the authors who have viewed the Buddha simply to be within the Brahmanical tradition. See also Swami Prabhavananda, *The Spiritual Heritage of India* (Chennai: Sri Ramakrishna Math, 2003) whose tone is much more moderate and accepting that Buddhism eventually became an independent sect through the political patronage of Asoka and moved out of Brahmanism.

the authority and sanctity of the Vedas, resulting in Buddhists being rejected by the religious authorities and largely leaving India for other more receptive destinations such as, Central Asia, then China and beyond.

The Buddha's and other nāstika groups' rejection of the Vedas meant replacing religious traditions with alternatives. Other nāstika groups emphasized physical, moral, or pleasurable acts or even seclusion as a means to soothe or manage the impulsive activities of the mind. The Buddha's singular alternative to the sacred Brahmanical scriptures was to expound on overhauling, excavating, and healing the mind's apparatus once and for all. The empirical mind replaced sacred scriptures as the source for taming deceptive thinking and incessant desires.

Clearly the Buddha's rebellious ideas replicated those of his contemporaries, such as the Çārvākas. Despite the fact that the Çārvākas and their literature did not survive beyond the fourteenth century, some of their ideas survived through Buddhism, such as nontheism, self-reliance, primacy of the body-mind over abstract metaphysical beliefs, irreversible process of death (parinirvana), and accepting the determinism built into unconsented birth and unasked death (samsara). Thus, the *methods* that the Buddha introduced were different from the Çārvākas, but not the goals.

However, despite the fact that the Buddha had in some radical ways dethroned the gods and taken away the authorities of the religious scriptures, the early Buddhists eventually fell prey to ritualism and textualism themselves. The entrapment this time was with Buddhist texts, not the Vedas.

The Stalemate of the Buddhist Scriptures – The Zen Rebellion

In order to reach the point of identifying the essential elements of Buddhist teachings, it is instructive to first review the tradition of Buddhist scriptures. The Buddha's teachings seem to have been written down not as a source of reference but rather as a continuation of the tradition of "sacredness" in the long history of Indian theistic culture. The volume of such writings is one problem. Their fixed meanings and interpretations is another.

It would be nearly impossible to read, comprehend, and master all of the existing Buddhist literature. Theravadan adepts wrote about six thousand pages beginning in the third century BCE, beginning with the *Tripitakas* ("three baskets"). These three canons were meant to lay the foundation for future Buddhist society by introducing the monastic rules (*vinaya*), the anecdotal teachings (*sūtras*) including the Buddha's rebirth stories (*jātakas*), and the highest teachings (*abhidharma*) of the Buddha.

Later, beginning around 50 BCE with the rise of the Mahayana school, a small circle of adepts appeared on the scene with the writing of the *Prajñāpāramitā Sūtras*,[7] and subsequently other sūtras (*Lotus Sūtra, Heart Sūtra*, etc.). Along with Nāgārjuna's *Mūlamadhyamakākārikā*, Buddhist textual materials increased up to fifteen thousand pages, mostly as newly conceived literature as well as commentaries on older literature. As Rupert Gethin puts it: "Subsequent centuries saw the production of vast expanded versions, such as those of 100,000 lines, 25,000 lines, and 8,000 lines, as well as shorter versions, such as the *Vajracchedikā* and *Hṛdaya* [the "Diamond" and "Heart" Sūtras]."[8] The Chinese, Indian, Tibetan, and Japanese Buddhist practitioners in their turn translated the old works and generated newer literature to supplement the Buddha's teachings. And further writings by individual Buddhist teachers and schools have continued to be produced over the course of time.

Buddhist scriptures are essential for knowing the principal teachings of the Buddha. There is, however, a dilemma of authority for scriptures from the different schools of Buddhism. Furthermore, when these scriptures become a set of inflexible beliefs, they block the freedom to interpret and apply them both in monastic and non-monastic communities. Stephen Batchelor is correct in saying that many Buddhist texts are both a blessing and a curse, leaving us in limbo in terms of interpreting the words of the Buddha.[9]

Even his very own message of independence ultimately was not enough for some to transcend the capture of the psycho-emotional tendency to cling, and much of Buddhism was eventually turned into a devotional belief system. Naturally, on a psychological level, there is no objection if the devotional practices "soothe and settle the mind."[10] But the "problem" of faith and belief in the Buddha's doctrine became a systematic institution, an oxymoron in light of his message of empirical thinking and living.

In light of what has been compiled and considered scholastically useful, the religiously-minded Buddhists have done a disservice to the Buddha's original, specific position against organized hierarchical religious establishments. The Buddha almost certainly did not intend to invent a new religion: he did not appoint a successor and did not write down his teachings. Perhaps he did not write down his teachings because it was not the custom in those days with

---

[7] The oldest and original *Prajñāpāramitā* is 8,000 lines (*Aṣṭasāhasrikā*).
[8] Rupert Gethin, *The Foundations of Buddhism* (Oxford: Oxford University Press, 1998), 234.
[9] Batchelor, *After Buddhism*, 20–21.
[10] Gethin, *The Foundations of Buddhism*, 169.

any teacher around the Buddha, but perhaps it was also due to the danger of the strong tendency to claim such words as sacred and inalterable.

Scripture-veneration and the development of a Buddhist belief system proceeded for almost 1,000 years after the Buddha until another consequential rebellion took place. The rise of Zen in some ways was a revolution against this conventional and scholastic Buddhism. The sixth-century Zen patriarch in China, Bodhidharma, abolished the use of texts in order to return to the authentic practice of the Buddha and to perfect wisdom (*prajñāpāramitā*). This was aimed against a corrupted thousand-year-old Buddhist tradition. Bodhidharma was no hair-splitting logician or a worshipped saint. Through "peaceful settling of the mind," he only wanted to reach the end of the road in Buddhist idealism and understand the nature of one's own being, beyond the individual and faulty self.[11] His famous message was clearly anti-textual and anti-scholastic, bypassing all other hierarchical authorities: "A special transmission outside the scriptures, not relying on words or letters; pointing directly to the human mind, seeing true nature is becoming a Buddha."[12] D. T. Suzuki goes as far as affirming that Zen was a "revolt of the Chinese mind against [scholastic] Buddhism."[13] Zen, indeed was an evolution out of the Chinese Chan-Buddhism influenced by Taoist philosophy as demonstrated in the mixture of their world views, idealism and writings.[14] Although the anti-scriptural attitude of Zen did not get immediate attention and took almost two hundred years after Bodhidharma to mature, it became a basis for combining oral theory and practice into one single guideline to free the mind.[15]

Other anti-textual and anti-ritualistic positions developed in other regions.[16] Japanese Buddhists made their own iconoclastic interventions in the waning tradition of Chinese Zen due to the Mongol invasion in the 13th century as well as text- and ritual-based Buddhism. As a result, they introduced innovative

---

[11] Daisetz Teitaro Suzuki, *The Awakening of Zen*, ed. Christmas Humphreys (1980; Boston: Shambhala, 2000), 15, 26.
[12] See "Zen," *Encyclopedia Britannica*, www.britannica.com/topic/Zen, accessed Sept. 17, 2018.
[13] Suzuki, *The Awakening of Zen*, 29, quoting an unnamed Chinese scholar.
[14] Heinrich Dumoulin, "Early Chinese Zen Reexamined: A Supplement to Zen Buddhism: A History," *Japanese Journal of Religious Studies* 20/1 (1993), 39, 41, 48.
[15] Ibid., 33.
[16] The Korean Sŏn tradition (of Zen) had also taken an anti-textual position. See Batchelor, *After Buddhism*, 257–258. The anti-Buddhist position in the Korean system can partly be attributed to the Confucianist campaign and policies, see Kim Jongmyung, "The Seon Monk Hyujeong and Buddhist Ritual in Sixteenth-Century Korea," *Korea Journal* 57/1 (Spring 2017), 7–34.

ideas and methods to understand and practice Zen-Buddhism. But even Zen began to fall prey to the age-long tendency to dogmatize teachings into rigid belief systems. From the twelfth through the fourteenth century, the great iconoclastic Zen teachers in Japan, such as Dōgen and Musō, tried to overhaul the depressing state of Buddhism and Zen, but after each round or reformation, the followers reverted back to dogma and ritual.

Eventually, the state of Zen in medieval Japan was nothing short of deception, simply relying on memorization of slogans and strictly following the teacher's way without reaching one's own enlightenment or thinking independently. This disarray and deviation from the Buddha's mandate of self-rule had much to do with an "age-old sickness of teaching Zen without being enlightened oneself."[17] It also had to do with the corruption in monastic institutions and the role of abbots in the Zen monasteries. As one leading Song dynasty master reported; "abbots ... with mind tricks manipulate and control the members of the community, while members of the community serve the abbot with the ulterior motives of influence, power, and profit."[18]

Another key impasse in the orthodoxy of Buddhism was that attaining nirvana, an ultimate level of liberation, became the monopoly of the monastic class. It was the typical expectation of Buddhist life that by precisely learning the scriptures and living a monastic life one would become awakened and liberated. However, Dōgen (d. 1253) was a prominent Zen teacher who opposed this attitude and the corruption in the teachings of the Buddha. He went so far as to divide the Dharma teachings into the true Dharma, the imitative Dharma, and the decayed Dharma, and took an iconoclastic position similar to that of the historical Buddha, speaking against a discriminatory position of who can or cannot attain nirvana.

Dōgen believed that in the past, not only Zen masters but also hunters, woodcutters, even bad people with wrong views, and individuals without ordination had become awakened. The real question of awakening for him was not a person's sanctity but a person's individual will.[19] Dōgen explained the simple reason as to why lay people have difficulty in being awakened had to do with their lifestyle and the obstacles they faced. He also added that worldliness and sanctity are not about being home-leavers (monks), or about

---

[17] Dōgen, *Rational Zen: The Mind of Dōgen Zenji*, trans. Thomas Cleary (Boston: Shambhala, 1995), 8.
[18] Ibid., introduction, 10–11.
[19] Ibid., 33–34.

the sentiment toward Buddhism, because there are lay people whose conduct is superior even to the formal home-leavers of the monastery.[20]

Additionally, he considered it unlikely that those monks who dedicate their lives to learning the scriptures are the only ones who possess the clarity of mind for understanding the teachings. But the implication of many of the scriptures is that non-monks engaged in worldly duties would be blocked from any direct experience or practice of awakening. Dōgen himself was a monk, but he was aware of the contradiction, and opposed the dogmatic memorization-repetition of texts among the Buddhist masters and their fellow monks.

In response to the dogmatism of Buddhism that barred people from attaining nirvana, in 1233 at the age of thirty-three Dōgen began to compose his life-long piece *The Treasury of the True Dharma Eye (Shōbōgenzō)*. He also founded a small center in Fukakusa, in the suburb of his native Kyoto.[21] This was an attempt to reform the ailing state of Buddhism.

On the dogmatic side, generally the authorities of the Buddhist scriptures and texts have been the basis for the devotional and faithful behavior of their followers. Rupert Gethin points out that the "Buddhist faith" similar to other religions is often based on what one reads or hears, other than direct experience or knowledge.[22] But the predominance in religiosity in Buddhism is when the monks and masses worship the Buddha, go on pilgrimage with offerings to the shrines and stupas, recite, chant, and even revere monks for their views. All are components of a religion.[23] The worship of the Buddha became another anomaly in the philosophy the Buddha presented.

Vedic beliefs in metaphysics, karma, rebirth, heavens, hells, and the supernatural that the Buddha originally rebelled against re-infiltrated Buddhism, particularly in Tibetan Buddhism after the 7th century. The traditional belief in *personal* karma that had been prevalent in faith-based Indian culture, such as the claim that each person lives through several successive bodies due to accumulated karma, eventually also made its way

---

[20] Ibid., 33, 35.
[21] Kazuaki Tanahashi, "Introduction," *Moon in a Dewdrop: Writings of Zen Master Dōgen*, ed. Kazuaki Tanahashi (New York: North Point Press, 1985), 7. Although Dōgen's teachings and writings were for the most part suppressed until early nineteenth-century Japan, they made a successful return in Japan as well as in the West.
[22] Gethin, *The Foundations of Buddhism*, 166–167, though the texts do not clearly counter the negative impact of faith, 169.
[23] Ibid., 168; see also Stephen Batchelor, *Buddhism Without Beliefs: A Contemporary Guide to Awakening* (New York: Riverhead Books, 1997), 14–15.

into scholastic Buddhism. The belief in karma meant that one's physical health and cognitive conditions, or success or failure in life, are all determined at the moment of conception, based on previous lives. Furthermore, suffering is not all undeserved. These claims, as argued by Paul Griffiths, are philosophically incoherent, deterministic, contradictory, and even empirically false.[24] The background goal of karmic theory in Buddhist communities was (and still is) to regulate a hierarchical as well as moral structure to maintain certain behavior, namely for lay people to support the monks, or to avoid harming sentient beings, or to gain enough merits to be born as a monk in the next life.[25] The wish to be born as a monk came from that old historical belief that *only* monks could attain nirvana, while lay people were barred from such privilege.

In the world of modern scholarship, Batchelor has arduously tried to demystify and demythologize the moralistic, poetic mythic, dramatic and dogmatic language of orthodox Buddhism by giving this doctrine a more lucid and rational interpretation than it has ever received.[26] He says that over time, ironically, more and more people worshiped the Buddha and uncritically accepted his teachings, something that was probably not the case in Buddha's early days, given the Indian style of challenging each other's views.[27] Gradually Buddha's pragmatic discourses bore the "truth claims," and by becoming tightly embedded in culturally dominated circumstances, people took them as the only understanding.[28] Therefore, Buddhism itself became increasingly a belief system, and Buddha's teachings on awakening became inaccessible to average people. Awakening became almost an exclusive privilege for the monastic resident and even that became rare. So, the far-flung idea of awakening became an object of worship rather than the everyday practice.[29]

Batchelor states that in the absence of any critical evaluation, karma and reincarnation have been converted into "beliefs." As reflected in the scriptures, Buddhism has itself turned into something almost unintelligible without these

---

[24] Griffiths, "Notes Towards a Critique of Buddhist Karmic Theory," 282–288.
[25] Ibid., 280, 290.
[26] Batchelor, *Buddhism Without Beliefs* and Batchelor, *After Buddhism*, 21. Batchelor's first book *Buddhism Without Beliefs* is absolutely common sense to those minds tuned to treating everyday life in a sensible and non-dogmatic, non-religious, and non-monastic framework. The follow up book, *After Buddhism* is a rather comprehensive approach to the worldliness of the Buddha and the Dharma by exploiting the primary and technical sources.
[27] Batchelor, *Buddhism Without Beliefs*, 15–16.
[28] Batchelor, *After Buddhism*, 1–3, 98–99, 118–119, 294.
[29] Batchelor, *Buddhism Without Beliefs*, 12–13.

concepts.³⁰ The 547 previous birth stories (*jātakas*) of the Buddha, sometimes as a human and others times as an animal, as recorded in the tripitakan scriptures (*Sutta Pitaka*), have to be viewed against the backdrop of belief in reincarnation. Needless to say, the belief in reincarnation infiltrated Buddhist doctrine, most probably a direct influence from the Brahmanical tradition, especially with the occurrence of animal allegories and imageries related to the previous births of the Buddha. But rationally thought, the Buddha must have been convinced that there could be no independent self that predates birth and survives death. Although the notion of reincarnation in the scriptures is introduced as part of a Buddhist belief system.

The ambitious claims in the Buddhist discourse on the origin of karma in the universe have no scientific or logical basis.³¹ In contrast, the Buddha's rebellion against the old-fashioned Vedic belief system of karma is clearly inherent in his message of taking charge of one's own destiny rather than subjecting oneself to fatalistic or ritualistic impositions. But the Buddha's words, Batchelor argues, have taken a permanent metaphysical turn in the canons, and this problem-solving philosophy instead became more like a truth-claiming Indian religion.³² Even using the term "Truth" in its literal interpretation stood for "ultimacy," "finality," and "solution forever," instead of using the term "Truth" to stand for "Real," which addresses the dynamic fluidity of Buddha's message about the non-fixed nature of things.³³

Furthermore, beliefs in heaven and hell also infiltrated Buddhism. As extreme as these absolutist religious views may have sounded to the Buddha, religiously-minded Buddhists later revived these images of reward and punishment. The most gruesome punishments in hell appear in the Chinese scriptures and later in a Sogdian text, "Sūtra of the Causes and Effects of Actions." In some of the sections of the Sūtra, the Buddha is the condemner of those who do not follow his Law (Dharma) or who do harm to the monks, including punishments that tongues be cut off or that such individuals be condemned to the hell of glaciers and so on.³⁴ The Buddhist *Naraka* is a

---

³⁰ Batchelor, *After Buddhism*, 16, 294.
³¹ Griffiths, "Notes Towards a Critique of Buddhist Karmic Theory," 281–282.
³² Batchelor, *After Buddhism*, chapter 5, especially, 117–19; see also Gethin, *The Foundations of Buddhism*, 168.
³³ Batchelor, *After Buddhism*, 118–119; see also Batchelor, *Buddhism Without Beliefs*, 4–5. See also Richard F. Gombrich, *How Buddhism Began: The Conditioned Genesis of the Early Teachings*, 2nd edn. (London and New York: Routledge, 2005), 4–5.
³⁴ D. N. Mackenzie (ed.), *The "Sūtra of the Causes and Effects of Actions" in Sogdian* (London: Oxford University Press, 1970), 3–33.

version of hell that it is divided into seven cold hells supplemented with a glacial one, and seven hot hells supplemented with a stinging blaze. The Tibetan purgatory is yet another intricate hell to pay for committed sins under the judgment of the priesthood.[35] Meanwhile, the Buddhist paradise is *Tushita*[36] where the divine buddhas reside, and where the last Buddha of time is currently residing, the Maitreya.

The Buddha cannot really be held responsible for inventing this religious afterlife and eschatological ideas. These elements were added on by later followers, revealing to us again the apparent need that many human minds have for religion and myth.

The Roots of Buddha-Worship

The human image of the Buddha did not begin to appear for several hundred years after his passing.[37] It seems to have started when Buddhism became more established among the people of Central and South Asia, and may very well have been due to religious competition caused by the Hellenistic introduction of Apollo-worship in the Seleucid era of the third-second centuries BCE in the same region. The theistic culture of the Indian subcontinent as a whole may also have influenced the future worship. The increasing prevalence of Buddha-worship may also be traced back to Asoka, the Mauryan king who around third century BCE declared Buddha's Dharma as state doctrine to be propagated in the neighboring territories. This was a crucial time when the Third Council was convened by the monks under Asoka to clarify and resolve the future of the Buddha's doctrine, and a *philosophy*

---

[35] Th. Schreve, "Ein Besuch im Buddhistischen Purgatorium: Aus dem Tibetischen erstmalig übersetzt." *Zeitschrift der Deutschen Morgenländischen Gesellschaft* 65 (1911): 471–486.

[36] *Tushita* is also considered by some practitioners to be a meditative state that can be accessed through the practice of mediation.

[37] The earlier emblem of the Buddhist communities was the "wheel of dharma," and or the Buddha's "footprint' (already borrowed from the Brahmanical tradition – the footprint of Viśnu). Or, potentially the Hindus borrowed the idea of footprint from the Buddhist tradition. The Buddha's image gradually appeared during the Kushan dynasty (first thru fourth centuries CE in present-day Afghanistan and its peripheries) and was developed in paintings, carvings, and statues, especially the sitting Buddha in meditation in the Gandhara school of art. See Vaziri, *Buddhism in Iran*, 68 (and 19). See also Simone Gaulier, Robert Jera-Bezard, and Monique Maillard, *Buddhism in Afghanistan and Central Asia* (Leiden: E. J. Brill, 1976), part I, introduction – Buddha-Bodhisattva, 5. See also Axel Michaels, *Buddha: Leben, Lehre, Legende* (München: C. H. Beck, 2011), 101, 102.

turned into a *religion*. Making the Buddha a quasi-divine figure and the construction of Buddhist metaphysical ideas evolved over the three centuries following his death.[38] Thus the problem of belief became more convoluted with deification of the Buddha and the worship of his image.

The worship of the Buddha may have arisen from a specific conceptual confusion: the doctrine of "*three bodies* of the Buddha, or *Trikāya*." Thinkers in the Mahayana school described the three "bodies" (*kāya*) or state of being of the Buddha comprising his physical person as well as his non-physical entity. The first body is the mind, which produces *joy* of being (*sambhoga-kāya*). The second body is the primordial state of existence, the state of suchness, and true consciousness – the *enlightened* state (*dharma-kāya*).[39] The third body is the *carnal* body of the Buddha, which manifested itself in the material world. This physical body of the Buddha (*nirmāna-kāya*) prepared to understand the state of now and joy. For worshippers, the three bodies of the Buddha could mean one and the same thing, a likeness that is noted in other forms of Buddha-worship, such as *Amitābha Buddha*, also known as Pure Land Buddhism.

Furthermore, the worship of the carnal body of the Buddha may have been erroneously associated with the concept of buddha-nature. The notion of *buddha-nature* represents the ultimate state of reality without the entanglement of change and time. Confusing the designation of *buddha-nature* with the Buddha implies that the ultimate reality or nature of everything contains a "buddha." The definition of buddha-nature is clearly described by the Mahayanists in the *Tathāgatagarbha Sūtra* using the term, *tathāgata-garbha*[40] (buddha womb, an embryonic state). The idea of *tathāgata-garbha* is that we all have the potential to become full-blown buddhas. The definition of *buddha-nature* is the same as *tathāgata-garbha*, or the embryonic understanding of the true nature of things beyond one's own mental tendencies, beyond being dependent on change and the passing of time. The embryonic mind is self-nature, the sun without clouds; it is the true mind and the buddha-nature, the nirvana without the cloudiness of false thoughts.[41] So, buddha-nature could easily have become entangled with the name of the historical Buddha – a confusion leading the masses to worship the Buddha as the mighty sun, moon, and god. These two designations of "buddha," one for a person and another for

---

[38] Batchelor, *After Buddhism*, 91–92.
[39] *Dharmakāya* concept also appears in the Theravada Pāli Canon.
[40] Gethin, *The Foundations of Buddhism*, 250–252.
[41] Dumoulin, "Early Chinese Zen Reexamined," 47–48.

a primordial awakened state, may have been another reason of confusion that led to his veneration as a 'divine' being.

From such divisions of the bodies of the Buddha, other metaphysical extrapolations were drawn. The scholastic adepts developed spiritual scenarios that enticed people to worship many Buddha-like deities such as bodhisattvas (the compassionate buddhas) such as Avalokiteśvara[42] or bodhisattvas who are yet to be born. By linking the three bodies of the Buddha (*Trikāya*) in an intricate fashion, all worthy of worship and offerings, laity continued its worship of the Buddha and other deities all under the guise of Dharma or Buddhism.

Buddha-worship also takes the form of having faith or commonly taking refuge in the three jewels: the Buddha (the enlightened historical Buddha), the Dharma (the teachings of the Buddha), and the Sangha (monastic community). Through taking refuge and having faith in these three jewels, ordained monks and nuns became more committed to adopt and practice the premise of their faith which is the belief in the three jewels. Similarly, the lay people by taking refuge in the three jewels would be declared Buddhist.[43]

This Buddha-worship is something that the Buddha probably never imagined, as he campaigned against taking refuge in anything other than the self and in one's own contemplative power. The paradox is that while the Buddha has been given supra-human titles such as "lord" and "god-like", and has been perceived as a "divine" entity, at the same time he has been presented as an ordinary man who never carried out miracles.[44] He was an ordinary man with a human side like everybody else. He failed to perform miracles, he failed to diffuse the crisis, and some people even turned against him.[45] He was not considered omniscient, and there is nothing about his life and teachings that points to the divine. According to *Majjhima Nikaya* "the Buddha denies possessing complete knowledge of everything at all times and defines the three-fold knowledge he does possess."[46]

---

[42] Avalokiteśvara, is a deity, a goddess of compassion, and a self-born bodhisattva whose appearance between the birth of the historical Buddha and the last Buddha (Maitreya) helps the sentient beings to attain enlightenment. See "Avalokiteshvara," www.britannica.com/topic/Avalokiteshvara, accessed Jan. 19, 2018.
[43] Gethin, *The Foundations of Buddhism*, 34, 167–168.
[44] Batchelor, *After Buddhism*, 173.
[45] Ibid., 152, 173, 174.
[46] *Majjhima Nikaya:* Tevijjavacchagotta Sutta (MN 71).

Helmut von Glasenapp in his *Buddhism – A Non-Theistic Religion* soundly lays out the evolution of Buddhism from a non-theistic tradition to becoming a religion with a number of gods. In the evolution of Buddhism, the status of the Buddha was gradually elevated from being a man to superman and then to the rank of god, which opened Buddhism to contradiction and criticism.[47]

In addition, by leaving many back doors open, Buddhism permitted a large number of native gods to enter its system. The Buddhist scriptures and popular culture developed parables including a pantheon of various gods and non-human beings, and even Brahma as the creator of the world.[48] These and similar Indian theistic beliefs should be suspected as having been put into the "mouth" of the Buddha, a sort of strategy of predating one's own dogma by inserting it in the "unalterable" scriptures. The non-theistic Buddhist message and theistic scripture along with popular culture contradict each other anyway. The idea of worshipping the Buddha is itself an oxymoron that has infiltrated what was originally a non-theistic empirical and pragmatic philosophy. Essential Buddhist principles such as dependent arising or the law of cause and effect makes it impossible to fit in an idea of god as the single cause for everything, especially if this god is the Buddha himself.

The Buddha's Stance Against Faith and Scriptures

It is in the *Kālāma Sutta* (*Kālāma Sūtra*) that the Buddha clearly rejects faith alone, and counsels against accepting scriptures, traditions, or even logic and reasoning merely out of respect for holy people and monks.[49] The Buddha advises the people of Kālāma: "Do not go upon what has been acquired by repeated hearing; nor upon tradition; nor upon rumor; nor upon what is in a scripture; nor upon surmise; nor upon an axiom; nor upon specious reasoning." He warns not to fall prey to "a bias towards a notion that has been pondered over; nor upon another's seeming ability; nor upon the

---

[47] Helmut von Glasenapp, *Buddhism – a Non-Theistic Religion*. With a Selection from the Buddhist Scriptures, edited by Heinz Bechert, translated by Irmgard Schloegl (New York: George Braziller 1966). Glasenapp alludes to the fact that the Buddha and later Buddhists may have believed in the existence of all kinds of impermanent gods. But these gods were incapable of bringing liberation and ending human suffering, see pages 30-31.

[48] *The Long Discourses of the Buddha*: A Translation of the *Dīgha Nikāya*, translated from the Pali by Maurice Walshe, (Boston: Wisdom Publications, 2012), introduction, 43-5.

[49] Gethin, *The Foundations of Buddhism*, 167

consideration."[50] In the same sūtra, the Buddha rejects the supernatural world as well as the belief in *karma*, by reiterating the power of here and now – being free from worry, intimidation, and grievance by living happily.[51] The powerful message of this sūtra promotes straight and free thinking for oneself, as well as gaining knowledge from the way things are in the reality around us. This is to avoid fanaticism and dogmatism by carefully examining and understanding all stages of the path to clarity.[52] The *Kālāma Sutta* is a short teaching yet a foundational teaching for self-rule.

The Buddha delineated a pragmatic, rational, utilitarian, non-absolutist, and skeptical philosophy. Even more exceptional than other nāstika members, the Buddha remained pragmatic by keeping matters of the mind in fluid states instead of framing them into fixed conceptions. The seductive illusion of reason being the source of salvation that leads to the true reality did not fool the Buddha, because in fact, the clever mind can reason things out in a way that serves its own gain: "Well-reasoned" does not always mean "right." Hence, the Buddha doubted that through logic everything could be accurately reasoned out, proposing that something could be: 1. well-reasoned and true (correct), 2. well-reasoned and false (incorrect), 3. ill-reasoned and true, and 4. ill-reasoned and false.[53]

Besides such conditions of reasoning, the Buddha also suggested conditions of verity, formulating that something can be: 1. true and useful, 2. false and useful, 3. true and useless, and 4. false and useless.[54] By this formulation, the Buddha wished to break away from moralistic absolutism and dogmatism, and do away with religious conventionalism. The Buddha espoused a well-reasoned, true, and useful scenario, while keeping things fluid based on circumstantial and arising causes and conditions. In the practical philosophy of the Buddha, universalistic and relativistic attitudes have had far greater value than the narrow and culturally religiously view of "right-wrong" or "true-false" dualism. Even a non-monastic and non-ritualistic way to enlightenment was preferred rather than fulfilling the cumbersome process of memorization or interpretation of the scriptures. This pragmatic attitude was at least prevalent among certain Zen adepts as well as the Buddha himself.

---

[50] *Kālāma Sutta: The Buddha's Charter of Free Inquiry*, translated from the Pali by Soma Thera (Kandy, Sri Lanka: Kandy Buddhist Publication Society, 1981; Online edition, 2008), "The Criterion for Rejection", 5, 6.
[51] Batchelor, *Buddhism Without Beliefs*, 34, 121. *Kālāma Sutta*, 7.
[52] *Kālāma Sutta*, introduction.
[53] McEvilley, *The Shape of Ancient Thought*, 339.
[54] Ibid., 339.

Buddha's Self-Rule Philosophy

The famous Zen saying is strongly indicative of this pragmatic objective: "Even false words are true if they lead to enlightenment; even true words are false if they breed attachment."

Against the background of the Buddha's rebellion in the theistic Brahmanical culture, as well as the backdrop of what has been described as anomalies of the dogmatic Buddhist practices, let us turn the discussion toward the *philosophy of self-rule* whose premise originates in Dharma or nirvana, as presented by the Buddha.

***

Dharma and Nirvana Defined

The Buddha wished to provide a psychological guide to help those tormented by their own minds or by others. His awareness of the human psychological reality is reflected in *Kandaraka Sutta*: The Buddha spoke of four general categories of people – one who torments himself, one who torments others, one who torments both himself and others, and finally one who torments neither and lives a truly righteous life.[55] A sense of incompleteness and dissatisfaction, consciously or subconsciously, troubles the mind in its deepest sense. Even when there is no outward sign of *dukkha* (dissatisfaction, sorrow, or pain), the compulsive mental inclinations can produce a lifelong and disquieting flickering flame.[56] In this way, the Buddha psychologized philosophy, or philosophized human psychology.

The Buddha's teachings in general took the designation of "Dharma." (The label "Buddhism" in Western sources is a concocted term, which we shall use only for convenience.) The verb *dhr* in Sanskrit means to "uphold" and *dharma* thus means "that which upholds" or "that which is upheld." Dharma in this context means upholding the order of the mind in relation to the dynamic laws of cause and effect. Dharma's content is therefore a toolkit, not a "truth," nor a belief system, nor something holy.[57] The mind is assigned to observe the constant change both in oneself and in the outer reality, a kind of awareness of measuring oneself against the fleeting forces of life. Dharma means living a fluid and dynamic life with rigorous psychological checks and

---

[55] *Majjhima Nikaya*: Kandaraka Sutta (MN 51).
[56] The allegory of the "flame" or "fire" of sensual passion stems from the Buddha's third sermon several months after his enlightenment.
[57] Batchelor, *After Buddhism*, 118–119, 206–207, 258–259; see also by the same author, *Buddhism Without Beliefs*, 6–7.

balances. In this chapter, our focus is on the end goal of Dharma, namely nirvana as self-liberation.

In general, nirvana can be defined as a quiet state of mind that is not contaminated with time, culture, religion, or linguistic conceptions – a sort of primordial state of being beyond anthropocentrism. The liberated, thirty-five-year-old Buddha experienced nirvana, and then conceptualized, taught, and lived it until the age of eighty. The Buddha's nirvana is "no imaginary place"[58] of happiness, nor is it a faith-based practice. Nirvana is a training of the mind in order to deal with life events with an unsullied attitude, an understanding of what lies outside time and all the births and deaths. At the same time, it is an observant understanding of physical reality, which is always in a constant state of flux. The coupling of the changing and unchanging reality in the mind is a realization of complete reality. The untrained mind not only fails to notice this fine understanding but is also prone to be confused and pained as a result.

The Buddha concretized his new philosophy in his initial three interrelated sermons. All three dealt with a deeper understanding of the insidious pain produced by one's own mind, and path of the release from it. The first sermon was "Setting in Motion the Wheel of Dharma," focusing on the roots of the pain of life and how to uproot it – the "Four Noble Truths".

The Buddha introduced his eightfold path (the fourth of the Four Noble Truths) in order to make one's life more purposeful after attaining liberation. The eight guidelines were meant as a life-long vocation in order to avoid extremes in thought and action, so that suffering and meaninglessness would end. Another aim of practicing the eightfold path was for practitioners to become useful and help others. The eightfold path is summarized in these terms: 1. right understanding, 2. right intention, 3. right speech, 4. right action, 5. right livelihood, 6. right attitude, 7. right awareness, and 8. right focus. In the language of the eightfold path, the use of the term "right" (*samyak*), or "noble" (*ārya*) is not intended as a moralistic and absolutist approach, but has a prudent and useful application. It has a broad-ranging application of being kind, beneficial to oneself and all sentient beings, compassionate, thoughtful, and pragmatic as well, taking the middle position between the extremes. It means seeing emptiness in all things, using the empirical reasoning method and wisdom, having a precision of mind.

The second sermon was on the conception of "Non-Self," an ever-changing self and reality without any concrete base. The third sermon was "Fire," which

---

[58] See Steven Collins, *Nirvana: Concept, Imagery, Narrative* (Cambridge: Cambridge University Press, 2010), 8, introduction.

emphasized the dangers of the flame of desire. In connection with these three sermons, the Buddha explored the three poisons of the mind (craving, aversion, and ignorance) and three components of reality (impermanence, non-self, and pain). In explicating nirvana, he began by focusing on the three poisons developed in the first three Noble Truths. Let us briefly put these ideas into perspective.

Dealing with the Three Poisons – A Foothold Toward Nirvana

Conventionally, the three poisons are known as greed, hatred, and ignorance. These poisons arise from insidious emotions and overpowering mental tendencies. Together they produce a sense of continually wanting and clinging (*rāga*), liking and disliking (*dveśa*), and an unclear view about reality (ignorance *avidyā*, delusion *moha*).

The insidious and obstructive character of these three poisons in one's mind is the reason that the Buddha formulated his 'four cognitive tools' (known as Four Noble Truths): 1. the recognition of *dukkha*, or dissatisfaction, 2. the causes of *dukkha* (which are the three poisons), 3. the possibility of nirvana (extinguishing the flame of *dukkha* and the three poisons), and 4. the path of a quiet life until death (the eightfold path leading to such a life). The first three of the Four Noble Truths are more urgent and *vital* to attend to, whereas the fourth is a *gradual* process of following a path.

Addressing the poisons was the Buddha's starting point. In one of the Buddha's powerful analogies, the three poisons of the mind block the untainted nature of the mind like clouds blocking the sun. True clarity of the mind without cloudiness is analogized as the original or "embryonic" (*garbha*) mind which once was and then "returned again" (*tathāgata* – thus gone-thus come) – meaning the return of the embryonic mind (*tathāgatagarbha*) to enlightenment and the Buddhahood. The mind that can return and be cleansed of the three poisons is a nirvanic mind.

The words of the Buddha about the three poisons are thus reflected in the *Tathāgatagarbha Sūtra*: "All beings, though they find themselves with all sorts of *kleśas* [poisons], have *tathāgatagarbha* that is eternally unsullied, and that is replete with virtues no different from my own."[59] These words point to the universal tendencies and the true nature of the mind regardless of its personal variations. The other important message is that everyone, literally everyone, just as the Buddha himself did, can eliminate the cloudiness of life, the *kleśas*, and

---

[59] Gethin, *The Foundations of Buddhism*, 251–252.

reveal the clear, ever-present reality of the mind. Everyone has a *tathāgatagarbha* and has the capacity to become a *Tathāgata* – the Buddha, awakened and liberated. (*Tathāgata* became an honorific title for the Buddha.)

Clarification of Nirvana and Pari-nirvana

In the eyes of the Buddha, the complexity of the mind is unknown to oneself and thus is inadvertently self-harming. He explicated that the mind is the powerhouse of all actions and all understandings, the source of pleasure and misery. The universal anomaly of the mind is that it is the source of blistering confusion, having no frame of reference or anchor in anything reliable and lasting. The more specific anomalies of the mind are its rampant obsessive cravings, which were determined by the Buddha to be the prime source of emotional disarray and catastrophic consequences in one's life. In addition, the mind, apart from its own intrinsic compulsions, is also conditioned by the formation of cultural and religious belief systems and idiosyncratic tendencies. The myth-making mind throughout the ages sublimated myths as beliefs and fervently labeled them as "truths."

So, for the Buddha, it became an issue of how one could *think*, not what one would *do* or *believe* to lessen or ease the existential torment. The Dharmic method of thinking and seeing the world offered a pragmatic philosophy of life and freedom in order to live rationally and happily without being bound to dogmatic ritualism. The Buddha's intention was to confront the mental confoundedness at the root of human depression and unhappiness, seeking the cessation of suffering by eliminating the three poisons of greed, anger, and delusion from one's life.

The Buddha labeled this liberation of the mind *nivvana* in his native dialect or Prakrit, or in its Sanskritized usage, *nirvana*. This term, as coined by the Buddha, is comprised of two parts: *ni* (out) and *vana* (blowing) – "blowing out" – together meaning "extinguishing the flame of the mind." But perhaps Richard Gombrich's proposal of the phrase "going out" is a more suitable formulation for addressing the three poisons, rather than an *active agent* extinguishing them.[60] This proposed definition is not just semantics but rather serves a deeper purpose. As we shall see later in the discourse of non-self, the five aggregates of a living self are constantly in a state of flux. This means there is no fixed "self" at any given time. Since the changing self cannot be a consistent agent to extinguish the flame, a more fitting definition for nirvana could be the notion of the flame of desires "going out" by itself

---

[60] Gombrich, *How Buddhism Began*, xv.

through the medium of awareness. Therefore, by the flame going out, no trace of pain, thought, or anxiety is left behind. The Buddha's nirvana is similar to the conception of the Ājīvikas that nothing is stored or can be stored, comparable to an extinguished fire.[61]

By coining nivvana or nirvana 'to extinguish the flame,' the Buddha focused on the psychological and philosophical healing of a troubled mind. The essence of the Buddha's solution was to develop a deeper understanding of oneself and extinguishing the never-ending mental "flame," a flame that sometimes brings a pleasurable warmth, and at other times, a burning fiasco. Both outcomes, good and bad, were viewed as harmful by the Buddha. The Buddha viewed the constant "bombardment" of the mind by feelings, ideas, temptations, sadness, happiness, craving, and choices as both a universal and yet personal incoherency of the mind. Thus, his solution – a relatively uncomplicated mental awareness to extinguish the grip of existential as well as self-inflicted disquiet – was a breakthrough toward lasting liberation.

A rather deeper experience of nirvana is through the reflection and assimilation of *non-self* and *emptiness*. As we will see later, non-self and emptiness are two interrelated experiences that become the strong foundation for attaining the nirvanic awareness. Furthermore, nirvana is said to transcend the dilemma of *samsara*, overcoming the riddle of *birth* and the pain of *death*. It is to transform dukkha (pain) into sukkha (the joy of existence). Nirvana also stands for accessing the pure mind. It is to overcome the karmic laws. Nirvana is an empty state without being bound to the laws of cause and effect. The awareness of nirvana signifies a valid perception of the phenomenal reality. Another aspect of nirvana involves recognizing perceptual reality and the law of interdependence, also called dependent arising. It is to perceive the state of suchness, is-ness, and recurring and never-ending nowness. In the experience of nirvana, impermanence is realized as the condition of existence. Furthermore, nirvana is to have a universal mind, to see others as self and, by virtue of compassion, help them to be liberated from painful conditions of life. Finally, when nirvana can no longer be articulated in conceptual language, it is an unconditioned state of the mind, which is perceived in the utter silence of the mind. The last stage of nirvana is the dissolution of body and mind at death, a permanent disappearance from the face of existence, also referred to as pari-nirvana – a state in which all the systems of cause and effect come to a complete halt and emptiness takes over.

---

[61] Kalupahana, "Consciousness," *Buddhist Psychology, Encyclopedia of Buddhism Extract,* 76–77.

Thus, nirvana is a multilayered, spatial and organic state of looking at life. It is a state when the mind and body live in a linear time and the supra-mind, free of the dominance of conditioned language, comprehends things beyond their spatio-temporal state. This mind fully realizes the experience of impermanence. In reality, nirvana is an impermanent experience of permanent emptiness. This experience happens when the body and mind are the fueling agents for the attainment of nirvana; however, the final nirvana at death (parinirvana) is without any substrate of life or fuel of body or mind. These elements are no longer subject to birth or death or temptation.

Nirvana is to make sense of our transient biological life, and parinirvana is a grasp of our permanent extinction. Parinirvana is a subject that is often overlooked in the Buddhist discourses.[62] Since death is the final station in samsara and all the causes and conditions for another birth of the same person are extinguished, it contradicts the traditional concept of reincarnation or a personal rebirth. Nirvana is a real experience but death puts an end to the body and to the experience of nirvana altogether. The Buddha spoke of his own experience of nirvana and saw death as the final station without rebirth: "Knowledge and insight arose in me; unshakable is my freedom. This is my last birth; now there will be no future becoming."[63] The traditional Buddhist perspective may argue the Buddha had reached enlightenment and no longer "needed" rebirth. But what can be argued is that any person (not only the Buddha) liberated from a deluded and belief-based mind, can die in peace without the anxiety of being born again.

The *Maha-Parinirvana Sūtra* in various Buddhist scriptures discusses the final days of the Buddha and his *Maha* or eternal[64] passing away. In the story of the Buddha's death, the disciples of the Buddha were sobbing and begging him not to enter parinirvana, not to die. The Buddha requested the crowed not to cry. He added; "this body is like a mirage in the hot season, ... a prisoner facing death, ripe fruit, a piece of meat, ... which is about to end. You should think that all created things are like poisonous food and that anything made is possessed of all worries."[65] By this, the Buddha quite clearly rejected

---

[62] Steven Collins, *Selfless Persons: Imagery and Thought in Theravāda Buddhism* (1982; Cambridge: Cambridge University Press, 1999), 83 (the reprint).
[63] David Kalupahana, *Ethics in Early Buddhism* (Delhi: Motilal Banarsidass, 2008), 28.
[64] *Maha-parinirvana:* "Maha" even though in Sanskrit means "great", in this case means "eternal," see *The Mahayana Mahaparinirvana Sutra*, Translated into English by Kosho Yamamoto. Edited, revised and copyright by Dr. Tony Page (Nirvana Publications, London, 1999-2000), Source: http://www.nirvanasutra.org.uk. 40.
[65] Ibid., 20-21.

a continuing self or rebirth – the frivolity of any belief about after death. Moreover, the notion of rebirth or more specifically reincarnation stands in contradiction to the notion of non-self (and emptiness).[66] The idea of reincarnation even seems absurd and void when all the dialectical modules of emptiness are taken into consideration. Given the importance of pari-nirvana and the irreversible fact of death, the beliefs in reincarnation and past-life karma are simply a cultural residue in traditional Buddhist cultures.

Parinirvana, does not have the same connotation of nirvana, "enlightenment"; it rather points to a complete emancipation from the worldly confusion and suffering – the eternal demise of the body and mind. Consequently, it should not be misunderstood: there are *not* two nirvanas. The notion of pari-nirvana is a technical term for biological and cognitive death without return – back to the "pure land" with none of the fluctuations of a living organism. Pari-nirvana puts everything ablaze, all the quandaries of life, its successes and failures; it is even the end of nirvana itself.

The Shape of a New Model: Nirvana and Ten Mini-nirvanas

Throughout texts on Buddhism, the descriptions of nirvana are so ubiquitous and varied that it demands to be brought into focus. Such descriptions have ranged from practical to abstract, from philosophical to poetical, from sentimental to idyllic. Due to the density of philosophical material, there has been difficulty in fusing together all the specific 'branches' of nirvana. But in exploring different definitions of nirvana, the commonalities among them become more and more evident. As a whole, nirvana can be viewed in the light of its conceptual, experiential and imagery.[67] Perhaps it is then possible to integrate and fuse together the crux of the scattered themes of nirvana in the context of self-liberation into one single interrelated and accessible model. In general, nirvana is not something to have or to gain, but rather it is a process of clearing oneself from unnecessary mental loads. This can happen through a series of awakenings as one proceeds through life.

From the Buddhist point of view, *samsara* refers to "birth and death" (in Sanskrit "same flow" – 'same serum') or coming to and going from the world. It is referring to the confusion and universality of our personal circumstances, with birth and death being the first source of confusion. At the same time, samsara itself is a life process for awakening. Along the way, the confusion and blunders of life often requires the intervention of the "wise self" in the

---

[66] *The Long Discourses of the Buddha: A Translation of the Dīgha Nikāya*, 36-7.
[67] Borrowing the words of Collins, *Nirvana: Concept, Imagery, Narrative*, chapters 2 and 3.

Buddhist sense. Such intervention can turn confusion into clarity and an experience of joyful and free living. As self-interventions continue to occur, they forge a path of liberation, with each intervention offering a new stage of awakening that can be called a 'mini-nirvana.' The peak results of these discrete "cognitive interventions" counter the effects of samsara as they unfold dynamically in real-life circumstances. The fruits of these minor-awakenings or "mini-nirvanas" are joy, clarity, and quietude of mind. As clarity assumes prominence, samsara or life circumstances continues in the background and nirvana itself develops. The mini-nirvanas can be seen as residing within an archetypal model of everyday life, with our personal mini-corrections as we move along. In a realistic perspective, the mini-nirvanas add up to become an all-encompassing awareness of the roots of our flaws and quandaries in various areas of the mind and life circumstances, leading to clarity and understanding.

Birth____*samsara*____..........____*samsara*____Death, final exit (*parinirvana*)

    mini-nirvanas   greater *nirvana* in the background

Thus, the model of ten mini-nirvanas presented here is an alternative narrative that repacks the essentials of Buddhist philosophy by leaving out the religious and metaphysical aspects, such as deities, reincarnation, and taking refuge in the Buddha, the Sangha and the Dharma. Instead, it is about nirvana as a model of self-liberation seen in a non-dogmatic way without a religious or cultural baggage.

The ten categories are analogous to the functions of the vital organs of the human body. The body's organs, even with their distinct and dissimilar functions, are the foundation of a single physiology. When the vital organs maintain high performance, a more holistic and enhanced function in the body is ensured. In the same way, the purpose of the model is to demonstrate that when the essential aspects of nirvana maintain high performance in the course of life, a more holistic, vigorous and liberated mind is ensured.

Another visual analogy of the model is to imagine the mind as a three-dimensional box on an axis. The box can rotate 180°. One side of the box reveals a turbid, cloudy side; the other side is clear and vibrant. Inside this large box of the mind are smaller boxes, each of which also stands on an axis of rotation, again able to show a cloudy side or a clear side. These rotating smaller boxes represent "mini-nirvanas." All of the mini-boxes begin with their cloudy side showing. But with each new inner realization, a box turns in the direction of its clearer face. The rotation of several such boxes, signifying the attainment of a number of mini-nirvanas, can have an effect on the entire frame of the mind until eventually, the large box of the whole mind would fully "rotate" into complete nirvanic clarity. Thus, the smaller and yet necessary understandings and stages of growth lead to attaining a deeper, more holistic understanding of oneself and the world.

In each of the mini-nirvana categories, there is a pair of opposites. On one hand, is the undesirable state, and on the other is the ultimate goal, and the mini-nirvana realization means shifting from one level of thinking to another – from unclarity to clarity. For example, such opposites could include shifting from "wanting to not wanting," from "selfhood to non-self," from "linguistic articulation to beyond language," etc. In the true essence of the Buddha's teachings, each stage should be experienced as an "unloading" the obsessive habits of mind to end a misunderstanding, not necessarily to accumulate a pile of new knowledge.[68] In other words, the experience of each mini-nirvana is to unload the old habits of thinking and judging rather than necessarily to reload new habits and new judgments. The continuity of the functioning person is never stopped, only the perspectives are enlightened.

For our purposes, in putting together a more holistic model of nirvana, we shall split nirvana into what can be characterized as "vital nirvana" and "gradual nirvana." We will use "vital nirvana" to refer to an awakening that can go into effect immediately upon the realization of all the sources of dissatisfaction (dukkha) as well as the three poisons in order to bring tranquility to one's life. To do this, it is necessary to assimilate the nature of "change-impermanency" in all mental and emotional transactions. Impermanency is the pillar of change in biological life; nothing stays the same, which then translates into nihility, final death, emptiness and beyond...

We shall use the term "gradual nirvana" to refer to a series of dynamics at work in cognitive, physical, and phenomenal reality. These dynamics need time to be experienced and integrated into daily life and the practitioner's awareness. They are part of actualizing the greater project of knowing the impermanent self and liberating oneself from all the misconceptions about reality. These dynamics range from an understanding of the concept of dependent arising (laws of causality or interdependency, *pratītyasamutpāda*), to perceiving the state of suchness (*dharmakāya*) of everything. Gradual nirvana encompasses a gradual understanding of the use and misuse of linguistic articulation, the logical knowledge of things (*pramāna*), the emptiness (*śūnyatā*) of things or the Middle Way (*mādhyamaka*). This gradual

---

[68] Ajahn Jayasaro, *Stillness Flowing: The Life and Teachings of Ajahn Chah* (Malaysia: Panyaprateep Foundation, 2017), 164.

process also entails the realization of non-self (*an-ātman*), and no-mind or embryonic mind (*tathāgata-garbha*). Gradual nirvana results in the development of a compassionate mind (*karunā*), seeing others as oneself.

It can be understood that vital nirvana is an experiential means of bringing the mind to its natural quietness, and gradual nirvana means making the mind insightful. This division of nirvana may be analogous to the two techniques of meditation, *śamathā* and *vipassanā*; calming and insightful meditations.

The connection between vital and gradual nirvana becomes apparent in the organic process of interacting with life conditions. The task before us here is to present a model in categories that are distinct and yet related to each other – a model that can be succinct and accessible, and integrates the themes that lead to broader nirvana. Through this integration, we can explore how stages of growth occur as 'mini-nirvanas' lead to greater growth overall.

Although we will be exploring ten essential mini-nirvana, the intention is neither to frame the themes into fixed and distinct discourses nor to limit them to ten. The purpose is to make the multilevel philosophy of nirvana more accessible in a single integrated flexible narrative. This model could actually be adapted, and enlarged, if other critical themes for mini-nirvanas are identified. The idea behind so much knowledge and scriptures, after all, is to remove personal dukkha and maintain clarity of mind.

Vital Mini-Nirvanas

1. Wanting → Not Wanting
2. Like/Dislike → Nonjudgment
3. Ignorance → Clarity
4. Dukkha → Liberation
5. Selfhood → Non-self
6. Realness → Emptiness
7. Rectilinear Time → Constancy of Nowness

Gradual Mini-Nirvanas

8. Self-interest → Compassion
9. Illogic → Proof
10. Language → Non-articulation

The Ten Mini-Nirvanas

1. From Wanting To Not Wanting

Grabbing, self-centeredness, or egocentric habits are common instincts that are born within us.[69] This innate tendency may go wild and become poisonous, or alternatively can be tamed. Unyielding and egocentric greed (the voice of "I want") systematically and insidiously manifests itself in different circumstances throughout the course of life. This poison in the Buddhist lexicon is known as greed (*rāga*), attachment (*upādāna*), and thirst or craving (*tṛṣṇā*). The "I want" phenomenon comes in imaginative and virtual cravings; sometimes they are possible to fulfill and other times remain in the realm of envy.

It is not always greed of the material world. Sometimes the ego dictates obtaining non-material things, such as fame, higher status, excelling at being better than others in ideas. Certain greed is also in play even in attaining knowledge and spiritual pursuits. The undesirable consequences of this poison arise not necessarily in "having" but rather through the enormity of constantly "wanting." The obsessive intention behind actions is where the harm arises.

Another detrimental tendency is "holding on" to the desires of the mind in the form of attachment, which leads to piling up mountains of material and non-material property. The emotional burden of these craving-attachment scenarios and their inevitable loss is quite heavy.

The challenge to subduing this poisonous instinct lies in the struggle against one's own capricious moods and the demands of society and culture. This psychological challenge has brought humans to the modern age with a seemingly incessant, insatiable desire for new things, and the accumulation of wealth without actual need. The realities of food, shelter, and security are needs, not desires per se. Attending to these needs are in fact necessities. However, greed, hoarding, and attachment, from the point of view of the Buddha's formulation of the first poison, can become so deeply entrenched that they create a negative and relentless cycle. As long as the eye sees the world through the window of an untamed mind, it wants. But one who does not look for something is free.[70]

The origin of greed and attachment is deep in the subconscious. Even the fact that the self is attached to itself is the work of a powerful ego and

---

[69] The self is born with three biological dispositions – greed, aggression, and sexual instinct – whose wild borders need to be tailored in the course of collective social cultivation.

[70] Kalupahana, *A History of Buddhist Philosophy*, 44–45.

materialism. It cannot extricate itself from itself. Freedom from the self, in a Buddhist sense, makes the self a "project" for oneself.[71] The challenge in this project arises when trying to distinguish the field of one's mind from all the cravings from the outer reality. If the inner and outer realities cannot be distinguished from each other and brought into some sort of harmony, then the opposition between a mentalistic idealism of within and realism of without takes the self in the direction of constant contradiction.[72] Self-love and attachment to oneself gradually become well-hidden in the background, yet they remain the driving force in one's life. Their negation is usually assessed against what utility selflessness may bring. Even a replacement of selfishness by selflessness can easily fail to be authentic enough and be suspected of being spiritual materialism, or piety in exchange for something else. One way or another, the attachment to self remains a reality until death.

However, the Buddha introduced the radical notion of non-self and impermanency, *not* as the negation of self but to emphasize the short-lived nature of cravings and the lack of ownership of even the self. All things in the world face demise and end in ultimate nothingness. The "philosophy" of non-self serves as a cognitive and rational tool to work out and reduce the impulsive tendency of holding on – to ego, objects, memories, opinions, family members, friends, pleasurable sensual experiences, emotionality or feelings, beliefs, and even ephemeral life itself. Nothing lasts and nothing has an inherent self; enough reason to treat matters of reality with shrewd common sense and not with emotionality or compulsiveness.

Attachment is an enormously powerful aspect of the poison of greed and wanting. The deft diagnosis of the Buddha targeted an even deeper anomaly: attachment to good things, such as his teachings (Dharma). The Buddhist texts refer to four kinds of attachments: attachment to sense-objects, to views, to precepts and vows, and to the doctrine of the self.[73] According to the teachings of the Buddha, all tools including the cultivation of virtues and morality, the practice of meditation, and even the Dharma can be compared with a vehicle (*yanā*) or raft. Once one reaches the opposite shore, the raft is no longer needed and should not be carried on the shoulder all the time. In other words, "ultimately, as the simile of the raft indicates, attachment to even the teaching and practices of Buddhism must be relinquished."[74] Thus,

---

[71] Keiji Nishitani, *Religion and Nothingness*, trans. Jan van Bragt (Berkeley: University of California Press, 1983), 11, 14, 25, 31, 33.
[72] Ibid., 17–18, 85.
[73] Gethin, *The Foundations of Buddhism*, 71.
[74] Ibid., 72, 80; see also introduction of, *Rational Zen*, 14.

any attachment to Dharma itself would be a contradiction and a lapse of judgment in dealing with this fundamental poison.

The anomaly of attachment has even led some Buddhist adherents into a blind spot. The Zen observation of the tendency to cling to Dharma illuminates the problem as an incongruity of the mind. In a Zen metaphor, the propensity of the mind is to run away from one "thorn" and resort to another as a proxy solution. The Zen allegory of the "first thorn" is clinging to absurdities of the world – excessive possession and other types of mental desires. Then the "second thorn" is supposed to be the solution, in this case, the teachings of the Buddha. The Zen allegory advises practitioners against using one "thorn" to remove another "thorn." The sound solution is to pull out the first thorn at once. Mishandling and dogmatically *clinging* to Dharma, even as useful as it might be up to a point, becomes "another thorn," a source of mental capture. This aphorism is a depiction of the undomesticated nature of the mind being captured by one thing or another, even Dharma.

The philosophy of liberation in the Buddhist context does not entail a complete dropping out of material existence and ignoring the reality of life in any given generation or culture. Liberation means instead to seriously address the compulsions of the mind, especially when it fails to fully realize the fleeting reality of life, of self, and the final annihilation of ego and all its objects. In the process of attaining an equanimous mind, connection with the world may not be lost but clinging to it certainly proves to be problematic. To appease the "I Want" urge with its inclination toward attachment is in one's own interest in order to reduce the conditioning and suffering of the mind. Thus, practical enlightenment or the lasting pleasure of the mind requires breaking away from the compulsion to cling. This undisturbed state of living also includes not being fixated on Buddhist doctrine.

In order to gradually turn 'wanting' into 'not-wanting,' there is another popular method for the identification and treatment of mental thirst, disquiet, and competitiveness. This Tibetan method towards liberation is called *Lamrim* (stages of the path) and developed out of the teachings of the eleventh-century Indian Buddhist scholar Atīśa. From Atīśa's point of view, the four dilemmas of *birth, illness, old age,* and *death* (similar to the Buddha) continue to produce bewilderment and fear, which demand radical illumination and fearlessness to overcome. However, Atīśa also identified suffering on four other fronts that equally require a complete awareness and intervention through the practice of *Lamrim*. According to this approach, the suffering of the mind stems from: 1. clinging to the pleasant and undesirably encountering what is unpleasant, 2. attaching to gratifying states and running away from dull and unkind circumstances, 3. running after desires and being disappointed for not acquiring what is desired, 4. seeking conditions to please the five senses without which one would feel discontent and resentful.[75] Obliviousness of these psychological immaturities may cause treacherous suffering, often quite insidiously.

An attitude of non-attachment can bring with it an altruistic wisdom of giving and not taking what belongs to others. This attitude of transformation (*parināmanā*) changes the course of events and breaks the vicious circle of one's destiny.[76] This is the separation point from suffering. For the equanimous mind, the stream of life represents the flow of a river. Like a river, a flowing life lets things come and go as they do. This may be coupled with keeping the nature of impermanency in mind. The constant urge of the mind's "I Want" tendency at some point loses its potency and meaning. Being unflustered by wanting could become the first advanced step in realizing the project of non-self and impermanency – the first mini-nirvana.

If one can succeed in uprooting the clumsiness of greed then a thoughtful, non-greedy personality may naturally be cultivated. In this way, one has already extinguished one of the treacherous mental flames of the poison of greed, achieved a mini-nirvana, and moved a giant step closer to a broader nirvana.

2. From Like/Dislike To Nonjudgment

Aversion (*dveśa*) is another mental poison. This impulse can take on a myriad of forms, including dislike, anger, antipathy, hatred, mental disquiet, belligerence, and violence through the three channels of body, thought, and speech. All of these cause harm to oneself and others and can cause ruinous events in life circumstances.

The mind throughout life continuously oscillates between "like" and "dislike," between being "pleased" and "displeased." The untrained and uncultivated mind experiences this flickering flame of duality in all emotive transactions. All dualistic emotions are the trajectory of the dualistic mind, which according to the Buddha, intrinsically produce opposites. However, it is clear that the Buddha was not interested in clinging to what is "liked" while

---

[75] Tsong-kha-pa, *The Great Treatise on the Stages of the Path to Enlightenment*, Vol. 1, trans. The Lamrim Chenmo Translation Committee (Ithaca, New York: Snow Lion Publications, 2000), 265–279.

[76] See *Mādhyamika and Yogācāra: A Study of Mahāyāna Philosophies*, Collected Papers of G. M. Nagao, edited, collated, and translated by L. S. Kawamura in collaboration with G. M. Nagao (Albany: State University of New York Press, 1991), chapter 8, 83–91. See also Suzuki, *The Awakening of Zen*, 9–10. The notion of *Parināmanā* is important in Pure Land, Mahayana Buddhism.

Buddha's Self-Rule Philosophy

opposing what is "disliked." Instead, as the Buddha put it, "What is good has to be abandoned, as does what is evil."[77] And so the Buddha's approach to this judgmental propensity of the mind was less moral and more cognitive.

To pacify the volatile mind through inspection is a step forward. A more rational adjustment means turning the mind away from its dualistic tendencies. To appease aversion through contemplative insights, the pure mind must emanate a levelheaded attitude. It is vital to understand that the "like and dislike" inclination emanates from one's mind; it does not exist in outer reality. For example, liking spring and disliking winter is not a recognizable matter to nature. Liking the birth of a child and disliking the death of a loved one or calling birth "good" and death "bad" is a sentimental duality not tenable in organic life.

The entanglement of like and dislike can manifest in innumerable ways. For example, the Buddha refused to become distraught in response to criticism, or to rejoice in being complimented, as stated in *Dhammapada*: "As a solid rock is not shaken by the wind, so the wise are not shaken by censure or praise."[78] Similarly in *Udāna* Discourses, the Buddha states this about a person who has defeated mental imprisonment: "Like a mountain standing unperturbed, he doesn't quiver from pleasures and pains."[79] Thus the equanimous mind does not judge or like people based on self-interest or dislike them because of self-interest. The quiet mind is generous in giving room to everybody and again, flows like a river. To subdue the ongoing inclinations of "like-dislike" is to subdue all "diabolical temptations" (*māra*),[80] and to assuage emotional agitation is to free oneself from heedlessness.

The Buddhist advice for attaining this mini-nirvana is to rid oneself from the dichotomous impulse of like-dislike or giving oneself the right to judge everything. To the Buddha, the disappearance of the influxes of passion is nirvana, and is at the same time the consequence of nirvana.[81] A well-composed and mature mind does not judge, or is not psychologically shaken, by life circumstances such as getting old, falling ill, or dying. The passion of the mind is

---

[77] Kalupahana, *A History of Buddhist Philosophy*, 101.
[78] *Dhamapada*, VI, 81.
[79] *Udāna: Exclamations*. A Translation with an Introduction and Notes by Thānissaro Bhikkhu (Geoffrey DeGraff), 2012, 3.3: *Yasoja Sutta*; see also 3.4: *Sāriputta Sutta*
[80] *Udāna: Exclamations*, 3.9: *Sippa Sutta*; 3.10: *Loka Sutta*; 4.2: *Uddhata Sutta*; 6.1: *Āyusama-osajjana Sutta*.
[81] *Dhammapada*, XVII, 226.

replaced by an insightful magistrate that sees itself on both ends of the spectrum of all dualities and avoids unqualified conclusions. The mental state of equanimity that the Buddha had in mind is a non-jittery, non-oscillating state of like-dislike that brings calmness and joy to mind.[82] The Buddha allegorized the transient exertions of the mind as clouds and the pure nirvanic mind as the spotless moon. The realization of the state of suchness (*dharmakāya*) in each moment and in life in general is through non-judgment.

In an ironic twist, it would seem that one should 'like' nirvana and 'dislike' the birth and death of samsara. But on the contrary, in the Buddhist understanding, both nirvana and samsara are equated as one inseparable entity – two sides of the same coin so to speak. Only the awakened mind knows nirvana without wishing to alter anything about the reality of samsara or life.

3. From Ignorance To Clarity

Ignorance, or false and confused understanding whether innate or acquired, is another poison that prevents clarity of mind, since clarity means having insight and wisdom about oneself and the world. The Buddha's diagnosis and treatment of "ignorance" was unprecedented and powerful, at a time when most seekers longed for knowledge and enlightenment.

The term *ignorance* is rather vague and first demands a clearer definition from the Buddhist perspective. The Sanskrit term for "ignorance" is *a-vidya* ("not-knowing" or "mis-knowing") which is the negative of *vidya* "knowing", and the Tibetan word for ignorance is *ma rigpa* meaning "not to know" or "deciding not to see," whether willfully or unwilfully. These definitions do not refer to the kind of ignorance that can be reduced by building knowledge or by learning from mistakes. The Buddhist notion of "ignorance" has nothing to do with bookish learning. In fact, the accumulation of more knowledge on top of a corroded foundation can render systemic ignorance even worse. It can also manifest as taking refuge in and repeating other people's opinions and knowledge rather than reflecting on one's own understanding and thus is, in fact, the starting point of nonthinking. "Mis-knowing" or true ignorance is when a person's knowledge is either distorted, incomplete, or wrong. Ignorance is like a warped lens in the mind that blurs and distorts, like an eye

---

[82] This quietude of mind has a Taoistic parallel in *Tao Te Ching* and was also replicated in the Hellenic world. The attainment of *ataraxia*, or anxiety-free state was familiarized by the Hellenic thinkers such as Epicurus and Pyrrho (the latter has been labeled as "the Buddha" of Hellenic world). See the previous chapter.

Buddha's Self-Rule Philosophy

trying to see through a cataract. Distortions are capricious or thoughtless suppositions. Suffering is the result of this distorted knowing.

The ignorant mind, in the view of the Buddha, is a mind which is deluded (*moha*) about the self and the world. It is a mind that is blind to cause and effect; it is a mythically oriented mind. It is a clinging and stubborn mind that refuses to undertake a new understanding. The Buddha's insights about ignorance refer to thoughtless persons sunk in negligence, those who consider themselves learned, laughing and jubilant while enveloped in burning desires. Ignorance is a non-steady mind which is the greatest of all impurities. The Buddha considers ignorance one of the five shackles in life: "The five fetters to be renounced are: craving for material existence, craving for immaterial existence, conceit, restlessness, and ignorance."[83]

The problem of ignorance lies in flawed reasoning and the lack of desire to fix it. The "chemistry" of ignorance means that the mind consumes itself with rash inclinations that can result in separation of mind from reality. The mind is also wrapped in imprudence by clinging to unexamined beliefs and is addicted and used to mis-knowing. The Buddha made ignorance a top priority to address because of the deep-seated destructiveness in this mis-knowing over the course of life.

The antidote to ignorance is to undertake the process of perfecting wisdom (*prajñā*). *Prajñā* means to overcome the bias inclinations of one's own personality which constantly interfere with the objective experience of things in the world. To perfect one's wisdom demands self-investigation in order to understand non-self, and that everything has a transient nature. Wisdom is not cultural or religious knowledge, nor is it a belief system. It demands distinguishing, as the Buddha put it, between the essentials and non-essentials of life: "Those who mistake the unessential to be essential and the essential to be unessential, dwelling in wrong thoughts, never arrive at the essential."[84] In the mind of the Buddha, all destructible phenomena, due to their non-lasting nature, cause emotional pain, and thus, they are to be deemed as unessential. This estimation is critical. The knowing of the nature of all earthly phenomena and their destructibility is a release from dissatisfaction and confusion.[85] Contemplation is a means to shed ignorance.

---

[83] *Dhamapada*, II, 26; III, 38; V, 63; XI, 146; XVIII, 243; XXV, 370. See also *Majjhima Nikaya*: Mahamalunkya Sutta (MN 64).
[84] *Dhammapada*, I, 12; also engraved on a stone at Deer Park in Śarnath, India.
[85] See David Burton, *Buddhism, Knowledge and Liberation: A Philosophical Study* (Aldershot: Ashgate, 2004), 1, 18–20.

Meditation

It is through meditation, or mental yoga (consisting of precision in focus without necessarily sitting), that the ignorance of one's own mind is confronted and the gentle shift from ignorance to wisdom can begin. Meditation is recommended in the fourth Noble Truth as one of the eight solutions, since to revert mis-knowing to knowing requires probing one's own ego and being willing to sit quietly and contemplate.

Meditation offers a means of reflecting and reexamining the mind's knowledge of itself and the knowledge of the transient world. Two essential kinds of meditations in Buddhism are *śamatha* and *vipassanā*. *Śamatha* meditation is for *calming* the flickering and anxious or confused mind. Its objective is achieved by letting tranquility take over chaos. With a gradual practice of calming the mind down by focusing on an object of meditation, a glimpse of the mind-control appears. It is during this stage of mastery that personal greed and attachment to objects or non-objects can be identified and dropped.

Vipassanā meditation is a more advanced technique of knowing the nature of the mind, a place where thoughts, feelings, and impulses can come in from one side and go out from the other, like a breeze blowing between two windows. It is a practice of clarity in which the true nature of everything is perceived to be empty, formless, and impermanent. One sees things with the same eye but perceives them to have no self and to be non-lasting. The interplay between calming meditation and insightful meditation enables one to see the roots of their own suffering as well as the emptiness of things, non-self, and impermanency. The combination makes it possible to see earlier beliefs as inherently flawed, and therefore to let go of the conditioned mind.[86]

The fruits of meditation as described by Buddha are five-fold: 1. application of thought, 2. examination of things, 3. joy (initial, feelings, momentary, body, and body-mind joy), 4. lasting lightheartedness, and 5. understanding the fruits of concentration. A mind which seeks no new objects of pleasure, becomes unified and satisfied.[87]

Dōgen pointed to "just sitting" (*śamatha* meditation). In sitting, a "right entrance" to the mind emerges. Then the mind and body are dropped off, and desires and ignorance subside.[88] Toshihiko Izutsu further describes the

---

[86] Gethin, *The Foundations of Buddhism*, 198–199.
[87] Ibid., 181, 183.
[88] Nishitani, *Religion and Nothingness*, 185, 186–187.

purpose of meditation: sitting cross-legged with closed eyes is to become familiar with the fleeting or impermanent nature of things. Through the energy of meditation, a sharper logic surfaces for the mind to 'see' itself or see the side of emptiness.[89] It is with this unique perspective that the mind detects the no-mind nature of everything, including the no-mind nature of self, or non-self. Thus, the mind in meditation is free to act in every form or no form, mind or no-mind, but the awareness should veer off from the fragmentary modification of "I" or "me." Instead, the entire field may be perceived in containing the dynamic and tranquil qualities, which are but two sides of a single Reality. In contemplation, one must 'see' both sides of this single Reality.[90] One of the goals of meditation is to use the self as a tool in order to see non-self and to see the emptiness of all identities. This power of empirical self removes all fantasies by equipping the mind with certain fine skills: the ability to see the self and the outer reality while at the same time seeing their interdependent and eventual empty nature.

The degree to which the ignorant mind has been rotated toward the clear side of clarity is measured through the person's virtuosity. But being virtuous doesn't always mean doing good or being attached to good actions but developing a judicious and composed mind. Instead, an enlightened mind focuses on wisdom as an engine for all actions, thus virtuous work is produced effortlessly; otherwise, each act, including a "good" one, is contaminated with ignorance.[91]

The fourteenth-century Zen master Musō Soseki (known as Kokushi, "national teacher") radically expresses the view of Zen of disapproval of intellectual knowledge or even Buddhist knowledge itself as neutralizers of ignorance. Both sets of knowledge are, in fact, obstacles to the natural mind to uncovering itself. This natural mind is free from theoretical knowledge and illusive thinking.[92] The Buddha's emphasis on understanding and uprooting mis-knowing was itself a cautionary warning not to build one's 'house' of knowledge upon the 'sand' of ignorance. Thus mind-investigation for perfecting wisdom is done through the methods of rational reasoning, power of retrospection, eradication of fallacious certainties, and meditation. Consequently, nirvana can be glimpsed only if the locked window of ignorance is unlocked.

---

[89] Toshihiko Izutsu, *Toward a Philosophy of Zen Buddhism* (1978; Tehran: Iranian Institute of Philosophy, 2003), 31–32.
[90] Ibid., 37, 39–40, 51.
[91] Musō Soseki, *Dream Conversations: On Buddhism and Zen*, trans. By Thomas Cleary, 9. PDF online: https://terebess.hu/zen/mesterek/MusoDream.pdf
[92] Ibid., 12, 13, 16, 18–19, 30, 37.

4. From Dukkha To Liberation

In the words of the Buddha, dukkha, impermanence and non-self are three perennial indicators of existence. All three are to be grasped and processed. Etymology can be a helpful place to start to understand the powerful role of the word dukkha. The Pāli word *dukkha* (*duhkha* in Sanskrit) is considered to be an evolved form of Prakrit, a popular spoken language,[93] potentially spoken by the Buddha. The evolution and the meaning of *dukkha* may be derived from Prakrit of *duś*[94] ("bad") -*stha* ("to stand"), *duś-stha* = "to stand bad," or *duś-kha*,[95] "to stand in a bad place." However, many Western sources have retained the old translation of dukkha as "suffering." The context in which the Buddha used the word in his psychological and philosophical deliberations makes it clear that he did not mean just an active "suffering" but rather in a sense of finding oneself in a bad place, meaning a place in one's mind or life circumstances. The word *duhkha* (दुःख) in modern vernacular Nepali and Hindi languages connotes the same meaning and intention: "trouble," "pain," "sorrow," "hardship," and so on. As for our purposes in this section, we must use different English words to express the same concept of dukkha in order to salvage the spirit of the Buddhist discourse, not just its form.

Dukkha, which is associated with worries, fears, and unrest, is the machination of a finite mind.[96] In other words, there is no dukkha in the outer reality. The mechanism of suffering is subjectivized according to one's actions, cognitive function and interpretation. The general and repetitive Western Buddhist mantra of "life is suffering" has a terrifying universal truth to it. The quintessence of the Buddha's philosophy was to uncover the universal sources of anxieties, misunderstandings of life's reality, and dissatisfactions, and then to uproot their causes. This natural decision to

---

[93] Prakrit is a name given to a popular spoken language, and different regions had different prakrits versus elitist Sanskrit or Pāli which eventually became written and fixed linguistic forms.

[94] In classical Persian, the prefix *duś* also means "bad.": for example, *duś-man* means "enemy," a person of bad intention. Another word is *duś-nām* means scolding someone with a "bad name."

[95] Monier Monier-Williams, *A Sanskrit-English Dictionary* (1899; London: Oxford University Press, 1964), 483. In Sanskrit the word *du* means "pain," "sorrow," and *kha* means "place," see www.sanskrit-lexicon.uni-koeln.de/monier/. See also Beckwith, *Greek Buddha*, 29.

[96] Suzuki, *The Awakening of Zen*, 18.

intervene philosophically came from an inclination to transform dukkha – from being in a "bad place" to being in a "good place" (*sukkha*[97]) in one's life.

Having pondered his experiences of seeing a sick person, an old person, and a deceased person in his earlier years, the Buddha developed a discourse about the *universal* pain of existence. The unavoidable conditions of birth, illness, old age, and death produce more grief for some[98] than others. The three poisons, however, cause *individual* suffering. All of these as well as other psychological conditions of life in every person demand a fresh and recurrent interpretation in order to release oneself from the acrimonies produced by the mind. Thus, the universality of dukkha relates to aging, dying, and existential anxiety, but the intensity and interpretation of such universal dukkha in life varies from person to person. Personal dukkha requires a deeper understanding of what causes dukkha which can then lead to the elimination of such causes, an approach that is a significant liberation (nirvana). The Buddha claimed that every action arises from a cause, and dukkha arises from the causes of actions.

Taking the three poisons of greed, aversion, and ignorance into consideration, based on their gripping effects, the shape of pain and affliction take different forms for each person, directly and indirectly, in one time or another. In quieting the mind, either gradually or suddenly, depending on the personality and psychic makeup, a freedom arises – a freedom that is decisive for living an integrated and complete view of life.[99]

Suffering is not a static or a black and white condition, nor was the Buddha's approach to it static. In his first sermon, the Buddha formulated his universal and personal analysis of dukkha and the cessation of dukkha under the title of "Four Noble Truths" (Sanskrit, *catvāri ārya-satyāni*). "Truth," as argued by Batchelor is not a "frozen view" or absolute and fixed[100] formulation. The Buddha's teaching alludes to a "shortcut" for finding solutions; it is not intended to depict any working solution as an unchangeable *truth*. Instead, the Buddhist lexicon of "Noble" (*ārya*) "Truths" (*satyāni*) could be alternatively expressed as "Authentic Realities": Four Authentic Realities.

---

[97] See Hermann Jacobi, "Ueber sukha und duhkha," *Zeitschrift für vergleichende Sprachforschung auf dem Gebiete der Indogermanischen Sprachen* 25/4 (1881), 438–440.
[98] Tsong-kha-pa, *The Great Treatise on the Stages of the Path to Enlightenment*, 265–278.
[99] Batchelor, *After Buddhism*, 74–82, 83–89.
[100] Ibid., 118–19n24; see also Batchelor, *Buddhism Without Beliefs*, 4–5. Instead, he proposes "Four Great Tasks" because "Tasks' is more relevant to the reality of a meditator's focus and is preferred over "Truth."

The three forms of dukkha in the Buddhist tradition include 1. sense of possession-separation, physical ailments, loss of youth, ordinary everyday difficulties (*dukkha-dukkhatā*), 2. the obstruction of impermanency for all the "permanent" expectations – neglecting change (*viparināma dukkhatā*), and 3. the struggle of selfhood by not understanding non-self and not understanding the conditioned and non-self-based existence in which everything is dependent on everything else (*sankhāra-dukkhatā*). This refers to the idea that there is no independent reality nor self.

Thus, the Buddha pinned down the nature of pain and its sources quite well.[101] On a deeper level, he created an awareness for the sources of cravings, obsessions, fears, aggravation, and the tendency to cling. The constant incoming and outgoing of thoughts are a source of disquiet and anxiety. The Buddha emphasized the detriment of hyper-reflection and warned about obsessive and agitated thinking. He advised extricating oneself from malicious and erroneous thoughts, otherwise, the mind would seem like an elephant sunk in the mud.[102] With dreadful cravings, thoughts can absorb the mind beyond control. A mind well-regulated in thoughts and free from the blame and the glory of the world increases in concentration. As a result, the mind experiences less agitation at its own hand.[103] In the Fourth Noble Truth, the Buddha promoted the cultivation of "right thought." This means measured thinking is beneficial so long as it does not trespass into the field of "wrong thought." The discernment of the double-edged sword of thinking is in itself the perfection of wisdom.

Suffering is sometimes misinterpreted through the lens of *karma* as seeing past-life karma to be the reason for dukkha in this life. The word and concept of "karma" is a matter of controversy as the basis for the pessimistic suffering. The word *karma* is rooted in *kr*, the Sanskrit word for "action." This means the fundamental laws of action and reaction (karma) should be sharply distinguished from a narrow "belief"[104] in reincarnation which is bound by karma. The idea of suffering as a result of karma simply refers to the natural consequences of the laws of action and reaction in one's life. Karma, in this case, does not mean carrying the psyche from a past life or lives. Even though the scriptures refer to the belief in karma, the Buddha's introduction of nirvana logically aimed to break away from the nature of this belief and the fatalism that

---

[101] Batchelor, *After Buddhism*, 71–73.
[102] *Dhammapada*, XXIII, 327, 339; XXIV, 349.
[103] Ibid., XXIII, 350; XXV, 378.
[104] For a critical analysis of belief system without question in "religious Buddhism," see Batchelor, *After Buddhism*, 16, 294. Batchelor, *Buddhism Without Beliefs*, 37–38.

was carried over from the Indian tradition. The uncomplicated philosophy of dukkha laid out by the Buddha is based on the laws of causality – the thought and behavior, not on the belief of karma that pain is an unchanging product of one's personal destiny. Instead, it is empirically based on mental inclinations and the outcomes of those inclinations. All manner of fatalism in regards to dukkha may be discarded in the context of cause and effect.

To understand personal *karma* is to understand the chain of cause and effect. This means one causes one's own suffering and in fact, one can end the chain of cause and effect (karma) and consequently attain nirvana. Suffering and nirvana are choices and products of cause and effect; they are not predetermined. Given the Buddha's "non-self" theory and the dialectics of "dependent arising," the unfolding of karma is about a chain of actions on a personal level that is filled with all kinds of possibilities, including the development of a will to attain nirvana. As a result, there is no predetermined personalized karma (of a previous life lived) that causes suffering other than one's own actions in this life.

The concept of *universal karma* addresses impersonalized birth and death, a phenomenon which has been taking place infinitely. This karma can be transformed through a deeper and broader interpretation of nirvana. Actually, this universal mechanism of birth and death, which can be karma or samsara, is the grounds on which one realizes there is no distinction between self and others, or between self and the world.[105] In reality, karmic suffering on an existential level applies to everybody. This type of karma is to be confronted by an ambiguous "death-nihility ahead" while living, or "self-being in time." The paradox is the discomfort of bearing this nihility while one has the freedom in joy of living and transformation. This freedom is to try to prevent too much focus on the angle of nihility or existential collapse.[106] In other words, existential suffering while facing the samsara of aging, illness, and death is countered by nirvana and its lightness and joy.

The Kyoto School philosopher, Keiji Nishitani, says that death (emptiness, nihility) itself, or even the effort to attain nirvana, is to escape and be detached from the constant karma of action and reaction that the world is uninterruptedly entangled with. In this confusion, nirvana means to become self-aware of our finitude existence in the infinity of birth and death (samsara).[107] It is the co-projection of the mind to *tathāgata* or "buddha-

---

[105] Nishitani, *Religion and Nothingness*, 256.
[106] Ibid., 246–247.
[107] Ibid., 171, 173–175, 176, 237, 242–243.

mind" and back to mind.¹⁰⁸ Furthermore, nirvana is an experience of dying to the "life" of birth and death and gaining a new life that makes true infinity (emptiness or *śūnyatā*) appear.¹⁰⁹ Allegorically put, the mirror of the finite life such as that of the Buddha faced the mirror of infinite birth-and-death cycles, and these two mirrors only reflected each other. Then the Buddha began to see his life in the context of the same repetition of humanity. This understanding of birth and death, according to Dōgen, is itself freedom and nirvana. Dōgen believes in order to understand the birth and death cycle, every day is a good day.¹¹⁰ In light of the irreversible birth and death, we all face diligent fearlessness and acceptance can transform the suffering of samsara into a reasonable flow in life.

Attachment to self and other entities causes fluctuations in feelings and eventually terrible suffering. The Buddha kept in mind that this personal suffering is not divorced from the broader universal suffering. Not understanding and having ignorance about the nature of change in self and others causes misperception, and can result in severe consequences and suffering. Since the precarious nature of the world cannot be stopped, Vasubandhu (ca. fifth century CE), the Yogācāra Buddhist philosopher, proposed a psychological solution. Vasubandhu proposed that it is necessary to change the nature of one's *relationship* with objects, restoring a non-grasping and non-wanting relationship because of the finite nature of the objects themselves in order to remove the suffering. He saw the conditioned mind as dependent on its own insubstantial sensory system that cannot perceive the change that occurs in objects. If the streams of mind vis-à-vis the changing objects cannot be comprehended by the individual, then the illusions are not comprehended either. Consequently, the nature of close relationships with physical and non-physical objects must be kept under scrutiny at all times.¹¹¹ This change of relationship with objects as well as with close people around us is because of the impermanent and empty nature of everything. The instability and demise of things causes emotional mayhem. But having clarity about this mind-emotion pattern epitomizes one of those realizations that can result in the rotation towards a mini-nirvana.

---

[108] Ibid., 178, 179, 181.
[109] Ibid., 176–177, 180.
[110] Ibid., 178, 179–182.
[111] *Abhidharmakośabhāsyam of Vasubandhu*, vol. 1, initially translated into French by Louis del la Vallée Poussin (1914–1918), English translation by Leo M. Pruden (1991; Fremont, CA: Jain Publishing, 2014), 119–20.

On the broader understanding of causality, change, demise, and suffering, Vasubandhu took a nontheist position and refused to accept a single cause, such as gods, for the existence and impermanence of objects and the resulting suffering. Vasubandhu "mocks the idea that a praiseworthy god should be satisfied with the evident suffering of sentient beings."[112] The theists, from his point of view, with all their beliefs and approximations, deny the causes and conditions of the world.

Vasubandhu was following the path of the Buddha who, by dethroning gods, proposed clarity of mind for detecting the continuous change experienced by all objects until they are eventually lost. In order to cope with and alleviate the suffering caused by change and mortality, the Buddha proposed finding the space between *engaging* and remaining *aloof*. This middle position was an epiphany that came to the Buddha upon overhearing the words of a music teacher to a pupil. While teaching one day, the music teacher advised his pupil how to tune the strings of the instrument in order to get a melody out of it. If pulled *too tight*, the string would break. If left *too loose*, no music would be produced. The story is that this epiphany became the reason that the Buddha broke his long ascetic fast, bathed, and came back to the world of ordinary people. He taught the avoidance of over-indulgence and self-torture in his *Samyutta Nikāya*.[113] He found that taking the middle path between engaging too deeply with the world and ascetically denying the world was the best place in which to pacify the fluctuating commotion of the mind.

To summarize, the Buddha viewed dukkha as arising on two tangible levels. First, it is the universal dukkha that arises from the irreversible conditions of illness, old age, and death. Second, it is the personal dukkha that arises from the flickering "flame" of the mind on an everyday basis, from one's own thought and actions. It goes without saying that the personal suffering and joy of everyday life cannot with any certainty be branded as black and white; it comes in different forms and intensities because humans are neither linear beings nor linear thinkers. As for old age, illness, and death, the Buddha pleaded for a peacemaking attitude with these processes of samsara, whose mechanism is universal and irrevocable.

After all, "joy-suffering" is simply a dichotomous interpretation that can be overcome and its contradiction removed. The pleasure of living beyond this

---

[112] See "Vasubandhu," *Stanford Encyclopedia of Philosophy*, first published Apr. 22, 2011 and substantive revision Apr. 27, 2015. Accessed Jan. 16, 2017. https://plato.stanford.edu/entries/vasubandhu/.
[113] *The Long Discourses of the Buddha*: A Translation of the *Dīgha Nikāya*, 21.

dualistic emotion is, in the end, the only goal; dukkha, as well as indulgence, are anomalies of the mind that can be appeased. Nirvana means remaining poised in the face of all changes, losses, and demises. The Buddha called "the end of stress" a state that is beyond the dualities of this state or that state: "And there, I say, there is neither coming, nor going, nor staying; neither passing away nor arising: unestablished, unevolving, without support [mental object]. This, just this, is the end of stress."[114]

5. From Selfhood To Non-Self

The Buddha rejected the existence of a consistent and permanent self, and all the awakened ones (buddhas) have rejected a permanent self.[115] Thus, according to the Buddha and Nāgārjuna, literally *no* entity in phenomenal reality, human included, has an inherent and fixed *self*, nor does anything come into or go out of existence on its own. The realization of these concepts of non-self and the mechanism of interdependency is itself an attainment of a mini-nirvana.

The Buddha was the original architect of this "non-self" (*an-atman*) philosophy, ahead of other materialist thinkers of ancient India. His second sermon was about non-self, aiming to deconstruct the linear thinking of those who had presumed the "self" to be something continuous that outlasts the body. He concluded that non-self is the relentlessly changing constituents of the mind and body manifested by the phenomenon of impermanency. A person's five psycho-physical aggregates (*skandhas*) – the physical body, feeling, volition, consciousness, and perception – continuously change from birth onward without any anchor that can concretely be called, "I," "me," "mine," or "self." These changing *skandhas* symbolize the sands of self being blown away every moment by the breeze of impermanency. The *Heart Sūtra* relates that the five aggregates are themselves empty of their own fixed identity. By understanding this, the non-self is understood, and therefore liberation and wisdom are the result.[116]

In other words, a person exists at a given time, but that person is constantly in a process of changing. The erroneous perception of self extends itself to

---

[114] *Udāna: Exclamations*, 8.1: *Nibbāna Sutta*.
[115] Bernhard Weber-Brosamer and Dieter Back, *Die Philosophie der Leere: Nāgārjunas Mulamadhyamakakārikās: Übersetzung des buddhistischen Basistextes mit kommentierenden Einführungen* (Wiesbaden: Harrassowitz Verlag, 1997), 69.
[116] Nishitani, *Religion and Nothingness*, 183. For the discussion of the *skandhas* see chapters four and five of Nāgārjuna's *Mūlamadhyamakakārikā*, see also page 140.

unawareness of the imperceptible changes in the self, thus the illusion of a continuous and permanent self exists ephemerally only in the memory of the individual, not in reality. The lack of "ownership" of the body and consciousness is due to its changing nature. This implies that a person is born without the ownership of a body and mind and without the prospect of future ownership, since after death all human constitution is irreversibly destroyed (parinirvana). All the physical and psychological components, in the Buddhist view, are formed through a chain of causes and conditions compounded by the lack of one's own knowledge of self.[117]

Sometimes lay people can misread this to mean that since the self is empty of its own essence, the self is therefore unreal. This conception is false; there is a self but it is constantly changing, and therefore has no ongoing or permanent identity. However, the opponents of Buddha's non-self philosophy believed that the self is real and eternal. This confusion led the Buddha to specifically avoid framing absolutist answers about "self," an entity that conventionally exists but lacks a stable anchor that can meaningfully be called self.[118]

By this reasoning, it means the principle of impermanency leaves no entity immune to the incessant flux; even the non-self is precarious and indefensible in the larger intermingled picture of the universe. Thus, the unrelenting *change*, even though concealed from the eye, is a blueprint for the mechanism of existence and a corroboration for non-self, or emptiness of all things.

The belief in a "soul" as something "sacred" that exists outside of the human constitution and that at birth is "inserted" into the human mind and then survives after death survives was completely rejected among the materialist thinkers of ancient India. The Buddha refuted anything lasting in the human constitution, even a soul. The soul as a separate "self" was considered an incredulous belief without any evidence and was thus rejected by the Cārvākas and other like-minded nāstika thinkers.

---

[117] Hans Wolfgang Schumann, *Buddhismus: Stifter, Schulen und Systeme* (München: Eugen Diederichs Verlag 1993), 88, 91; see also Hans Wolfgang Schumann, *Handbuch Buddhismus, Die zentralen Lehren: Ursprung und Gegenwart* (Kreuzlingen/München: Heinrich Hugendubel Verlag, 2008), 193.
[118] Gethin, *The Foundations of Buddhism*, 160, 161.

The Buddha's instructions to "take refuge in yourself"[119] alongside his discourse of non-self in one single paradigm may seem to contradict each other, at least on the surface. The Buddha, however, did not reject an *empirical* self who emerges moment to moment and who must act upon the emerging thoughts, events and sensation, a self who eventually must understand non-self-concept and act upon it by attaining nirvana. What seems to be a "real" self, the Buddha argued, is an illusion of self, not the logic of self. The biological determinism for the Buddha was samsara, which demanded human interpretation to make it a willful and joyful endeavor. It is therefore this "temporary self" that needs to attain nirvana in order to understand the nature of all fleeting substances including the very self that inhabits the realm of impermanent experiences in time and space.

The Buddha proposed that there is no celestial entity other than self to help self. This self is responsible for introspection and fixes its own problems. Yet his proposition also entailed that there is no entity less reliable than the self due to its unstable sensory and cognitive activities. There is simply no stage in the changing self that can be considered stable enough to grasp the reality of self.

The recognition that a permanent self is only an illusion itself is the stepping stone in the awakening of the mind. The logical experience of non-self is not an illusion; it is only the fixity of self that is an illusion. Illusion is when the self is perceived to be a continuous and permanent entity. The generations who have passed away represent the "illusion" that the people of those generations once upon a time held as being "real" to them. If the two interrelated *self* and *non-self* experiences are kept distinct from one another, they would no longer clash and contradict each other, nor would the self be seen as fictitious and non-self as real, or vice versa.

To understand the notion of non-self is to understand the notion of emptiness (relentless change) inherent in everything. This awareness can potentially be realized in meditation as a conduit for the passage of multiple and yet parallel lines in the mind, such as; *prajñā* (wisdom), "non-discriminatory knowledge," "special eye," "buddha-nature," "the illumination

---

[119] The Buddha in speaking to his long-time friend and disciple, Ananda, pointed out these words: ""Therefore, Ananda, be islands unto yourselves, refuges unto yourselves, seeking no external refuge; with the Dhamma as your island, the Dhamma as your refuge, seeking no other refuge." See *Maha-parinibbana Sutta* (in *Dīgha Nikāya*): Last Days of the Buddha. Translated from the Pali by Sister Vajira & Francis Story, 1998. Online: https://www.accesstoinsight.org/tipitaka/dn/dn.16.1-6.vaji.html.

of the 'see' itself," seeing the side of emptiness, and a consciousness without distinguishing self from others and the world.[120]

In *Shōbōgenzō*'s first chapter called Genjokoan, Dōgen makes an iconic statement which simplifies the psychological goal of Zen, something that the Buddha also succinctly laid out in his non-self philosophy. Dōgen said: "To study the Way [Dharma] is to study the self. To study the self is to forget the self.... It is to let the body and mind of the self and the body and mind of others drop off."[121]

More concisely, Dōgen treats everything, including the body, mind, the world, non-self, and even nirvana as destructible. Once destroyed, all become traceless and join the nihility of existence. By grasping this penetrable reality then the impenetrable reality of non-self and emptiness of all things can be realized as well.

6. From Realness To Emptiness

As much as the self seems real, it lacks any inherent and permanent substance. In the same way, as much as the world seems real, it also lacks inherent and permanent substance. Phenomenal reality, similar to the non-self, is also empty of its own identity and is not substantial or eternal. The self and the world follow the same destinies of shifting and changing, only in different time intervals.

The manifesting world, in the Buddhist notion, is the mirror of a changing world, in a constant state of transmutation. Because there is no real fixed anchor in things, they are considered to be empty of an "agent" that can be identified as an intrinsic *essence* of things. A thing before it came into existence was not a thing and after vanishing will be no more a thing.

The world and everything in it arises because of an interdependent chain of causes and conditions. This principle that everything exists in interdependence is called "Dependent Arising" (*pratītyasamutpāda*) in the Buddhist dialectics. Because of this law of interdependence, things exist neither in absolute existence nor in complete annihilation. There is no origination nor cessation of things. Things exist because of the previous causes, not from or out of

---

[120] Izutsu, *Toward a Philosophy of Zen Buddhism*, 27–31, 69, 72.
[121] See Shohaku Okumura, *Realizing Genjokoan: The Key to Dogen's Shobogenzo* (Boston: Wisdom Publications, 2010), 2.

themselves – no self-causation.[122] It is important to become aware that the world did not appear by its own willpower, just as the self did not come into existence by its own spirit. Realizing this principle means liberation from all dogmatic presumptions of constancy and the absoluteness of the world. Consequently, the self and the world have no firm terrain to stand on since they constantly transmute due to the laws of causality – simply the pace of change is slower in the heavier, more complex world than in smaller and more fragile living bodies.

No absolutist articulation makes sense when the shifting nature of reality points to the lack of an "ultimate reality" in any meaningful way. Each moment of reality that seems so real has, a moment later, already turned into a "pseudo-reality." There is no station in the physical or cognitive realm that can be considered a concrete state in which the object and subject are fixed. To avoid absolutist formulation, this attitude was adopted: the world that was is no longer. The experience of the emptiness of the self and the world find true meaning in the shifting stages of things from their previous to the new stages until their demise and disappearance.

Nāgārjuna was the third-century Buddhist thinker who developed such thoughts, namely by applying the Buddha's non-self discourse to the larger phenomenal reality of the world. He called his non-self philosophy *śūnyatā*, or "emptiness."[123] Nāgārjuna's notion of emptiness does not refer to the emptiness of an isolated existence. There is no such isolation; emptiness is a mechanism of this "real" world.

Dynamic phenomenal reality, whether of the individual self or other levels of existence, is a shift from "pseudo-reality" to the "decisive or definitive reality." The only decisive state is the middle state, between the previous and the next state. This middle state between "is" and "is not" is a neglected or shifting state – the middle state that Nāgārjuna calls *emptiness* (analogous to

---

[122] Nāgārjuna, *Mūlamadhyamakakārikā of Nāgārjuna: The Philosophy of the Middle Way*, Introduction, Sanskrit Text, English Translation and Annotation by David J. Kalupahana (1986; Delhi: Motilal Banarsidass Publishers, 1999), 105. The eyes can see and ears can hear, not because of themselves or a metaphysical reason, but for the reason of the causes and conditions that existed prior to the existing eyes and ears. Nāgārjuna, *Mūlamadhyamakakārikā*, 188-190.

[123] So often, emptiness is equated with nihilism, which is not the case. Nineteenth-century Europeans equated nirvana with just "nothingness," "atheism," "pantheism," or "nihilism," which led to a misunderstanding of Buddhism for a long time. See Bernard Faure, *Chan Insights and Oversights: An Epistemological Critique of the Chan Tradition* (Princeton: Princeton University Press, 1993), 39–40.

non-self). This middle state of *shift*, or a state where and when the previous state is being emptied of itself ("emptiness") may potentially be realized with an awareness of the middle state or deep reflection or meditation. But the continuum of time and changing reality can block a deeper cognitive understanding of the middle state. The causes and conditions are blurred from view; nothing concrete is evident in fleeting objects.[124]

The Mahayanists in general argue that the underlying *vehicle of change* for everything in the phenomenal world is the middle state between is and is not, or *emptiness*. Because all things share the same mechanism of change, this points the arrow in a direction of "non-discriminatory knowledge." It is a critical point to learn that self and objects are not in their last stage; they are non-surviving and inherently carry an "empty" identity.[125] In fact, the main teaching of *Prajñāpāramitā* (perfecting wisdom) is that all things have relative existence and are eventually empty of their own real and independent materiality. This knowledge of the world is a stepping-stone toward experiencing a far-reaching nirvana.

Madhyamika is one of the Mahayana sub-schools and was founded by Nāgārjuna. The goal of the Madhyamika ("Middle Way") school was to make a satisfactory argument that would avoid the extreme position of denying perceptible reality a proper and deserving recognition, while at the same time, not neglecting the chain of changes due to cause and effect, and ultimate reductionism. The goal of Madhyamika was thus to keep things uncategorized and non-absolute, between reality and non-reality. Nāgārjuna's proposition of "two truths"[126] or "two realities" distinguishes between the conventional truth that can be perceived by the sensory system and expressed through language, and the ultimate truth which is concealed from view. The latter is independent from any cause and condition and cannot be described by language.

In other words, the world we existentially, externally, and pragmatically see is not truly the way this world is. It is dynamically (causally) outside of human assessment. To understand the latter truth (emptiness) requires *no observing mind*. This is due to the continuous causation, and thus inherent emptiness, of all things. The former truth (conventional reality) is *mind-dependent* – experienced by the sensory system. This truth means seeing the bigger picture of things, the façade which seems fixed and unchanging; a rather

---

[124] Nāgārjuna, *Mūlamadhyamakakārikā*, 107, 117-122.
[125] Izutsu, *Toward a Philosophy of Zen Buddhism*, 26–28, 29–30.
[126] Nāgārjuna, *Mūlamadhyamakakārikā*, 331, 333.

deceiving truth since changes are imperceptible and yet are happening. The other, ultimate, truth is the undeceiving nature of things, which changes and shifts on the minutest levels – not observable with the naked eye. The two truths should not be mistaken as one being more valid and the other one less valid; they are two sides of the same coin.

In the formulation of Nāgārjuna's discourse of Dependent Arising, or dependent origination, as part of Madhyamika discourse, three interrelated notions are identified: 1. There is no inherent and independent self. 2. All selves and entities come into existence, become, and leave existence due to causes and conditions (*pratītyasamutpāda*), not on their own. 3. There is a position against the proponents of a substantialist view (the world is real and solid) or eternalist view (the world is eternal) as well as against annihilationist epistemology (final destruction of the world). On this last topic, Nāgārjuna proposed a middle position between substantialism and annihilationism, between something and nothing, between self and non-self, all of which is rooted in the non-self philosophy of the Buddha. The Middle Way is the "middle" station of the extremes of eternalism and annihilationism; the two are linked together through the process of dependent arising.[127]

Through his elaborations, Nāgārjuna tries to help his readers not to fall into the trap of seeing the world in one way or another and falsifying reality. He warns, if emptiness is wrongly perceived, it would be like a snake that is wrongly perceived; a malignant knowledge to cultivate.[128] He rejects anything permanently fixed or sacred. Nāgārjuna also avoids a dichotomous approach to one single Reality.[129] The two wings of existence live side by side without one side dispossessing the other. Nevertheless, this coexistence does not rule out the fact that non-self or emptiness is the ultimate and decisive reality of all substantial things in the world.

The laws governing phenomenal reality cause the shifts and changes. These laws also assure that things do not exist independently, but rather interdependently. This mode of operation requires causes and conditions for the objects to come into and go out of existence. There is never a moment that an entity can anchor itself concretely and indefinitely. From the ontological and conceptual point of view, large objects are made out of smaller objects, all the way to the smallest units, down to where there is nothing else to be detected.

---

[127] Gethin, *The Foundations of Buddhism*, 145, 238–239.
[128] Nāgārjuna, *Mūlamadhyamakakārikā*, 335, 336-7.
[129] Izutsu, *Toward a Philosophy of Zen Buddhism*, 37, 106. Nāgārjuna, *Mūlamadhyamakakārikā*, 132-133.

Thus, every object is empty of solid and unified substance. In an infinitesimal breakdown of everything, in the end, there is no part left and thus emptiness arises. Furthermore, all animate and inanimate objects inherently go through the process of decay, break down, and become empty of what they once were. Emptiness, in this case, appears to be both the template and the final destiny of everything, and could even be compared to entropy as the physicist's version of emptiness, defined as disorder and change.[130]

On the contemplative level, to retreat from "I" and the world is to let them both merge into each other, an experience that the Zen practitioners and phenomenologists would refer to as the real experience of inseparability of time with self and the world. In this fluid experience, the rise and the fall of things happens without the feeling of any sharp beginning or termination.[131]

More on the Nature of Emptiness

It was actually Nāgārjuna, who later became known as the second Buddha almost 750 years after the Buddha's death, who fully developed the dialectics of emptiness in his famous text and most important work, *Mūlamadhyamaka-kārikā* (*Fundamental Verses on the Middle Way*).[132] The realization of emptiness is such a powerful tool for self-liberation that it warrants further understanding through a brief survey of the intellectual evolution of this idea in the world of Buddhism.

The idea of emptiness is extrapolated from the notion of *suñña* or 'empty'. It is asserted in the later Sanskrit texts that the term emptiness or *śūnyatā* is more specific not just in individual but also universal emptiness, particularly after the third century CE and the new interpretation by Nāgārjuna. Buddha's second sermon on non-self reasoned that everything is empty of a real self or true identity, which paved the way for the Mahayana Buddhists to expound

---

[130] The same process of flux has been studied in evolutionary biology and physics as it became an established fact that nothing stays itself; all animate and inanimate beings are governed by the excitation of the change and through interactions of all the irreducibly smallest particles and fields of energy become something else in the course of time. Thus, the illusion of solidity, especially memorizing the solid object, is an anomaly of the mind.

[131] Shizuteru Ueda, *Wer und was bin ich?: Zur Phänomenologie des Selbst im Zen-Buddhismus* (Freiburg: Verlag Karl Alber, 2016), 11–24.

[132] Other works examine Nāgārjuna's concepts of emptiness (*śūnyatāsaptati*) and reasoning (*yuktiṣaṣṭikā*). A shorter treatise discusses the notions of emptiness and dependent arising (*pratītyasamutpāda*). See https://plato.stanford.edu/entries/nagarjuna/, accessed Jan. 29, 2018.

on it further in their earliest text, the *Prajñāpāramitā Sūtras* (*Sūtra of the Perfect Wisdom*) around the first century CE.

The discourse on *śūnyatā* as a greater Philosophy of Emptiness for both the individual and universal level was systematized centuries after the Buddha. In one way or another, the various assertions of originality in the Buddhist texts base their arguments on the original teachings of the Buddha himself. While it may be true that the teachings of the Buddha do not contain all the claims of the sūtras and commentaries, the core messages can be traced back to him.

Technically, the Buddha is not believed to have used the term "emptiness" in the same philosophical context as Nāgārjuna. The Buddha's discourse of non-self in the Pāli sūtras refers to all things being empty of self – a meaning that may be encompassing the definition of non-self, emptiness of everything, as well as nirvana.[133] The Buddha, according to two sūtras in *Majjhima Nikaya*, recommended contemplation on emptiness (*suññata*).[134] This being said, the Buddha may be the source of the idea, but he did not prodigiously philosophize the subject of emptiness the way Nāgārjuna did.

The Pāli texts speak of empty *suñña* in regards to non-self, that is to say, that everything is empty of self. Nevertheless, the greater claim outside of just "self" being empty is in realizing a broader application of *śūnyatā* (especially in Madhyamika school). The application of *śūnyatā* is also for both the physical *reality* and the *mind*, both of whose contents are passing and empty. In other words, there is neither a solid world nor a dependable mind; both are in reality empty.

The disagreements and inconsistencies in the claims of the term "emptiness" is a matter of philological as well as philosophical interest. The collision among the Buddhist dialecticians occurred when the essentialist Buddhists such as the Sarvāstivādin school, an extinct branch of Buddhism (between ca. 3rd century BCE and 7th century CE), maintained their strong position about the realness of the world. They argued, for example, X is X, therefore X cannot be anything other than X because it has its own inherent

---

[133] See Abraham Velez de Cea, "Emptiness in the Pāli *Suttas* and the Question of Nāgārjuna's Orthodoxy," *Philosophy East & West* 55/4 (Oct., 2005), 507–528. The author of the article, Velez de Cea supports the notion of emptiness to have appeared in the Pāli texts first, which supersedes Nāgārjuna's texts. In other words, this view challenges the Mahayana sect's claims to be the first to extrapolate the Buddha's discourse of emptiness. Thus, according to the article, it was the Theravada, the earliest Buddhist sect, that first referred to the discourse of emptiness.

[134] *Majjhima Nikaya*: Cula-sunnata Sutta, Maha-sunnata Sutta (MN 121, 122).

and permanent essence of being X. This essentialist view had to confront the non-essentialist view put forward by Nāgārjuna.[135] By proposing his Middle Way, Nāgārjuna wished to point out the neglected areas between the two points or two assertions of reality. His non-essentialist position is laid in his non-absolutism that something can be either this and that, neither this nor that, and perhaps even none of the propositions assumed.

The perception of everything being solidly itself is an ingrained perception in the mind due to the fallacy of the sensory system. This illusive perception is challenged by Nāgārjuna who asserted that everything vibrates and changes. Solid things move in the direction of non-solid, not being self – toward becoming empty of its own individuality. The conventional (solid) reality and the empty reality are two levels that are not identical and their relationship necessitates contemplation. The change from moment to moment is an indication of the object that seems solid to the eye but is not solid and it is not itself. The object constantly interacts with a greater field and ceaselessly "becomes" something other than it was a moment ago. This composed paradox of nature is picked up and elaborated on by the Buddhist Mahayanists and, of course, can be traced back to the Buddha and Nāgārjuna.

The Mahayana-Madhyamika standpoint on the question of reality of the world is a two-fold perspective: it is real but constantly changing; thus, it is real and unreal. It is relative and dependent on the causes of the change. Yet its ultimate and true reality is empty. The problem with this two-fold formulation of reality is that neither the comprehensive causes and conditions of the change are readily detectable to the naked eye, nor is the emptiness apparent in any given moment. The perceptible world is valid moment by moment by the sensory system, and its emptiness can be detected by the deductive reasoning. Things consequently have their own intrinsic existence until they become extinct, and yet things demonstrate themselves to us on certain cognitive levels. The optical illusion lies in this discrepancy. By challenging human faculties more radically, the philosophy here took on the task of greater responsibility in restoring a deeper logic in the cognitive system.

Therefore, Nāgārjunian logic cannot be dependent simply on the sensory system but must also depend on deductive reasoning. The agent of change or the annihilation of the entities are not apparent in the initial perception. Nāgārjuna corrects this optical illusion logically by stating the middle and neglected position of all changes is between "is" and "is not." This middle position is the emptiness of all quantifiable things (dharmas). This emptiness

---

[135] Izutsu, *Toward a Philosophy of Zen Buddhism*, 108.

or middle position cannot be framed in the linguistic and conceptual articulation. When something is in the state of becoming, it neither is nor is not, and more succinctly Nāgārjuna said, it is both and it is neither. The following is an opening verse in *Mūlamadhyamakākārikā*, offering a summary of his Middle Way philosophy dedicated to the Buddha: "there is neither cessation nor origination, neither annihilation nor the eternal, neither singularity nor plurality, neither the coming nor the going."[136]

Nāgārjuna's tetralemmas are comprised of both negative and positive positions, contained among these four possibilities: 1) True (exists), 2) False (does not exist), 3) Both True and False (existent and non-existent), 4) Neither True nor False (nothing is existent or non-existent). In other words, there is an area of transition neglected between self and non-self which confirms both experiences to be true and false at the same time, yet neither one to be true. The flow of existence does not stop at any fixed position in order to pinpoint it didactically. Regardless of our sensorial and cognitive inabilities, the principle of relentless cause and effect is established.

As abstruse as these states sound, they are intended to make his formulation of the two truths of *dependent arising* and *emptiness* understood, while also freeing himself from asserting anything absolute.[137] The state of experience of the middle way is to bridge or avoid extreme annihilationist and eternalist thinking – as "it" ends yet "it" continues – a middle ground that the Buddha and Nāgārjuna called indefinable and undeclared.[138]

On the topic of non-origination and emptiness, we can look briefly two offshoots of Madhyamika schools, the Prāsaṅgika and Svātantrika; both emerged in Tibet in the eleventh century. These two sub-schools of Nāgārjuna's Madhyamika school of philosophy were popularized in medieval and modern Tibet, particularly Prāsaṅgika. The proponents of Prāsaṅgika follow the dialectical reductionism, while Svātantrika uses syllogism for proving the ultimate reality. The use of syllogistic construction by the followers of Svātantrika for their mode of reasoning is countered by followers of Prāsaṅgika's mode of deconstructionism. The dominant Tibetan school of Buddhism, namely Gelug holds to Prāsaṅgika's reasoning and ridicules the

---

[136] Nāgārjuna, *Mūlamadhyamakakākārikā*, [the translation of this verse is taken from Nāgārjuna's Middle Way *Mūlamadhyamakakākārikā* by Mark Siderits and Shōryū Katsura (Somerville, MA: Wisdom Publications, 2013), 13.]
[137] Jay L. Garfield and Graham Priest, "Nāgārjuna and the Limits of Thought," *Philosophy East & West* 53/1 (Jan., 2003), 13-14.
[138] *Nāgārjuna Mūlamadhyamakākārikā*, introduction by David J. Kalupahana, 16.

Svātantrika school on the ideological grounds, even though Svātantrika's constructionism is used in the Tibetan dialectics.[139] Since Nāgārjuna's infinite reductionism and divisibility is believed to end at the point of its origination, it created a dilemma in dealing with reductionism.[140] He asked: "Does the originating thing exist prior to its origination?" But there is no point of origination in his reasoning; everything is dependently originated and nothing has originated independently. In other words, there is no starting point per se. So, the point of origination has to infinitely regress following the origination of the origination and so forth all the way back to emptiness.[141] This is a point when emptiness itself is also empty.

The dispute between the schools of Prāsangika and Svātantrika was an attempt to logically bridge the appearing reality and the empty reality, as well as to address whether one's worldly cognition of reality is valid and should be the only cognition and source of knowledge (pramāna).[142] Ultimately, however, the heated debates between the followers of Prāsangika and Svātantrika, even considering the escalation of contradictions in their language and philosophical positions, did not by and large derail the principle of non-self and emptiness that the Buddha and Nāgārjuna put forward.[143]

The Nature of Mind is Empty

> No beginning,
> No end.
> Our mind
> Is born and dies:
> The emptiness of emptiness.

-Zen master, Ikkyū Sōjun (d. 1481)

Emptiness, in an ironic twist on the word, is in fact a very full, rich and transformative concept. The Madhyamika Buddhist school delved further into

---

[139] McEvilley, *The Shape of Ancient Thought*, 421; Gethin, *The Foundations of Buddhism*, 240.
[140] Nāgārjuna, *Mūlamadhyamakakārikā*, 170, 174.
[141] McEvilley, *The Shape of Ancient Thought*, 423.
[142] Helmut Tauscher, "Phya pa chos kyi seng ge as a Svātantrika," in *The Svātantrika-Prāsangika Distinction: What Difference Does a Difference Make?* Ed. George B. J. Dreyfus and Sara L. McClintock (Boston: Wisdom Publications, 2003), 207–238.
[143] Gethin, *The Foundations of Buddhism*, 240.

the idea of emptiness by using it as a way to explore the relationship between the mind and the objective, external world. They came to the view that the mind and object reflect each other through the law of interdependence. Thus, Madhyamika is known as the "No-Mind, No-Object" school, since in the absence of this interdependent relationship, only emptiness remains; neither the object remains, nor the mind. When there is no mind to view the object, the world of objects does not exist independently from the mind. And the mind would not exist if there were no world to perceive; it would be an empty mind. The inner reality of emptiness is the only reality that does not require the mind and is outside of mind-and-object duality.

So, since the mind and the world are interdependent, one without the other would be meaningless. On a meditative and experiential level, emptiness envelopes the mind-object relationship. Thus, an understanding of emptiness is possible through meditation. However, the Yogacāra school, another branch of Mahayana, holds that the world is inherently empty but there is and has always been a mind-stream, regardless of the object. For this reason, this branch of Mahayana is known as the "Mind-Only" school, meaning that the mind is real and the world is a mental reflection that is empty and unreal.[144]

In his deft and straightforward work *Muchū Mondō* (*Dream Conversations*), the fourteenth century Zen Buddhist monk-scholar Musō provided many valuable insights about Madhyamika of the "No-Mind" school. In one instance, Musō using *The Enlightenment Sūtra* said; when the transient body vanishes, the transient mind also vanishes; and when the transient mind vanishes, all objects also vanish.[145] That is to say, the body and mind temporarily appear and the ignorant minds think the body-mind has concrete existence.[146] The conventional mind perceives the phenomenal reality, and the no-mind (nirvanic mind) realizes emptiness. The key focus in both Madhyamika and Zen specifically is to avoid an absolutist perception of objects as being permanent and existing without the laws of causality. Musō tersely again put this matter in perspective by emphasizing that all phenomena appear conditionally and in due course come to an end. He cautioned his audience to be fully aware of the impermanence and emptiness of all existing things.[147]

---

[144] Ibid., 248.

[145] Musō, *Dream Conversations*, 41, quoting *The Complete Enlightenment Sutra*. See https://terebess.hu/zen/mesterek/MusoDream.pdf.

[146] Ibid., 38.

[147] Ibid., 25.

Musō endeavored to make emptiness more understandable on a human level in another contemplation. He described bodies and minds come and go because they have no independent reality and have no ownership of self. The true mind is formless and is never born nor does it die. Once this true mind is realized, then in death the conventional mind is forgotten and the true mind merges with the cosmos.[148]

In the ultimate reality of things, the self, the mind and the world become extinct, just at different time intervals. Making absolute statements about the phenomenal reality is doomed to change or be erroneous. In safeguarding oneself not to fall into essentialist and absolutist thinking, the Zen master Seung Sahn Sohn Sa kept his students under the guidance of "keep a 'don't-know' mind." Nāgārjuna also stated: "'Don't-know' mind is an empty mind. There are no words, no speech. So, there is no one, no god, no nothing, no mind, no emptiness. ... This is your true self. So always keep 'don't-know' mind."[149]

The Enlightened Mind

In his early days of learning Zen, the mind of the young thirteenth-century monk Dōgen was quite confused by one puzzling statement in the Buddhist literature: all persons have a pure mind, or "buddha-nature." Why then would a person who already has a buddha-nature need to practice Dharma or seek enlightenment? "If I am already enlightened, why must I practice?"[150] This is rephrased by Kazuaki Tanahashi: "If each moment is complete, why do we need to practice?"[151] This puzzle led Dōgen to go to China and study Zen, and return to Japan with a deeper reflection.[152] The answer for Dōgen was that the inner workings of the conventional mind inflame the pure mind (buddha-nature). This confused mind goes through layers of thoughts, and thus the pure mind becomes prey to the conditioned mind. It became clear to Dōgen that due to this taxing of the mind, one needs to practice Dharma to reach one's own buddha-nature.

---

[148] Ibid., 12.
[149] McEvilley, *The Shape of Ancient Thought*, 483.
[150] Leesa S. Davis, *Advaita Vedānta and Zen Buddhism: Deconstructive Modes of Spiritual Inquiry* (London and New York: Continuum International, 2010), 93.
[151] See the youtube teachings by Kazuaki Tanahashi: https://www.youtube.com/watch?v=ebh2C0avDlo.
[152] Tanahashi, "Introduction," *Moon in a Dewdrop*, 4. See also Dumoulin, "Early Chinese Zen Reexamined," 50.

Although Musō came from the Rinzai Zen school and Dōgen from the Sōtō Zen school, Musō followed in the footsteps of Dōgen[153] and questioned a version of the same oxymoron about the purpose of practicing the Dharma. Musō made a deft and similar allusion by saying, if all the Buddhas taught in order to liberate our minds, what about someone who has no mind, why should he need any of the teachings?[154]

Musō found it challenging to label or give a proper name to the buddha-nature, the primordial mind: "true mind," "no mind," "natural mind" – as opposed to the "conditioned mind," "illusory mind," "false mind." He went on to quote the Buddha by saying that the original mind has been lost to humans and the current cognizing mind is not their own mind.[155] Thus it seems that at a bifurcation point, the conditioned mind of the lay people came into prominence, while the natural mind remained in the background.

The repression of the natural mind/buddha-nature happens in the course of sociocultural evolution while dealing with the distracting everyday circumstances. The clever and industrious mind takes over without recognizing or even distinguishing between the natural mind and the conditioned mind. The original, luminous awareness continues to be lost to the conditioned-illusory mind. The buddha-nature has always been there, but the mind has veered off toward its own interests. Musō advises that to attain the original "Buddha" mind does not require abandoning the body and mind as some ascetic monastic Buddhist or Hindu sects prescribed.[156] He states that the quintessence of all the Buddha's teachings is how to trace back to the true mind. If such an approach is taken, the empty land of the natural "no mind" would then appear. Musō, similar to Dōgen, believed that the goal of all Buddhist teachings is to reach this natural mind, an enlightened mind.

The Buddha, and even more so the Zen adepts, advised using the mind to locate the no mind. To locate the no-mind is to locate buddha-nature, the emptiness, the natural mind, and the supreme *prajñā* (wisdom). Knowing this

---

[153] Dōgen is the founder of the Sōtō school in thirteenth-century Japan. Musō is from Rinzai school whose patronage from the mid-1300 to mid-1500 influenced painting, landscape design, gardening, and the tea ceremony. Sōtō, on the contrary, had very little cultural influence in Japan. Meanwhile the Sōtō school between 1400 to 1800 kept Dōgen's work and his teachings in the margins, even secret, until his *Shōbōgenzō* (*The Treasury of the True Dharma Eye*) was published in 1816 for the first time. See Tanahashi, "Introduction," *Moon in a Dewdrop*, 23.
[154] Musō, *Dream Conversations*, 51.
[155] Ibid., 40.
[156] Ibid., 41.

mind is a radical awakening, a nirvana. The discovery of this natural mind to Dōgen is the discovery of the three scopes of the workings of the mind: the universal mind, the joyful mind, and the caring mind, all of which enables the person to see the whole spectrum or reality not just the narrow self.

All things (dharmas) exist the way they ought to exist in the world. The enlightened mind, as Dōgen explained, does not confirm any permanent self or identity in anything. All things hold the world together, but the laws of cause and effect keep the things transitory by shifting existence moment to moment. All pasts are therefore wiped out.

As the metaphorical Zen saying puts it: "Bodhidharma never came to China."[157] In fact, Bodhidharma did go to China but because the past has been wiped out, the Zen saying is a reminder to treat past events as forgotten bygones, as if they never happened. This points to the destructible, non-existent quality of past bodies and events.[158] For the Buddha, liberation from the past-oriented, erroneous mind was enlightenment. All ownership of the past, whether remote or immediate, must be relinquished, and even transcendental experiences must be relinquished for the sake of liberation. Complete liberation in the Rinzai Zen school means even removing the Buddha from the equation: "If you meet the Buddha, kill him ... only then you will obtain liberation and dwell in complete emancipated freedom, without getting emotionally caught up in things."[159] "Kill" refers to killing the dependency on the bygone Buddha for enlightenment, killing all egos and seeing the world in a different light of nowness and suchness. Radical enlightenment is to validate the world on one hand and to see it as inherently empty on the other, a position which provides a rational and judicious inclination to live happily and to die unreservedly.

The realization of the emptiness of all things in the mind of a prudently wise thinker is the mental experience that will revise all the previously held conceptual thinking. This means the final liberation is the mature state that is detached from all concepts and all beliefs, even from the very concepts of emptiness and nirvana.

7. From Rectilinear Time To the Constancy of Nowness

The opposite of nowness is the past and future. Nowness receives its significance in the world of impermanence by recurrently happening. The

---

[157] Nishitani, *Religion and Nothingness*, 189, 191, 196.
[158] Ibid., 190.
[159] Ibid., 262–263.

Buddha identified impermanence (*anitya*) to be one of the three indicators of life alongside non-self (*an-ātman*) and the pain of existence (*dukkha*). Since there is no independent reality other than the reality we live in, the experience of impermanence is the only currency of time in human perception. Phenomenal objects are in constant transit of time. There is, however, another interpretation of time outside of this conventional linear experience of time in which birth and death, or samsara, takes place. It is a dimension of time that the Buddha referred to as non-origination in which no birth, no death, no movement of time, no beginning, and no end take place, the recurrent permanence of nirvana – all free from cause and effect.

Impermanence is the common realm of existence, which we share with other animals. We share our birth, life, and mortality with all sentient beings. But the answer the Buddha looked for can be sought in this very public impermanence. Reality in flux has no beginning or origin and will have no end (*an-utpada:* "no-origination" in Mahayana doctrine). This means the buddha-mind unambiguously experiences never-ending impermanency. This perception of time nullifies any marker that time shall end abruptly and shows no beginning or origination of time. There is no beginning nor end of time, there is only eternal-present time.

The notion of a creator is strongly linked with the theory of "origin" and the linearity of time. This means the world had an origin and consequently will have an end. Rectilinear time is given a direction and an implied end, at least in a religious and conventional sense. But the theory of origin and a creator is a metaphysical speculation and belief is therefore unverifiable. The Buddha, having disempowered belief in the gods, intended to abandon anything mysterious and incomprehensible for the empirical mind. In the core Buddhist discourse of Madhyamika, all sensory, material, and intuitive clues point to non-origin (non-createdness) of objects and existence altogether, an ongoing process of change in a more cyclical or recycling mode rather than linear. Never-ending impermanence is the shift of one moment to another, laden with the dynamics of causes and conditions through the constant making and unmaking of things.

Addressing the idea of time is one of the tasks in the Buddha's teachings, a concept which was elaborated upon later by the Buddhist philosophers and Zen masters. In revisiting an understanding of time in a Zen context, one faces two dimensions of time which deal with two levels of consciousness. One is the movement of consciousness in time-space like an arrow points to a unidirectional path. The other level is the experience of eternal-present time, as if time is the same time repeating its nowness. It is and always remains now; it is a non-directional time. In the experience of nowness, it is as if impermanence and passing time lose their effect. Nirvana and nowness point to no change of time, always the same, outside of time (*nitya*, or permanently). Even though the physical body travels through time and impermanence causes change and ages the body, the nirvanic mind experiences the unchanging permanence of nowness that nothing changes – the constancy of always the same. Dōgen stated that each moment carries all of time and the actual experience happens in the present, and the tranquility of nirvana is timeless. He writes:

> As usual
> cherry blossoms bloom
> in my native place,
> their color unchanged –
> spring.[160]

In the Zen context, there are mutual interactions between the two dimensions of time, one upon another, as Izutsu put it, which may be ready to tilt to either direction. The eternal-present is in view, but the next moment time-space may intervene and hide the eternal-present behind it.[161] The goal of the pure mind is to understand the whole phenomenal world beyond the limitation of time-space, outside of its temporary identity.[162] It is a pre-human, pre-mind, pre-time, and pre-concept phase – a state of empty time and empty mind.

Time-space is one level of reality, but it is a factor that veils the non-moving time. The eternal-present is another level of reality that submerges all the temporalities of what has been perceived as past, present, or future. Even in terms of emotional experiences linking the past and present, all joy and pain are from the condition of the mind that stems from the causes and effects belonging to another scale of time.[163] This understanding of the eternal-present is not just tightly linked with the experience of the original mind, but it is also a product of it. The eternal-present time is the original state of all things that operate in pre-cognitive, pre-linguistic, and pre-phenomenal conditions and circumstances. But linear time-space is the most familiar thing to the human cognitive faculty. Nevertheless, both dimensions of time live side by side, intertwined; the grasp of eternal-present time depends only on the mental training of the perceiver.

---

[160] Kazuaki Tanahashi, "Introduction," *Moon in a Dewdrop*, 13–14.
[161] Izutsu, *Toward a Philosophy of Zen Buddhism*, 37.
[162] Ibid., 54–55.
[163] Musō, *Dream Conversations*, 7.

The distracted mind cannot detect the eternal-present time nor can it explore the authentic state of pure existence readily at hand. This existence differs from the existence that has its basis in the forms of birth and death as well as in changes detected by the sense organs. The Buddha's extrapolation of nirvana countered the linearity of birth and death as the only experience of mind. This does not mean the Buddha could influence the physical and biological laws or stop the movement of time. His nirvana entailed having a momentary glimpse or experience of the eternal-present dimension of time that transcends birth and death, referring to the stoppage of all other temporal activities in a new perception of nonlinear and formless time.

Nishitani offers further insights about the Buddhist circular and rectilinear sequence of time. The infinite recurrence of now makes existence burdensome, which keeps everyone "being-at-doing"; otherwise rectilinear time and eternal nowness is nothing but boredom.[164] It is perhaps this boredom and the burden of infinite nowness that makes it possible to explore creativity and freedom for the great liberation. Thus, time, on a deeper level, is the medium for participating in the field of changes, and even the experience of emptiness. Inversely, given our psychological frailty, facing impermanence may bring us to the brink of existential collapse even though in reality we are free.[165] The quiet mind, even though it maintains "being-at-doing," makes use of impermanence to *process* all actions and thoughts and to keep grueling compulsions at bay. In a practical sense, rectilinear time and looming death perhaps can be seen as a blessing for some since it shortens the suffering and confusion. So, the outright understanding and the acceptance of impermanence in life may seem like common sense, but after all, is a nirvana in its own right.

The recognition of the impermanency of life is just the beginning of understanding Buddhism, and by this, it is meant to create an awareness that impermanence and nowness are inseparable.[166] Impermanence may in itself seem to be a sad experience, a sign of attachment and denial of the truth of change, but impermanence proves itself useful when it is used to observe cause and effect. Dōgen indicated it is impermanence which allows suchness and buddha-nature to manifest.[167]

The clarity in distinguishing rectilinear time from the ever-present nowness is itself a mini-nirvana offering insight into nirvana. Miscalculations about the

---

[164] Nishitani, *Religion and Nothingness*, 220–222.
[165] Ibid., 220, 222, 231.
[166] Kazuaki Tanahashi, "Introduction," *Moon in a Dewdrop*, 14.
[167] See Joan Stambaugh, *Impermanence Is Buddha-Nature: Dogen's Understanding of Temporality* (Honolulu: University of Hawaii Press, 1990).

permanency of self and the world, attachment to insubstantial-empty things, and dissonance between our views of the world and the way things are all lead to suffering.[168] Clarity in the mind provides a vista of impermanence that links with the infinite recurrence of now.[169] Impermanence is a "teacher" to learn from, about non-attachment, non-self, dependent arising, freedom from anxiety, joyful living, and how to transform burdensome samsara to liberating nirvana. Impermanence can entice everyone to seize the abundance of nowness as a token of the greater reality of time and freedom.

8. From Self-Interest To Compassion *(proceeding into the gradual nirvana category)*

The true goal of nirvana is to liberate oneself and others, and among other things, nirvana means seeing no distinction between self and others. Compassion, or *karuna*, is a natural product of nirvana. The ideal of compassion is not sentimentalism or charity, but means holding a broader view of the interconnectedness of all things. It is also based on the philosophy of non-self in which in essence all sentient and non-sentient beings are in the same boat, interdependent. There is no self for itself. Each self is dependent on and lives for others: the earth, the sun, water, animals, trees, humans, and so on. Through this reflection, interdependency is fully comprehended and externalized in attitude.

In the Zen tradition, the distinction between an idea's intent and expression can be confusing for the non-enlightened. The intent is the root of the tree and the expressions are the branches of it.[170] Compassion may be present in the intent, even though wordless or expressionless. *Compassion* toward sentient beings, objects, and objectless thoughts would also have to be distinguished between its sentimental characteristic and its causal relations. One category of help can fix the *surface*, another can address the *root* cause by understanding the underlying recurrence of the problem. In this context, the first category of help is non-liberative compassion while the other is a true and liberative compassion.[171] The dynamic and conscientious intention, in the Buddhist sense, is in caring for all sentient beings. Doing good deeds or *parināmanā* (transfer of merits) is to break away from one's own life

---

[168] Gethin, *The Foundations of Buddhism*, 235.
[169] Nishitani, *Religion and Nothingness*, 219.
[170] Musō, *Dream Conversations*, 17–18.
[171] Ibid., 6–7.

quandary toward healing the wounds of others.[172] Sometimes a decent deed is in intention, other times in expression.

Mahayana Buddhism has compassion at the cornerstone of its teachings. Although all teachings go back to the Buddha, the prime draftsman of compassion in Buddhism is undoubtedly Shāntideva, the eighth-century Mahayana-Madhyamika monk[173]. Shāntideva offered a model of Buddhist enlightenment through wholehearted methods. It entails the metamorphosis of a gloomy mundane person into a *bodhisattva*, or awakener of sentient beings, whose vibrant participation in every generation is aimed at making life enriching for oneself and for others.

The bodhisattva is a person or type of mind whose enlightenment is inextricably linked with helping others live up to their potentials. Shāntideva called this a path of the bodhisattva, or a path to patience and compassion, healing the compulsion of anger, conducting a meaningful life, and living for and sharing with others. It became a guide to the cultivation of virtues and a measuring stick for benefit in attitude and behavior in the process of awakening.

For Shāntideva, being a bodhisattva was the ultimate goal of everyday life and the ideal of Mahayana Buddhism. He authored nine hundred verses in *The Way of the Bodhisattva* (*Bodhicharyāvatāra*), contributing another altruistic dimension to Buddhism that compelled both adepts and lay people to observe their collective behavior and to cultivate honorable virtues as a way to reach and socially externalize nirvana.

Shāntideva addressed two levels of help: self and other. On the personal level, he put the three poisons of the Buddha in perspective by warning that desirous and self-absorbed minds suffer, and happiness moves farther away. In his social discourse, he maintained that benefiting others is the same as benefiting oneself. Shāntideva's formulations are succinct and clear about the interdependent relationship between oneself and others' suffering and liberation. The Mahayana idealism of compassion (*karunā*) becomes realized and turns into practical wisdom with the work of Shāntideva.

Shāntideva epitomized humanism in Buddhism. He brought the intellectuality of Nāgārjuna's Madhyamika treatment of emptiness and the

---

[172] Suzuki, *The Awakening of Zen*, 9–10.
[173] In section IX of his *Bodhicharyāvatāra*, Shāntideva conducts an argumentation between the Madhyamika and Yogācāra schools. See Shāntideva, *The Way of the Bodhisattva* (A Translation of the *Bodhicharyāvatāra*), trans. Padmakara Translation Group (Boston: Shambhala, 2011).

Buddha's doctrine of non-self down from their instructive, theoretical levels to a practical and societal level. Emptiness and non-self philosophy came to mean a non-egocentric experience[174] of the world, existing in harmony with all living beings, who are subject to the same life as we are. In an interesting historical parallel, the notion and practice of *love* has been the cornerstone in Sufi thinking since beginning in the eighth century in the Eastern Iranian world and Iraq. The notion of *love* also took a creative and poetic dimension in the world of Buddhism as presented by Shāntideva in India in the same time period.

In the eighth section of his book, Shāntideva emphasized that the self and others are equal, providing the universalistic approach to sentient beings, something that the founder of the doctrine, the Buddha, had developed.[175] Love and compassion toward other sentient beings is *the practice* of attaining a reasonable and kind state of being. Clarity is only reached by seeing others rejoice in the same joy as oneself. Clarity on a deeper intellectual level means seeing that the craving for things, even happiness itself, has no lasting or intrinsic anchor. The bodhisattva is aware that all things reside in the impermanence and the non-substantiality of the world.

The type of altruism that Shāntideva introduced is clearly not designed to attain personal merits for oneself but is a collective endeavor to bring existence into harmony as an interconnected unit. The wisdom of compassion in the words and imagination of Shāntideva is the culmination of simplicity, generosity, egalitarianism and impermanency of all things, all of which are summarized in his archetypal individual: "A bodhisattva thinks of everything as belonging to someone else and does not own anything. Why? Because ownership is fear."[176] In the same section of his work, he declared that sanity and wakefulness of the mind is the priority over all other banalities – it is actually the mind that "pays the body" to carry out its tasks.[177]

The psychology of anger and resentfulness is framed by Shāntideva as a trajectory for causing insomnia, illness, restless heart, mental despair, conflict, and the loss of protecting oneself and others. He went on to explain that the pleasure of mind, on the contrary, creates patience, insight to the emptiness of ego, friendship, sacrifice and service to the needy, and a path

---

[174] "Shantideva," https://plato.stanford.edu/entries/shantideva/, accessed Jan. 31, 2018.
[175] See *Majjhima Nikaya*: Kosambiya Sutta (48).
[176] https://plato.stanford.edu/entries/shantideva/, accessed Jan. 31, 2018, quoting *The Way of the Bodhisattva* (*Bodhicharyāvatāra*), section V, verses 9–10 (see also verse 83).
[177] Shāntideva, *The Way of the Bodhisattva*, V, verses 14–35, 41, 47–54, 69.

toward becoming the Buddha, the *Tathāgata*.[178] His diligent guidance toward happiness is an embodiment of nirvana, which in itself is unique both in style and content in all of Buddhist literature.[179]

The restorative impact of Shāntideva's words is to make mind and heart reflect again and again on a different non-self level. Restoration of non-self, in the form of impermanency and interdependency, is the goal. To him, the act of meditation is not always sitting cross-legged. To perfect one's meditation, according to Shāntideva, is to meditate for and on behalf of others who cannot meditate. Supreme compassion, the ultimate and the highest platform that the human species can stand on, is expressed in a few words from Shāntideva:

> Since I and other beings both,
> In wanting happiness, are equal and alike,
> In fleeing suffering, are equal and alike,
> What difference is there to distinguish us,
> That I should strive to have my bliss alone?
> That I should save myself and not the others?[180]

Shāntideva wrote to jolt his audience. His advice to Buddhists and non-Buddhists alike was that by exercising empathy toward others, one can become liberated from the web of self-entanglement. Sacrifice for others, and decency, have never failed to be the trend for enlightenment and a candle to show the path to others. The words of Shāntideva are echoed by Musō who articulated the same notion for liberation in a fundamental sense, beyond any label of Zen or even Buddhism. He, in essence, thought those who care to help themselves alone and not others, they will in fact harm themselves and will never be enlightened. The true liberation is in helping others.[181]

9. From Illogic To Proof (pramāna)

The Buddha doubted whether knowing the answers to metaphysical or philosophical questions was fruitful or applicable on the path towards

---

[178] Ibid., VI, 1–133.

[179] There have been tens of minor replicates of his opus magnum on the way of bodhisattva. Among them, the fourteenth-century writer Tokmé Zongpo produced thirty-seven verses on the practices of a bodhisattva, see Tokmé Zongpo, *Reflections on Silver River*, trans. Ken McLeod (Los Angeles: Unfettered Mind Media, 2013).

[180] Shāntideva, *The Way of the Bodhisattva*, VIII, 95, 96.

[181] Musō, *Dream Conversations*, 6–7.

realization. Instead, the Buddha and later adepts tried to rid people from believing in fictitious constructions of the world learned through the medium of religion or culture, or even asking unanswerable questions. In order to alleviate the cognitive dissonance that comes with such beliefs and questions, a logical system was needed to put people in direct contact with the world. Thus, another gradual component on the path to nirvana is the development of a system of logic about physical reality.

The proponents of logical Buddhism did not want their doctrine to be an insular mystical or otherworldly school but rather a materialist, empirical, and rational school. Buddhist logicians endeavored to encourage people to base their understanding of the changing world on evidence rather than beliefs. This meant that one's understanding of the world should be based on *pramāna*, or proof, leading to the development of Buddhist epistemology. In this epistemology, proof can come from two sources: *sense perception*, and *inference* which is a deductive reasoning from the verifiable sources. Such sources must be provable or have evidence to back them up. With these requirements as a foundation, metaphysics and beliefs can no longer be supported.

Sensory *perception (pratyakṣa)* refers to the direct contact and experience that the sensory system has with an object or phenomenon. The source of knowledge is direct interaction between the person and the object, a method tersely borrowed from the Çārvākas' system of thinking (see Chapter 5). The authorities of texts or obscure interpretations in religious sources due to their unverifiable nature are rejected as the basis of perceiving the coherence of the world. *Inference (anumāna)* refers to using deductive or inductive logic drawn from particular processes and indicators that are known and are supportable knowledge such as sunset and the cycle of seasons. In inference, syllogism can be used to reach a conclusion.

The pre-Buddhist Çārvākas settled for sense perception as the primary source of knowledge about the world, although they did accept deductive reasoning or inference depending on the premise of the argument. Both the Buddhists and Çārvākas preferred an uncomplicated and nonmetaphysical explanation of the material world based on a reliable logic that most people could relate to. In contrast, an esoteric or numinous experience of the world would be subjective, mysterious, illogical, and built on the premise of imagination. Such experience cannot be verified, nor can it be explained to a wider public.

The science of cognition that the Buddhists continue to uphold is based on a verifiable perception of one's own body, surrounding objects, and the nature of the greater reality from stage to stage. The methods of investigation make sure to verify the soundness of one's experience of the external reality is not absolute but rather moment by moment through sense perception, and deductive reasoning.

In this logic, sense perception is the key source of knowledge about the world. Inference is just a technique of deductive reasoning to *support* sense perception and the laws of cause and effect. This convincing epistemology directly challenged metaphysical speculations. But given the psychologically conditioned and religious environment in which the Buddha lived, he was often cornered and asked specific metaphysical questions, such as whether the world is eternal or non-eternal. He was asked about the existence of the soul beyond the body, about the afterlife, and even whether the Buddha himself actually exists in essence, will exist in the future, or will not exist.[182]

The Buddha significantly offered no replies to such metaphysical questions. Although it remained an enigma as to exactly why he refused to entertain these questions and remained silent,[183] it may have been because one set of answers would leave out another, so it would be a treacherously one-sided, speculative, and slanted debate. Furthermore, the Buddha considered that these scenarios all stem from mere curiosity about topics that are essentially unverifiable and non-testable, and such claims and their proof extend beyond human life experiences. Arbitrary answers to such questions from the Buddha's perspective would lead to severe errors and self-convincing speculations.[184] Similarly, in a lesson learned from the Buddha about avoiding cardinal errors in uttering conceptual ideas, Nāgārjuna said: "If I would make any proposition whatsoever, then by that I would have a logical error. But I do not make a proposition, therefore I am not in error."[185]

Other Zen masters contributed their share of euphemistic astute wisdom regarding the dangers of focusing on things one-sidedly. The Chan (Zen) master, Huan Po allegorically cautioned: "Beware of clinging to one half of a pair."[186] In the same logic, Dōgen pointed out the value of balancing opposite

---

[182] Gethin, *The Foundations of Buddhism*, 66, 68.
[183] J. Abraham Velez de Cea, "The Silence of the Buddha and the Questions about the Tathāgata after Death," *The Indian International Journal of Buddhist Studies* 5 (2004): 119–141.
[184] See A. K. Warder, "On the Relationships Between Early Buddhism and Other Contemporary Systems," *Bulletin of School of Oriental and African Studies* 18/1 (1956): 58–59; see also McEvilley, *The Shape of Ancient Thought*, 339–340.
[185] McEvilley, *The Shape of Ancient Thought*, 456.
[186] Ibid., 468.

forces: "One who falls to the ground gets up with the help of it."[187] There is a danger in dogmatically clinging to either one set of answers or another.

The Buddha refused to accept fixity of the self-and-reality coupling by any stretch of the imagination, let alone accepting a hidden and independent reality other than the one in which we live. By this conception, the reality that the Buddha and Buddhist adepts described clearly omitted the beliefs in the celestial mysteries that, despite the total lack of direct experience, had been passed down over the generations.[188] The Buddha also expressed strong opposition to the imagery of the end of the world. The knowledge of the world is between the mind and the physical world, not outside of their interaction, and thus he renounced any belief in hidden mysteries.

Sensorial perception can be enhanced by deductive and inductive reasoning in determining whether something is false or true, exists or does not exist, is verifiable or non-verifiable, and so on. Buddha warned that the deceptively well-reasoned argument does not necessarily make something *true* or even offer *useful* knowledge; the claims have to be well-reasoned, true, and useful.

The intention of this Buddhist logic is to have a personal and direct experience of the world without being dogmatic, emotional, or irrational. Knowledge is not based on faith or on the interpretation of someone else's authority. For every old or new claim about the world, valid proof would be required. The claims of heaven and hell, karma and reincarnation and so on, are metaphysical beliefs that cannot be verified by sense perception or deductive reasoning. In this case, a great deal of unverified past claims or spectacularly omnipotent and miraculous claims are of dubious nature.[189] This realism, from the Buddha's point of view of liberation, is a source of freedom, no longer being bound to sacred scriptures or priests to interpret the world and its purpose or direction. By developing this logical knowledge, the Buddha's nirvana comes one step closer. The foundation of awakening takes on another dimension, which is the task of inquiry and relying on the evidence provided by one's own logical experience.

---

[187] Tetsuaki Kotoh, "Language and Silence: Self-Inquiry in Heidegger and Zen," in *Heidegger and Asian Thought,* trans. Setsuko Aihara and Graham Parkes (1987; New Delhi: Motilal Banarsidass Publishers, 2010), 205.

[188] David Kalupahana, "Pratityasamut pada and the Renunciation of Mystery," In *Buddhist Thought and Ritual,* ed. David J. Kalupahana (1991; Delhi: Motilal Banarsidass, 2001), 21, 31.

[189] The laws of nature and mechanics are quite routine and predictable. Any acts of "singularity" that happen in the material world do not demonstrate any particular known pattern and *may* randomly or non-randomly repeat again.

Dharmakīrti, the Systematizer of Pramāna (Epistemology)

Buddhist dialecticians opened the gate for further such debates about verifiable cognition or pramāna. The most important scholars of the Buddhist pramāna are Dignāga and the later Dharmakīrti. The seventh-century Dharmakīrti is the author of *Pramāna-vārttika* ("Illumination of Proof," or "Explanation of Means of Knowledge"), perhaps the foremost work on Buddhist logic and epistemology. In this opus, he dealt with valid cognition, sense perception, syllogism, deductive reasoning, relativizing, and the reasoning of debate. This became part of Tibetan tradition in epistemology – being factual, rhetorical and persuasive. The focus of Dharmakīrti, apart from basing his argument on the discourses of the Buddha, was on the two sources of cognition, namely perception and inference. Nāgārjuna, in comparison, listed four instruments for more reliable knowledge and a more logical answer by using perception, inference, *analogy,* and testimony.[190]

Dharmakīrti in the second part of his work viciously attacked the Cārvākas' use of perception as the *only* source of knowledge. This exclusivist attitude of Dharmakīrti and his attack can only be understood in terms of the Cārvākas' refutation of omniscient people, such as the Buddha and hidden entities such as gods (e.g., Īśvara) as well as the Cārvākas' rejection of past and future births and karma.[191] Otherwise, in empiricism and as an investigative approach, the Cārvākas were the forerunners of and a likely source of influence on the Buddha.

The contribution of Dharmakīrti to the Buddhist epistemology has been enormous. According to Dharmakīrti's approach to logic, the key to unlocking the tangled mind is being able to distinguish between unverifiable *belief* and verifiable *knowledge.* The former is untenable due to lack of proof while the latter is compatible with the flow of the world, regardless of the dominancy of culture and religion. Proof pre-empts illogical thinking. Topics that are impossible to verify and prove, such as the metaphysical and unseen claim of "what happens after death" is not seen as something useful or relevant in the daily experience of the world. The actualization of another angle of nirvana is the knowledge of moment-to-moment about the world around us. By this

---

[190] See "Nāgārjuna," https://plato.stanford.edu/entries/nagarjuna/, accessed Jan. 29, 2018.
[191] The Second Chapter, Dharmakīrti, *Pramanavarttika,* trans. Venerable Kelsang Wangmo (McLeod Ganj, Dharamsala: Institute of Buddhist Dialectics, 2014), 31, 60–32, 65, 147–149, 151. This author has personally attended and benefited from the seminars of Kelsang Wangmo on Dharmakīrti's *Pramānavārttika* in the Spring of 2015 and 2016 in Dharamsala, India.

Buddha's Self-Rule Philosophy

token of logic, nirvana may be attainable when credulous and fixed beliefs about the fleeting world are dropped.

10. From Language To Non-articulation

The natural world has always existed wordlessly, long before the rise of language. The processes that the natural world have been going through with all of its fine structures and fluctuations cannot be fully articulated or framed in human language. Instead, words and languages have locked many concepts and processes into inflexible and inadequate borders that have often become the origin of misperception and distortion of reality on finer levels. Awareness of how language manipulates the mind and deludes the perception of reality is central in Buddhist debates, particularly in Zen. In contrast, true realization is not verbally dependent. The nirvanic mind should know the border between linguistically conditioned and non-linguistically conditioned reality.

In the Zen school, the attitude towards language finds its roots in the Madhyamika school, which believes language has no relation to reality. It is therefore not surprising that Dōgen assigns a new and different role to language, taking a poetic direction. And the Yogacāra school also holds that language induces a false view of reality. Why is that? Because the dominant view of these schools is that the impermanent and fluid reality of things are framed and fixed into solidly and permanent concepts through language. But in fact, both the perceiver and the perceived go on changing their actual contents from moment to moment although the speed of the change is not perceptible.[192] In the same context, Nāgārjuna believed that a word does not indicate the real object – the word is a baseless construct whose meaning is only determined by its relation to other words. Vasubandhu believed the mind is accustomed to falsely imagined forms that are not existent. Vasubandhu added, "as the mind perceives no object it remains as Pure Awareness."[193]

Zen Buddhism was fundamentally founded on the idea that true reality can be understood outside of scriptures, words, and language, a radical idea traceable back to the Buddha and picked up by Bodhidharma in the sixth

---

[192] Izutsu, *Toward a Philosophy of Zen Buddhism*, 103–105.
[193] Ibid., 75, 105–106.

century. It is believed that the Buddha himself picked out words[194] to suit the subjective circumstances but that words were not his original intentions.[195] For the Buddha, the comprehension and application of Dharma was believed to lie both within the borders of language and yet also be non-language-based (meditative). This is evidenced when the Buddha was asked ten metaphysical and philosophical questions about which he remained silent by neither negating nor affirming them. This paradoxical position vis-à-vis articulation was intended to weaken the conceptual thinking. Meanwhile, it suggests that perhaps part of the reason he did not respond – because he did not want to get bogged down in the traps of language.

As we have explored earlier, the Madhyamika-Zen school portrays the imagery of the phenomenal world as being the reflection of the mind while the mind is equally the reflection of the phenomenal world. They are mirroring each other as one and the same thing. Meanwhile, if there is no mind, there is no object and vice versa. In this formulation of reality, language is nothing but a defective anomaly which distorts this interrelationship between the mind and the essence of the world. Language falsely frames the essence, which is neither part of the pure mind nor part of the essence, of the phenomenal world. To confirm these views of language that stem from a conditioned mind, Musō gave an example of water freezing into ice, and ice melting into water. He implied, they seem to differ each time because of the conditioned mind, whereas the enlightened mind would not be fooled by this confusion.[196]

Buddhism is interested both in the true nature of the mind and the true nature of reality, but language gets in the way. By using names for objects, the mind becomes conditioned through conceptual notions of what each object or entity represents in its image, form, and function. Dōgen elaborated, regarding the falsification of essence in the configuration of the arbitrary use of language. He deftly described the sense organs as being unable to "see" water in things when water is not apparent in them, such as in trees, stones, humans, flowers, etc. These entities are not labeled as "water" nor are they labeled in a way that includes "water" in the composition of those entities. Therefore, the objects are mislabeled because the essence is not in the

---

[194] The non-wasteful and precise use of words at least would deliver a heart-changing message as the Buddha states: "A single word full of meaning, upon hearing which one becomes at peace, is better than a thousand words which are empty of meaning." See *Dhamapada*, VIII, 100, 101, 102.
[195] Musō, *Dream Conversations*, 46.
[196] Ibid., 41.

interest of the language.[197] Nāgārjuna similarly referred to mislabeling of things by saying; "fuel is not fire." And if there is no fuel there is no fire, meanwhile, fire is not fuel either. So, fuel and fire depend on each other yet receive different labels.[198]

What linguistic designations miss in the true representation of each entity is the larger Field that each entity operates in and with. The interaction of the bird with the flower is missed in using the name of "flower" or "bird" or even the larger Field of interactions that a flower or a bird comes from.[199] The singular labeling of an object called "eye" similarly disregards the connection of the eye to a larger Field of head, nervous system, the body, and much more. The "eye" does not live in isolation as an independent entity, nor does anything else for that matter. Thus, the limitations of language can be seen to hide the true nature of interdependency. The division, separation and isolation of all objects seems to emerge as a consequence of the simplification that comes with language.

The use of language without linguistic awareness may entail obstructions that inherently exist within the fixed words. Such anomalies are: 1. Names and designations are too fixed; 2. They do not describe the true nature or essence of the objects; 3. They neglect the constant state of flux in those objects and the flux of consciousness itself – the impermanency of all things is not understood in the context of giving fixed designations to things; and 4. Features and fields that cannot be detected by the sensory organs are left out, labeled partially, or not labeled at all.

Zen practitioners, in order to curb linguistic and conceptual thinking, established a three-step method to be vigorously observed. The first was to recognize the flaw of language and articulation. The second step was to go through silence and non-articulation. By practicing silence, language stops functioning, during which time reality begins to appear as it is without names

---

[197] Izutsu, Toward a *Philosophy of Zen Buddhism*, 137–143. Musō, in a similar way uses the imagery of water: "A sutra says, "When the spirit of fire enters into water, water also becomes fire. When the spirit of water enters into fire, fire also becomes water." This is the way it is with Buddhism: when seen with the eye of Zen, the doctrinal teachings also turn into the message of Zen; when seen with the eye of the doctrines, the message of Zen and the doctrinal teachings are no different." Musō, *Dream Conversations*, 46. Lao Tzu has a fascinating part about the nature of water in his *Tao Te Ching*. It seems the metaphor of "water" had been popular among the sages of Zen Buddhism which may have borrowed from Taoism.

[198] Nāgārjuna, *Mūlamadhyamakakārikā*, 204.

[199] Izutsu, *Toward a Philosophy of Zen Buddhism*, 130–132.

and labels. The third step was to use the same language pragmatically as in the first step, with the same names and labels, *but* with an awareness of how precarious and artificial such articulations may be.[200] It is this paradoxical approach to language that resulted in Zen *kōans*, a sort of meaningless and nonsensical use of words and questions designed to chaotify conceptual thinking. So, poetry was used as a means of reality appearing "in a momentary flash of words."[201] Musō added that only duller students linger over words, those who cannot even work them out intellectually.[202]

Language consequently has to do with our "pattern of thinking" inside, versus outside in the frame of the replication of the human mind. The purpose of Zen is to stop the mind from running after 'outward' phenomena by turning it 'inward' in exploring the 'inner' reality.[203] The anthropocentric use of language in the Buddhist sense is to ascribe reality to ourselves versus knowing that the pre- or non-linguistic reality does not recognize this human propensity. Though a language-based reality cannot be totally excised, as social human beings it must be understood, the way Nāgārjuna put it, as a superimposition on the reality of the original and non-articulated. The articulated world is sheer imagination and the pre-linguistic reality is the reality.[204] With Nāgārjuna's "two truths," language describes the conventional and everyday reception of reality, whereas the deepest reality, which is emptiness of everything, contains no concept or name. Finally, by lowering the status of language, it allows amateur minds to run their conventional affairs, but should not delude the thinker that the language is a gate to the authentic reality.

If we understand Martin Heidegger correctly, he once said that the language speaks us, not we the language. In other words, we are not the master of language; language is the master of humans. We only respond by listening to the appeal of the language.[205] In the same frame of thinking, it can be said that invented words and concepts in cultural and religious realms have mastery over us rather than vice versa.

Deeper cognitive liberation means cutting oneself loose from the limited conceptual thinking that is wrapped within language. In introspection,

---

[200] Ibid., 98, 124, 125–28.
[201] Ibid., 87, 96, 98, 123; see also Musō, *Dream Conversations*, 31–2.
[202] Musō, *Dream Conversations*, 31, 35, 46.
[203] Izutsu, *Toward a Philosophy of Zen Buddhism*, 190–191.
[204] Ibid., 106, 107.
[205] Martin Heidegger, trans. Albert Hofstadter, *Poetry, Language, Thought* (New York: HarperCollins, 1971), 144 (in the essay of "Building Dwelling Thinking"); also, see the essay "The Language" 205, 213–214.

The empirical proof that this philosophy is functional comes only when one's own experiences turn out to be true; by reflection then, the Buddha's experiences become true.[212] This means that this philosophy, like other pragmatic philosophies, becomes a living experience instead of a belief in someone else's experiences.

Such a multilayered philosophy can only be understood in accessible and digestible doses if people from all walks of life and from various cultures are able to relate to it. The Buddhist philosophy, with content that deals with the self and the dynamic world, may have more transcultural appeal after being secularized. For this practical reason, the ten mini-nirvanas in this chapter are presented in order for the readers to integrate them into a broader dialectic of nirvana. It is also to suggest that the accumulation of mini-nirvanic realizations may lead the way to a greater whole nirvana. One by one, the small mini-nirvana boxes of the mind turn from their 'cloudy' side to their 'clear' side, until finally the entire "box of the mind" turns on its axis, shifting to the clarity of nirvana. After all, nirvana is a transformation of mind and heart (*metanoia*). The long battle of philosophy has been aimed at fostering a transformation from mis-knowing to knowing, and for cultivating cognitive self-reliance independent from external events (*autarkia*).[213]

The secular nature of this philosophy can serve the cognitive needs of people whether they are working in a shop, office, or sitting at home – so long as they keep the three poisons of greed, anger, and delusion at bay, and they keep impermanence, non-self, and a non-fluctuating state of mind in perspective. The Buddha's universal advice, to "take refuge in yourself", was meant to make nirvana a paramount and unsullied cornerstone of the human ideal, a practical method for self-liberation in one's own innovative ways without offending any tradition. The crux of the Buddha's teaching or "liberation philosophy" was to become the master of one's own destiny with a deeper understanding of the world – to become a knower of one's own consciousness. "Take refuge in yourself" also meant that suffering-happiness, ignorance-enlightenment, selfishness-compassion, and so on all exist inside the human mind. Which one triumphs depends on our personal choice between confusion and awakening in life.

---

[212] Suzuki, *The Awakening of Zen*, 94.
[213] The followers of the Hellenic schools of Cynics and Stoics as well as Epicurean believed in attaining peace of mind and inner freedom, a kind of self-sufficiency (*autarkia*) by relying on inner sources independent from external events.

Chapter 7

Omar Khayyam's Model of Liberation: Construction, Pleasure and Nothingness

Martin Heidegger, using the words of Hölderlin, once asked, "Wozu Dichter?" - "and *what are poets for* in a destitute time?"[1] In a destitute time in the twelfth century, Persian poet Omar Khayyam appeared, a remarkable poet and a philosopher who encouraged people to stand firm in comprehending the fleeting stream of life in its totality. He has remained a poet for the destitute time of the twenty-first century as well. So, Heidegger's question, "What are poets for?" in this case, is answered by Khayyam's undertaking. Khayyam's poetry was meant to help those who have been left behind or have gone emotionally astray in difficult and confusing times in life. He presented us with an understanding of the material world which he was convinced would produce clarity, confidence, and pleasure in life.

Omar Khayyam was born ca. 1048 in Neishābur in northeastern Iran and died there in 1131.[2] Khayyam was a brilliant mathematician and astronomer as well as a lettered philosopher-poet.[3]

His existential approach as reflected in his *Rubā'īyyāt* (quatrains)[4] is a fundamental philosophy in its own right.[5] To understand and practice

---

[1] Heidegger, *Poetry, Language and Thought,* 89; see also Hwayal Jung, "Martin Heidegger and the Homecoming of Oral Poetry," *Philosophy Today* 26 (1982): 148–170.
[2] These dates have been astrologically calculated and suggested by Swami Govinda Tirtha and agreed upon by the scholarly community. See Peter Avery and John Heath-Stubbs, *The Rubā'īyyāt of Omar Khayyam* (London: Penguin Books, 1981), 10.
[3] In the last century and half, biographies about Khayyam have focused on his hedonism, carpe diem, and images of drinking wine and carousing. The exception to many popular sources on Khayyam is the master and impressive work of Mehdi Aminrazavi. Mehdi Aminrazavi, *The Wine of Wisdom: The Life, Poetry and Philosophy of Omar Khayyam* (Oxford: Oneworld, 2007).

Khayyam's rational-didactical principles, which were mainly presented in the form of poetical quatrains,[6] there is no need for deep meditation or priesthood, neither asceticism nor altered reality. There is no sanctity attached to his words, no need for serving a master, and Khayyam himself was no lord or saint. His words are simple to understand and require no esoteric interpretation by a master. Each and every literate or illiterate person upon hearing Khayyam's quatrains can relate them to their own life reality, serving as a truly accessible source of self-liberation.

His hundreds of poetic quatrains are loaded with substantial insights about many profound topics and yet these lines have been read over the last nine hundred years with very little attempt to systematize them into a philosophy. In fact, Khayyam put existential matters in perspective in a way that is no less significant than by the Buddha, Epicurus, Çārvāka thinkers, Pyrrho, and Lucretius, the thinkers who influenced their societies and beyond. Like his predecessors, Khayyam addressed diverse and fundamental topics including

---

[4] Persian *rubā'ī* is an Arabic word derived from *arba*, meaning "four"; its plural is *rubā'īyyāt*. Khayyam composed *Rubā'īyyāt*, or four-line stanzas in twelfth-century eastern Iran. This followed a strong Buddhist precedent from centuries before, since the time of the Buddha (after fifth century BCE). In the *Prajñāpāramitā Sutra* (Perfection of Wisdom Sutra), the earliest Mahayana scripture, the Buddha is claimed to have valued wise ideas being expressed in "four-line stanzas." According to chapter 13 of the *Vajracchedikā* (Cutting Diamond) [from *Prajñāpāramitā Sutra*], the Buddha suggested that extracting, teaching and internalizing four-line verse (*gāthā*) merits greater virtue than anything else. See The Diamond Sutra *Vajracchedikā Prajñāpāramitā Sūtra*, trans. Edward Conze, 3–6, 13, 17, www.universaltheosophy.com/pdflibrary/Diamond%20Sutra_EC.pdf; see also B. N. Puri, *Buddhism in Central Asia* (New Delhi: Motilal Banarsidass Pubishers, 1987), 201. The Buddha himself outlined his own teachings in four intertwined extracts called the *Four Noble Truths* – a sort of Khayyamian *rubā'ī* of its own kind. Many of the Buddha's words in the *Dhammapada* (a collection of his anecdotes and sermons, see *Dhammapada: The Sayings of the Buddha*, A Rendering by Thomas Byrom (Boston: Shambhala, 1993), were written down in four or five lines. A seminal four-line verse transmission is attributed to Bodhidharma, the first Zen patriarch in sixth-century China. The tradition of four-lined Buddhist teachings in Tibet and Japan picked up momentum in the course of Buddhist history.

[5] Some poetry outside of the Persianate world was bound to become the basis of newly found philosophical schools. The pre-Socratic Greek thinkers such as Parmenides would write philosophy in hexameter, in the same fashion of poetry/philosophy as the work of Lucretius' *Nature of Things*. In addition, Lao Tzu's *Tao Te Ching*, the *Upanishads*, and much more were written in poetical style.

[6] Khayyam had also written a few treatises on various philosophical themes but the premise of his quatrains takes a radical turn in being forthright and open.

biological and mechanical processes, atomism, the philosophy of pleasure, rejection of the metaphysics of an afterlife, and an episto-ontological discourse on nothingness. Such topics deserve more rigorous philosophical scrutiny than just calling them "merely" poetry. It must be borne in mind that the "poetry" of Lao Tzu, the Upanishads, Lucretius, and Rumi[7] have also been treated as philosophies, and so although Khayyam's writings were and still are read as poetry, analysis of his quatrains in the philosophical context presented here is an attempt to cement his edifying words more systematically.

Besides the philosophy inherent in his poems, Khayyam's fluid poetry is linguistically unique, sweet, jolting and direct from mind to mind. He does not seem to force words in order to make his poetry rhyme. He avoids the banality of poetical jargon. He composed tersely with clearer and more straightforward connotations than almost any other well-known Persian poet. He seemed to be quite aware that humans need clarity more than decorative words. He immersed himself in addressing human pain, confusion, and perplexing life circumstances in his literal and allegorical poetry. The goal of his poetry in its core was the liberation of the human mind from misperception and false indoctrination.

He accomplished this by addressing the basic aspects of human life. His philosophy of pleasure particularly addressed the absence of pain – the pain of existence. Pleasure (*khoshī*, *kām*, or *neshāt*) is the antidote to doubt and anxiety. He was aware of the fact that humans are more prone to feel and respond to displeasure than to be conscious of or consider what is not displeasure. The human propensity to react to pain and to be oblivious to states of no-pain, or pleasure, was pinpointed and discussed by ancient Indian and Hellenistic giants, such as the Çārvākas, the Buddha, Democritus, Epicurus, and Pyrrho, and even Arthur Schopenhauer in his *Die Welt als Wille und Vorstellung* (1818).

Another particularly strong quality of Khayyam's poetry is his communication of the doctrine of atomism. Atomistic thought claims that all animate and inanimate objects are made of small indivisible and indestructible blocks (atoms), and ultimately all objects return to these basic elements. The demolished bodies release their atoms in a dance for new reconfiguration, leaving no qualities of the previous entities behind. It is highly possible that Khayyam read and was familiar with the atomist philosophy of Democritus, a

---

[7] Rumi is another Persian poet whose poetry has recently been taken out of the realm of literature and placed in the world of philosophy. See Mostafa Vaziri, *Rumi and Shams' Silent Rebellion: Parallels with Vedanta, Buddhism and Shaivism* (New York and London: Palgrave Macmillan, 2015).

doctrine which was passed down to other important atomist thinkers such as Epicurus and Lucretius. These classical atomist thinkers subscribed to cultivating pleasure in the natural setting before death, since a return to life would not be possible. One of Khayyam's compatriots and contemporaries, al-Shahrastāni (d. 1153), who in fact studied in Khayyam's native city of Neishābur, covered the ideas of Democritus and Epicurus in his volume of twelfth-century heresiography.[8] An important Sunni theological school, Ash'arites of Neishābur had also a well-developed theory of atomism.[9] So, given Khayyam's erudite education in Avicennian-Aristotelian and other Hellenic philosophies and sciences, it is reasonable to assume that atomism was known to him and his intellectual circle.

Interestingly, not far from his native Neishābur, atomism had another precedent in the Indian subcontinent, especially in the Nyaya-Vaisesika school as well as among the Çārvākas. Having probably benefited from the influences of the Hellenic and Indian schools of atomism, Khayyam drew upon the same paradigm for the behavior of nature and the dance of atoms when crafting his poems about the nature of existence.

Khayyam's Own Beliefs, If Any?

Many existing monographs cover Khayyam's biography and poetry, therefore there is no need for redundancy here. It suffices to briefly refer to his personal inspiration or belief system. Regarding his personal faith in any religion or philosophy, he seems to have despised such labeling.

However, some have attached Khayyam to some sort of religious or mystical faith.[10] Khayyam's name is often associated with the Malāmatī, an antinomian

---

[8] See Abdulkarim, Shahrastāni, *al-Milal wal-Nihal*, vol. II, trans. and ed. M. R. Jalali Na'ini (1387; Tehran: Entesharat Iqbal, 2008), 167–171, 178–80.

[9] See Richard T. W. Arthur, "Time Atomism and Ash'arite Origins for Cartesian Occasionalism Revisited," Department of Philosophy McMaster University Hamilton, Ontario Canada. See PDF online: https://www.humanities.mcmaster.ca/~rarthur/papers/AshariteOrigins.pdf.

[10] H. M. Batson unwaveringly would like to prove his point that Khayyam by no means was the follower of Epicurean thought, and it is an impossibility for Khayyam to deny God and for us to label him an atheist. Khayyam's skepticism was "within the confine of faith and has in it an infinite yearning for truth." See H. M. Baston, "Commentary," in *The Ruba'iyat of Omar Khayyam* (London: Elibron Classics, 2005), 130, 133. Even the Indian guru Yogananda felt compelled to address the incoherence of FitzGerald's translation while he strangely did not have access to the original Persian of Omar Khayyam himself. See Sri Sri

ascetic group in his native city of Neishābur. Khayyam's simple lifestyle and his rebellious views against false spiritualism may indicate that he was a secret adherent and follower of the Malāmatīs.[11] But this influence is slightly likely from the point of view that Malāmatī's doctrine had taken a stance against traditional Sufism and scholastic Islam.[12]

The Malāmatīs were the progenies of Balkh asceticism. Ibrāhīm ibn Adham was the Malāmatīs' iconic figure who both broke new ground and symbolized the continuation of Buddhism in Balkh and later in Neishābur (the depiction of Adham is a "proto-Buddhist" prince who travels from Balkh to Neishābur[13]). Considering Ibrāhīm ibn Adham's life and spiritual aspiration, as reported by 'Attār (d. ca. 1220) in his *Tadhkirat ul-Aulīyā*, it is a narrative that parallels with that of the biography of the historical Buddha. The Malāmatīs of Balkh and Neishābur in brief inherited elements of fading Buddhism in their emergence and in their doctrine.[14] Thus, if Malāmatī was the basis of Khayyam's poetry, then Buddhism may have indirectly infiltrated into *Rubā'īyyāt*. Khayyam, however, left no tangible trace of whether he was a Malāmatī adherent, a Buddhist, or a member of another outcast group in Neishābur.

Additional influences were likely to swirl around Khayyam in the rich spiritual environs of Central Asia where he grew up. He may have been exposed not only to the esoteric Buddhism of Central Asia, but also to Manichaeism.[15] The Dīnāvarī Manichaean groups were concentrated in

---

Paramahansa Yogananda, *The Wine of the Mystic: The Rubaiyat of Omar Khayyam – A Spiritual Interpretation* (Delhi: Macmillan Limited, 1997).

[11] Aminrazavi, *The Wine of Wisdom*, 63, 151–152; it is also suggested that Khayyam may have belonged to an independent Sufi order of Uwaysī, 145, 152.

[12] See Vaziri, *Buddhism in Iran*, 141–144 (see chapter 8).

[13] Neishābur was the capital of medieval Khurāsān and was also home for many centuries to the followers of Vedanta, Zoroastrianism, Mazdakism, neo-Platonism, Pantheism, and Buddhism. See Otto Rothfeld, *Umar Khayyam and His Age* (Bombay: D. B. Taraporevala Sons & Co. 1922), 20–22. Neishābur's people, before the large-scale conversion to Islam, were still mainly Zoroastrian, Christian, Jewish, or possibly even Buddhist. See Richard Bulliet, *The Patricians of Nishapur: A Study in Medieval Islamic Social History* (Cambridge: Harvard University Press, 1972), 15. At the time of Khayyam, the Turkish Seljūq dynasty of the eleventh through twelfth centuries had begun the persecution of many shaman (Buddhists), Manichaeans, and Christians that sent them underground. See Richard N. Frye, *Bukhara: The Medieval Achievement* (Norman: University of Oklahoma Press, 1965), 115.

[14] See Vaziri, *Buddhism in Iran*, chapter 8.

[15] For further discussion on Manichaeism and Buddhism, see Vaziri, *Buddhism in Iran*, chapter 3.

Samarqand and Neishābur[16] whose ideas were known in Neishābur at the time of Khayyam, a city lying on the Silk Route.

And so, with all of these diverse perspectives likely affecting him, even though Khayyam was said to be the son of a Zoroastrian who converted to Islam and was thus a first-generation Muslim,[17] there is no trace of either his alleged paternal Zoroastrianism or of Islam in his poetry.

Regarding Khayyam's position against conventional Islamic belief, one of the earliest commentators on his life and poetry in twentieth-century Iran, Sādiq Hedāyat, believed Khayyam had refuted the power of the "Semitic God" who is capable of doing everything but had left humanity in despairing confusion about the purpose and direction of life.[18] The sweeping freethinkers such as Khayyam were known for tackling broader existential fronts, not just the abilities of the "Semitic God."

Instead, Khayyam maintained a scientific and philosophical life, preoccupying himself with Hellenic and Avicennian (and perhaps Indian) philosophies. Because of his unconventional views, however, he suspected others may lay a tag on him, so he composed a quatrain to reject all libelous speculations. He said essentially: everybody is suspicious of my creed; whether I am an unbeliever, or believer of some form of atheism, it really does not matter. "I am who I am." He considered such labeling as a lapse of judgment in those who misread him (*rubā'īs:* 104, 74, 75).

Khayyam must have certainly been a unique, compelling character. Unlike most learned people of the day, he was not interested in teaching any of his ideas to the public or to a large audience, and thus nobody would know his true

---

[16] Werner Sundermann, "Dīnāvarīya," *Encyclopaedia Iranica*, 1995, accessed Dec. 2010. http://www.iranicaonline.org/.

[17] Aminrazavi, *The Wine of Wisdom*, 19, Omar Ali Shah based on his contentious manuscript claims Khayyam was a Sufi master and asserts that he was born to Afghan parents from a Sufi community of Balkh. C. E. Bowen, "The Rubā'iyyāt of Omar Khayyam: A Critical Assessment of Robert Graves' and Omar Ali Shah's Translation," *Iran: British Institute of Persian Studies* 11 (1973): 63–73, Bowen debunks all the arbitrary assertions made by Omar Ali Shah and R. Graves; see also Aminrazavi, *The Wine of Wisdom*, 154–156.

[18] Cf. Sāiq Hedāyat, *Tarāneh-hāye Khayyam* (1313; Tehran: Entesharat Javidan, 1934), 22, 32, 50. The anti-Islamic or anti-Arab sentiment of Khayyam is what certain modern authors would like to emphasize, see also Friedrich Rosen, *Die Sinnsprüche Omars des Zeltmachers* (1919; Wiesbaden: Marixverlag, 2008), 132.

belief.[19] This distinctiveness, including his vegetarianism and celibacy, raised a few eyebrows among Muslims.[20] It is therefore not surprising that Khayyam kept his *rubā'īyyāt* a secret until after his death out of fear of the conformists on one hand, and simply because of his withdrawn personality on the other.[21]

From the impressions given by his quatrains, Khayyam is apparently not concerned about anti-religious thinking. Instead, he took a great interest in enhancing intellectual and rational thinking exercises. This rational position inherently debunked many archaic religious beliefs. His fusion of rational thinking and the pursuit of happiness was made in such a way that the knowledge of the world and its processes relinquished the pressure of constant personal judgments.

It has been argued that Khayyam's poetic adversarial views on religion were influenced by the Syrian poet Abul 'Alā al-Ma'arrī (973–1057), a blind, ascetic, strict vegan who had composed poetry against the Koranic teachings.[22] His parodies of Koranic verses as well as heaven and hell demonstrated his religious skepticism.[23] Khayyam's name was first mentioned in association

---

[19] Alireza Qaragozlu, *Omar Khayyam* (1381; Tehran: Entesharate Tarhe Nou, 2000), 12, 14, 20–21; see also Sādiq Hedāyat, "Muqqadame-yee bar Rubā'īyyāt-i Khayyam," in *Neveshtehā-ye Farāmoush Shodeh-i Sādiq Hedāyat*, edited by Maryam Dānā'ī Boromand, (Tehran: Mo'asseseh Entesharat Negah, 1376/1997), 58.

[20] Ja'afar Aghyani Chawoshi, "Āyā Khayyam va Abul 'Alā Ma'arrī Zandīq Budeh-and?" in *Nineteen Maqāleh dar bāreh Hakim Omar Khayyam Neishāburī* (Khurasan: Neishābur Shenāsī, n.d.), 6–7.

[21] Mohammad Mohammadian, "Der oblique Blick: Zum Verhältnis von Philosophie und Religion in den Robā"iyât von Omar Khayyâm," in *Atheismus im Mittelalter und in der Renaissance* (Wiesbaden: Harrassowitz Verlag, 1999), 99, 105.

[22] Even anti-religious poems and reputation of Abul 'Alā were widespread at the time of Nāsir Khosrau Qubādiānī. See *Safar Nāmeh* (1344; Tehran: Amir Kabir, 1965), 16. For the poems of Abul 'Alā Ma"arrī, *Ash'ār-e Abul 'Alā Ma'arrī*, trans. Amir Chenari (1385; Tehran: Zavvar, 2006).

[23] Due to his religious skepticism al-Ma"arrī goes on to write a parody of Koranic verses of which only the first third remains. Muhammad Abū al-Fadl Badran, "denn die Vernunft ist ein Prophet – Zweifel bei Abū'l-'Alā' al-Ma'arrī," in *Atheismus im Mittelalter und in der Renaissance*, ed. F. Niewöhner and O. Pluta (Wiesbaden: Harrassowitz Verlag, 1999), 78, 80–81. This parody was probably an imitation of the tenth-century Ibn Rāwandī's work of *Dāmigh* (*Refutation*), which was designed to discredit the miraculous style and content of the Koran. See Reynold Nicholson, *A Literary History of the Arabs* (New York: Charles Schreibner's Son, 1907), 375; Majid Fakhry, *A History of Islamic Philosophy* (1970; New York: Columbia University Press, 2004), 97. Then Abul 'Alā further moves on to make a mockery of heaven and hell in his book of *al-Ghofrān* (*Book of Forgiveness*).

with Abul 'Alā Ma'arrī by the twelfth-century philologist Az-Zamakhsharī. Az-Zamakhsharī mentioned that Khayyam, as a student visiting his classes, was familiar with the Syrian poet's Arabic stanzas.[24] Al-Ma'arrī is known for his rebellious position and empirical reasoning, which has a great deal in common with Khayyam's later writings. In particular, Al-Ma'arrī claimed that reason is humanity's prophet.[25] The incredible similarities in the themes which both poets treat, one in Arabic the other in Persian, lead us to suspect certain cross-influences. There is however one substantial difference between the two poets. From the attitudes reflected in their poetry, it can be asserted that Khayyam's optimism, hedonism, and world-affirming diverged from al-Ma'arrī's pessimistic, ascetic, and reclusive stance.

A Word About FitzGerald's Translation Mishap

Edward FitzGerald unleashed an unwarranted impression of Khayyam in 1859 with his quasi-translation of the *Rubā'īyyāt* into English. FitzGerald offered an extremely limited, distorted and unchallenged view of Khayyam's writings. Apart from incorrect translation, FitzGerald also derailed the meaning and the philosophical orientation of Khayyam's messages. (The French translation, which followed in 1867, though critical of FitzGerald, was itself not free from errors.[26]) Thus Khayyam's logic and lyric was highly inaccurately translated.

---

[24] Avery and Heath-Stubbs, *The Rubā'īyyāt of Omar Khayyam*, 18.

[25] Al-Ma'arrī espoused three conditions in regard to the relationship between human beings and God. First, the Supreme God remains inaccessible. Second, God shows no sympathy for humans and then occasionally decides to send angels and prophets to forbid things for them. The third condition is the staggering human rationality versus human foolishness. See Badran, "denn die Vernunft ist ein," 70–71. See also Ignaz Goldziher, "Abū-l-Alā al-Ma'arrī als Freidenker," *Zeitschrift der Deutschen Morgenländischen Gesellschaft* 29 (1875): 637–641; A. von Kremer," Philosophische Gedichte des 'Abū-l 'alā' Ma'arrī," *Zeitschrift der Deutschen Morgenländischen Gesellschaft* 38 (1884): 40–52.

[26] The image constructed of Khayyam through FitzGerald's translation was, however, challenged and argued by later works of J. B. Nicholas, *Les Quatrains de Khèyam, traduit de Persan* (1867), and T. S. Eliot, although not free from criticism. See Giuseppe Albano, "The Benefits of Reading the Rubáiyát of Omar Khayyám as Pastoral," *Victorian Poetry*, 46/1 (Spring 2008), 63, 65. J. B. Nicholas was the French consul in Rasht, Iran, see "Les Quatrains de Khèyam, traduits du Persan by J. B. Nicolas; Rubáiyát of Omar Khayyám,the Astronomer-Poet of Persia," *The North American Review*, 109/225 (Oct. 1869): 565–84; for T. S. Elliot, Khayyam was a great influence and source of his philosophical passion, but the pessimism transmitted through FitzGerald was criticized, see William H. Martin and Sandra Mason (eds.), *Edward FitzGerald's Rubáiyát of Omar Khayyám: A Famous Poem and Its Influence* (London: Anthem Press, 2011), 118; see also M. A. R. Habib, *The Early T. S.*

The discrepancy is noticed between the mindset of Khayyam and that of the translator, FitzGerald.²⁷ The sources that FitzGerald used for his free interpretation of Khayyam were problematic as well.²⁸ FitzGerald's English words and meanings depended more on his effort of rhyming and not the content of the poems. A poet such as FitzGerald had used his poetic license to change the original meaning and intent of Khayyam's poetry.

The translation also did not correspond to Khayyam's Persian words and messages. Peter Avery says of FitzGerald's translation: "His work is more in the nature of a fantasia than a translation. It is often very free and occasionally not precisely accurate."²⁹ Arthur J. Arberry also believed that FitzGerald shaped the translation of the *Rubā'īyyāt* according to his own poetical taste and the romantic demands of the Victorian era.³⁰ One can construe that FitzGerald was not a translator but instead created an "English Khayyam"³¹ rather than presenting an original "Persian Khayyam." Even the Indian guru Yogananda,³² who tried to make up for the *Rubā'īyyāt's* lack of moral teaching, he could not avoid using the very same words and the poor translation of FitzGerald. The translation of FitzGerald can be respected simply as an obsolete work of Orientalism, but definitely *not* as a reference to the intellectual pondering of Omar Khayyam.

Now before we delve into a model of Khayyam's philosophy, the time is well overdue to purge the stubborn labels of "hedonism" and "nihilism" attached

---

Elliot and Western Philosophy (Cambridge: Cambridge University Press, 1999), 161. Two German translations also appeared in the nineteenth century from Adolf Friedrich von Schack, *Strophen des Omar Chijam* (1878) and Friedrich Bodenstedt, *Die Lieder und Sprüche des Omar Chajjam* (1881).

27 See William Cadbury, "Fitzgerald's Rubáiyát as a Poem," *ELH* 34/4 (Dec. 1967), 541–563.
28 See Parichehr Kasra, "FitzGerald's Recasting of the Rubāiyāt," *Zeitschrift der Deutschen Morgenländischen Gesellschaft* 130 (1980), 458–459.
29 Avery and Heath-Stubbs, *The Rubā'īyyāt of Omar Khayyam*, 32.
30 A. J. Arberry, "Omar Khayyam," in *Nineteen Maqāleh dar bāreh Hakīm Omar Khayyam Neishāburī* (Khurasan: Neishābur Shenasi, n.d.), 89–91; see also A. J. Arberry, *The Rubaiyat of Omar Khayyam and Other Persian Poems* (London: Everyman's Library, 1954), vii.
31 See Ali Taslimi, *Rubā'ī-hāye Khayyam: Va Nazarīeh Kamīyyat-e Zamān* (1391; Tehran: Ketab Āmeh, 2012), 75–76.
32 It is not clear as to why Yogananda felt compelled to address the incoherence of FitzGerald's translation while he strangely did not have access to (nor the linguistic knowledge of) the original Persian of Omar Khayyam himself. See Yogananda, *The Wine of the Mystic*. Regarding Yogananda's interpretation, see also Aminrazavi, *The Wine of Wisdom*, 139.

to Khayyam and his *Rubā'īyyāt*. There is so much more to Khayyam than simply "carpe diem, bread and wine, and the emptiness of life."

Hedonism and Nihilism as Debatable

Let us begin by saying that in the past, some religious and ascetic traditions have frequently demonized and overblown self-indulgence or hedonism as sheer sensual joy, and therefore linked it with wicked immorality and heresy. Ironically, the longing to have an eternal and pleasurable life in Heaven in the Judeo-Christian-Islamic traditions itself can be seen as a disguised hedonistic rumination.

As for Khayyam, his approach to life is affirmatively hedonistic, but not in the sense of indulgent sensory pleasure without a deeper grounding in life matters. His hedonism is not an active, non-thinking, pleasure-seeking enterprise. It is rather a non-reactive state of awareness, a trouble-free state, a thankful and persevering state. The pleasure and "hedonism" that Khayyam expounds on can be extrapolated to be analogous to what the Buddha,[33] Epicurus,[34] and Lucretius[35] or even Stoics expressed. Such hedonism by and large implies to a psychological wellness, trouble-free mind, and a spirited sense of governing one's pleasure in life.

Khayyam's poetic metaphors such as "drinking wine" may initially sound like an active sensual pleasure, but it is simply a poetical metaphor for escalating one's own body-mind to a tranquil and unperturbed state when life takes its challenging turns. The wine metaphor is equal to grasping the pleasure of living here and now and dropping the anxiety of tomorrow.

---

[33] Buddha's idea of pleasure as mentioned in the Pāli Canons was *sukkha* as opposed to suffering dukkha.

[34] Epicurus's notion of pleasure, *hédone*, is basically an unperturbed state of mind, *ataraxia*.

[35] Lucretius being the follower of Epicurean school of pleasure had the same idea as Epicurus. For an interesting introduction comparing Khayyam's and Lucretius' views, the author of the following book puts the ideas of Lucretius creatively in the *rubā'ī* form. See W. H. Mallock, Lucretius on Life and Death: In the Metre of Omar Khayyam, 1900. See also George Sarton in 1927. Sarton in brief makes suggestion that Khayyam's philosophy is similar to that of Lucretius and Voltaire, in *Introduction to the History of Science: From Homer to Omar Khayyam*, Vol. 1 (Baltimore, MD: The Williams and Wilkins Co., 1927), 760. Sadiq Hedāyat also suggests Khayyam's philosophy with Epicurus, Lucretius, Shakespeare, Goethe, and Schopenhauer, *Tarāneh-hāye Khayyām*, 16. He also mentioned Çārvāka's dialectics of not knowing the maker of the Universe with our limited senses, and there is no life after death, thus let us cultivate happiness, 30–31.

Furthermore, the idea of *carpe diem*, "seize the day," although it is a fitting authentication of living a joyful life every day, is too superficial to use for Khayyam. It is too limiting, because the mind requires a deeper and more panoramic map of life than just the pleasure of today. In this map of life, which begins with the birth of things and ends in death, all conventional contracts within a lifetime must be compatible with the last "contract" of death. So, the attitude of *carpe diem* must carry with it a more farsighted rationality, and a more responsible conduit in order to view the beginning, the middle, and end of all things. Thus, the *carpe diem* of Khayyam represents a broader consciousness, more of "let the day proceed as it will, and move on in serenity" rather than enthusiastically clinging to the day. The notion of *hédoné* or pleasure in the Khayyamian model is not an action-based pleasure but it is in one's insightful perspective-interpretation of life circumstances. It is a maintaining of a quiet mind which is the highest pleasure. The dialectics of Khayyam's philosophy of pleasure can be described as resolving the paradoxes of happy-sadness, religion-disbelief, past-future, and birth-death by living outside of them in an authentic state of nowness, a state of never finishing today. Khayyam's poetic metaphors such as, 'drink wine,' 'live joyfully,' 'happy heart,' and 'sit in delight,' are the solutions to the dualities that the human mind has developed outside of a true reality of existence.

The second unfortunate misconstruction about Khayyam regards negative nihilism.[36] Generally, nihilism is associated with the sense of life as being purposeless and meaningless, ending in death. Khayyam's use of the word *hīch* (nothingness or emptiness) in his poetry may be the source of such interpretation. But this is largely a misreading of the term *hīch*. This misreading dislocates his larger reflection on the theme of nothingness. The primary and most common use of the word *hīch* is not for nihilism per se, referring to purposeless living, but rather a dialectical reductionism: after death, the individual disintegrates into a "non-individual" and to the minutest elemental level. It implies that everything ceaselessly emerges into existence from no-thing, and it also repetitively vanishes into no-thing, or nothingness. As Khayyam put it, the natural process of rising and falling does not stop anywhere along the way; all phenomena regardless of their size and lifespan are destined to disintegrate and lose their individuality, from microorganisms to galaxies. *Hīch*, therefore, is an epistemological *awareness* of the single destiny of all things in the factory of existence.

---

[36] An interesting and engaging article has been dedicated to Khayyam's nihilism from the Western point of view. See Mostafa Abedinifard, "Nihilism dar Rubāʿī-haye Khayyami," *Faslnameh ʿElmi-Pazhoheshi*, 3/10 (Summer 1389/2010), 143–74.

On a psychological level, because the end of all existing phenomena is nothingness or *hīch*, Khayyam suggested dropping all fantasies of immortality and all thoughts of an afterlife, whether it meant the fear of hell or the striving for heaven. He rejected an eternal individual life. Importantly, this is not a negative connotation about the present life. Instead, the concept of *hīch* offers clarity on the work of natural processes – the non-stop recurrence. This understanding can orient individuals in exploring the reality of things without being misled. In this vein, Khayyam warned against viewing one's own personal biography with too much self-importance. The fatal end renders one's life story valueless (*hīch*) along with all the other perished individuals and entities, millennia after millennia. And since all things end in *hīch*, Khayyam advises, be aware of the opportunity and participate in the celebration of nowness before the end nears.

A secondary misreading of *hīch* is that it suggests the idea of a complete "void" after death. Yet there is no such thing as absolute nothingness in Khayyam's view, nor was it the conception adopted by Democritus, Epicurus, or Lucretius. Instead, in death, the four permanent elements of water, earth, air, and fire survive, so there is no complete void. Khayyam's notion of *hīch* implies that almost "nothing disappears" in death. Khayyam's atomism is clear in his quatrains when he expressed the regeneration of the world occurring through the salvaging and reusing of the same old atoms of decomposed corpses, carried "in the mouths of ants" (*rubā'ī*: 40).

Thus, Khayyam's notion of nothingness or *hīch* concludes that there is an annihilation of all forms and identities, even though their *atoms* survive and swirl around to form new entities. Things do not end up in an absolute vacuum, nor does their raw material disappear completely after demolition. Khayyam's *hīch* refers to the nullification of the biological constitution that was once enjoyed. *Hīch* is neither nihilism nor total emptiness but rather a transition from identity to no identity, and from some-thing to no-thing, from the old-thing to new-thing. *Hīch* does not mean the world is emptied of its old molecules and fragments. The earth and cosmos do not import raw material from "elsewhere"; they reuse the old material creatively, over and over. Hence, there is never nothingness or a void in the universe. *Hīch* simply means the individual constitution is lost. Nevertheless, Khayyam himself pondered about the frivolous process of construction-demolition without a particular purpose or direction. He focused, however, on cultivating pleasure instead of pondering about the cosmic purpose and direction.

The notion of *hīch* can also be correlated with the Indian-Vedanta-Buddhist notion of *maya*, meaning fleeting phenomenon or illusion in Sanskrit. According to *maya* all phenomena always remain unstable, subject to constant change until complete obliteration. Phenomena did not exist before, but they will arise, and then they will cease to exist at some later point, as if they never existed at all. Regardless of the speed of change, the processes of decline, decay, and disappearance are inevitable in everything. These dynamic movements mimic an *illusion*, or *maya:* entities whatever they might be in a "snapshot" come from nothingness and pass away to nothingness. This impermanent picture of phenomena is referred to as *maya*, an elusive perception of objects that plunge into the realm of nothingness or *hīch*. The Khayyamian intention of *hīch* is just that: an object which once was, is not anymore. The biological perspective of *hīch* also points to the complete dissolution of human consciousness, with its childhood memories, experiences, and other recollections, not just the dissolution of the carnal body alone.

Even though each generation of humans seems to be new or even "foreign" to the world, Khayyam's clarity leaves no room for an ambivalent relationship with the transient world. Through his invitation to move from an impulsive anthropocentric view to an empirical and universal approach to life, Khayyam intended to keep human emotionality and confusion at bay. His genius also lies in bridging the mechanics of existence with human reason, and thus disengaging from any serious misreading of how things work. His holistic model invites his readers to consider that the collapse and reprocessing of existence is not personal but is an all-inclusive orchestration of the universe.

Having provided an introduction to some of Khayyam's ideas, it is time to scrutinize his quatrains for their philosophy as well as the guidelines they offer for governing one's own cognitive insights through experiential inspection. Khayyam's quatrains are not necessarily didactic like those of Lucretius, nor do they follow a preset and sequential flow. They are simple, lucid, potent, lyrical, and persuasive and provide a bedrock for the tangible landscape of life. So, the task here is to rearrange, deepen, and connect the logic of these poems systematically into a methodic and accessible model.

The objective of such a model is to view the uninterrupted cycle of construction and demolition of existence without personalizing its mechanism. By understanding this, Khayyamian philosophy can be viewed as a model of clarity. This model of existence directs perplexed minds to live life without misreading the implications of birth and death on the walls of every corner of existence. It is to keep people away from their ancient tendencies toward the supernatural by exempting themselves from the rest of nature. In the Khayyamian perspective, the mind can open up to a broader view rather than just being entangled with one's own personal and constricted obsessions. Fanatical beliefs and information about the world, the self, an afterlife, and other such matters are rendered into unimportant ambiguous human gossip. He replaced beliefs and misinformation with a new set of invigorating perspectives in his quatrains.

Finally, Khayyam proposes free will to delight in life at one's own pace in the face of an uncontrollable and deterministic universe. And so, having the knowledge of this dynamic model in mind, the Khayyamian message of *pleasure* becomes more imperative and brings it closer to the heart as the path to skillful living.

***

The Model: The Confluence of a Five-Spoked Wheel

By taking a different approach to Khayyam's poetry, reading it with a new awareness and looking for philosophical themes, a metaphorical model of existence begins to emerge. His quatrains begin to reveal five thematic categories. We will explore these categories and assess how they are interrelated to create a dynamic and powerful model of existence:

1. Construction
2. Becoming
3. Nowness-Pleasure
4. Return to Atoms
5. Nothingness

When we look at how these five categories are related to each other, we can see that each one leads to the next in the cycle of existence. We can create a model of an incessantly spinning apparatus of existence, each category representing an invisible spoke on a spiraling, whirling wheel. The conceptual spokes spin, each leading to the next, an unremitting and steady round of existence from the first spoke of construction to the last spoke of nothingness and oblivion. Granted, the use of a wheel for analogizing Khayyam's elegant poetry sounds rather coarse. Five petals of a flower would have been more poetic. The choice of a wheel as the vehicle for this model, however, provides a better representation for a dynamic universe: a wheel is constantly moving just as existence is constantly changing. Existence could not be modeled with five identical, finite petals of a flower.

While applying the idea of a wheel[37] to Khayyam's philosophy (and his poetry) seems crude, the notion of a wheel is perhaps not completely far-fetched nor alien to the Khayyamian depiction of the universe. He in fact, in his poetry, refers to the mechanism of existence *Charkh*, "Wheel." As an astronomer, mathematician, and the founder of a magnificent solar calendar that he calculated one thousand years out, Khayyam was intimately familiar with the turning of the cosmos and the orbiting motions of its celestial bodies. His philosophical ideas are the product of his scientific and mathematical mind, rather than being matters of idealistic formulations. Based on the structure and relationships among the ideas presented in his poetry, Khayyam could have easily imagined a turning wheel when he articulated the flow of the processes of existence starting with birth, growing up, adulthood, death and ending in complete annihilation of the human body.

Let us briefly introduce each of the five spokes before exploring them in more depth alongside Khayyam's quatrains:

1. *Construction:* The first spoke represents the causes and conditions that lead to the birth or rise of things (*āmadan* = coming) and their natural growth (and implicitly includes the engine of demolition or death that will inevitably come later).

2. *Becoming:* The second is the process of growth and becoming that has no identifiable maker-destroyer. Khayyam speaks of the universe as the "pot-maker" in mixing the "clay" in order to make a new "pot." (*kuzeh-gari* = pot-making). With this, he is in line with process philosophy and the scientific notion of *process* instead of *creation*, or *becoming* instead of *being*.[38] Things do not suddenly burst into existence; their becoming is due to change and transmutation. In the Khayyamian system, the operator of the universe or a lawful universe keeps repeating an unstoppable cycle.

---

[37] The idea and model of wheel is simply introduced by this author in order to give Khayyam's veiled poetry a philosophical vibration.

[38] There is a league of mostly modern philosophers, particularly Alfred North Whitehead, who have described process philosophy by proposing an organic process of *becoming* rather than just static *being*. See his seminal work: *Process and Reality* (1929). The dialectics of *Becoming* have had an Indian and Hellenic precedent – the dialectics of Madhyamika, the Buddhist school of the Middle Way.

3. *Nowness:* This realm is the product of the previous spokes (analogous to the Buddhist notion of causes and conditions). This third, middle spoke represents the present, the fleeting realm of existence in which human beings and other objects live *right now*. For humans, this surfacing "middle stage" represents nowness (*hāl* or *dam*), the unique opportunity of the coupling of a person with existence and the opportunity to live a life of natural pleasure. Khayyam uses the allegory of "wine" as a reminder to transcend the duality of sadness-happiness and rejoice in "nowness."

4. *Return to Atoms:* The fourth spoke is the time of demolition, death, a stage in which objects return to the basic atoms (*zarreh, khāk*) and particles of their original construction.

5. *Nothingness:* The fifth spoke is the final blow to the identity of the previously existing objects. It is the spoke of traceless nothingness (*hīch*), a complete obliteration of any previously held individuality. Identity ceases to be. Even though the elements of the physical body do not disappear, no trace of beings whether memory, consciousness, or thought survives the decisive last spoke. No individual object after its obliteration can ever return to the original state – heaven-and-hell and the resurrection of the bodies or reincarnation of the souls are discarded in the Khayyamian worldview.

The Rationale for the Wheel

In a more philosophical context, the five-spoked model of the wheel can also represent the five features of philosophy: ontology (construction), epistemology (becoming), ethics (pleasure of nowness), physics (back to atoms), and metaphysics (nothingness). These five aspects all come into play in the entire existence as well as in a human life. People grapple with this spinning wheel in one way or another.

The dynamic imagery of a wheel describes the constant movement and shifting in the mechanics of existence. Although the five spokes are independent in their individual utility, when spinning they all blend and turn into one single indistinguishable unit in the unremitting motion of the rise and fall of birth and death. The unit in motion contains two main constituents: the physical elements (visible components) and the metaphysical elements (the intangible processes of degeneration and regeneration due to invisible factors such as time, temperature, motion, and pressure). As a result of this spinning, the reality of existence comes into being, and gradually slips out of existence through aging, entropy, decay, and death. Through motion and change, each spoke performs its task and the stages pass on to the next and so on; the holistic wheel in this arrangement keeps spinning for every single object of creation.

The allegory of a wheel applies no matter the form or size of the organism, from the largest to the smallest; the mechanism of the spinning five-spoked system is the same for everything. Khayyam draws our attention to the rise and demise of each human being as visible ontological evidence of this process. By extrapolating from this highly accessible observation of human life, one can also see the wheel at work with objects with much shorter life spans such as flowers, bacteria, and insects, as well as far-flung, enormous, nonliving, slow-change objects such as stars and planets.

By looking at the leaves on a tree, we can see how this model of the spinning spokes demonstrates the stages of existence. In the spring, the wheel begins to "spin," the first spoke of *construction* goes into action, and buds emerge. By late spring, the buds have matured through the second spoke of *becoming*; the leaves are lush and full and green. From late spring through summer the leaves can enjoy their existence and take pleasure in the sunshine, the breeze, and the birds. The wheel continues to spin as time passes, and as the fourth spoke of *return to atoms* takes over, the leaves lose their vitality and fall to the ground; they disintegrate and are absorbed into the soil. With the final spin of the wheel in winter, the fifth spoke of *nothingness* takes over; no trace of the individual leaves remains. They have gone into oblivion and have already been forgotten by nature, but their atoms exist, having been transformed into other forms, other materials. The next spring the cycle is repeated with a new set of leaves; the wheel spins again as the generation changes. In this way, the process of the wheel is obvious and perceptible as leaves on a tree come and go out of existence each year. This process is for each leaf to enjoy the nowness of existence before being doomed. Critically, this impermanent and recurring process has no identifiable maker or destroyer.

Through the five spokes of the wheel, two broad levels of reasoning can be attributed to Khayyam's rational thinking. The *first* level of reasoning is the human cognitive faculty of observing nature and the environment with the capacity to understand the rise and fall of things as much as can be perceived. Observation allows humans, without resorting to incredulous beliefs and fantasies, to assess the indiscriminate rise, fall, and demise of all animate and inanimate entities around them. Through this observation, one can corroborate the causes and conditions as well. For example, one can reasonably follow the cause of pregnancy and how a fetus is formed. One can also understand how death occurs – whether a prey is killed by a predator or whether death results from disease or being struck by a cobra or from hunger or from other causes.

In understanding the causes and conditions of construction-demolition on a simpler mechanical level, one realizes there is no hidden hand, or any capricious randomness. It is important to bear in mind that the physical world did not come into existence in a sudden flash of light nor will it all abruptly stop existing, but rather its objects come in and go out of existence in different time intervals.

By this reasoning, Khayyam abandoned the credulity of randomness or divine selective interventions, because he believed in the predictability and changelessness of the fundamental laws of physics.

The *second* level of reasoning, something deeply rooted in Khayyam's quatrains, is to keep emotionalism at bay in dealing with life matters, particularly death. To Khayyam, this psychological awareness of life's panorama from the birth of things to their death enables a person to veer away from one's own frozen predicament between birth and death into a stream of joyful living and free will on an everyday basis. Khayyam was aware of human error in the clash of free will and the physical and impersonal determinism that can produce irrational results and therefore unhappiness. So, in short, Khayyam projected a reasonable autonomy within the permissible boundaries that allow a person to maintain a joyful state in life without a false hope about the determinism and the end of life. The beginning and the end do not fluctuate. Khayyam, however, recognized that it is the emotion of fear and uncertainty about death and the afterlife that causes psychological mayhem and spoils the peace at hand.

Combining these two set of reasonings, therefore, the "philosophy of tranquility" proposed by Khayyam entails having a panoramic view of the cycle of existence in which one can more easily find mental peace. The wheel model shows the destiny of all things from their construction to their end, which is complete oblivion; this clarity has the highest value to Khayyam because it is the source of liberation.

What draws his attention the most is the non-repeatable, entirely unique construction of oneself in this massive and uncontrollable universal juggernaut, an opportunity which cannot be taken for granted nor treated with distress and anxiety. Khayyam urged that before we decompose into *khāk* or dust, *zarreh* or atoms, and before we return to traceless nothingness (*hīch*), we should take pleasure in this transient "middle" station (the third spoke of nowness).

In the texts that follow, the original Persian *Rubā'īyyāt* of Khayyam is translated and interpreted. Sometimes the stanzas are paraphrased by using the subject pronoun of "I" when Khayyam is speaking in the first person. Other times his poems appear in literal translation within quotation marks.[39] Thus, this work is not a verbatim poetic translation, but is designed to highlight the philosophical aspects of Khayyam's poems.

Let us now embrace and delve into this new Khayyamian model of the five-spoked wheel of existence, according to his *Rubā'īyāt*.[40]

1. Construction

Khayyam disparaged those who are obsessed with solving the metaphysical riddle of emerging phenomena and the origin of all things. Although

---

[39] All poems are freshly translated from the original Persian by this author.
[40] The following analysis will be based on 143 Persian *rubā'īs* presented by Hedāyat's *Tarāneh-hāye Khayyām*, Tehran: Entesharat Javidan, reprinted from 1313/1934 version with almost one third marked with asterisk as potentially inauthentic. A 7-year later Iranian source is M. A. Foroughi and Qasim Ghani, *Rubā'īyāt Khayyam*, Tehran: Entesharat Asatir, 1371/1972 (first published 1941) with 178 *rubā'īs*. The twenty scattered historical sources of the *rubā'īs*, see Qaragozlu, *Omar Khayyam*, 190–1. As for the authenticity of the quatrains actually being composed by Khayyam, it is hard to verify them all for their historicity. On the actual number and authenticity of *rubā'īs*, there are all kinds of speculations. Denison Ross, "Omar Khayyam," *Bulletin of the School of Oriental Studies* 4/3 (1927), 433, indicates that the number of *rubā'īs* can reach 800. Some debates explore whether some of the *rubā'īs* attributed to Khayyam were actually composed by Ibn Sīnā (Avicenna), but those claims cannot be supported with evidence, see Soheil Afnan, *Avicenna: His Life and Work*, (London: George Allen & Unwin LTD, 1958), 82; [The poetry of Ibn Sīnā seems to follow the style of his Mu'tazila mentor, Abdul Jabbār from Hamadān, see Frank Griffel, *Apostasie und Toleranz im Islam: Die Entwicklung zu al-Gazālīs Urteil gegen die Philosophie und die Reaktion der Philosophen* (Leiden: Brill, 2000), 151–52.] Rothfeld, *Umar Khayyam and His Age*, 14. It is indicated that the Paris manuscript of 1448, next to Khayyam's shows a few *rubā'īs* to be from Ibn Sīnā, see Christian Rempis, *Beiträge Zur Hayyam-Forschung* (Leipzig: Deutsche Morgenländische Gesellschaft, 1937), 14; see also Friedrich Rosen, "Zur Textfrage der Vierzeiler Omar's des Zeltmachers (Rubā'īāt-i-"Umar-i-Khayyām)," *Zeitschrift der Deutschen Morgenländischen Gesellschaft* 80 (1926), 312–13. Aminrazavi, however, suggests that we must abandon the search for the composers of the uncertain *rubā'īs* attributed to Khayyam and instead establish the fact that the consistency in the message of the poems compel us to categorize them in the "Khayyamian school of thought' – that the message is more important and takes precedence over the messenger. Aminrazavi, *The Wine of Wisdom*, 13–14, 97–8; Ali Dashtī indicates the number of the *rubā'īs* increases in the historical writings, see Ali Dashtī, *Damī bā Khayyam* (Tehran: Entesharat Asatir, 1377/1998), 22–30. This means for us, Khayyam as a person is not under scrutiny here, but his school of philosophy is.

flamboyant religious and mythical assertions claiming to have solved this enigma have emerged in cultures from the primitive human history onward, Khayyam did not engage with any of them. Like the Buddha, he dismissed the mystery of trying to know where everything comes from, and shifted his attention to the larger picture of humans as miniscule entities in this colossal endeavor of existence. He formulated his thoughts on the premise of a deterministic apparatus, which is beyond the human domain. The "operation" of this apparatus is clear to Khayyam. In each cycle the universe constructs something new and elegant, it then breaks it down and reduces it to the original elements again. This process solely depends on the existing raw material without any new raw material imported from "somewhere" else. Khayyam was absolutely clear about this dynamic of recycling. This is a *physics* of nullification through constructing and demolishing and infusing creativity each time around. Khayyam's use of metaphor of pot-maker points to an unknown source of construction and becoming. This representation of pottery points to a continual and creative making of new things ('pots') from the recycling of the old raw material.

Despite being an astronomer-mathematician, Khayyam's philosophy of existence left out scientific curiosities. He by no means claimed to know the metaphysics behind the generation, flux and transmutations of things. Instead, Khayyam challenged those who have claimed to know. He did not acknowledge any distinction between natural and human chemistry; they are one and the same, following identical laws of making and unmaking. In his compositions, he pointed out that the reality of physics begins with the four permanent elements from which all things are crafted and come into being. It is a singular and enchanted birth (*rubāʿīs:* 29, 32).

Khayyam took a challenging position against the belief of a traditional creator god. He calls the mystery, *dahr,* the material world itself. Although defiant, he replaced the idea of god with numerous rational insights and set the intellectual dynamic in motion for innovative thinking in the Islamic and Persianate world.

Yet Khayyam pointed cynically to the lofty claims of those who think the cosmos has an actual creator. If this is the case, then the creator who laid the foundation of this earth and heaven caused much aching in the hearts of those who now lie in the graveyard of existence (*rubāʿī:* 24). The construction without an anthropocentric purpose is only the work of emotionless cosmos. So, for Khayyam, as he explained in a quatrain, the reality of endless spinning does not carry any particular meaning, nor does the cosmos seem to be nervous by collapsing its own stars and giving their places to newer ones (*rubāʿī:* 33). Human life is only a shred of a greater example that lies on the fringes of this massive juggernaut of existence. Khayyam is crystal clear in putting in context the larger picture of the moving, churning stars in relation to human life, which is nothing but a subservient shadow of this massive enterprise (*rubāʿī:* 105). He attempted to remove humans from the center of attention by saying that the dynamic and manifold domain of existence has been well-maintained before we came into existence and would not be perturbed without having us around (*rubāʿīs:* 51). In one way or another, there will never be any extinction of reality; it is we who needs to change perspective and put away our sorrow. The joy of being here is the supreme goal before the sun of our body sets (*rubāʿīs:* 138).

The central push of Khayyam here was to criticize the errors in the minds of our human ancestors for not having realized this massive and inalterable law of existence. Out of one single giant reservoir of material, the factory of existence produces versatile forms, which are in fact fragments of the same system with no special priority of one over another. As Khayyam portrayed it, the drop of water goes back to the ocean, the atom of earth returns to its source, and human life, like the life of a fly, comes in and goes out of reality in the same way (*rubāʿī:* 41). As every wise person knows, life with its splendid decorations is not just for and about humans. If this were the case, then there would be a friendlier treatment of those came before us and those who shall come after us (*rubāʿī:* 45). There is no rational explanation for the symmetry of this process. Khayyam's reflection daringly admitted that "no religion, no Islam, no theology or search for the truth" can explain this (*rubāʿī:* 104).

Khayyam spoke adamantly: There is no other choice except to surrender to the principle of a predetermined cosmos, therefore "I cannot be more than what I already am" (*rubāʿīs:* 30). He penned this by saying, it is curious that there are so many rituals in the synagogues and the mosques in order to change the rules of the universe. People convince themselves of reward in heaven and punishment in hell. According to him, those believers need to understand that they cannot override the carvings on the wall of existence (*rubāʿīs:* 31).

Besides being replete with concise imagery, Khayyam's poetic philosophy regarding this topic is also full of sarcasm against those who have preoccupied themselves with the puzzle of the world's origin and its construction and where it is heading. He cast off and abandoned even the most flamboyant language attempting to decipher the mystery. Each group, he inferred, has been absorbed in its own esoteric interpretation, but have been unable to produce any evidence to solve the puzzle. All assertions have perished with those who championed them (*rubāʿī:* 14). Khayyam finds it bizarre how people during their short stay in the world can somehow know whether the world has a "creator" or not. Let us assume, Khayyam alleged, one is right and proves the other wrong. Nonetheless, our imminent mortality renders all assertions void again. The solution is simpler: leave behind all anticipation by grasping the life that is within reach – wine and joy (*rubāʿī:* 93).

Khayyam reasonably admitted that human feelings and the search for purpose in life are part of our psychic makeup, but at the same time he warned against the cosmic tyranny that knows no boundary between its laws and human emotions. He said that the uttering of "good or bad" is completely useless in this robust and endless cosmic mechanism (*rubāʿī:* 26). Khayyam declared both qualities ('good and bad') as having already been intertwined and determined by the turning wheel; there is no need to intellectualize it (*rubāʿī:* 34). To appease our overriding joy at the event of birth and the inevitable personal anxiety and fear of death, Khayyam deftly pointed out that even massive galactic entities that come into being in an unknown way are also unable to avoid or stop this endless revolution and collapse. If the cosmos could itself stop this construction-demolition, it surely would. In other words, we and the cosmos journey on the same ship of existence; we just embark and disembark at different intervals.

2. Becoming

Following the process of Construction, we come to the second level of Khayyam's discourse. In our model, the second spoke of the spinning wheel is responsible for the dynamic *fluctuation* and *change* of all cosmic and natural processes. Traditional religions tended to attribute the *processes* of the world to gods or mythical beings. But Khayyam took a challenging position against the belief of a traditional creator god in charge of such processes. He replaced the idea of god with numerous insights and set the intellectual dynamic in motion for innovative thinking in the Islamic and Persianate world, using powerful allegories to demonstrate how the material world flows naturally, following its own natural laws, without the hand of god or any other being.

The ancient world prior to humans seems to have operated properly without human consciousness. With the arrival of humans, none of the laws of the cosmos appear to have changed, except that religious and mythological claims came into existence. Khayyam takes us inside a "godless" material engine that continues its function no matter what humans perceive, or think they perceive. Although many alterations and modifications in the world are detectable, the inner operating mechanisms of the world such as temperature, motion, time, pressure and so on, are inapparent. The human experience is the trajectory of birth, growth, decay, and death, all of which can be detected, and yet the very vibrant fundamental mechanism remains hidden from the sight. Is it god who makes humans age, their bones deteriorate, their hair turn gray, and then finally succumb to death? How does the mechanism of Spring bring fresh green leaves on the trees and then by Autumn cause them to become yellow and fall off?

The quatrains treating this subject are precise, simple, and cogent. One of Khayyam's most powerful metaphors casts the material universe as the "pot-maker" (*kuzeh-gar-e dahr*) that crafts and embellishes all kinds of "pots," (becoming) and after a while smashes them into the smallest possible pieces, time and time again. It is important to recognize that the "pot-maker" in Khayyamian quatrains is not "god," but is an allegory for the mysterious dynamics following the same set of laws in the cosmos and nature that "make" things, let them be for a while and "destroys" them over and over. Nobody has seen or can figure out by which force(s) the making, becoming and unmaking takes place – although religions conveniently attribute it to a god-figurehead. But Nature or the material universe (*dahr*) meanwhile has no central headquarters, nor obvious traceable localized intelligence. Khayyam undoubtedly recognized the mystery, saying that the enigma of existence is as if things emerge from the ocean and submerge again to its floor and no one knows how or why! (*rubā'ī:* 42).

Khayyam by challenging the creationist theology, stated we all become and die in this anonymous physical process and become raw material for the next construction. In one *rubā'ī*, he allegorically called the world a "pot factory" and humans the "pots." The 2,000 pots anxiously look around and whisper, "Has anyone seen the pot-maker?" The fascinating questions persist: who is the pot-maker, pot-buyer, and where is the pot-seller anyway? (*rubā'ī:* 73).

The process of becoming, beginning with no identity and going to identity and then back to no identity is the work of the material world or the pot-maker of the universe. Khayyam's fictional pot-maker constantly needs clay for his new pots. But this pot-maker only has a fixed amount of raw material to work with. In manufacturing newer pots, the pot-maker has to demolish the old ones to make new clay to throw at the pottery wheel. Khayyam is quite clear that the pot-maker does not discern between one old pot and another; all old phenomena must be smashed and turned into clay regardless. The vigorous beginning in the youth is deceitful; the bitter truth of the matter comes only at the end. No matter how dear we appear to the world, the pot-maker waits for our turn to come to demolish us as it has done with all the others (*rubā'īs:* 39, 43).

In other poems, the pot-maker uses the "clay" of a human body to make a wine cup. In this allegory, the cup represents the human body and wine is the joyful mind. But also, at the same time, the allegory implies the transference of raw material from one animate to another inanimate thing. The wine cup voices these words to a person: "I was once you, and one day you'll be me" (*rubāʿī:* 67). Khayyam took this to a higher level by showing how inconsequential the human perception is about one's own body with all its sensual experiences; after death it all becomes irrelevant. The body of a man is turned into a goblet, and his arm, which once had cuddled the neck of a darling concubine, becomes the handle of the goblet (*rubāʿī:* 72).

He cynically asks whether the pot-maker cares to know that some of his "pots" have held supreme positions in the workshop. The hierarchy seems to be neglected as well. The "pious," the "beautiful and moon-faced," and the "kings" are put in the same category, or on the same shelf, with the "beggars." Indiscriminately, all are turned into one cluster of clay under the feet of the pot-maker, preparing it for the construction of new pots. It is an existential callousness to witness a clay from the head, hand, and fingers of a once a majestic king indifferently treated on a pottery wheel (*rubāʿī:* 70). It is even more preposterous when the master pot-maker crafts a new pot from the king's skull mixed with the beggar's hand, a distasteful thought for a king[41] (*rubāʿī:* 71).

Khayyam pointed to the capriciousness of this "creator" and the process of becoming. In his allegorical style, Khayyam pretended that "god" is a perfect "painter." Khayyam complained, this painter painted me in such a rush. After the painting job was done, the painter then fervently wiped me off without any idea of why he painted me in the first place, other than to add to my undeserved confusion (*rubāʿīs:* 1, 2). Khayyam then imagined a debate with the painter, exclaiming, If I were worthy of the art why would you remove me? If you weren't pleased and I didn't fulfill your criteria, then whose imperfection would it be, mine or yours? (*rubāʿī:* 11).

In order to jolt his readership, Khayyam takes a courageous leap: is coming and departing from the world significant at all? To whom would this matter the most, and what is the purpose of this amusement? (*rubāʿī:* 3). This incessant making and destroying are disconcerting to the human mind. When something is made and it is a joyful creation, then why destroy it, unless the maker is vehemently angry or intoxicated? Khayyam mused over the contradiction: If constructing something comes from sweet love, does destroying it come from abhorrence? (*rubāʿī:* 44). Is this a circus, he asks, and we are simply the puppets for a theatrical performance in the hands of the magician? It appears we are taken out of the box for a short act; once the show has ended, we are then put away in the box of oblivion (*sandouq-e ʿadam*) (*rubāʿī:* 50).

---

[41] This allegory may have been extracted from a Buddhist *Jataka* (Buddha's previous birth stories), for cross-references see Vaziri, *Buddhism in Iran*, 47–8.

In hypothesizing about the matter, he says that if we have to deal with this incomprehensible predicament on a human level, he would run the affairs of the cosmos differently. He proposed that "if I had been the maker of the world like god (*yazdān*), I would have first gotten rid of the present world, and then I would have made a pioneering world in which everyone could just celebrate life in pure pleasure" (*kām*) (*rubāʿī*: 25). In imagining being an ideal god, Khayyam longs to make a world where humans and non-humans would be spared from sudden death, savage killing, earthquakes, floods, and other calamities. Having projected his ideal world, he in his poetry captured the scenario of the involuntary construction-demolition of the dynamic world. Khayyam sealed his case by disclosing that the passing of time during our youth and adulthood is so insidiously slow that we struggle to pinpoint how it all started and how it is all coming to an end (*rubāʿī*: 35). Khayyam's main goal, however, was to caution his readership to drop all inefficient approximations about the identifiable *producer* of the world and instead focus on the wonderful *product*, which is to be savored each time around.

As much as the wheel spins slowly, even imperceptibly from our perspective, at some point the blade of demolition will take each human, each creation, out of existence. Until then, the coming third spoke is kind enough to allow us to live in peace and joy for a finite period of time.

3. Nowness – Pleasure

This is the most applicable segment in the Khayyamian philosophy. The third spoke of the wheel brings the new constructions to the surface in order to enjoy their generation and their turn to be in the world. 'Now' is to be valued before the wheel of existence tosses everything out of existence once again. Nowness is the philosophy of mind and pleasure, and Khayyam was an enthusiastic proponent.

His dialectics focused on removing the duality and fluctuations between happiness and sadness. In order to attain a level of serenity, Khayyam had to eliminate the paradox and constant opposition of pain-and-pleasure. Khayyam was aware that the apparent contradictions of past and future, or pain and pleasure are found in the human mind. His outstanding poetical effort aims to free the human mind from this duality and bring into focus the reality of things. By providing humans with such a roadmap of existence, he encourages deeper understanding along with savoring the momentary time given to each one of us.

The nature of existence itself is neutral regarding the experience of "pain and pleasure," but the dichotomy seems to dominate the human mind and triggers much ambivalence. Keeping the dichotomy of pain and pleasure in mind, the Khayyamian version of enjoying pleasure or converting pain into pleasure has three elements. The first is the kind of knowledge about existence that brings clarity and tranquility to mind. This knowledge is almost like reading the mind of existence even before it acts or fluctuates. The second is to delight in the psycho-physical realm by enjoying the beauty of nature and the privilege of being in the world as well as savoring bodily comforts such as drinking water when thirsty, eating food when hungry, and sleeping when tired. The third is the state of life that one experiences when there are no specific difficulties, confrontations, or pain. This subtle state of pleasure can be mistakenly labeled as "boredom" (especially in the modern world). But in a deeper sense, this state of pleasure can be appreciated when one does not crave anything further. In other words, the state of suchness and being, in itself, is a pure state of pleasure without anything additional being needed. By using the allegory of 'drink wine', Khayyam alludes to leaving behind the anxious and dualistic mind – to loosening the mental tension and existential confusion.

This three-fold outlook on pleasure all implicitly expressed in Khayyam's quatrains demonstrates the need for precision of the mind in the precarious conditions of construction-demolition and psychological fluctuation. Thus, Khayyam's counsel of pleasure attempted to reduce the tyranny of the anthropocentric mind and bring it into a composed state and in harmony with the world, which operates in a non-anthropocentric rhythm.

The language of the quatrains about human pain and pleasure also aimed at releasing oneself from the fear of death, afterlife uncertainties, and other mental agonies. The impulse to live longer and return after death, according to Khayyam, triggers a trajectory of unquiet mental pursuits and illusions. The experience of pleasure for Khayyam was the prosperity of mind in a composed fashion that accepts the fleeting world with its laws of cause and effect and entropy. This means neither clinging to the world nor antagonizing it with dissonant personal opinions and expectations – simply living the world with a lesser and lesser dichotomous mind.

The heart of Khayyamian philosophy takes an interest in the practice of pleasure, living an anxiety-free life with calmness of mind, living with the awareness of now, and abandoning the past and future in one's idle thoughts. To make his argument lucid and accessible, he uses different metaphors in the quatrains such as; attain pleasure (*kām*), drink wine (*sharāb* or *mai*), be aware of now and the breath (*dam*), be happy (*khosh*), play the melody of harp (*chang*), and other poetical combinations. The crux of his approach is freedom from the deceptive and impulsive mind that searches for happiness outside of itself.

Khayyam used the power of language for a deeper psychological purpose, like a key to unlock the reluctant mind. He focused with precision on the rift between the self-absorbed mind and fleeting life. In purging the confusion of the mind, Khayyam tackled the pleasure of life on two levels: one level was to become aware of the very celebration of life in its totality and elegance, and the second level was to disentangle the obsessive mind from the bygones as well as the unarrived future.

For Khayyam, the ideal situation would be if our cognitive faculty would not have to deal with all the dichotomous opposites such as birth/death and pain/pleasure. The quatrains speak of an indeterminate free will wrapped between the determinate life facts of birth and death. In several quatrains, he divulged that since our unconsented birth has already happened and this one-way path cannot be undone, then we need to make a vow to perform positively in life and live joyfully (*rubā'īs*: 17, 32, 94). No matter in which land or family we are born, whether rich or poor, fortunate or unfortunate, all such characteristics eventually become irrelevant in this pulsating dynamic world. Our talent for turning pain into pleasure is the final victory (*rubā'ī*: 95).

Khayyam was aware of the amount of anxiety and mental torment that people sustain as a whole. His clear visualization of the existential process was designed to help myopic, entangled minds. Since both pain and pleasure originate in the dichotomous mind, Khayyam proposed an "antidote" – wine – to neutralize the poison of displeasure and thus overturn the bitter mindset and replace it with the pleasure of joy (*kāmranī*) in one strike (*rubā'ī*: 16).

Khayyam remarked that people tend to rot in their compulsive minds. This type of mind leads to a path of perpetual anxiety that brings ruinous results. He described ignorance as one who does not savor the fleeting moments of life (*rubā'ī*: 84). Khayyam went on to criticize even the most upscale knowledge as pathetic if it cannot rescue a person from anguish and offer a reinvigorating soothing joy (*rubā'ī*: 99). Life is designed such that we oscillate between two breaths, so why then should we allow our own mentally forged fantasies to rob us of the precious breath of now? (*rubā'ī*: 108, 137). It is ludicrous to think of "there" when one is already "here,"[42] wine in hand to enjoy. (*rubā'ī*: 4)

The following *rubā'ī* beautifully expresses the philosophy of nowness: Craving for longevity is nothing short of absurd when one is not even able to appreciate in tranquility the time at hand. The pleasure of living does not happen through wishful thinking or having more time; even adding a

---

[42] For an interesting article about "thereness" (being here) of Khayyam, see Mehdi Aminrazavi, "Martin Heidegger and Omar Khayyam on the Question of "Thereness" (Dasein)," in *Islamic Philosophy and Occidental Phenomenology on the Perennial Issue of Microcosm and Macrocosm*, edited by Anna-Teresa Tymieniecka (Dordrecht: Springer 2006), 277-288.

hundred years to one's life will not help. The quintessence of longevity is hollow (rubāʿī: 103).

Khayyam continues to layer his messages: The beast of mortality swallows everything. The good time and bad times will be swallowed, no matter what. Wise is he who relinquishes the memory of the past, and concedes that all bygones are inalterable (rubāʿī: 123). Under this celestial constellation of dust, we are also made out of dust. Before we turn back into dust ourselves, there is only today to cultivate pleasure (rubāʿī: 131).

Khayyam warned of the dream of the future in the face of the abrupt dissolution of our organism (rubāʿī: 20). In other words, as much as it paves the opportunity for newcomers, the passage of time shortens the future of the old-timers. Those who spoil their opportunity to have a pleasurable mindset (kām), regardless of joy and regrets, will be razed from the face of reality and their components will become traceless in the cycle of existence, like all previous generations (rubāʿīs: 18,19). This world faces two doors of coming and going. One door is: "suffer and leave," and the other is: "the joy of not having been born" (rubāʿī: 23). From his 'antinatalist'[43] position, Khayyam says, if those unborn knew what we endure in our lifetime they would never come to this material world (rubāʿī: 28). He allegorizes the joy of life yet another way: if my comrades died one by one, I raise my wine cup and utter cheers to those who enjoyed life before us (rubāʿī: 38). Is there any higher purpose other than inhabiting the territory of sound reason and a happy heart? (rubāʿī: 76).

The *Rubāʿīyyāt* is never short of allegorical images.[44] The ingenious analogies in the following quatrains speak for themselves as they offer experiential poetic images, allegories, and wisdom for dealing with the ups and downs of the world, and how to find joy within. The following represent Khayyamian philosophy of happiness: The day of release from religion is a day of an untainted joyous mind, free from all labels. On the same day, I married the bride whose name is the "world," I asked her, what is your dowry? She said I want nothing but a happy "husband" (rubāʿī: 75). In my union with joy, tonight I shall entirely break up with my anxious mind and religion so that I can revitalize my state of life (rubāʿī: 77). Grief exhausts, but a happy mood is

---

[43] Antinatalism is a philosophical position among many creeds which rejects or discourages procreation on various grounds.
[44] In fact, his pioneering impact can be seen in the poetic inspirations of the Persian poets who followed him, including the master of allegories and metaphors such as the fourteenth-century Hafiz. See Hedāyat's *Tarāneh-hāye Khayyām*, 41, 42–3.

abundant, and growing older can be only magnificent in a well-groomed mind and heart (*rubāʿī:* 97).

The moonlight is terrific tonight. Tomorrow the moon will be around but it may not find us here anymore. Due to this uncertainty, thinking of tomorrow is absurd when the moon turns my sadness into a happy heart tonight – drink wine to her glory (*rubāʿī:* 112). Bear in mind, the brightness of the moon slashes the darkness of the sky open. If you don't treasure this moonlight tonight, the moon then is obliged to throw its light on the darkness of your last resting place. (*rubāʿī:* 111)

The caravan of the days and years keep passing by us. Take heed to value each moment, otherwise, each night passes without joy while the apprehensive mind ruminates about tomorrow. (*rubāʿī:* 113)

Do we know why the rooster crows at dawn? It is to awaken us to another fresh morning of life, and jolt us from our unawareness of another night has passed (*rubāʿī:* 114). During the crisp morning is the time to grasp the essence of life and repudiate any imprudence we have partaken. It would also be the time to make a vow to fine-tune our mind for another melody of life. (*rubāʿī:* 117)

The passing years have thrown thousands of kings to the ground without the shred of a trace. Bearing this fact in mind, each morning should be treated respectfully and joyfully as a new composition of life (*rubāʿī:* 116). The art of living in the present is when the world is considered to be one's own sovereign kingdom, and the moments as melodic tunes. Err not to think of the ever-returning bygones; the purpose of life is to live here and now, not in the past (*rubāʿī:* 134). The entire cosmos through the labyrinth of its evolution has brought us here with the wine of the present moment. I wonder, if we were to sell this wine of joy, what would we buy to replace it?! (*rubāʿī:* 110).

Unfetter yourself from idle thoughts and reawaken, since the long journey of life has brought you to this moment. Look around and see the assembly of nature; all is for you to celebrate life (*rubāʿī:* 133). The day is impeccable, and the flower's shiny face is a witness to it. The nightingale sings in Persian to the gold-leaf flower: be merry, drink wine (*rubāʿī:* 118). The breeze of the spring day is soothing for the flower, unlike the memory of winter. Stop the talk of yesterday when today is enchanting (*rubāʿī:* 120). Whichever way life is assessed, only wine and music are the source of jubilation; the rest are overexaggerated details (*rubāʿī:* 136). Remember that even pleasure itself becomes passé and simply a metaphor at the end. But until the last breath, joy is renewable (*rubāʿī:* 21).

Khayyam expressed the *will* to live strong, even though the elements of the body are decaying. Although reaching the end of life is certain, and living in the world taxes our system, there is still a magnificent source left, and that is the sparkling joy of the hour (*rubāʿī*: 100). He exhorted readers to live like the courageous Qalandars (a group of antinomian wandering ascetics) who were fearless; they danced, drank, and gave up sinister talk. (*rubāʿī*: 96). Khayyam resisted the conventional materialism by preferring simplicity in living over living dangerously like kings. To him, half a loaf of bread with wine and the wholehearted self in a destitute house were more satisfying than living in the palaces of the emperors (*rubāʿī*: 98).

Khayyam categorically debunked the mind which constantly worries and has a gloomy picture of life. Nature finds it disgraceful to witness those beings sitting abject and melancholic in search of the past. He exhorted: get up and dance to the melody of life - it's the way to go before our turn comes to an end (*rubāʿī*: 127). It is obvious that seasons come and go and it feels like fast-paced impermanency. But my advice to you is to relax and use the antidote for the poison of grief, which is to maintain an unconfined mind – drink wine! (*rubāʿī*: 128). To view life by intellectualizing is not comparable to living it joyfully. Don't waste time by always pondering anxiously. Before the end begets us, we must beget the joy of tranquility while at hand (*rubāʿī*: 126). An incongruous outlook on life must be abandoned. He relays that even though he is in his old age, he must forsake all discombobulations coming to mind. I wonder, if I don't do it minute by minute, who will do this for me!? (*rubāʿī*: 141). The "postponing-mindset" and the feelings of grief with regret have damaged every fiber of our existence. It is time to make a soldierly vow and arise in order to embrace joy which has been so near all along. Our treasurable innovation of life lies between our own birth and death with a knowledge that this attraction of birth-death will continue after we are gone (*rubāʿī*: 138).

Khayyam talked about the danger of impulsively coveting tomorrow, referring to the yearning for or being anxious about the future. This compelled him to encourage disentangling from such a future-oriented mind. It is a sort of abstraction of one's own existence in illusory time that has not arrived yet. This mindset is contemptuous toward the present moment. The uncontrolled anxiety of "tomorrow" causes the nervousness of unarrived future, and the spoiling of now and today. All tomorrows become yesterdays.

An awakened mind values the present time. This aware mind prevents diluting one's valuable existence between the two tails of time, leaving a person in limbo before death arrives (*rubāʿī*: 135). Because the nature of time is fluid, Khayyam allegorized that time is therefore unfaithful. Rest assured, he said, time will not make any exception in treating you differently. Since it is impossible to outlive the passing world, have joyous moments while it is still possible (*rubāʿī*: 124). In this massive cosmos, no entity cares how we live our lives. Thus, each opportunity is for our pleasure; don't sigh and choose sadness. The signature of finitude is surely on every wall, although you are not yet at the end (*rubāʿī*: 125).

Inevitably, your name will be brushed off the face of existence. But before that time, drink wine to brush the despair from your heart. This splendid decision loosens the fibers of anxiety one by one, before the fibers of your existence deteriorate one by one (*rubāʿī*: 129). Time here in this world has a real existence, and our body and our contentment are real. The time after death is abstract, as if time stands still. This is why the moment after our death we are on the same par without any time difference with those who have passed away seven thousand years before us. "So, my friend, come and let us not lament about tomorrow" (*rubāʿī*: 130). Khayyam destroyed any fantasies about the fixity of time and forms in the theater of life: all is in a state of flux. In between this unremitting construction-demolition there is a miniscule opportunity to be in our present profile; why waste it when we know we shall also be swallowed by formlessness? (*rubāʿī*: 101)

In a series of quatrains, Khayyam elaborated on the uninhibited flow of life regardless of our fantasies about heaven and hell. The claims of heaven and hell for Khayyam symbolized an unrealistic suspension of the flow of the universe. To inspire empirical contemplation for sobering the mind, Khayyam presented heaven as being right here around us. He rejected the common speculations that celestial bodies or places are responsible for our personal pleasure and final destiny. He said that it is certain we are in charge of our pleasure which is here and now; we need to let go of the ruminations about far-flung heaven and hell (*rubāʿī*: 92). He tersely rejected any religious belief in heaven and hell. Heaven is nothing more than the true tranquility of mind; hell is the pointless suffering in life (*rubāʿī*: 142). If in Paradise, the darling beloveds are promised, I'd prefer my cup of wine here and now. "It is indeed wiser to remain firm with the present life than vouching for the seductive promises of some nebulous future" (*rubāʿī*: 90). If the aim of toiling of life is to land in heaven to enjoy milk, honey, wine, sweets, and angel-faced creatures, it seems an absurd lapse of judgment to leave all these things unconsumed here on earth and instead ruminate on their replication in another dimension (*rubāʿīs*: 88–89). Khayyam categorically refuted the claims of the monotheists or polytheists, that the virtuous go to heaven and the wicked to hell. Here he called himself as a witness: "Khayyam! Who said there would be hell? Tell me, whom can you name who has already gone to hell, and who has recently returned from heaven to visit us here?" (*rubāʿī*: 6).

Khayyam in due course had to bring up the most-feared phenomenon, death. There will obviously and eventually be a time in each person's life to say "yes" to death; death can be denied and repressed only for so long. But Khayyam gave an optimistic twist to the event of death: The subject of death in the quatrains is consistently defined to be nothing but the juncture between worldly joy and the natural dance of the atoms. Khayyam wrote: "The day I depart from this world, without a doubt my body would decompose and return to atoms and dust. Make sure the ashes of my corpse are thrown into the clay of pottery to make a wine flask, which will enliven those who drink from it. Though death seems the end, the life of joy is reproducible" (*rubāʿīs:* 81–82). His unrestricted presentism is clear when he says; don't expect to find me on resurrection day; I shall be in the tavern. In death, also make sure first to bathe my corpse in wine, then bury me. This way, my tomb will emanate so much intoxicant of joy that the people passing by will become affected and overwhelmed, especially those like me who seek the same in life (*rubāʿīs:* 79–80).

Before departing the world and being thrown into the oblivion of existence, Khayyam petitioned his audience to be vigilant with the weeks of life that come and swiftly disappear. Be mindful before another week slips away, take a walk in an open and beautiful field with lush grass and flowers. The singularity of this occasion will not be repeated. The odyssey of this turning wheel of life (*charkh* - the wheel) causes the constant disintegration of our existence, as well as that of the grass and flowers. Before withering away and turning into mud, the red tulip awaits your company (*rubāʿīs:* 121–22).

Khayyam's final advice was to live in the world as if it is a terrific reward that requires no payback. Let us sit with rosy-cheeked companions and be merry. Act as if you have not been in the world, and instead you were just born today – don't let the feeling of emptiness in this world stop you from living delightfully (*rubāʿī:* 140). This body which we possess indicates no turning back of time; it is the world ending in nothingness at the end. Let us not waste this "something" focusing on the world of nothingness. Just a whisper of music in the background and a delightful heart would amount to good living; the rest is not important (*rubāʿī:* 136). Before the winter of life begins, with the mayhem of our physical and mental disintegration, there is no task more important than responding in harmony to the rhythm of life.

4. Return to Atoms (Mechanical Philosophy: Entropy and Demise)

What humans consider "death" is an everyday task of the cosmos in which all differentiations and distinctions of the manifold world are inexorably lost and transmuted. The third spoke of nowness throws the all things onto the fourth spoke, to demolish them into the essential four elements with the return to atoms. Human birth and becoming are also processes that continue into adulthood, old age, death, and decomposition, and all are the involuntary work of the mechanical laws of nature. The stage-to-stage work of nature is certain, precise, and forward-looking.

In our Khayyamian model of existence, the fourth spoke of the wheel spins and blows by, converting the phenomenal objects that have enjoyed existence for a period of time back to fragments and dust. This spoke of transition brings everything down in different time intervals, depending on size, density, and form. The trajectory of emergence and submergence of all entities is being constantly repeated, which Khayyam recaptured in the "mechanical philosophy" of his quatrains. The role of this fourth spoke is thus quite clear as he acknowledged this process to be irrefutably irreversible.

In this section of our discussion, Khayyam's "mechanical philosophy" explains how all bodies follow a two-step rule: *annihilation* and *irreversibility*. The first is the complete annihilation of all entities, humans included, into atoms, a complete destruction of what was once a magnificent and complex constitution. During this stage, the bulk of the atoms of the disintegrated bodies are salvaged for future construction. The second step is the "law" of no return to the previous and identical state. Due to the characteristics of these two steps, any psychological hope of a return after death must be abandoned. The unfolding messages in Khayyam's quatrains lay out a panoramic map of nature and natural processes that dismantles the human perception of immortality.

In this map, Khayyam rejects the claim that human consciousness predates its own body or survives after its own death. This Khayyamian thesis rejected the ancient belief in resurrection and reincarnation. Due to the intricate phenomenon of the physical body, the eyes can see, the brain can memorize, the hands can produce art, and so on. However, after death, none of these organs will be functional. This includes the "organ" of the mind. However, the raw material will be left behind, the atoms from the body and the brain will be rescued, mixed with other bodies, and reused for new constructions.

Although it may seem that death is the point here, that is less of the focus for Khayyam. It is rather the "law of demolition and conversion." Because birth and death matter to humans, Khayyam tries to alleviate the preoccupation and fear of death. He put reality in perspective by making it clear that humans are not special and are not exempt from the ongoing law of cosmos. Culturally manufactured death and afterlife scenarios were rejected by Khayyam because it seemed obvious that all animate and inanimate bodies in nature follow the same laws. The eyes can see, according to the quatrains, that our decomposed bodies end up in the mouths of ants, being transported in different directions, and that the dust from our bones mixes indistinguishably with the soil for the grass grow.

To make the goal of his radical poetry clearer, Khayyam used a set of "atomistic" metaphors in his vibrant quatrains, including dust (*khāk*), clay (*gehl*), block (*khesht*), and atom-particle (*zarreh*). The following paraphrased quatrains epitomize how Khayyam makes forgotten atomism vibrant again, and demonstrates the absolute clarity of natural recycling:

Every atom (*zarreh*) on the ground or hovering above may have been the body parts of an alluring sweetheart; no one can distinguish those atoms from one another anymore (*rubā'ī*: 58). Once your, and my body pass away, our tombs become the storage of raw material for the reconfiguration of newer bodies (*rubā'ī*: 57).

In this direct quote from Khayyam, we can confirm his atomism and his perspective about the four permanent elements of water, earth, air and fire: "Your construction is out of four [elements], and seven [planets]. Through the four and seven you are continuously in upheaval." Be merry, drink wine! I have told you more than a thousand times, you shall not return. Once you pass away, the process is irrevocable (*rubā'ī*: 29).

The number "seven" in the astrological convention of Khayyam's time referred to the belief that the seven planets influenced the state of affairs. (The astronomers knew of only seven planets at that time). It is clear that Khayyam had no belief in such astrological conventions. He captured in a *rubā'ī* the irrelevance of astrology to a joyful living and to the natural processes: Since the wheel of the cosmos did not spin favorably in bringing permanent pleasure to even the wisest among us, it does not matter whether one considers the influencing planets be seven or eight. And since death is a debt to pay back and give up all our yearnings, in this case, we say it really doesn't matter whether the ants in our grave consume our corpse, or the wolves in the field (*rubā'ī*: 40).

Khayyam reminded us time and again that this world is an old cemetery which has entombed hundreds of kings who once upon a time rejoiced in their own glory (*rubā'ī*: 53). He tells of a Persian king Bahram, who all his life fancied hunting zebras and gazelles. Then a time came when those beasts witnessed Bahram himself being hunted down by the beast of death in his own turn (*rubā'ī*: 54). A king's haughtiness prevents him from imagining his own inevitable demise and permanent disappearance from the face of the earth. Khayyam poeticized this tragic misperception of those who desire to be the "kings" of their own life. He tells us: I saw a bird picking up a fragment of the skull of a glorious king whose glamour was unrivaled in his time. The bird chirped, "Alas, alas, what happened to all your royal maneuvering and indulgence?" (*rubāʿī*: 55).

Khayyam continued with eloquent allegories presenting the two-step rule of annihilation and irreversibility. He provided a number of persuasive reminders: The assets of life were spent, the end neared, and I awaited somebody to come from the world of beyond so that I could ask, 'How are the worldly travelers doing on the other side'? (*rubāʿī*: 36). In the long journey of life, has anybody approached us from the afterlife with an auspicious message? Khayyam cautions that no one has ever come back, so don't accumulate or leave anything behind, because you won't come back a second time either (*rubāʿī*: 46). Celebrate sitting with a blossoming tree as your company, because you and the flower shall wither away for a common destination without a comrade to keep you company. Don't be confused by nature, nor shout this enigma in public: "Any tulip that withers will never blossom again" (*rubāʿī*: 47). The spring breeze soothes the flower bud; the nightingale enjoys the company of the flower. We are also invited to sit in the shadow of the blossoming tree, a tree which once sprouted out of the earth and in due time shall recede back into the earth (*rubāʿī*: 60).

The news of those who passed away before us continues to preoccupy the wise masters. According to Khayyam, once a master in his supreme wisdom uttered this message: drink wine and be merry, because many like us have left and none have come back (*rubāʿī*: 48). The act of nature is universal without nepotism or favoritism – I have verified this fact for myself. It is a one-way road; once unmade it cannot be made again (*rubāʿī*: 49). Khayyam declares that the illusion of immortality or a glamorous return to a perfect individual state is incompatible with natural processes and therefore unfounded.

Here Khayyam takes another turn, showing us how the mechanism of "atomism" operates in nature. By employing a powerful allegory of grass growing, he attempted to demonstrate how the atoms of a deceased human body are transferred to nurture the grass. Since grass is ubiquitous and organic, it feeds on the deposits of all organic matters, whether animal corpses, human corpses, or other plants in the soil. Khayyam's grass parallel reduced the human ego by making it equal to the grass. In other words, grass and the human body, although different in their constitution, are interchangeable, using up similar atoms. When one is destroyed, another is constructed, the chain of food in full action. In his atomism, Khayyam took humans out of their erroneous exceptionalist illusion, pointing out that they are of no special fabric distinct from nature – they too are constructed and then consumed again.

Khayyam also offered delicate imageries: The clouds poured droplets of fresh water on the grass and a sound whispered, "Don't go on living without being merry (without wine)." Then the grass and I gazed at each other for a moment, and I pondered, "If someday this grass sprouts out of the ashes of my body, who it would be gazing at in the next round?" (*rubāʿī*: 61). As I witnessed the tulip being showered in lush rain, I thought it would be absurd if I don't lift my wine glass and be cheerful like the tulip. Imagine if I don't delight in the moment. The grass which is gazing at me today will be feeding on and growing from the components of my decomposed body tomorrow (*rubāʿī*: 62). All the green grass growing alongside the streams has taken its food from the lips of angel-faced, rosy-cheeked girls – beware where you place your feet as you walk, since all this grass has gotten its life from those gorgeous girls (*rubāʿī*: 63). Cultivate pleasure since at the end the "mechanistic" world will degrade and reduce us to pieces. Go lie down in tranquility on the grass and be alive blissfully before the grass consumes you (*rubāʿī*: 64).

Other quatrains also offered experiences with atomism: The turning wheel has already, hundreds of times, transformed the glamorous bodies of the moon-faced idols into clay for wine jugs. Take your wine jug and wander around in nature. When one day I smashed my wine jug, the jug cautioned me by uttering these words: 'I was once like you, as you'll someday will be like me' (*rubāʿīs*: 66,67). The wine flask is full of wine; it is time to enjoy it. Soon the ashes from our bodies will be trampled on in the alleys and roads, and finally we become the clay for the pot-maker (*rubāʿī*: 68).[45]

Khayyam continued by providing us with more imagery of how the atoms of the decomposed bodies become dispersed and used everywhere: The other day I passed by the pottery workshop and witnessed an inconspicuous pot-maker producing alluring pots in every spin of the wheel. I saw this for myself although other unobservant people did not. I bore witness to my father's ashes being dispersed in every pottery workshop (*rubāʿī*: 69). Another time, at a construction site, while the clay was prepared to make bricks, I saw a solitary man stomping in the mud. The mud under the feet of the man demanded gentleness: "Stop! You will yourself be stomped upon by someone else one day" (*rubāʿī*: 65).

Take heed in this – all the atoms (*zarreh*) in our bodies may have once been the atoms of the bodies of kings. The human story is nothing but an unreliable

---

[45] This particular *rubāʿī* has a Hafizian parallel, when Hafiz literally advises his audience; before you become the clay of the pot-maker, hurry up filled up your own wine jug (body) and live vigorously and joyfully.

account with many seductive promises of the future. Consequently, what is real in this moment at hand is to live mindfully and peacefully (*rubāʿī:* 109).

Having conceptualized the recurrent process of dancing atoms, Khayyam wanted to counsel those who dwell in uncertainty. He used himself as a symbolic example. He advised that in his death we should treat the ashes of his body unremarkably and make the course of his life cycle a cautionary lesson for the newcomers. He wished the dust of his corpse to be mixed with wine in making caps for the wine flasks (*rubāʿī:* 78).

In this unchangeable reality, Khayyam's point is that specific atoms cannot be selected and stored individually and exclusively for humans' sake. Nevertheless, there should be no room for despair or abjection in this physical process, whether the fourth spoke of annihilation takes away the form of a human being, a fly or a magnificent object in the galaxies. The mechanism is such that the world of multiplicity is reduced to the uniformity of dust, and then is reconstructed, and returns to multiplicity, time and again. Appreciation of this mechanical philosophy presented by Khayyam can only occur when spirited logical thinking transcends the typical sensational human reactions to birth and death.

5. Nothingness (*hīch*)

Khayyam found the purpose of existence difficult to understand. For him, the ultimate meaning of life points to nothingness, *hīch*.[46] Death at the end further adds to the nothingness of the whole existence. In this conundrum, the impersonal wheel of existence spins without an apparent particular terminus in sight, and finally, the fifth spoke gives a fatal blow to all the remaining characteristics of the individual, leaving behind no sense of what was once called an entity or a self. Through the fourth spoke, the material existence returned to atoms, and with the fifth spoke, the existence of a cohesive identity returns to nothingness. This complete obliteration plugs into a vacuum in which all notions of selfhood become futile, void of all differentiations.

The odyssey of the natural world, the earthly chain of food as seen in the animal kingdom and the continual need for the raw material for new construction leaves no one and nothing immune from final annihilation. In this segment, Khayyam revealed his discourse on the ontological construct of

---

[46] Hafiz had also composed poems about the same notion of nothingness: "The world and its inner working is nothingness in nothingness (*hīch dar hīch*), I have made certain of this transaction a thousand times by thinking over it."

the universe which emerges from nothingness, materializes transiently, and then submerges to nothingness again. Thus, the substantial world that exists in each moment is in a constant state of flux and operates intrinsically and keeps spinning and returning to the same course of action (construction-demolition). Khayyam calls the end stage *hīch* (null, point zero, nothing). The quantifiability of previously existing objects become unquantifiable after their demise and disappearance. Their formal memory is also erased from all forms, and in the end, no trace of them can even be retrieved after their complete obliteration. Prey which is devoured by the predator can no longer come back to life, nor can its individuality be traced back in the labyrinth of uninhibited and continuous obliteration process. A withered flower will not blossom a second time. Is this an absurd cycle with no ultimate goal in sight? Is there something sinister in this affair?

Khayyam in the *Rubā'īyyāt* did not entertain any metaphysical speculations whatsoever. He directs his readership to pay attention to the following thoughts. The enigma of constant annihilation has long been the object of investigation of the wise masters. The irony of the matter is that the speculations and insights of these wise masters die with them when they fall prey to death and we return to nothing again (*rubā'īs*: 7, 8, 9). For the enthusiasts of life, the imagination of nothingness is unimaginable and thus humans have done everything to circumvent and purge the thought of nothingness from their biographies. To counter this, Khayyam purported, because the ceaseless construction-demolition is pre-human and its extension seems endless in either direction, no one has been given the privilege to anchor himself in existence. And no one has been able to figure out the motivation or destination for this ever-recurring being and nonbeing (*rubā'ī*: 10).

Khayyam moved away from arbitrary speculation and washed his hands of abstract metaphysical oversights. He overturns all kinds of guess approximations by resorting to reason and the power of observation. He believed that all things at the end of their phenomenal existence lose their individual identities, and nothing is left except for their raw material. Nothingness, in Khayyam's perspective, is the final complete obliteration of the body and the consciousness. In regard to consciousness, Khayyam declined to accept consciousness as a separate entity from the body, let alone something that survives after death. Human identity and personality after death are all lost forever and join the traceless machinery of recycling. He called upon people to take into account of all the past physical objects which have vanished indefinitely. Thus, even giant rocky planets will vanish in their own turn. Khayyam deemed this mechanism of demolition and oblivion to be dissonant with all our fantasies and wishful thinking. Hence, he suggested dropping the fantasies and enjoying the time within reach (*rubā'ī*: 101).

To stimulate our mind, he poeticized about the world of nothingness: I put the jug to my lips and made a wish for immortality. The jug silently whispered a secret to my lips: 'Drink wine that you shall not come back to this world anymore' (rubāʻī: 139). No hour is more suitable than this one to let go of the anguished heart. Life begins with youth as if it is the fountain of immortality; the passing time, however, dissolves this unthinking. The finish line of this long journey is an eternal sleep (rubāʻī: 132). Although in the earth's heart lies the buried bodies, in my glance at the vast plain land of traceless nothingness (sahrāy-e ʻadam), I can only see the empty places of those gone before, and the unarrived ones (rubāʻī: 52).

Khayyam again rejected all guesswork coming from the mortals who speak of and promise immortality: Those who arrogantly claim to have access to the mystery of existence, where are they? They are covered with dirt. Listen to me: go dwell nicely in the world. It's all empty air what others have alleged (rubāʻī: 13). Those metaphysicians may always sound erudite, but their chatter is only in the darkness. In actuality, no one can survive this darkness to have a glimpse at the light of truth (rubāʻī: 12). How can we be certain of all the metaphysical claims of afterlife? If we can't know this insidious cycle while we are alive, how can we know it after death when the consciousness is obliterated? (rubāʻī: 5).

The dialectics of nothingness point to non-locality. There is no any other independent reality where things, consciousness, "souls," or "bodies" can be stored. Death is final, generating empty space. Khayyam made certain that his point about nothingness or the non-substantiality of all things, including human existence, is clearly understood. He imparted: "I wish there were a solid place in existence in which we could lodge, or that at least after a long journey we would reach our destination. We would rejoice after a waiting of even hundred thousand years when we would sprout out like lush grass out of earth and breathe again" (rubāʻī: 22). Those who feel firmly stationed in this world and have important people around them will eventually learn the bitter fact of mortality: no return and no trace left behind (rubāʻī: 115).

An archetypal rubāʻī about nothingness (hīch) is expressed: Look insightfully at all our toiling in life which will eventually evaporate into being nothing. Even though we excel in order to become an alluring intellectual powerhouse in the circle of intelligent ones, the gloomy end of life will doom us to nothingness. Even though we once were the most precious gem in the world, once we shatter, we are reduced to nothing (rubāʻī: 107). Khayyam went on to forewarn those who may have some illusive imaginations about the end of life. He said, I was a child tutored in the sciences and when I grew up, I was enchanted to have become a learned scholar. But, pay attention to the end of my story: I emerged as a fountain of water, and at the end, I dried up in the air (*rubāʿī:* 37). I advise the wise ones to teach farsighted prudence to the new generation so that their lives are based on the sound experiences of the former times (*rubāʿī:* 59).

Khayyam confronted and challenged the credibility of an independent reality other than the present one, particularly regarding the idea of resurrection in heaven or hell: Those who assert the existence of another world sound as if they have just returned from one. Our hopes and fears are simply out of our beliefs; otherwise, heaven and hell are only names without any visible clues (*rubāʿī:* 81). Those who are fluent in the languages of heaven and hell have the task of explaining how the physical body could withstand the heat of hell. Let us assume the claim of hell being true, what then after hell? All would be extinguished and flattened, commencing all over again (*rubāʿī:* 87).

Khayyam made it clear that contrary to the common belief, Armageddon will not happen in the afterlife – it is in *this* life. Nothingness is so apparent in this world; the writing is on every wall of existence. It only requires stopping by the ruins of the palaces where once the kings erected their magnificent kingdoms. In this quatrain, Khayyam makes a play on the word *coo*, which is both the sound a bird makes, but also means "where" in Persian: "Once I saw a bird sitting on the shattered arch of a ruined royal palace, singing: 'coo coo, coo coo...'" Where are they? Where are they? the birds said, referring to the once celebrated kings, now gone (*rubāʿī:* 56).[47]

Khayyam condensed his view of nothingness into one notional *rubāʿī:* "Since all things are doomed to become extinct to themselves, nothingness (*hīch*) is their final destiny." Owing to this fact, none of the existing things can self-sustain; they decay and shatter at the end. In this case, it is perhaps appropriate to deem what has not come into existence as existent, and deem what exists today as non-existent in the future (*rubāʿī:* 106). In this way, the human mind persistently tends to ponder on being and nonbeing. Khayyam tersely advises: Don't let your harmful ego whisper in your head about how long you might live, or what will happen after you die. Be delighted to stand here and now with wine in hand. The life which I see ends in heartbreak. So, your liberation in real life can be attained in the joyful state of now, and then in your long sleep of oblivion (*rubāʿī:* 143).

Regardless of what we believe, the wheel of the universe inevitably eradicates all the traces of our existence. And yet, with the final turning of the

---

[47] The parallel of this *rubāʿī* can be found in Khaqani's (d. 1190) Persian poem "*Eivān-e Mādāʾen*".

blade, Khayyam's philosophy of nothingness (*hīch*) inspires let go of self. In his view, the universe is without self despite its relentless addition and subtraction of objects. Our coming and departing is another addition and subtraction leading to a greater juggernaut of nothingness. He warned that the universe keeps forgetting all the entities as their bodies are disconnected from the cord of existence. Khayyam's underlying message is directed at every one of us, suggesting that we must become aware of the obliviousness of the world as the universe will forget us for sure.[48]

Conclusion

Although Khayyam's quatrains may seem rigidly materialistic, they encompass very fine psychological angles. His craftsmanship in such short compositions is decisively dense, and encompasses much of the same content that the Buddha, Çārvākas, Democritus, Epicurus, Lucretius, al-Ma'arrī, and similar thinkers addressed. He was perhaps right to believe that there is nothing evil about the world, that death is a fact of existence, that the dance of atoms is a spectacular performance of the cosmos, and that in between, we humans are here to delight in this spectacle of life without leaving a trace of pain or regrets behind. By pointing to the process of nothingness, and urging us to cultivate joy in life at the same time, Khayyam permitted no paradox of despair in his liberating philosophy. He realized that if impermanence is the rule of existence, then humor must be its reason. His philosophy of happiness cancels out the nihilism that is encoded in existence.

He single-handedly and tersely challenged the cultural and psychological mindset of fearing death, venerating the dead, and hoping to return after

---

[48] Interestingly, the tremendous message of oblivion was formulated almost 100 years after Khayyam. The prominent Zen master, Dōgen (1200–1253), offered a similar teaching in his book of *Shōbōgenzō*. Dōgen's message was that the purpose of Zen is to study the self in order to forget the self, because at the end all selves shall become unintelligible and traceless. Through this idea of Dōgen, the Buddhist dialectical philosophy of *sunyāta* (emptiness) is epitomized. *Sunyāta* is a concept which explains that all phenomena without exception inherently lack a self-sustaining and fixed *self*, and are therefore subject to change, decay and destroy without any control. The awareness of traceless oblivion is the focus of meditation. Based on this remarkable similarity, there is nothing closer to Khayyam's philosophy of *hīch* than its equivalent: the Buddhist *sunyāta*. (Although it is important from the epistemological point of view to differentiate the Buddhist concept of *emptiness* of existing objects which lack an intrinsic self, and *nothingness* which means things that once were are destroyed, absent and become traceless. [In Japanese Zen context, emptiness is Kü and nothingness is Mu])

death. He moved away from *temporal* anxiety, avoiding visualizing the self either in the past or future. He also moved away from *existential* anxiety, avoiding the fantasy of life after death, and instead accepting death as the final stage. Far more importantly in liberating ourselves from imagination and false hope, Khayyam tried to deemotionalize our interpretation of natural processes, and encouraged us to enjoy each moment and remember the repetition of the greater reality of construction-demolition, without resorting to living our lives based on mythological, religious, or cultural fabrications.

Epilogue - Enlightenment Revisited: The Second Enlightenment

In light of the nature of the rational and empirical philosophies, we have explored from the Indian, Greek and Iranian worlds, it is now a natural progression to reflect on the Western Enlightenment. The Western Enlightenment could easily be called 'liberation philosophy' in a European context. We will review the trajectory that philosophy took in the West during the Renaissance and Enlightenment, and see how that path was influenced by the ancient thinkers Epicurus and Lucretius specifically, in order to explore the sociopolitical effects of a revival of past philosophies. Along the way, it will be easy to see European philosophical parallels with the thinking of the Asian liberation philosophers we have been exploring thus far as well. The European philosophers of the Enlightenment were responding to the culturally and religiously oppressive conditions of their time, and their emergence reminds us of how and why the Çārvākas, the Buddha, Khayyam and Rumi emerged in their own times as well. Maybe it's also time now for a modern resurgence of these powerful philosophies.

The European Enlightenment: A Fresh Return to the Past

Given the carnage and ongoing conflict, despotism, depression and the manifestation of religious oppression in European societies at the close of the Middle Ages, Enlightenment thinkers each in their own capacity tried to remedy the dire conditions entrapping people. But what is particularly intriguing in those European circumstances between the 15th and 19th centuries is that the search for solutions went deep into the past, to pre-Christian times. The shattering of the absolute domination by the Catholic Church with the advent of the Reformation, the revival of skepticism, and the groundbreaking scientific revolution made it possible to doubt the existence of god - and the existence of god was even assumed implausible. As a result, this god was gradually replaced by an impersonal Nature.[1] The guilt, devout

---

[1] Anthony Pagden, *The Enlightenment and Why It Still Matters* (Oxford: Oxford University Press, 2015), 79, 79-124.

sentimentalism and oppression of religion gradually lost their holds on the minds of the literati of the time.

The influence that Epicurus and his philosophy had on Renaissance and Enlightenment philosophers during this time is absolutely undeniable.[2] The Epicurean idea of free thinking and happiness gradually brought European thinkers past their religious inhibitions as they began to write openly about the rights of citizens to be happy in life; hundreds of essays and books appeared on the topic of 'happiness' during this time.

Another of the major tenets explored in the Enlightenment movement was the ideal of free and independent thought. The power structure of the Church, with a clergy that thought for and decided for individuals (as religion had been doing for millennia), had compromised human reasoning power for centuries and now it was being challenged. Blind belief and obedience, that pernicious partnership of regressive thinking, was shaken to the core. Eventually, intellectual maturity and philosophical dexterity paved the way for people to have the right to reason their own understanding and be able to express themselves without fear of condemnation of religious or political authorities. Immanuel Kant called this self-liberation *Selbstbestimmung*:[3] 'self-determination,' 'self-rule,' 'deciding for oneself,' and using one's own reasoning power. It also signified being free, self-organized, without inhibition from external circumstances. While Kant made no distinction between self-organization and morality, both were tightly connected with personal will, reason and ethical considerations.[4]

This was truly liberation philosophy. Independent thinking and decision-making without the interference of self-appointed ruling classes was the fruit of the new logic of the Enlightenment. The goal of this new logic was multi-layered: it was designed to understand and test the laws of nature through scientific methods, minimize human suffering, create a tolerant and beneficial society, introduce a new political mechanism of checks and balances, provide free access to knowledge, and finally develop a society that could challenge and debate the authority of religious institutions,

---

[2] See Neven Leddy and Avis Liefschitz (eds.), *Epicurus in the Enlightenment* (Oxford: Voltaire Foundation, University of Oxford, 2009). Those who were definitely influenced by Epicureanism were Malebranche, La Mettrie, Diderot, Helvétius and Hume.

[3] Immanuel Kant, *Grundlegung zu einer Metaphysik der Sitten*, 1786. See also Volker Gerhardt, "Selbstbestimmung: Zur Aktualität eines Begriffs," *FIPH Journal 8* (September 2006), 1-7.

[4] See Jacqueline Karl, *Selbstbestimmung und Individualität bei Platon: Eine Interpretation zu frühen und mittleren Dialogen* (Freiburg: Verlag Karl Alber, 2010), 22.

superstition, and the belief in god. Thus, to understand the natural world and human nature, reason, science, humanism and progress were and still are the basis of the Enlightenment.[5]

The new thinkers of the time recognized the power of a supreme logic out of which mathematics emerged, and this trajectory led to the discovery of the laws of nature and universe. These thinkers understood this natural logic to be greater than god per se, since god can't even change its own laws.[6] The power of observation and experimentation led to the conclusion that there is no counterevidence against the predictable rule of logic. Reason therefore became the law for logicians to follow, both to understand what was not previously understood, and, by the power of reason, to improve the conditions of life on various levels for everyone by overturning the power of dogma through scientific proof.

To implement the philosophy of liberation and to make the 'renaissance' of new ideas a reality, the ancient atomist and modern scientific theories needed to be proven empirically correct. The microscope, telescope, thermometer, barometer, and pendulum clock, sometimes known as "philosophical" instruments, gave the natural philosophers (who would become known as scientists) the ability to measure quantities that had never seen or understood before.[7] In a sense, those instruments that measured the physical realms were also indirectly testing the human capability of logical thought: if the instruments measured correctly and theories were proven correct, then the human logic behind them was also correct. Perhaps it is not without reason that science was called 'natural philosophy.'

The first scientific and empirical challenge to the old dogma began with a telescope. Galileo's telescope brought forward a revolutionary idea. In 1632 he published his manuscript claiming that the sun is in the center of the 'universe' and the earth revolves around the sun, in breach of the Church's 1616 agreement that he should not state such a thing. Galileo's 'heretical'

---

[5] See the new book by Steven Pinker, *Enlightenment Now: The Case for Reason, Science, Humanism and Progress* (New York: Viking-Penguin, 2018).
[6] William S. Cooper, *The Evolution of Reason: Logic as the Branch of Biology* (Cambridge: Cambridge University Press, 2001), 178.
[7] Jean-François Gauvin, "Instruments of Knowledge," *Oxford Handbook of Philosophy in Early Modern Europe*, edited by Desmond M. Clarke and Catherine Wilson (Oxford: Oxford University Press, 2011), 316-18 (315-337).

statement undermined the doctrine of the Church as the possessor of the only logical truth.[8]

Some 50 years after Galileo, in 1687, Newton used the calculus that he had invented for calculating infinitesimal units of speed and time and to work out the laws of motion using geometrical, mathematical interpretations. Using such mathematics, Newton could describe and even predict the motion of objects. This enterprise transformed reasoning power by taking humans beyond their natural and visual faculties.[9] The realization that mathematics could be used to describe the workings of the orderly universe overturned the medieval magical thinking that all is in god's hands. 'Progress' began to mean moving beyond merely understanding the causes of finding patterns and laws, such as the mathematical laws governing the universe. And although there was still the tendency among the religious crowd to attribute all causes and laws to god, human knowledge and existence were destined to be revolutionized by the renaissance of reason and science.[10]

In the same way, that science was leading the way to logic, philosophy also began to free people from superstition and subjugation. A number of philosophers of the Western Renaissance and Enlightenment drew their didactic philosophies from the Epicurean school, whose teachings had been demonized and stigmatized as hedonistic and immoral during the Church's medieval domination of Europe. The works of Epicurus had been destroyed or had gone missing, yet somehow, in the fifteenth century the single major work representing the teachings of Epicurus, Lucretius' *The Nature of Things*, resurfaced and was quickly copied and circulated (see chapter 5). Since its views were antithetical to the Church, Lucretius' text remained on the list of forbidden books. But despite such attempts at suppression, the ideas within could not be contained. Its time had finally come in the intellectual and scientific life of the European Renaissance, and philosophers of that time emphasized several major Epicurean principles (even though Epicurus or Lucretius were not always or directly mentioned in their works). These

---

[8] Desmond M. Clarke, "The Epistemology of Religious Belief," *Oxford Handbook of Philosophy in Early Modern Europe*, edited by Desmond M. Clarke and Catherine Wilson (Oxford: Oxford University Press, 2011), 549-559 (548-570).

[9] Stephen Gaukroger, "Picturability and Mathematical Ideas of Knowledge," *Oxford Handbook of Philosophy in Early Modern Europe*, edited by Desmond M. Clarke and Catherine Wilson (Oxford: Oxford University Press, 2011), 338-9, 350, 352, 354 (338-360).

[10] Tad M. Schmaltz, "From Causes to Laws," *Oxford Handbook of Philosophy in Early Modern Europe*, edited by Desmond M. Clarke and Catherine Wilson (Oxford: Oxford University Press, 2011), 32-50 (32-50).

principles later dominated the Enlightenment atmosphere: the power of reason, relying on one's own nature, appreciating pleasure, avoiding useless knowledge, and liberating the oppressed mind.[11]

Philosophical propositions such as the atomism of Epicurus-Lucretius not only regained momentum in the philosophical materialism of the seventeenth century onward, but triumphed from being a hypothesis to becoming a sound epistemological model in the domain of the sciences and philosophy.

Generations of Enlightenment philosophers brought about an incredible upheaval on the continent, but a number of prominent ones captured the spirit of ancient atomism, empiricism and rationalism. For example, the mechanical philosophy of Newton is inherently atomistic. It has been adduced that Newton's atomistic views appear in the *Principia Mathematica*, where Newton claimed "the least parts of bodies to be—all extended, and hard and impenetrable, and moveable, and endowed with their proper inertia."[12] "There is no doubt that Newton shared the assumption of the ancient and mechanical atomists that there is just one kind of homogeneous matter of which all atoms are composed. This is clear from the way in which Newton explained the differing densities of observable matter in terms of the amount of space intervening between the component atoms."[13]

Newton had established another logical niche: the predictable, orderly, mathematical natural laws that govern the universe. John Locke, a friend of Newton's, took this idea further, stating that if the universe and nature are governed by laws, then societies should be governed by such order as well, not by the arbitrary and absolute power of the elites.[14] The very same political spirit influenced a series of French revolutionary thinkers and philosophers such as Voltaire, Montesquieu and Rousseau. The sciences and philosophy, in reflecting one another, relentlessly emphasized the value of thinking and reason over belief and superstition, especially about matters in the public realms.

Besides logic and materialism, the liberation philosophy essentials of reason, happiness and self-rule were powerful themes among Renaissance and Enlightenment philosophers. The number of philosophers who espoused

---

[11] Pagden, *The Enlightenment and Why It Still Matters*, 58-61.
[12] "Atomism," https://plato.stanford.edu/entries/atomism-modern/. Accessed October 30, 2018.
[13] See https://plato.stanford.edu/entries/atomism-modern/. Accessed October 30, 2018.
[14] See G.A. J. Rogers, "Locke, Newton and Enlightenment," *Vista in Astronomy* 22/4 (1978), 471-76. While some debate whether both thinkers influenced each other, it is clear that they both laid the foundation of the Enlightenment in the 17th century.

and wrote about ideals that seem almost copied from the work of ancient liberation philosophers is more numerous than can be included here. But a brief survey of a handful of these thinkers demonstrates the power and infiltration of liberation ideas.

The Renaissance philosopher Michel de Montaigne built upon Lucretian and the Epicurean philosophies by emphasizing that living well is not dependent on our intellectual arrogance, or when we patronize non-literate people. Instead, he claimed that the power of reason is the highest-level tool to be used in order to attain happiness and pleasure of life, not to gain so much dull knowledge. Philosophy was in fact the source of living well and virtuously. Living happily also meant being physically strong in order to withstand heat, cold, pain, difficulties and other pressures in life. It meant maintaining a temperate mood, thinking honorably, traveling, studying philosophy for attaining an adequate knowledge of life, and dealing with death using soundness of mind. Montaigne's idea of happiness aimed at ridding oneself of the fear of death, hell and suffering.[15]

In the work of Nicolas Malebranche, an influential seventeenth-century philosopher, we see the effort to liberate people from the constricting influences of religion and myth. In endorsing the rejection of superstition and medieval metaphysics, Malebranche argued that in an orderly and empirical world even a genuine god cannot save a good person from drowning.[16] All the evidence points to this fact, as opposed to blind belief. The illusion that god is punishing human beings through natural disasters, commonly known as "acts of god," is anthropomorphized in one's own mind.[17]

In the same period, Spinoza accelerated the disputation of belief versus reason, holding the opinion that the scriptures and prophets offer no knowledge; they only heighten the imagination.[18] The character of the 'god' of religion was challenged by Spinoza's point that 'god' as a nomenclature may

---

[15] José R. Maria Neto, "Scepticism," *Oxford Handbook of Philosophy in Early Modern Europe*, edited by Desmond M. Clarke and Catherine Wilson (Oxford: Oxford University Press, 2011), 230, 241 (227-248). (Charron, of course, was accused of being an atheist.)
[16] Steven Nadler, "Conceptions of God," *Oxford Handbook of Philosophy in Early Modern Europe*, edited by Desmond M. Clarke and Catherine Wilson (Oxford: Oxford University Press, 2011), 528-9.
[17] The presence of Epicurean ideas in Malebranche's disputation against Christian dogma has been debated. See Elodie Argaud, "Bayle's Defence of Epicurus: The Use and Abuse of Malebranche's *Méditations chrétiennes*," in *Epicurus in the Enlightenment*, Neven Leddy and Avis Liefschitz (eds.) (Oxford: Voltaire Foundation, University of Oxford, 2009), 13-30.
[18] Richard H. Popkin, *Spinoza* (Oxford: Oneworld Publications, 2007), 59.

have originally been intended to represent the harmony and mystery of nature. Spinoza meant that god is *natura naturans*: nature is natural; it cannot be supernatural. In this sense, nature is reality, and reality is harmony. "Spinoza pragmatically was an Epicurean materialist. As in Epicurus and Lucretius, Spinoza's God is scarcely distinguishable from Nature, and is altogether indifferent to us, even to our intellectual love for him as urged upon us by Spinoza."[19] This was a major breakthrough in challenging the Judeo-Christian god and introducing a new concept of god based on visible nature and the harmony around it.[20] The Epicurean-Lucretian lens filtered Spinoza's reading of the Hebrew Bible.[21] Spinoza defended freedom of thought, speech and belief and refused to allow the priesthood to have power over communities.[22]

The pendulum of thought could not be stopped; rebellious empirical ideas were pouring in, such as from the eighteenth-century figure Denis Diderot. His endorsement of the cultivation of pleasure is directly draw from Epicurus' notion of enjoying life.[23] As with other philosophers of his time, Diderot's atomism and the manifestation of nature based on the dance and configuration of atoms was most probably inspired by Epicurus and Lucretius.[24] Through undertaking the monumental work of his *Encyclopedia*, Diderot also became a major proponent of the mass popularization of knowledge that was previously held in the monopoly of the church, the state, and the artisanal classes. His cause also became the power of reason over belief, which gradually created a wide rift between him and the Church. He claimed that there is no god and the creation story is only a fiction (all reflected in his *Pensées*). Meanwhile, Diderot also rejected all public claims of

---

[19] Harold Bloom "The Heretic Jew," a book review "*Betraying Spinoza* by Rebecca Goldstein," *New York Times*, June 18, 2006.

[20] Spinoza's religious enemies suspected that his pantheistic outlook came from plagiarizing and combining the ideas of the Kabbala with the terminologies of Descartes to make it look original. See Popkin, *Spinoza*, 1, 37, 82.

[21] Warren Montag, "Lucretius Hebraizant: Spinoza's Reading of Ecclesiastes," *European Journal of Philosophy*, (Feb. 27, 2012): Wiley Online Library.

[22] Ursula Goldenbaum, "Sovereignty and Obedience," *Oxford Handbook of Philosophy in Early Modern Europe*, edited by Desmond M. Clarke and Catherine Wilson (Oxford: Oxford University Press, 2011), 500, 502, 505, 509, 512-13 (500-521).

[23] Natania Meeker, "Sexing Epicurean Materialism in Diderot," in *Epicurus in the Enlightenment*, Neven Leddy and Avis Liefschitz (eds.) (Oxford: Voltaire Foundation, University of Oxford, 2009), 85-104.

[24] See Gerhardt Stenger, "L'atomisme dans les *Pensées philosophiques*. Diderot entre Gassendi et Buffon," *Dix-Huitième Siècle*, (Fait partie d'un numéro thématique: L'épicurisme des Lumières 2003), 76 (75-100). See also by the same author, *Diderot, Le combattant de la liberté* (Paris: Perrin 2013).

mystical experiences and miracles. Through his skepticism, he declared that god is only found within the compounds of sanctuaries, while the members of society are suffering and in tears.

Diderot's other cause was *freedom* – of religion, thought, and eventually self. The thinking self symbolizes one's own religion and one's own god, as he put it. The self and nature were for Diderot the most authentic sources for the clarity that humans sought, but only if humans could leave their blind views behind. Diderot's intellectual mandate in defense of freedom, free information-encyclopedia for all, reason, and atheism impacted the philosophical and social realms tremendously. The rising intellectual change of attitude worried the Church. Diderot's approach, with the naturalism and atheism that stemmed from Epicurean and Lucretian thought, was feared by the establishment. Not surprisingly, his ideas were condemned and his book ordered burned in public. Philosophers were suspect; their books were banned. Yet despite this, two more important philosophers influenced by Epicurean thought swayed the European way of thinking enormously as seen in the works of Claude Adrien Helvétius and Julien de La Mettrie in the 18th century.

The essays of Claude Adrien Helvétius in "On the Mind" (*De l'Esprit*) were of such a utilitarian, rational and atheistic nature that they caused outrage in the Church and resulted in the burning of his works on the basis of heresy. The very same aims of happiness and pleasure of life that Epicurus-Lucretius emphasized, Helvétius developed by different methods. He believed birth and the mental propensities of people are sheer chance and haphazard, but that people are free to avoid pain and explore new potentials. His poetry on "Happiness" (*Le Bonheur*) symbolizes his hedonistic philosophy and his promotion of a new self-education regardless of birth and environment – all in the pursuit of happiness despite the inequalities and the despotism of religion, state and universities. Thus, his political ideas were also influenced by Epicurean notions.[25]

Julien de La Mettrie was another Enlightenment atheist-materialist-hedonist philosopher-physician. One cannot fail to notice the Epicurus-Lucretius influence on his ideas about mind as matter, and that humans are just another animal in nature in pursuit of pleasure. It is said that La Mettrie did not necessarily give atheism a good name in his day, bluntly claiming the guts of human and those of animals to be identical, thus published in his

---

[25] Pierre Force, "Helvétius as an Epicurean Political Theorist," in *Epicurus in the Enlightenment*, Neven Leddy and Avis Liefschitz (eds.) (Oxford: Voltaire Foundation, University of Oxford, 2009), 105-118.

treatise, *Man a Machine*.²⁶ Nevertheless, he outlines a treatment for the self through cultivating pleasure without religion,²⁷ a 'medical Epicureanism'²⁸ (*Discours Sur le Bonheur*), and describes the human biochemical constitution as a machine that drives human life.²⁹

The philosophies of Democritus, Epicurus and Lucretius continued to revolutionize the view of the human condition based on those ideals of freedom and pursuit of happiness. Thomas Jefferson admitted that he was an Epicurean, and it is not at all difficult to recognize how the American Declaration of Independence and the Constitution arose out of Epicurean elements. Despite the 2100-year gap between the two men, Epicurus and Jefferson both believed that all people deserve "life, liberty and the pursuit of happiness." For Epicurus, all people, included women and slaves, poor and rich, were equally capable of learning and enjoying the wisdom of life – all attended his Garden academy in pursuit of knowledge. The paradox between Jefferson's ownership of slaves and his ideal of "pursuit of happiness" for all demonstrates that he was still entangled by the discrimination and limitations of his generation, and not fully able to implement his Epicurean imagination and idealism.

Two other personalities who benefited in one way or another from the Epicurean philosophy were Karl Marx and Friedrich Nietzsche. Both of these figures in their own distinct ways influenced European thought. In his writings in the nineteenth century, Karl Marx relied on Hegelian philosophy but his doctoral dissertation was based on Epicurean fundamentals, entitled: "The Difference Between the Democritean and Epicurean Philosophy of Nature." Marx's materialism, egalitarianism and happiness for all found their roots in the naturalism and rationalism of Democritus and Epicurus. For Marx, Epicurus represented the Greek enlightenment, and was a blissful and

---

[26] Pagden, *The Enlightenment and Why It Still Matters*, 111-12.
[27] Ibid., 112.
[28] See Charles T. Wolfe, "A Happiness Fit for Organic Bodies: La Mettrie's Medical Epicureanism" in *Epicurus in the Enlightenment*, Neven Leddy and Avis Liefschitz (eds.) (Oxford: Voltaire Foundation, University of Oxford, 2009), 69-84.
[29] This empirical and hedonistic influence of the Epicurean school of thought *Système d'Epicure* (The System of Epicurus) in La Mettrie's *Philosophical Works* has been edited and published in 1996. See Julien de la Mettrie, "The System of Epicurus," in *Machine Man and Other Writings*, edited by Ann Thomson (Cambridge: Cambridge University Press, 1996), 89-116.

satisfied philosopher.[30] Marx himself embraced the power of philosophy as a vehicle of awakening as well as social and intellectual transformation.

To consider further the potency of Epicurean pleasure and didactic thinking, we can see that Nietzsche's life and writing in the nineteenth century were also influenced by the example of Epicurus as well. "For Nietzsche, Epicurus is one of the greatest human beings to have graced the earth, and the inventor of 'heroic-idyllic philosophizing'."[31] The philosophy of Epicurean pleasure, peace, good will, self-cultivation and liberation is certainly reflected in Nietzsche's *The Joyful Science* or *The Gay Science* (*Die fröhliche Wissenschaft*), but particularly in his *The Wanderer and His Shadow* (*Der Wanderer und sein Schatten*).[32] Nietzsche, perhaps noting that although Epicurus's teachings have been rejected politically in the past, they were fundamentally sound, and alive and well, had this to say about Epicurus: "Epicurus has been alive in all ages and lives now, unknown to those who have called and call themselves Epicureans, and enjoying no reputation among philosophers. He has, moreover, himself forgotten his own name: it was the heaviest burden he ever cast off."[33] Nietzsche, although an atheist himself, was first and foremost searching for philosophical and psychological methods to liberate himself and his audience from the bondage of religion. Nietzsche was searching a philosophical position beyond theism and atheism, where the autonomy of the mind is rooted.[34]

It was the confluence of streams of thought that made the Enlightenment a critical bifurcation and an influential era. Consequently, a new mindset with a new language outside of the traditional theistic cultural life was adopted. Arguments debating logic and the power of god led to rationalist and anti-rationalist discourses.[35] Logical "ideas," were defined, given status, and believed to emanate from self-reflection.[36] The power of abstraction and the

---

[30] Keith, Ansell-Pearson, "Heroic-idyllic Philosophizing: Nietzsche and the Epicurean Tradition," *Royal Institute of Philosophy* Supplement, 74 (2014), 237, 242, quotes from Marx's dissertation. (237-263).
[31] Ibid., 237. The author quotes F. Nietzsche, *The Wanderer and His Shadow*, trans. Gary Handwerk (Stanford: Stanford University Press, 2013), section 295.
[32] Ibid., 238-41.
[33] Ibid., 239, quoting Nietzsche, *The Wanderer and His Shadow*, section 227.
[34] Keiji, Nishitani, *Religion and Nothingness*, trans. Jan van Bragt (Berkeley: University of California Press, 1983), 64.
[35] Nadler, "Conceptions of God," 525-547.
[36] Pauline Phemister, "Ideas," *Oxford Handbook of Philosophy in Early Modern Europe*, edited by Desmond M. Clarke and Catherine Wilson (Oxford: Oxford University Press, 2011), 142-159 (142-159).

dialectics of deductive reasoning led to strong philosophical traditions. Not only just the sciences, but the language of metaphysics also had to be adjusted along these new lines of thought. The "abuse of words", whether religious threats, or the use of disturbing and insulting jargon by the authorities which had affected the way of thinking of the population had to be purged from the public sphere. "Artificial ignorance and learned gibberish" were to be replaced with "charm of eloquence" and "reason and eloquence" to modify the minds, and lead humans out of obscurity.[37] And thus, the unfolding of the Enlightenment and its resulting achievements became a river of thought arising out of the confluence of many minor streams, including the 'stream' of Epicurean philosophy and its offerings of liberation philosophy.

***

Given the intellectual power of hundreds of thinkers and scientists, Enlightenment ideals had the potential for global effect, but instead remained limited to parts of Europe and North America. Nowadays, however, due to our knowledge of the world, extensive traveling, translation of Asian texts, and knowledge of liberating schools of philosophy, the world can now learn more about Epicurus, Lucretius, and modern European philosophers who were influenced by them. Having said that, perhaps even Europe itself, despite having passed through its "first" Enlightenment, is ready to embrace and integrate older ideas from within the Asian philosophies in revitalizing a "Second" Enlightenment.[38]

A critical paradox (and weakness) in the European Enlightenment was that despite such lofty goals of happiness, they still saw humanity in terms of 'us' and 'them'. Despite the fact that the Enlightenment was a secularized phenomenon, its values were primarily endorsed relative to Europe's overseas settlers due to their shared Christian background, and were rarely applied to those people being colonized.[39] The Enlightenment's 'search for happiness' only referred to the Europeans' own happiness and those like them; it didn't apply to the happiness of everyone. They were aiming for the

---

[37] Jaap Maat, "Language and Semiotics," *Oxford Handbook of Philosophy in Early Modern Europe*, edited by Desmond M. Clarke and Catherine Wilson (Oxford: Oxford University Press, 2011), 272, 277, 278, 291 (272-294).

[38] The designation of "Second Enlightenment" here in this chapter is not to be confused with the German translation of Neil Postman's book title, *Die zweite Aufklärung: von 18. Ins 21. Jahrhundret* with the original English title of *Building a Bridge from the 18th Century: How the Past Can Improve Our Future*, 2000.

[39] Pagden, *The Enlightenment and Why It Still Matters*, 83.

pursuit of 'happiness' of their own people and countries actually at the expense of others' happiness. They couldn't yet see the humanity of the Africans, Asians, South Americans, Native Americans or the original people of any other colonies. It was not a universal humanism. Gender inequality, racism, national-chauvinism, eurocentrism and colonialism remained uninhibited and malicious despite the Enlightenment ideals. This fundamental paradox led to a fatal flaw of inequality and inhumanity which we continue to see manifesting even today around the world.

Considering this, there is an even more compelling necessity for a Second Enlightenment. This time around, though, philosophy can and should take a more practical and humane direction, supporting the "pursuit of freedom and happiness" not just for one's own people, religion, nation or continent, but for all.

Perhaps the teachings of the unique schools of Çārvāka, Buddhism, Khayyam and Rumi among others can help remedy this weakness, if brought forward in a Second Enlightenment in the same way the European Enlightenment thinkers referred to Epicurus and Lucretius. To integrate the prime ideas of these philosophies into a fresher and fuller interpretation of European philosophical and intellectual culture might bring the West and Asia and Africa closer to each other in an attempt to bring about a broader global Enlightenment – a gradual liberation from dogma of all kinds, in a true sense.

***

Liberation Philosophy Today: Çārvāka, Buddhism, Khayyam and Rumi as "New" Sources for a Second Enlightenment

We have seen how ancient Epicureanism wielded a great influence on the revolution of thought in the Western Renaissance-Enlightenment. Thus, the great focus and challenge of this century will be to explore whether the East is also capable of relying on its past philosophical traditions in order to salvage modern, secular, rational and democratic ideals, and whether the West, as well as other parts of the world, can also continue to progress by tapping into the wisdom of the ancient East. Let us then, in the context of the Second Enlightenment, put the empirical and advanced ideas of Çārvākas, Buddhist, Khayyam and Rumi in perspective.

A pioneering empirical and pragmatic philosophy emerged with the emergence of the Çārvāka school in the Indian subcontinent around the 6th century BCE. The proponents of this important school put forward several powerful, practical ideas which were progressive back then, and forward-thinking even in our modern times.

Their epistemology was an empirical one, similar to what John Locke and David Hume adopted in the Enlightenment period. The experience of the sensory system is a valid perception of the world and the immediate reality with which one is surrounded. For the Çārvākas as well as for Hume and Locke, all other speculations, testimonies, interpretations, sacred texts and what priests claimed were invalid sources for our knowledge of the world. Fundamentally, as Locke argued, direct experience is the most evident knowledge that needs no further proof, a conception which is no different from the Çārvākas' naturalism.[40] In broader terms, the epistemology of the Çārvākas, Buddhist, Locke and Hume are extremely close to each other.[41] The knowledge of *self* over metaphysics or god is the epicenter of a remarkable philosophy which was represented by Hume and Buddhism,[42] not to mention the Çārvāka philosophy. The Çārvākas as a whole offered enough potent and logical ideas that they could have been a vehicle of Enlightenment some 2,000 years ago.

The question is whether the Çārvākas' once-powerful philosophy can make a return, not just in the form of a few websites or scholarly monographs, but in such a way that Asian, European, and other non-European social and political thinkers of today could draw upon the Çārvākas' intellectual achievements. Perhaps the similarities between Çārvākas, Epicureanism and empiricism of Locke and Hume are not a coincidence but suggest a prototypal, perhaps even archetypal, model of the human craving to know based on the experience of the world in an empirical manner, moment to moment.

Buddhism too was and is a philosophical powerhouse, out of which an evolutionary and empirical philosophy emerged. Although Buddhism in the course of centuries has turned into various religious traditions, as a philosophy it emphasizes *thinking*, not merely *believing*. The core of such thinking, as discussed in chapter 6, deals with an empirical self. This school of philosophy frees people by emphasizing there is no need to *believe* in any truth.

In its 2500-year old history, Buddhism has been mixed with many indigenous cultures and native religions and is still largely entangled with truth-based and religious attitudes. However, new secular approaches may have certain success

---

[40] Dale Maurice Riepe, *The Naturalistic Tradition in Indian Thought*, (1961; Delhi: Motilal Banarsidass 1964), 63-64.
[41] Riepe, *The Naturalistic Tradition in Indian Thought*, 63. See also Arunjit Gill, "In Search of Intuitive Knowledge: A Comparison of Eastern and Western Epistemology," Doctoral Dissertation submitted to Simon and Fraser University, Canada, 2006, 18-19. Online PDF.
[42] Pagden, *The Enlightenment and Why It Still Matters*, 126-29.

in salvaging the major didactic aspects of this shrewd philosophical stream, such as the inner workings of the mind and the notion of emptiness.

In enhancing the detailed discussion of Buddhist liberation philosophy, the six-point summary below may help us better appreciate understand secular Buddhist principles and their applicability on a broader intellectual level for our modern times:

1. **Interdependence and Compassion:** The reminder of the interdependence of all things, brings with it a responsibility, a sense of others in the world. This critical principle of interdependence among all beings plays a major role in overcoming the 'us vs. them' mental trap that has led to so much human suffering.

2. **Buddhist Psychology of Happiness and Individual Freedom:** The central goal of Buddhism is liberation from all sources of entrapment, be it self or religion. Thus, deep joy and equanimity in life is the end goal.

3. **Rejection of Absolutism, and Embrace of Impermanence:** Buddhism rejects dogmatism, including the rejection of supernatural claims, and the idea of absolute truth. The Buddha considered suspect any *truth* that would point to an entity as real, fixed, infallible, finality, ultimate, or a solution forever.[43] Due to impermanency, all things of the world are in the state of flux, and no-thing remains fixed and final forever. Pleasure is therefore the result of an awareness of each moment rather than clinging to things that will produce anxiety

4. **Logic and Epistemology:** Buddhism is both empirical and rational. The *pramana* or the *proof* of the world is not based on abstract or metaphysical truth-claims. It is based on two empirical criteria – sensory perception and deductive reasoning. Such epistemology can help reduce dependence on supernatural or mythical claims which so often lead to divisive and ambiguous belief systems. This and similar empirical-rational systems of knowledge can enhance the prospect of a new universal Enlightenment.

---

[43] See Stephen Batchelor, *After Buddhism: Rethinking the Dharma for a Secular Age* (New Haven: Yale University Press, 2015), 118-120.

5. **Ontology of Emptiness**: The transition from one moment to another, from one state to the next, suggests the lack of an absolute state. Instead, such never-ending transitions point to an impersonal mechanism in the larger interdependent world. Self-perpetuating mechanical laws lead all things to the point of their annihilation, and the rise of new things. Nothing remains permanently itself. The concept of emptiness in Buddhist dialectics continues to be an intriguing theme for the modern theoretical physicists and a theme for deeper intellectual as well as scientific explorations.

6. **Death is Final**: The notion of parinirvana is a complete dissolution of body and mind with the final exit from the cycle of existence – all traces will be irreversibly destroyed. Parinirvana should have put an end to any fantasies or speculative beliefs of return to life. The Buddha found it irrelevant and unpragmatic to ponder about heaven and hell, reward and punishment. Among all uncertainties, two things are certain from the Buddhist point of view: the present time to live pleasurably, and death.

Unlike Buddhism, Khayyam's philosophy did not become a religion, and in fact thoroughly countered religion and religious thinking. His poetical philosophy, despite its incredible potential for enlightenment due to its non-religious themes, was considered abhorrent by the religious establishment and various medieval authors.[44] In fact, free and dialectical philosophy after the time of Khayyam sank to its lowest level. With the emergence of the dogmatic philosophy of al-Ghazzālī in the twelfth century and the propagation of a number of theological streams of thought, the chance for the Khayyamian philosophy to take root in intellectual and free-thinking circles was largely repressed and gradually lost ground altogether over the course of centuries.[45]

---

[44] See many available works on the biography of Khayyam, namely Mehdi Aminrazavi, *The Wine of Wisdom: The Life, Poetry and Philosophy of Omar Khayyam* (Oxford: Oneworld, 2007), 40-66.

[45] The ongoing tyrannical environment undermined philosophy as well as the culture of scientific research. The destruction of many valuable philosophical and unruly works such as the works Ibn Rāwandī (d. 911) and Zakarīyā Rāzī (d. 925) among others by fanatical religious rulers left little chance for further intellectual exploration and debates. See Vaziri, *Buddhism in Iran*, 170-172. See also Sarah Stroumsa, *Freethinkers of Medieval Islam: Ibn*

It is not at all difficult to see similarities parallels between Khayyam and the philosophers of Çārvākas, the Buddha, Epicurus, and Lucretius. Although typically thought of as a poet, Khayyam stands alongside these philosophers not only as regards his empirical-rationalist philosophy but also with his scientific achievements. Given his high achievements in the sciences of his time along with his lucid philosophy, he could easily be designated as a prime architect of Eastern Enlightenment whose time was completely missed. Khayyam belonged to the epoch of 800-1,200 CE which encompassed an intellectual region whose Golden Age pioneers of mathematics, astronomy, music, medicine, art, poetry and philosophy collectively could have brought about an extraordinary Central Asian Enlightenment. But due to political and religious demagogy, the demise of intellectualism became inevitable and thus the downfall of a *Lost Enlightenment in Central Asia*.[46] Nevertheless, Khayyam stood tall as one of the last great Central Asian scholars whose poetry is still guiding us.

Given that content of his well-equipped and philosophically loaded poetry, Khayyam could also be considered the groundbreaker of Process Philosophy in the Persianate and Islamic world, whose focus is to study the dynamic and changing nature of reality. The ancient giants such as Heraclitus, Lao Tzu and Chuang Tzu were the forerunners of Alfred North Whitehead and William James among the prominent Process Philosophers of modern times.

Thus, we can see how relevant Khayyam's foundational principles are for an emerging Enlightenment, both in the East and the West:

1. **Humanism:** Cognitive growth and human dignity in the Khayyamian world means to uproot ignorance and illusory

---

al-Rawandi, Abu Bakr al-Razi and Their Impact on Islamic Thought (Leiden/Boston/Koln: Brill, 1999). Thus, Sufism and poetry became outlets for the literati to express their shrewdest intellectual and spiritual experiences. The dying philosophical tradition in Iran made a strong return with the School of Isfahan in the seventeenth century, but this revival was short-lived as the hard-core theologians of the time and those who followed suppressed such challenging philosophies, and dogmatic theologians even demonized research in the areas of mathematics and chemistry in particular.

[46] S. Fredrick Starr, *Lost Enlightenment: Central Asia's Golden Age from the Arab Conquest to Tamerlane* (Princeton, NJ: Princeton University Press, 2015). Starr basically argues that it was the Central Asian scientists and thinkers who by and large brought about the Golden Age between 800 to 1,200 CE, not the commonly known Arabs of Arabia. Since these Central Asians wrote their works in Arabic language and any Arabic work would be associated with the Arab-Islamic culture of Baghdad, it became a common misnomer by calling it Arab or even Islamic Golden Age, which in fact it should be known as the Central Asian Golden Age.

beliefs of return to life. Freedom and happiness is above all the knowledge of metaphysics.

2. **Empiricism:** Khayyam's empiricism vividly emphasized human sensory observation and the real experience of how the world operates. The existential processes of construction and demolition seem to be the rule. In his natural philosophy, Khayyam treated nothing beyond the physical world, life and the experience of joy.

3. **Rationalism:** His rationalism took into consideration logical physics. To avoid treating matters of life with emotionalism, Khayyam supported utilizing logic to deduce the unalterable laws of existence and the irreversible laws of biology.

4. **Skepticism:** Khayyam remained emphatically skeptical about metaphysical and religious truth claims and speculations. The utopia of immortality and a better life in the underworld of afterlife met his strongest ridicule and criticism. Any knowledge that contradicts the experience of here and now even though claimed by holy people as truths must be suspected.

5. **Hedonism: The Joy of Now;** Khayyam prioritized the awareness of here and now and the realness of this life. He dialectically tried to remove the clashing paradox of constant joy-sadness in human emotions by resolving and replacing it with a higher understanding of natural processes.

Khayyam's philosophy can undoubtedly be catalogued as timeless and universal. Insightfully, he detected a universal psychological friability among the crowd which needed to be purged. He saw how some become highly religious with the hope of influencing the course of affairs through prayers and intercession and bargaining with god, ignoring the fact that no natural law can be abandoned for the sake of some expressive wishes. By undoing the old nagging mind, Khayyam introduced a robust attitude of living freely and wholeheartedly. He advised embracing a life similar to that of a flower: it buds, blossoms, radiates its fragrance and beauty through joyful living, accepts its impermanency, and withers away without clinging. The gorgeous flower that once was vanishes from the face of existence without regret or memories, and yet has graced the earth with its color, scent, and being, and through its interaction with the rest of the world.

Khayyam's poetry had already initiated an "Age of Reason" in his time and geography the way Lucretius' writings did in his. Khayyam's poetical legacy with its unprecedented imageries and messages prompted and influenced a new genre of literature in Persian. His philosophy demands a rescue from its stagnant position to a dynamic everyday life. As a thinker with an unbreachable universal logic and realism, he brilliantly bridges Western Epicureanism with Eastern Zen. Khayyam's teachings can support the intellectual progress of the future and be one of the key sources of the new Enlightenment.

Rumi: A Secular Enlightener

It is important to briefly mention Rumi, the great Persian poet of the thirteenth century, in the list of Enlightening men of Asia.[47] The relevance of Rumi in today's world may be assessed from two perspectives: 1. After almost 800 years, he has made an incredible comeback in the popular East-West popular culture. 2. His iconoclastic and secular thinking resonates with the modern political and social ideals of the twenty-first century as delineated in this book.

Here, for our purposes, it is important to emphasize a few key points relevant to the context of liberation philosophy Rumi represented. Liberation first found true meaning in Rumi's personal life when at age 37 he experienced that life-transforming meeting with Shams. Rumi then abandoned his profession and scholastic circle, fearlessly rebelling against his past and his culture's ancestral belief system. His new approach to life symbolized a first step to self-liberation.

Over the course of years, Rumi toiled to reinvent himself despite his clash with the theological establishment and the fervent Sufi circle around him. By ignoring such clashes, he went on to produce magnificent literature that laid a pioneering and inclusive foundation for human evolution. Over 60,000 verses of poetry backed his new reasoning of life. By immersing in the world of cognitive experiences, he realized self-liberation is simply a conduit to

---

[47] For a detailed discussion of Rumi and Shams, see Mostafa Vaziri, *Rumi and Shams' Silent Rebellion: Parallels with Vedanta, Buddhism and Shaivism*, (New York & London: Palgrave Macmillan 2015). Those who have linked Rumi narrowly with Sufism and Islamic mysticism have done him a disservice. This labeling has obscured his ideals of secularism, universalism and humanism, and his role as a liberation philosopher. As happened with Khayyam, Rumi's contribution to philosophy and a broader sociocultural renaissance in the Islamic world was missed. Instead, after his death Rumi was anachronistically reduced to being the "founder of Mevlevi Sufi order". The error in lumping the universality of Rumi's and his teacher Shams' universal philosophies and their erudite rebellion into the simple category of 'Sufism' have been fully discussed in a separate book. See Vaziri, *Rumi and Shams' Silent Rebellion*.

liberate others. His secularism, humanism and universalism are his most forceful messages that are reflected in the verses of his *Divan* and *Masnavi*.[48]

At some point, Rumi became aware of the limitation and failure of religion in being exclusivist and non-egalitarian. The declaration of inclusivism and universalism in religions is inherently meant to believe in and follow these religions, not to doubt them. Islam, like some other religions, not only excludes those who do not belong to the faith but also takes a harsh position against the infidels, apostates and heretics. Without any ambiguity, Rumi composed hundreds of poems in his *Divan* and *Masnavi* to in fact *include* the infidels (*kāfir*), apostates, heretics, non-Muslims, and all ethnic groups of humanity known to him from Zanzibar of Africa to the Romans, Indians, Turks, Persians and others – all as one *secular* human family without denominational or ethnic discrimination. Rumi, as a wise and critical thinker, did not want to take sides, and welcomed universal equality for humanity without keeping Islam or Sufism as his criteria. His anti-violence message was also universal, heralding to protect all sentient beings, including plants. His cardinal message was that all humanity receives their life not through their native gods or their parochial surroundings but through a universal source, Love,[49] a source to which we all belong. This is the reason for which that Rumi's transcultural appeal has enjoyed an unprecedented triumph over the centuries.

He defied religious severities and self-righteousness. His continuous defiance bothered the theologians of his time. Due to their horror at witnessing Rumi playing musical instruments, dancing, and adopting a receptive attitude towards heretics and non-Muslims, the religious orthodoxy of the time gave him several warnings.

Nevertheless, by re-establishing the culture of music in human life after years of rejection by the Islamic theological establishment of the time, Rumi laid a new foundation for generations to tune in to the moving and exhilarating sound of music. The large number of his poems on the subject of happiness (*shādī*) makes him a philosopher who, like Epicurus and Khayyam, fostered the cultivation of tranquility and freedom as a pleasurable state of

---

[48] His production of *Masnavi*, is nothing short of an encyclopedia; a unique integration of literature and anecdotes from many different regions and cultures about so many useful social themes from around the world. His *Masnavi* is a master work and impressive scholarship; a work to wake the monolithic thinkers up.

[49] Love is defined to be a nameless, placeless, timeless and immortal field of energy, a force of life which makes life and its beauties manifest themselves. For an alternative discussion and meaning of "Love" in the Rumian context see, Vaziri, *Rumi and Shams' Silent Rebellion*, 85-96.

being. The primacy of self took precedence over god. Moreover, Rumi's humanist position supplanted any religious and ethnic discrimination, a rather modern approach to human value for the difficult century he lived in. This egalitarianism and universalism are repeatedly emphasized in Rumi's philosophical poetry.

In his collection of poetry, he brings certain disarray in the Islamic monotheistic thinking, sometimes the world is god, other times Shams is god, or self is god and sometimes there is even no god. Through this language play with heterogeneous meanings, he brought monotheism into a certain disarray. He confronted the purity-seeking men of religion by using profanity. Even leaving out Rumi's metaphoricity, paradoxality and contradictability,[50] we must acknowledge that he radically de-emotionalized the religious and mystically-oriented mindset. He did this to show us that in living in this real world with all its diverse people, we should not allow mystical states take over in an anesthetizing way but rather we should harness and make use of these spiritual experiences in solving problems. Rumi has a highly esteemed place in the West in modern times because his language is the language of Enlightenment and cosmopolitanism.

Rumi's prodigious philosophy, similar to those of the other philosophers addressed in this book, focused on emancipating the natural self from the fictitious self and the deception of the everyday social-cultural environment. His philosophy of mind advocates a sensible and healthy psyche which knows its own makeup as well as the nature of the world. Rumi addressed the mind's dangerous propensity to run after ideas, opinions and beliefs while seeking distractions and temporary anchors. He saw that religious impulsiveness causes a moving away from the center of one's own existence. In transcending thousands of years of cultural and religious beliefs, Rumi sought to locate the natural mind of the universe, free from beliefs buried in the human mind. The emanation of this pure and wise mind is the primordial mind of the universe, *Love*. Thus, the primacy of locating the natural self over metaphysics, and valuing scrupulous thinking over sentimental mysticism, remained the focus of the poetry of this master of liberation.

Rumi's philosophical and social positions are the most appealing in his poetry especially when they address the dilemmas of this turbulent and tribalistic century:

---

[50] "Metaphorizität, " "Paradoxalität, " "Widersprüchlichkeit," borrowing ideas and these terms from Reinhard Margreiter, *Erfahrung und Mystik: Grenzen der Symbolisierung*, (Berlin: Akademie Verlag, 1997), 68.

1. **Universalism and Cosmopolitanism**: All ethnicities, all cultures, all people of the world belong to the same human family. To Rumi, different skin colors, traditions and languages are nothing but a façade.

2. **Secularism**: Keeping religious dogma, discrimination and stigmatization out of intercultural and human affairs – dismantling the use and application of the label *heretics* or *heresy* in public and private spheres.

3. **Humanism**: Dissolving the hardest of dogmas in the alchemy of Love – the longing for coexistence not out of force but out of loving one another, the world and nature.

4. **Non-Violence and Environmental Respect**: Violence among nations and religious communities is absolutely discouraged by Rumi. Non-violence also includes going beyond human affairs. One should not cut trees or damage nature as we and nature are interwoven.

5. **Promotion of the Culture of Music and Dance**: In playing several musical instruments and performing dance, Rumi was a strong proponent of this performing art in human society, regardless of religious or cultural inhibitions.

6. **Personal Freedom and Independent Thinking**: Individuals are free to make choices and be able to reinvent themselves – liberation of self from the self and from the entanglement of taxing social and religious conventions – the way he did in his time.

Final Reflections

The key concepts in the four Asian schools of Çārvākas, Buddhism, Khayyam and Rumi range from the psychological to the existential. These concepts in conducive circumstances have great potential to be developed on the individual as well as on broader sociopolitical life. These philosophies carry a wide range of intellectual application in the modern world without misplacing the achievements of modernity. Until these philosophies take root on broader social, political, economic and scientific levels in the same way Epicureanism evolved and spread during the Enlightenment, it falls to individuals to make changes by modernizing and secularizing Buddhist principles, for example, or creatively reviving Çārvāka, Khayymian and Rumian principles through empirical lenses. The purpose of this modernization and secularization is to make these ideas more viable for the broader multicultural and rational needs of our ever-evolving societies.

As we have explored, over the course of history literally thousands of religious claims have served to appease the fear and emotional vulnerability of individuals and groups around the globe. At the same time, the same religious systems have also caused the suffering of their opponents, including the secular thinkers. Despite such sufferings caused by religions and religious people, progressive people have been chivalrous and gracious towards religious claims, endorsing our world to be a place of multiculturalism and religious pluralism for the sake of peace and harmony. And generally speaking, the current generation of anthropologists and social scientists have also tried to understand cultures and religions as respectfully as they could without offending the followers.

Yet the vast and at times irreconcilable differences in our religious traditions continue to cause clashes and stereotyping. Dictators and religious authorities still have much power, and in some cases have the authority to order the shedding of the blood of their opponents under the guise of defending the interest of the so-called tribe, land or god. We know where this tribal thinking comes from, its ancient submission to myth and power still so ingrained in many human minds. Thus, technological *modernization* alone is not enough. Empirical thinking, laws, social justice, gender equality, human value and pursuit of happiness are the fruits of *modern thinking*. Enlightenment, reform, and a deeper understanding of our current circumstances are indispensable necessities, not optional laidback choices. On a broader level, many pending issues that still need to be resolved include; gender equality, human value, human rights,[51] self-determination, animal rights, removal of religious and political dictatorships, preventing female genital mutilation, equitable distribution of wealth, healthcare for everyone, abolishing war including

---

[51] Much of the world still lacks democratic process, intellectual freedom and religious freedom; there is still abject human exploitation, despotism, and the absence of universal tools protecting human values and human rights, let alone gender equality. Any radical improvements in regards to human values and human rights, of course must first take place locally before going universal. For a broader and a more structural debate on Asian values, Islamic system of thinking in regards to human rights and human value, see Marie-Luisa Frick, *Menschenrechte und Menschenwerte: Zur konzeptionellen Belastbarkeit der Meschenrechtsidee in ihrer globalen Akkomodation* (Weilerswist-Metternich: Velbrück Wissenschaft, 2017). For future discussions, see Marie-Luisa Frick, *Human Rights and Universal Relativism* (New York: Palgrave Macmillan, 2019).

complete disarmament and denuclearization, all the way to domestication of our personal and national greed.

Now a greater task lies ahead in order to vigorously tackle our disagreements, particularly our discriminatory and religious conflicts. Using simplistic jargon such as embracing "religious harmony" and "religious pluralism" to address this field of profound human conflict that is rife with serious confrontation only serves to prolong the problem.[52] The Tibetan spiritual leader, the Dalai Lama, also finds the idea of "religious differences" hard to deal with, saying, "It is time for all the religious Chiefs to meet openly, and not in secret as happened some time previously." He favors a global submit to resolve the religious conflicts. But then he detects the nature of "religious differences" are inherently "paradoxical" and hard to reconcile.[53] The Dalai Lama makes the point about the "paradox" of our religious differences (himself included) while longing for peace despite them. This paradox and religious division will remain unless there is a universal shift in dropping individual dogma, be it the Buddha, Moses, Jesus or Mohammad. Pacifying the religious dogmas on a global level and finding common logic will have to come to the fore in order for people and religious leaders to transcend these dogmas of gods, religions, and parochial inflexible beliefs.

Liberation philosophy does not mean making an ambivalent choice of one idea or another for one's intellectual hobby, or liberation of oneself, but is a

---

[52] Ulrich Beck, the contemporary German sociologist, coined the term "risk society" (*Risikogesellschaft*) when writing about the 1986 Chernobyl disaster, noting the fact that neither the rich nor the poor can escape horrendous global and local crises. Problems of modernity, pollution, inequality, lack of knowledge, and insecurity are risks and side effects of standard and poorly developed modernization. Leaving the poor destitute and the illiterate unschooled enhances risk on a global level. In the Beckian context, superstition and fanaticism have increased level. The tern "risk society" was coined by Ulrich Beck and Anthony Giddens in the 1980s. For more details see, Ulrich Beck, *Risikogesellschaft: Auf dem Weg in eine andere Moderne* (Frankfurt: Suhrkamp, 1986).

[53] This is part of a letter put out by the Dalai Lama's office in Dharamsala: "H.H. the Dalai Lama has directly mentioned the necessary presence of the highly admired Catholic Pope, saying (during the Livestream) that it is time for all the religious Chiefs to meet openly and not in secret, as happened some time previously. This Summit should be held in order to analyze together what to do, with the purpose of cooling down all fighting, reducing and then extinct all of those conflicts, paradoxically based on the religious differences (!) of which the human history is tragically witness." The source of this letter is: Subject: From Dharamsala – In a couple of worldly proposals put forward on 25 October 21018 by H. H. the XIVth Dalai Lama of Tibet, Tenzin Gyasto, at his personal residence in Dharamsala (Himachal Pradesh) India.

cognitive tool to think of peace and liberation on a collective level. It is a deeper understanding of interdependence and empathy for others. Liberation means perhaps to snap out of our 'medieval minds,' whether in the West or the East, and orient ourselves towards a more scrupulous, non-persecutory and non-divisive attitude in understanding issues and people. It is the triumph of ethical reason over dishonorable irresponsibility, from our personal choices all the way to our public life.

Introducing a new order of reasoning is exactly when philosophy can play a mature and practical role in the development of a society. Offering universal reasoning with an adjusted secular language can help ordinary people to apply their minds to attend everyday psychological or social issues. For example, *nirvana* no longer need to be perceived as something abstract that is barely understood, or something haphazardly ethereal that can only be experienced in a cave. It is no longer enough for meditation towards the attainment of nirvana to consist of repeating the mantra of "may all sentient beings know peace" without actually taking action. The significance of nowness and reality of the world demands concrete and pragmatic reasoning within such reality not outside of it. As Thomas Merton once eloquently said, in cautioning Buddhists and non-Buddhists alike: "A purely mental life may be destructive if it leads us to substitute thought for life and ideas for actions."[54]

The advantage we have over our ancestors is that in our modern global setting we are more literate than ever and can free ourselves from the bondage of myths, existential fear, and keep our emotionality over our native gods and holy scriptures at bay. Literacy and scientific-intellectual progress have brought us to a point where we are able to read, learn, reflect and even rewire our brain in order to become free-thinkers and be awakened to our responsibilities in the interconnected world around us. The ancient philosophers taught us that the pleasure of life comes when fear and dogma is replaced with insightful knowledge. As Epicurus said: "It would be impossible to banish fear on matters of the highest importance if a person did not know the nature of the whole world but lived in dread of what the legends tell us."[55]

---

[54] Thomas Merton, *Thoughts in Solitude* (New York: Farrar, Straus and Girous, 1999), 16.
[55] Diogenes Laertius, *Lives of Eminent Philosophers*, trans. R. D. Hicks (London: William Heinemann and New York: G. P. Putnam's Sons, 1925), X, 667.

Bibliography

Abedinifard, Mostafa. "Nihilism dar Rubāʿī-haye Khayyami." *Faslnameh 'Elmi-Pazhoheshi*, 3/10 (Summer 1389/2010): 143–74.

Abhidharmakośabhāsyam of Vasubandhu. Vol. 1, initially translated into French by Louis del la Vallée Poussin (1914–1918), English translation by Leo M. Pruden, 1991; Fremont, CA: Jain Publishing, 2014.

Abhinandan, M. S. *A Journey Through Jainism.* Delhi: Indialog Publications, 2005.

Achtner, Wolfgang. "The Evolution of Evolutionary Theories of Religion." In *The Biological Evolution of Religious Mind and Behavior,* ed. E. Voland and W. Schiefenhövel, Berlin, Heidelberg: Springer Verlag 2009.

Adolphs, Ralph. "The Biology of Fear." *Current Biology* 23/2 (Jan. 21, 2013): 82–88.

Adorno, Theodor W. *The Jargon of Authenticity (Jargon der Eigentlichkeit: Zur deutschen Ideologie).* Trans. Knut Tarnowski and Federic Will, Evanston, IL: Northwestern University Press, 1973.

Afnan, Soheil. *Avicenna: His Life and Work.* London: George Allen & Unwin LTD, 1958.

Albano, Giuseppe. "The Benefits of Reading the Rubáiyát of Omar Khayyám as Pastoral." *Victorian Poetry,* 46/1 (Spring 2008): 55-67.

Aminrazavi, Mehdi. *The Wine of Wisdom: The Life, Poetry and Philosophy of Omar Khayyam.* Oxford: Oneworld, 2007.

___. "Martin Heidegger and Omar Khayyam on the Question of "Thereness" (Dasein)." In *Islamic Philosophy and Occidental Phenomenology on the Perennial Issue of Microcosm and Macrocosm,* 277-288, edited by Anna-Teresa Tymieniecka, Dordrecht: Springer 2006.

Andrae, Tor. *Mohammed: The Man and His Faith.* Trans. Theophil Menzel, 1936; Mineola: Dover Publications, 2000.

Ansell-Pearson, Keith. "Heroic-idyllic Philosophizing: Nietzsche and the Epicurean Tradition." *Royal Institute of Philosophy* Supplement, 74 (2014): 237-263.

Arberry, A. J. *The Rubaiyat of Omar Khayyam and Other Persian Poems.* London: Everyman's Library, 1954.

___. "Omar Khayyam." In *Nineteen Maqāleh dar bāreh Hakīm Omar Khayyam Neishāburī.* 89–91, Khurasan: Neishābur Shenasi, n.d.

Argaud, Elodie. "Bayle's Defense of Epicurus: The Use and Abuse of Malebranche's *Méditations chrétiennes.*" In *Epicurus in the Enlightenment,* Neven Leddy and Avis Liefschitz (eds.), Oxford: Voltaire Foundation, University of Oxford, 2009.

Armstrong, Karen. *A History of God: The 4,000-Year Quest of Judaism, Christianity and Islam.* New York: Ballantine Books, 1993.

Arthur, Richard T. W. "Time Atomism and Ashʻarite Origins for Cartesian Occasionalism Revisited." Department of Philosophy McMaster University Hamilton, Ontario Canada. See PDF online: https://www.humanities.mcmaster.ca/~rarthur/papers/AshariteOrigins.pdf.

Assmann, Jan. *The Invention of Religion: Faith and Covenant in the Book of Exodus.* Princeton: Princeton University press, 2018.

___. *Totale Religion: Ursprünge und Formen puritanischer Verschärfung.* Wien: Picus Verlag, 2016.

___. "Transkulturelle Theorien – am Beispiel von Jaspers' Achsenzeit-Konzept." In *Theorietheorie. Wider die Theoriemüdigkeit in den Geisteswissenschaften,* ed. Mario Grizelj, Oliver Jahraus (Hg.) München 2011.

ʻAttār, Fariddin. *Mokhtār Nāmeh.* Section 18. http://www.nosokhan.com/Library/Topic/0QNV.

"Atomism." https://plato.stanford.edu/entries/atomism-modern/. Accessed October 30, 2018.

"Avalokiteshvara." www.britannica.com/topic/Avalokiteshvara, accessed Jan. 19, 2018.

Avery, Peter and Heath-Stubbs, John. *The Rubāʻiyyāt of Omar Khayyam.* London: Penguin Books, 1981.

Badran, Muhammad Abū al-Fadl. "denn die Vernunft ist ein Prophet – Zweifel bei Abū'l-ʻAlā' al-Maʻarrī." In *Atheismus im Mittelalter und in der Renaissance,* ed. F. Niewöhner and O. Pluta Wiesbaden: Harrassowitz Verlag, 1999.

Baily, Kent. *Human Paleopsychology: Applications to Aggression and Pathological Processes.* Hillsdale, NJ: Lawrence Erlbaum Associates, Inc., 1987.

Balcerowicz, Piotr. *Early Asceticism in India: Ājīvikism and Jainism.* Abingdon, Oxon and New York: Routledge, 2016.

Basham, A. L. *History and Doctrines of the Ājīvikas: A Vanished Indian Religion.* 1951; Delhi: Motilal Banarsidass, 2009.

Baston, H. M. "Commentary." In *The Rubaʻiyat of Omar Khayyam.* London: Elibron Classics, 2005.

Batchelor, Stephen. *After Buddhism: Rethinking the Dharma for a Secular Age.* New Haven: Yale University Press, 2015.

___. *Buddhism Without Beliefs:* A Contemporary Guide to Awakening. New York: Riverhead Books, 1997.

___. "Greek Buddha: Pyrrho's Encounter with Early Buddhism in Central Asia by Christopher I. Beckwith." Book review article in *Contemporary Buddhism* 17/1 (2016): 195-215.

Beck, Ulrich. *Risikogesellschaft: Auf dem Weg in eine andere Moderne.* Frankfurt: Suhrkamp, 1986.

Beckwith, Christopher I. *Greek Buddha: Pyrrho's Encounter with Early Buddhism in Central Asia.* Princeton, NJ: Princeton University Press, 2015.

Bennett, James O. "Karl Jaspers and Scientific Philosophy." *Journal of the History of Philosophy* 31/3 (July, 1993): 437-453.

Bergson, Henri. *The Two Sources of Morality and Religion.* Notre Dame: University of Notre Dame Press, 1977.

"Bergson Henri." https://www.britannica.com/biography/Henri-Bergson#ref202567, accessed October 28, 2018.

Bhattacharya, Ramkrishna. "Development of Materialism in India: The Pre-Çārvākas and the Çārvākas." *Esercizi Filosofici* 8/1 (2013): 1-12.

___. *Studies on the Çārvāka/Lokāyata.* London: Anthem Press, 2011.

Bhupender, Heera. *Uniqueness of Çārvāka Philosophy in Traditional Indian Thought.* Delhi: Decent Books, 2011).

Bloom, Harold. "The Heretic Jew." Book review *"Betraying Spinoza* by Rebecca Goldstein." *New York Times,* June 18, 2006.

Blumenberg, Hans. *Paradigms for a Metaphorology.* Trans. Robert Savage, Ithaca, NY: Cornell University Press, 2010. The first German edition was published in 1960.

Bodenstedt, Friedrich. *Die Lieder und Sprüche des Omar Chajjam.* 1881.

Bodewitz, H. W. *The Jyotiṣṭoma Ritual: Jaiminīya Brāhmaṇa* I. Leiden: E. J. Brill, 1990.

Bouchard Jr., Thomas J. "Authoritarianism, Religiousness, and Conservatism: Is "Obedience to Authority" the Explanation for Their Clustering, Universality and Evolution?" In *The Biological Evolution of Religious Mind and Behavior,* ed. E. Voland and W. Schiefenhövel, Berlin, Heidelberg: Springer Verlag 2009.

Bowen, C. E. *"The Rubā'īyyāt of Omar Khayyam: A Critical Assessment of Robert Graves' and Omar Ali Shah's Translation." Iran: British Institute of Persian Studies* 11 (1973): 63–73.

Boyer, Pascal. *The Naturalness of Religious Ideas: Cognitive Theory of Religion.* Berkeley, Los Angeles: University of California Press, 1994.

Brüne, Martin. "On Shared Psychological Mechanisms of Religiousness and Delusional Beliefs." In *The Biological Evolution of Religious Mind and Behavior,* ed. E. Voland and W. Schiefenhövel, Berlin, Heidelberg: Springer Verlag 2009.

Bulliet, Richard. *The Patricians of Nishapur: A Study in Medieval Islamic Social History.* Cambridge: Harvard University Press, 1972.

Burkert, Walter. *Creation of the Sacred: Tracks of Biology in Early Religions.* Cambridge: Harvard University Press, 1998.

___. *The Orientalizing Revolution: Near Easter Influence on Greek Culture in the Early Archaic Age.* Trans. Margaret E. Pinder and Walter Burkert, Cambridge: Harvard University Press, 1992.

___. *Greek Religion.* Trans. John Raffan, Cambridge, MA: Harvard University Press, 1985.

Burton, David. *Buddhism, Knowledge and Liberation: A Philosophical Study.* Aldershot: Ashgate, 2004.

Cadbury, William "Fitzgerald's Rubáiyát as a Poem." *ELH* 34/4 (Dec. 1967): 541–563.

Callahan, Tim. "The Triumph of Christianity" *Skeptic,* 8/4 (2001): 82–6.

Callaway, Ewen. "Mystery Humans Spiced up Ancients' Sex Lives." *Nature* (Nov. 19, 2013), accessed Jan. 3, 2016. https://www.nature.com/news/mystery-humans-spiced-up-ancients-sex-lives-1.14196.

Campbell, Joseph. *The Power of Myth*. New York: Anchor Books, 1991.

___. *The Hero with a Thousand Faces*. Princeton: Princeton University Press, 1968.

___. *The Masks of God: Primitive Mythology*. London: Secker & Warburg, 1960.

Carruthers, Peter and Chamberlain, Andrew (eds.). *Evolution and the Human Mind: Modularity, Language and Meta-cognition*. Cambridge: Cambridge University Press, 2000.

Chandra Jain Kailasha and Jaipur, M. A. "Antiquity of Jainism." www.fas.harvard.edu/~pluralsm/affiliates/jainism/article/main.htm, accessed Jan. 15, 2017.

Chattopadhyaya, Debiprasad. *Lokāyata: A Study in Ancient Indian Materialism*. New Delhi: People's Publishing, 1959.

Chawoshi, Ja'afar Aghyani. "Āyā Khayyam va Abul 'Alā Ma'arrī Zandīq Budeh-and?" In *Nineteen Maqāleh dar bāreh Hakim Omar Khayyam Neishāburī*. Khurasan: Neishābur Shenāsī, n.d.

Clarke, Desmond M. "The Epistemology of Religious Belief." In *Oxford Handbook of Philosophy in Early Modern Europe*. Edited by Desmond M. Clarke and Catherine Wilson 548-570, Oxford: Oxford University Press, 2011.

Cline, Eric H. *From Eden to Exile: Unraveling Mysteries of the Bible*. Washington DC: National Geographic Society, 2007.

Collins, Steven. *Nirvana: Concept, Imagery, Narrative*. Cambridge: Cambridge University Press, 2010.

___. *Selfless Persons: Imagery and Thought in Theravāda Buddhism*. 1982; Cambridge: Cambridge University Press, 1999.

Conger, George P. "Did India Influence Early Greek Philosophies?" *Philosophy East and West* 2/2 (July 1952): 102–128.

Coolidge, Frederick L. and Wynn, Thomas. *The Rise of Homo sapiens: The Evolution of Modern Thinking*. West Sussex: Wiley Blackwell, 2009.

Cooper, William S. *The Evolution of Reason: Logic as the Branch of Biology*. Cambridge: Cambridge University Press, 2001.

Coriando, Paola-Ludovika. *Metaphysik und Ontologie in der abendländischen und buddhistischen Philosophie*. Berlin: Duncker & Humblot, 2011.

Crespi, Bernard. "The Kin Selection of Religion." In *Oxford Handbook of the Evolution of Religion*, ed. J. M. Liddle and T. Shackleford (in press).

Dashtī, Ali. *Damī bā Khayyam*. Tehran: Entesharat Asatir, 1377/1998.

Davis, Leesa S. *Advaita Vedānta and Zen Buddhism: Deconstructive Modes of Spiritual Inquiry*. London and New York: Continuum International, 2010.

Davis, Wade. *Shadows in the Sun: Travels to Landscapes of Spirit and Desire*. New York: Broadway Books, 1999.

Dawkins, Richard. *The Blind Watchmaker: Why the Evidence of Evolution Reveals a Universe Without Design*. 1987; New York: W. W. Norton and Company, 2015.

___. *The God Delusion*. London: Bantam Press, 2006.
___. *The Selfish Gene*. Oxford: Oxford University Press, 1987.
Dhamapada: The Wisdom of the Buddha. Trans. Harischandra Kaviratna. www.theosociety.org/pasadena/dhamma/dhammapada.pdf, accessed Feb. 18, 2018.
Dharmakīrti. *Pramanavarttika*. Trans. by Ven. Kelsang Wangmo, McLeod Ganj, Dharamsala: Institute of Buddhist Dialectics, 2014.
Dōgen. *Rational Zen: The Mind of Dōgen Zenji*. Translated by Thomas Cleary, Boston: Shambhala, 1995.
Dumoulin, Heinrich. "Early Chinese Zen Reexamined: A Supplement to Zen Buddhism: A History." *Japanese Journal of Religious Studies* 20/1 (1993): 31–53.
Eliade, Mircea. *Myths, Dreams and Mysteries: The Encounter Between Contemporary Faiths and Archaic Realities*. New York: Harper & Row, 1961.
Empiricus, Sextus. *Outlines of Pyrrhonism*. Trans. Benson Mates, New York and Oxford: Oxford University Press, 1996. www.sciacchitano.it/pensatori%20epistemici/scettici/outlines%20of%20pyrronism.pdf.
Fakhry, Majid. *A History of Islamic Philosophy*. 1970; New York: Columbia University Press, 2004.
Farhadi, A. G. Ravan. *Abdullāh Ansārī of Herāt (1006–1089 CE): An Early Sufi Master*. Surrey: Curzon Press, 1996.
Farringto, Oliver C. "The Worship and Folk-Lore of Meteorites." *Journal of American Folklore* 13/50 (July–Sept. 1900): 199–208.
Faure, Bernard. *Chan Insights and Oversights: An Epistemological Critique of the Chan Tradition*. Princeton: Princeton University Press, 1993.
Feierman, Jay R. "How Some Major Components of Religion Could Have Evolved by Natural Selection?" In *The Biological Evolution of Religious Mind and Behavior*, ed. E. Voland and W. Schiefenhövel, Berlin, Heidelberg: Springer Verlag 2009.
Fetchenhauer, Detlef. "Evolutionary Perspective on Religion – What They Can and What They Cannot Explain (Yet)." In *The Biological Evolution of Religious Mind and Behavior*, ed. E. Voland and W. Schiefenhövel, Berlin, Heidelberg: Springer Verlag 2009.
Flintoff, Everard. "Pyrrho and India." *Phronesis* 25/1 (1980): 88–108.
Force, Pierre. "Helvétius as an Epicurean Political Theorist." In *Epicurus in the Enlightenment*, Neven Leddy and Avis Liefschitz (eds.) 105-118, Oxford: Voltaire Foundation, University of Oxford, 2009.
Foroughi, M. A. and Ghani, Qasim. *Rubā'īyyāt Khayyam*. Tehran: Entesharat Asatir, 1371/1972 (first published in 1941).
Frankl, Viktor. *The Will to Meaning: Foundations and Applications of Logotherapy*. New York: Meridian, 1988.
Frey, Ulrich. "Cognitive Foundations of Religiosity." In *The Biological Evolution of Religious Mind and Behavior*, ed. E. Voland and W. Schiefenhövel, Berlin, Heidelberg: Springer Verlag 2009.

Frick, Marie-Luisa. *Menschenrechte und Menschenwerte: Zur konzeptionellen Belastbarkeit der Meschenrechtsidee in ihrer globalen Akkomodation.* Weilerswist-Metternich: Velbrück Wissenschaft, 2017.

Fromm, Erich. *On Disobedience and Other Essays.* London: Routledge & Kegan Paul, 1984.

___. *The Sane Society.* 1956; London: Routledge & Kegan Paul, 1976.

Frye, Richard N. *Bukhara: The Medieval Achievement.* Norman: University of Oklahoma Press, 1965.

Garcia, Elenita. "Immortality Lost: Existential Themes in Gilgamesh and Other Hero Epics." *Philosophia: International Journal of Philosophy,* 31/2 (2002). https://philpapers.org/rec/GARILE.

Garfield, Jay L. and Priest, Graham. "Nāgārjuna and the Limits of Thought." *Philosophy East & West* 53/1 (Jan., 2003): 1-21.

Gaulier, Simone, Jera-Bezard Robert and Maillard, Monique. *Buddhism in Afghanistan and Central Asia.* Leiden: E. J. Brill, 1976.

Gaukroger, Stephen. "Picturability and Mathematical Ideas of Knowledge." In *Oxford Handbook of Philosophy in Early Modern Europe.* Edited by Desmond M. Clarke and Catherine Wilson 338-360, Oxford: Oxford University Press, 2011.

Gauvin, Jean-François. "Instruments of Knowledge." In *Oxford Handbook of Philosophy in Early Modern Europe.* Edited by Desmond M. Clarke and Catherine Wilson 315-337, Oxford: Oxford University Press, 2011.

Gerhardt, Volker"Selbstbestimmung: Zur Aktualität eines Begriffs." *FIPH Journal* 8 (September 2006): 1-7.

Gethin, Rupert. *The Foundations of Buddhism.* Oxford: Oxford University Press, 1998.

Gill, Arunjit. "In Search of Intuitive Knowledge: A Comparison of Eastern and Western Epistemology." Doctoral Dissertation submitted to Simon and Fraser University, Canada, 2006.

Glasenapp, Helmut von. *Buddhism – a Non-Theistic Religion.* With a Selection from the Buddhist Scriptures, edited by Heinz Bechert, translated by Irmgard Schloegl, New York: George Braziller 1966.

Gokhale, Pradeep P. "The Cārvāka Theory of Pramāṇas: A Restatement." *Philosophy East and West* 43/4 (Oct. 1993): 675–682.

Goldenbaum, Ursula. "Sovereignty and Obedience." In *Oxford Handbook of Philosophy in Early Modern Europe.* Edited by Desmond M. Clarke and Catherine Wilson 500-521, Oxford: Oxford University Press, 2011.

Goldziher, Ignaz. "Abū-l-Alā al-Maʿarrī als Freidenker." *Zeitschrift der Deutschen Morgenländischen Gesellschaft* 29 (1875): 637–641.

Gombrich, Richard F. *How Buddhism Began: The Conditioned Genesis of the Early Teachings.* 2nd edn. London and New York: Routledge, 2005.

Goody, Jack. *The Logic of Writing and the Organization of Society.* New York: Cambridge University Press, 1986.

Gorman, James. "Prehistoric Massacre Hints at War Among Hunter-Gatherers." *New York Times: Science,* Jan. 20, 2016.

___. "The Big Search to Find Out Where Dogs Come From." *New York Times: Science*, Jan. 18, 2016.

Greenblatt, Stephen. "How St. Augustine Invented Sex: He Rescued Adam and Eve from Obscurity, Devised the Doctrine of Original Sin – and the Rest Is Sexual History." *The New Yorker: Annals of Culture*, June 19, 2017.

___. *The Rise and Fall of Adam and Eve*. New York and London: W. W. Norton and Company, 2017.

___. *The Swerve: How the World Became Modern*. New York: W. W. Norton, 2011.

Gregersen, Niels Henrik. "The Naturalness of Religious Imagination and the Idea of Revelation." *Ars Dispuntandi* 3 (2003), 1–27.

Griffel, Frank. *Apostasie und Toleranz im Islam: Die Entwicklung zu al-Gazālīs Urteil gegen die Philosophie und die Reaktion der Philosophen*. Leiden: Brill, 2000.

Griffiths, Paul J. "Notes Towards a Critique of Buddhist Karmic Theory." *Religious Studies* 18/3 (Sept. 1982): 277–291.

Habib, M. A. R. *The Early T. S. Elliot and Western Philosophy*. Cambridge: Cambridge University Press, 1999.

Harmon, Katherine. "New DNA Analysis Shows Ancient Humans Interbred with Denisovans." *Scientific American*, Aug. 30, 2012, 1–4, accessed Jan. 3, 2016.

Harris, Erica and McNamara, Patrick. "Neurologic Constraints on Evolutionary Theories of Religion." In *The Biological Evolution of Religious Mind and Behavior*, ed. E. Voland and W. Schiefenhövel, Berlin, Heidelberg: Springer Verlag 2009.

Havelock, Eric A. *The Muse Learns to Write: Reflection on Orality and Literacy from Antiquity to the Present*. New Haven: Yale University Press, 1986.

Hedāyat, Sāiq. *Tarāneh-hāye Khayyam*. 1313; Tehran: Entesharat Javidan, 1934.

___. "Muqqadame-yee bar Rubā'īyyāt-i Khayyam." In *Neveshtehā-ye Farāmoush Shodeh-i Sādiq Hedāyat*. Edited by Maryam Dānā'ī Boromand, Tehran: Mo'asseseh Entesharat Negah, 1376/1997.

Heidegger, Martin. *Poetry, Language, Thought*. Trans. Albert Hofstadter, New York: HarperCollins, 1971.

Horard-Herbin, Marie-Pierre, Tresset, Anne and Vigne, Jean-Denis "Domestication and Uses of the Dog in Western Europe from the Paleolithic to the Iron Age." *Animal Frontiers*, 4/3 (2014): 23–31.

Hylen, Torsten. "Closed and Open Concepts of Religion: The Problem of Essentialism in Teaching about Religion." In *Textbook Gods – Genre, Text and Teaching Religious Studies*, ed. Bengt-Ove Andreassen and James R. Lewis, Sheffield: Equinox Publishing, 2014.

"Israfil." www.britannica.com/topic/Israfil, accessed Apr. 26, 2018.

Izutsu, Toshihiko. *Toward a Philosophy of Zen Buddhism*. 1978; Tehran: Iranian Institute of Philosophy, 2003.

Jacobi, Hermann. "Ueber sukha und duhkha." *Zeitschrift für vergleichende Sprachforschung auf dem Gebiete der Indogermanischen Sprachen* 25/4 (1881).

James, William. *Pragmatism: A New Name for Some Old Ways of Thinking.* 1907. Reprinted by Floatingpress.com, 2010.

———. *The Varieties of Religious Experience: A Study in Human Nature.* 1902. Reprinted by Seven Treasures Publication, 2009.

"James William." https://plato.stanford.edu/entries/james/, accessed May 3, 2018.

Jayasaro, Ajahn. *Stillness Flowing: The Life and Teachings of Ajahn Chah.* Malaysia: Panyaprateep Foundation, 2017.

Jongmyung, Kim. "The Seon Monk Hyujeong and Buddhist Ritual in Sixteenth-Century Korea." *Korea Journal* 57/1 (Spring 2017): 7–34.

Joshi, Lal Mani. *Brahmanism, Buddhism, and Hinduism: An Essay on Their Origins and Interactions.* Kandy, Sri Lanka: Buddhist Publication Society, The Wheel Publication No. 150/151. https://what-buddha-said.net/library/Wheels/wh150.pdf.

Jung, Hwayal. "Martin Heidegger and the Homecoming of Oral Poetry." *Philosophy Today* 26 (1982): 148–170.

Kahneman, Daniel. *Thinking, Fast and Slow.* New York: Farrar, Straus and Giroux, 2011.

Kālāma Sutta: The Buddha's Charter of Free Inquiry. Translated from the Pali by Soma Thera, Kandy, Sri Lanka: Kandy Buddhist Publication Society, 1981; Online edition, 2008.

Kalupahana, David. "Pratityasamut pada and the Renunciation of Mystery." In *Buddhist Thought and Ritual.* Edited by David J. Kalupahana, 1991; Delhi: Motilal Banarsidass, 2001.

———. *Ethics in Early Buddhism.* Honolulu: University of Hawaii Press, 1995.

———. "Consciousness." In *Buddhist Psychology, Encyclopedia of Buddhism Extract,* Dehiwala, Sri Lanka: Ministry of Buddhasasana, Department of Buddhist Affairs, 1995.

———. *A History of Buddhist Philosophy: Continuities and Discontinuities.* 1992; Delhi: Motilal Banarsidass, 1994.

Kant, Immanuel. *Grundlegung zu einer Metaphysik der Sitten.* 1786.

Karl, Jacqueline. *Selbstbestimmung und Individualität bei Platon: Eine Interpretation zu frühen und mittleren Dialogen.* Freiburg: Verlag Karl Alber, 2010.

Kasra, Parichehr. "FitzGerald's Recasting of the Rubāiyāt." *Zeitschrift der Deutschen Morgenländischen Gesellschaft* 130 (1980): 458–459.

Kessler, David A. *Capture: Unraveling the Mystery of Mental Suffering.* New York: Harper Collins, 2016.

Keown, Damien. *Buddhism: A Very Short Introduction.* Oxford: Oxford University Press, 1996.

Kotoh, Tetsuaki. "Language and Silence: Self-Inquiry in Heidegger and Zen." In *Heidegger and Asian Thought.* Trans. Setsuko Aihara and Graham Parkes, 1987; New Delhi: Motilal Banarsidass Publishers, 2010.

Krause Johannes, et al. "Neanderthal in Central Asia and Siberia." *Nature* 449 (Oct. 18, 2007): 902–904.

Krause, Johannes, et al. "The Derived FOXP2 Variant of Modern Humans Was Shared with Neanderthals." *Current Biology* 17 (Nov. 6, 2007): 1908–1912.

Kuzminski, Adrian. *Pyrrhonism: How the Ancient Greeks Reinvented Buddhism.* Lanham, MD: Lexington Books, 2008.

La Mettrie, Julien de. "The System of Epicurus." In *Machine Man and Other Writings.* Edited by Ann Thomson, 89-116, Cambridge: Cambridge University Press, 1996.

Laertius, Diogenes. *Lives of Eminent Philosophers.* Trans. R. D. Hicks, London: William Heinemann and New York: G. P. Putnam's Sons, 1925.

Lanchester, John. "The Case Against Civilization: Did Our Hunter-Gatherer Ancestors Have It Better." *The New Yorker,* Sept. 18, 2017.

Leaman, Oliver. "Hiob und das Leid: Ursprung des Bösen, Leiden Gottes und Überwindung des Bösen im talmudischen und kabalistischen Judentum." In *Diskurs der Weltreligionen: Ursprung und Überwindung des Bösen und des Leidens in den Weltreligionen,* ed. Peter Koslovski, München: Wilhelm Fink Verlag, 2001.

Leddy, Neven and Liefschitz, Avis (eds.) *Epicurus in the Enlightenment.* Oxford: Voltaire Foundation, University of Oxford, 2009.

Leviton, Richard. "Through the Shaman's Door." *Yoga Journal,* (July–Aug., 1992): 52-102.

Lieu, N. C. *Manichaeism in the Later Roman Empire and Medieval China.* Tübrigen: J.C.B. Mohr, 1992.

Lilienfeld, Scott O., Jay Lynn, Steven, Ruscio, John and Beyerstein, Barry L. *50 Great Myths of Popular Psychology: Shattering Widespread Misconception about Human Behavior.* Chichester: Wiley Blackwell, 2010.

Lillegard, Norman. *On Epicurus.* New York: Thomson Wadsworth, 2003.

"Lokayata/Carvaka – Indian Materialism." *Internet Encyclopedia of Philosophy,* accessed Jan. 11, 2017.

Lorenz, Konrad. *The Waning of Humaneness, The Waning of Humaneness.* Trans. Warren Kickert, Boston and Toronto: Little Brown and Co., 1987.

Lovecraft H. P. Quotes. BrainyQuote.com, BrainyMedia Inc, 2018. https://www.brainyquote.com/quotes/h_p_lovecraft_676245, accessed November 28, 2018.

Lovejoy, C. Owen. "Evolution of Human Walking." *Scientific American* (Nov., 1988): 118-125.

Lucretius. *The Nature of Thing.* Trans. A. E. Stallings, introduction by Richard Jenkyns, London: Penguin Classics, 2007.

Ma'arrī, Abul 'Alā. *Ash'ār-e Abul 'Alā Ma'arr.* Trans. Amir Chenari, 1385; Tehran: Zavvar, 2006.

Maat, Jaap. "Language and Semiotics." In *Oxford Handbook of Philosophy in Early Modern Europe.* Edited by Desmond M. Clarke and Catherine Wilson, 272-294, Oxford: Oxford University Press, 2011.

McEvilley, Thomas. *The Shape of Ancient Thought: Comparative Studies in Greek and Indian Philosophies.* New York: Allworth Press, 2002.

Mackenzie D. N. (ed.). *The "Sūtra of the Causes and Effects of Actions" in Sogdian.* London: Oxford University Press, 1970.

Mādhyamika and Yogācāra: A Study of Mahāyāna Philosophies. Collected Papers of G. M. Nagao, edited, collated, and translated by L. S. Kawamura in collaboration with G. M. Nagao, Albany: State University of New York Press, 1991.

Maha-parinibbana Sutta: Last Days of the Buddha. Translated from the Pali by Sister Vajira & Francis Story, 1998. Online: https://www.accesstoinsight.org/tipitaka/dn/dn.16.1-6.vaji.html.

Majjhima Nikaya: The Middle Length Discourses of the Buddha. Translated by Bhikkhu Ñāṇamoli and Bhikkhu Bodhi, Somerville, MA: Wisdom Publications, 1994.

Majlisi, Mohammad Baqir. *Bihar ul-Anwar.* Vol. XIII, Tehran: Dar ul-Kutub al-Islamieh, n.d.

Mall, Ram Adhar. *Indische Philosophie – Vom Denkweg zum Lebensweg: Eine interkulturelle Perspektive.* Freiburg: Alber, 2012.

Mallock, W. H. *Lucretius on Life and Death: In the Metre of Omar Khayyam.* 1900.

Mâr Élijah Bar Israël, H. E. Hadrian. *The Twelve Commandments and the Egyptian Book of the Dead.* Nazarani Foundation, 2013.

Margreiter, Reinhard. "Mythos versus Religion?: Über eine Denkfigur bei Cohen und Cassirer." *Philosophisches Jahrbuch,* Freiburg, München: Verlag Karl Alber 2003.

___. *Erfahrung und Mystik: Grenzen der Symbolisierung.* Berlin: Akademie Verlag, 1997.

Martin, William H. and Mason, Sandra (eds.). *Edward FitzGerald's Rubáiyát of Omar Khayyám: A Famous Poem and Its Influence.* London: Anthem Press, 2011.

Meeker, Natania. "Sexing Epicurean Materialism in Diderot." In *Epicurus in the Enlightenment.* Neven Leddy and Avis Liefschitz (eds.) 85-104, Oxford: Voltaire Foundation, University of Oxford, 2009.

Merton, Thomas. *Thoughts in Solitude.* New York: Farrar, Straus and Girous, 1999.

Merzenich, Michael. *Soft-Wired: How the New Science of Brain Plasticity Can Change Your Life.* 2nd ed., San Francisco: Parnassus Publishing, 2013.

Michaels, Axel. *Buddha: Leben, Lehre, Legende.* München: C. H. Beck, 2011.

Milgram, Stanley. *Obedience to Authority: An Experimental View.* 1974; Printer & Martin Ltd., 2010.

Mirazón Lahr. Marta, et al. "Towards a Theory of Modern Human Origins: Geography, Demography, and Diversity in Recent Human Evolution." *Year Book of Physical Anthropology* 41 (1998): 137–176.

Mohammadian, Mohammad. "Der oblique Blick: Zum Verhältnis von Philosophie und Religion in den Robâ"iyât von Omar Khayyâm." In *Atheismus im Mittelalter und in der Renaissance* Wiesbaden: Harrassowitz Verlag, 1999.

Monier-Williams, Monier. *A Sanskrit-English Dictionary.* 1899; London: Oxford University Press, 1964.

Montag, Warren. "Lucretius Hebraizant: Spinoza's Reading of Ecclesiastes." In *European Journal of Philosophy*, (Feb. 27, 2012): Wiley Online Library.

Montagu, Ashley. *Man: His First Million Years.* Cleveland, OH: The World Publishing Co., 1957.

Mooallem, Jon. "Neanderthals Were People, Too." *The New York Times Magazine*, Jan. 11, 2017.

Morris, Desmond. *The Human Zoo.* 1969; London: Vintage, 1994.

Nadler, Steven. "Conceptions of God." In *Oxford Handbook of Philosophy in Early Modern Europe*, edited by Desmond M. Clarke and Catherine Wilson 525-547, Oxford: Oxford University Press, 2011.

Nāgārjuna. *Mūlamadhyamakakārikā of Nāgārjuna: The Philosophy of the Middle Way.* Introduction, Sanskrit Text, English Translation and Annotation by David J. Kalupahana, 1986; Delhi: Motilal Banarsidass Publishers, 1999.

Nāgārjuna's Middle Way Mūlamadhyamakakārikā. Mark Siderits and Shōryū Katsura, Somerville, MA: Wisdom Publications, 2013.

"Nagarjuna." https://plato.stanford.edu/entries/nagarjuna/. Accessed Jan. 29, 2018.

Nāsir Khosrau Qubādiānī. *Safar Nāmeh.* 1344; Tehran: Amir Kabir, 1965.

Neto, José R. Maria. "Scepticism." In *Oxford Handbook of Philosophy in Early Modern Europe.* edited by Desmond M. Clarke and Catherine Wilson 227-248, Oxford: Oxford University Press, 2011.

Nicholas, J. B. *Les Quatrains de Khèyam, traduit de Persan.* 1867.

___. "Les Quatrains de Khèyam, traduits du Persan by J. B. Nicolas; Rubáiyát of Omar Khayyám, the Astronomer-Poet of Persia." *The North American Review*, 109/225 (Oct. 1869): 565-84.

Nicholson, Reynold. *A Literary History of the Arabs.* New York: Charles Schreibner's Son, 1907.

Nishitani, Keiji. *Religion and Nothingness.* Trans. Jan van Bragt, Berkeley: University of California Press, 1983.

Nixon, Gregory M. "Myth and Mind: The Origin of Human Consciousness in the Discovery of the Sacred," *Journal of Consciousness Exploration and Research*, 1/3 (2010): 10-37.

Okumura, Shohaku. *Realizing Genjokoan: The Key to Dogen's Shobogenzo.* Boston: Wisdom Publications, 2010.

Ong, Walter J. *Orality and Literacy.* Oxon: Routledge, 2012.

Osman, Ahmed. *Moses and Akhenaten: The Secret History of Egypt at the Time of Exodus.* 1990; Rochester, VA: Bear and Co., 2002.

Ostler, Nicholas. *Passwords to Paradise: How Languages Have Re-invented World Religions.* New York: Bloomsbury Press, 2016.

Pääbo, Svante. *Neanderthal Man: In Search of Lost Genomes.* New York: Basic Books, 2014.

Pagden, Anthony. *The Enlightenment and Why It Still Matters.* Oxford: Oxford University Press, 2015.

Palmer, Craig T., Ellsworth, Ryan M. and Steadman, Lyle B. "Talk and Tradition: Why the Least Interesting Components of Religion May Be the Most Evolutionarily Important." In E. Voland and W. Schiefenhövel (eds.), *The Biological Evolution of Religious Mind and Behavior*. Berlin, Heidelberg: Springer Verlag, 2009.

Phemister, Pauline. "Ideas." In *Oxford Handbook of Philosophy in Early Modern Europe*. Edited by Desmond M. Clarke and Catherine Wilson, 142-159, Oxford: Oxford University Press, 2011.

Piaget, Jean. *Play, Dreams and Imitation in Childhood*. 1951; Oxon: Routledge, 2007.

Pinker, Steven. *Enlightenment Now: The Case for Reason, Science, Humanism and Progress*. New York: Viking-Penguin, 2018.

Pollan, Michael. *How to Change Your Mind: What the New Science of Psychedelics Teaches Us About Consciousness, Dying, Addiction, Depression and Transcendence*. New York: Penguin Press, 2018.

___. *Cooked: A Natural History of Transformation*. New York: Penguin Press, 2013.

Poole, Steven. "Behave by Robert Sapolsky Review – Why Do We Do What We Do?" Book Review of Robert Sapolsky, *Behave: The Biology of Humans at Our Best and Worst* in *The Guardian*, June 9, 2017.

Popkin, Richard H. *Spinoza*. Oxford: Oneworld Publications, 2007.

Prabhavananda, Swami. *The Spiritual Heritage of India*. Chennai: Sri Ramakrishna Math, 2003.

Prinz, Wolfgang and Meltzoff, Andrew N. "An Introduction to the Imitative Mind and Brain." In *The Imitative Mind: Development, Evolution, and Brain Bases*, ed. Andrew N. Meltzoff and Wolfgang Prinz, Cambridge: Cambridge University Press, 2002.

Puri, B. N. *Buddhism in Central Asia*. New Delhi: Motilal Banarsidass Pubishers, 1987.

Qaragozlu, Alireza. *Omar Khayyam*. 1381; Tehran: Entesharate Tarhe Nou, 2000.

Quinn, Daniel. *Ishmael: An Adventure of the Mind and Spirit*. New York: Bantam Turner, 1992.

Ramachandran, V. S. "Mirror Neurons and Imitation Learning as the Driving Force Behind 'the Great Leap Forward' in Human Evolution." *Edge* (2000).

Reardon, Sara. "Neanderthal DNA Affects Modern Ethnic Difference in Immune Response: Two Studies May Explain Why People of African Descent Respond More Strongly to Infection, and Are More Prone to Autoimmune Diseases." *Nature* (Oct. 20, 2016), first published as "Neanderthal and Infection," in *Scientific American*.

Reason, James. *Human Error*. 1990; New York: Cambridge University Press, 2003.

Reich, David, et al. "Genetic History of an Archaic Hominin Group from Denisova Cave in Siberia." *Nature* 468 (23/30 Dec. 2010).

Rempis, Christian. *Beiträge Zur Hayyam-Forschung*. Leipzig: Deutsche Morgenländische Gesellschaft, 1937.

Richerson Peter J. and Newson, Lesley. "Is Religion Adaptive? Yes, No, Neutral, But Mostly, We Don't Know." In *The Evolution of Religion: Studies, Theories, & Critiques*, ed. Joseph Bulbulia, Richard Sosis, Erica Harris, Russell Genet, and Karen Wyman, Santa Monica, CA: Collins Foundation Press, 2008.

Richert Rebekah A. and Smith, Erin I. "Cognitive Foundations in the Development of a Religious Mind." In *The Biological Evolution of Religious Mind and Behavior*, ed. E. Voland and W. Schiefenhövel, Berlin, Heidelberg: Springer Verlag 2009.

Riepe, Dale Maurice. *The Naturalistic Tradition in Indian Thought*. 1961; Delhi: Motilal Banarsidass, 1964.

Rizzolatti, Giacomo, Fadiga, Luciano, Fogassi, Leonardo and Gallese, Vittorio. "From Mirror Neurons to Imitation: Facts and Speculations." In *Imitative Mind: Development, Evolution and Brain Bases*, ed. Andrew N. Meltzoff and Wolfgang Prinz, Cambridge: Cambridge University Press, 2002.

Rogers, G.A. J. "Locke, Newton and Enlightenment." *Vista in Astronomy* 22/4 (1978): 471-76.

Rossano, Matt. "The African Interregnum: The 'Where,' 'When,' and 'Why' of the Evolution of Religion." In *The Biological Evolution of Religious Mind and Behavior*, E. Voland and W. Schiefenhövel, Berlin, Heidelberg: Springer Verlag, 2009.

Rosen, Friedrich. *Die Sinnsprüche Omars des Zeltmachers*. 1919; Wiesbaden: Marixverlag, 2008.

___. "Zur Textfrage der Vierzeiler Omar's des Zeltmachers (Rubā'īāt-i-"Umar-i-Khayyām)." *Zeitschrift der Deutschen Morgenländischen Gesellschaft* 80 (1926): 312–13.

Ross, Denison "Omar Khayyam." *Bulletin of the School of Oriental Studies* 4/3 (1927): 433-439.

Rothfeld, Otto. *Umar Khayyam and His Age*. Bombay: D. B. Taraporevala Sons & Co. 1922.

Rubalcaba Jill and Robertshaw, Peter. *Every Bone Tells a Story*. Watertown, MA: Charlesbridge, 2010.

"Samuel Clarke." https://plato.stanford.edu/entries/clarke/. Accessed October 15, 2018.

Sankararaman Sriram, et al. "The Genetic Landscape of Neanderthal Ancestry in Present-Day Humans." *Nature* 507 (March 20, 2014).

Sapolsky, Robert. *Behave: The Biology of Humans at Our Best and Worst*. New York: Penguin Press, 2017.

Sarma, Deepak. *Classical Indian Philosophy*. New York: Columbia University Press, 2011.

Sarton, George. *Introduction to the History of Science: From Homer to Omar Khayyam*. Vol. 1 Baltimore, MD: The Williams and Wilkins Co., 1927.

Schack, Adolf Friedrich von. *Strophen des Omar Chijam*. 1878.

Schmaltz, Tad M. "From Causes to Laws." In *Oxford Handbook of Philosophy in Early Modern Europe*. Edited by Desmond M. Clarke and Catherine Wilson 32-50, Oxford: Oxford University Press, 2011.

Schreve, Th. "Ein Besuch im Buddhistischen Purgatorium: Aus dem Tibetischen erstmalig übersetzt." *Zeitschrift der Deutschen Morgenländischen Gesellschaft* 65 (1911): 471–486.

Schumann, Hans Wolfgang. *Handbuch Buddhismus, Die zentralen Lehren: Ursprung und Gegenwart.* Kreuzlingen/München: Heinrich Hugendubel Verlag, 2008.

___. *Buddhismus: Stifter, Schulen und Systeme.* München: Eugen Diederichs Verlag 1993.

Scott, James C. *Against the Grain: A Deep History of the Earliest States.* New Haven, CT: Yale University Press, 2017.

Segal, Robert A. "Jung on Myth." In *Teaching Jung,* 75–92, Kelly Bulkeley and Clodagh Weldon (eds.), New York: Oxford University Press, 2011.

Shahristānī, Abdulkarim. *al-Milal wal Nihal (Tozih al-Milal).* Trans. Seyed M. R. Jalali Naini, vol. II, Tehran, 1387/2008.

Shāntideva. *The Way of the Bodhisattva.* A Translation of the *Bodhicharyāvatāra.* Trans. Padmakara Translation Group, Boston: Shambhala, 2011.

"Shantideva." https://plato.stanford.edu/entries/shantideva/, accessed Jan. 31, 2018.

Shree Madh Bhagvad Maha Purāna. n.d.

Shreeve, Jamie. "Mystery Man." *National Geographic* (Oct. 2015): 30–57.

Soseki, Musō. *Dream Conversations: On Buddhism and Zen.* Trans. By Thomas Cleary. PDF online: https://terebess.hu/zen/mesterek/MusoDream.pdf.

St. Fleur, Nicholas. "Starting Fires to Unearth How Neanderthals Made Glue." *New York Times:* Science, Sept. 7, 2017, reporting from the journal *Scientific Report.*

Stambaugh, Joan. *Impermanence Is Buddha-Nature: Dogen's Understanding of Temporality.* Honolulu: University of Hawaii Press, 1990.

Starr, S. Fredrick. *Lost Enlightenment: Central Asia's Golden Age from the Arab Conquest to Tamerlane.* Princeton, NJ: Princeton University Press, 2015.

Stenger, Gerhardt. *Diderot, Le combattant de la liberté.* Paris: Perrin, 2013.

___. "L'atomisme dans les *Pensées philosophiques: Diderot entre Gassendi et Buffon.*" In *Dix-Huitième Siècle,* Fait partie d'un numéro thématique: *L'épicurisme des Lumières* (2003): 75-100.

Strohl, G. Ralph. Dundas, Paul and Premanand Shah, Umakant. "Jainism." *Encyclopaedia Britannica,* www.britannica.com/topic/Jainism, accessed Jan. 15, 2016, and Jan. 15, 2017.

Stroumsa, Sarah. *Freethinkers of Medieval Islam: Ibn al-Rawandi, Abu Bakr al-Razi and Their Impact on Islamic Thought.* Leiden/Boston/Koln: Brill, 1999.

Sundermann, Werner. "Dīnāvarīya," *Encyclopaedia Iranica.* 1995, accessed Dec. 2010. http://www.iranicaonline.org/.

Supplementary Information, "Map of Neanderthal Ancestry: Supporting Information," na. 15, 2014, 10, 90, DOI: 10.1038/*Nature* 12961.

Suzuki, Daisetz Teitaro. *The Awakening of Zen.* Edited by Christmas Humphreys, 1980; Boston: Shambhala, 2000.

Tablan, Ferdinand. *Early Philosophical Atomism: Indian and Greek* (2012), Online PDF. www.academia.edu/9514956/Early_Philosophical_Atomism_Indian_and_Greek, accessed Jan. 15, 2017.

Tafażżolī, Ahmad. "FERĒDŪN: Iranian Mythic Hero." *Encyclopedia Iranica*, Dec. 15, 1999, accessed Dec. 23, 2016.

Tanahashi, Kazuaki. "Introduction." In *Moon in a Dewdrop: Writings of Zen Master Dōgen*. Edited by Kazuaki Tanahashi, New York: North Point Press, 1985.

Tanahashi, Kazuaki. https://www.youtube.com/watch?v=ebh2C0avDlo.

Taslimi, Ali. *Rubā'ī-hāye Khayyam: Va Nazarīeh Kamīyyat-e Zamān*. 1391; Tehran: Ketab Āmeh, 2012.

Tattersall, Ian and Schwartz, Jeffrey H. "Hominids and Hybrids: The Place of Neanderthals in Human Evolution." *Proceedings of the National Academy of Sciences, USA* 96 (June 1999): 7117.

Tauscher, Helmut. "Phya pa chos kyi seng ge as a Svātantrika." In *The Svātantrika-Prāsangika Distinction: What Difference Does a Difference Make?* Ed. George B. J. Dreyfus and Sara L. McClintock, Boston: Wisdom Publications, 2003.

Taylor John H. (ed.). *Ancient Egyptian Book of the Dead: Journey Through the Afterlife*. Cambridge: Harvard University Press 2013.

The *Circle of Ancient Iranian Studies* (CAIS) (School of Oriental and African Studies – SOAS London: www.caissoas.com/CAIS/Religions/iranian/Mithraism/mithraism_and_christianity.htm, accessed Dec. 29, 2016.

The Long Discourses of the Buddha: A Translation of the *Dīgha Nikāya*. Translated from the Pali by Maurice Walshe, Boston: Wisdom Publications, 2012.

The Mahayana Mahaparinirvana Sutra. Translated into English by Kosho Yamamoto. Edited, revised and copyright by Dr. Tony Page, London: Nirvana Publications, 1999-2000. Source: http://www.nirvanasutra.org.uk.

Thomson, J. Anderson, Aukofer, Clare and Richard Dawkins (Foreword). *Why We Believe in God(s): A Concise Guide to the Science of Faith*. Charlottesville: Pitchstone Publishing, 2011.

Thurow, Joshua C. "Does Cognitive Science Show Belief in God to be Irrational? The Epistemic Consequences of the Cognitive Science of Religion." *International Journal for Philosophy of Religion*, 74/1 (2013): 77–98.

Tillemans, Tom J. F. *Scripture, Logic, Language: Essays on Dharmakirti and his Tibetan Successors*. Boston: Wisdom Publications, 1999.

Tremlin, Todd. *Minds and Gods: The Cognitive Foundations of Religion*. New York: Oxford University Press, 2006.

Tsong-kha-pa. *The Great Treatise on the Stages of the Path to Enlightenment*. Vol. 1, trans. The Lamrim Chenmo Translation Committee, Ithaca, New York: Snow Lion Publications, 2000.

Udāna: Exclamations (80 Utterances of the Buddha). A Translation with an Introduction and Notes by Thānissaro Bhikkhu (Geoffrey DeGraff), 2012. PDF Online: https://www.accesstoinsight.org/lib/authors/thanissaro/udana.pdf

Ueda, Shizuteru. *Wer und was bin ich?: Zur Phänomenologie des Selbst im Zen-Buddhismus.* Freiburg: Verlag Karl Alber, 2016.

Ulansey, David. "The Mithraic Mysteries." *Scientific American* 261/6 (Dec. 1989): 130–135.

Vaas, Rüdiger. "Gods, Gains, and Genes on the Natural Origin of Religiosity by Means of Bio-cultural Selection." In *The Biological Evolution of Religious Mind and Behavior,* ed. E. Voland and W. Schiefenhövel, Berlin, Heidelberg: Springer Verlag 2009.

Van Eyghen, Hans. "Religious Belief is Not Natural. Why Cognitive Science of Religion Does Not Show That Religious Belief is Rational." *Studia Humana* 4/4 (2016): 34–44.

"Vasubandhu." *Stanford Encyclopedia of Philosophy.* First published Apr. 22, 2011 and substantive revision Apr. 27, 2015. Accessed Jan. 16, 2017. https://plato.stanford.edu/entries/vasubandhu/.

Vaziri, Mostafa. *Rumi and Shams' Silent Rebellion: Parallels with Vedanta, Buddhism and Shaivism.* New York and London: Palgrave Macmillan, 2015.

___. *Buddhism in Iran: An Anthropological Approach to Traces and Influences.* New York and London: Palgrave Macmillan, 2012.

Velez de Cea, J. Abraham. *The Buddha and Religious Diversity.* London and New York: Routledge, 2013.

___. "Emptiness in the Pāli *Suttas* and the Question of Nāgārjuna's Orthodoxy." *Philosophy East and West* 55/4 (Oct., 2005): 507–528.

___. "The Silence of the Buddha and the Questions about the Tathāgata after Death." *The Indian International Journal of Buddhist Studies* 5 (2004): 119–141.

Vigne, Jean-Denis. CNRS-Paris "Lecture," published Dec., 14, 2017 in Youtube: https://www.youtube.com/watch?v=5o1JZ5wo_Qs.

Voland, Eckart. "Evaluating the Evolutionary Status of Religiosity and Religiousness." In *The Biological Evolution of Religious Mind and Behavior,* ed. E. Voland and W. Schiefenhövel, Berlin, Heidelberg: Springer Verlag 2009.

von Kremer, A. „Philosophische Gedichte des 'Abū-l 'alā' Ma'arrī." *Zeitschrift der Deutschen Morgenländischen Gesellschaft* 38 (1884): 40–52.

Waldman, Marilyn R. "Primitive Mind/Modern Mind: New Approaches to an Old Problem Applied to Islam." In *Approaches to Islam in Religious Studies,* ed. Richard C. Martin, Tucson: University of Arizona Press, 1985.

Warder, A. K. "On the Relationships Between Early Buddhism and Other Contemporary Systems." *Bulletin of School of Oriental and African Studies* 18/1 (1956): 58–59.

Weber-Brosamer Bernhard and Back, Dieter *Die Philosophie der Leere: Nāgārjunas Mulamadhyamakakārikās: Übersetzung des buddhistischen Basistextes mit kommentierenden Einführungen.* Wiesbaden: Harrassowitz Verlag, 1997.

Wilford, John Noble. "Skull Fossil Offers New Clues on Human Journey From Africa." *New York Times: Science,* Jan. 28, 2015.

Wolfe, Charles T. "A Happiness Fit for Organic Bodies: La Mettrie's Medical Epicureanism." In *Epicurus in the Enlightenment,* Neven Leddy and Avis

Liefschitz (eds.) 69-84, Oxford: Voltaire Foundation, University of Oxford, 2009.

Wrangham, Richard. *Catching Fire: How Cooking Made Us Human*. New York: Basic Books, 2009.

www.researchgate.net/publication/45589599_Primate_Sleep_in_Phylogenetic_Perspective.

"Yahweh." *New World Encyclopedia*, accessed Dec. 17, 2016, www.newworldencyclopedia.org/entry/Yahweh.

Yin, Steph. "Cold Tolerance Among Inuit May Come from Extinct Human Relatives." *New York Times: Science*, Dec. 23, 2016.

Yogananda, Sri Sri Paramahansa. *The Wine of the Mystic: The Rubaiyat of Omar Khayyam – A Spiritual Interpretation*. Delhi: Macmillan Limited, 1997.

Zehm, Günter. *War Platon in Asien?: Adnoten zur Globalisierung des Geistes*. Schnellroda: Anthaios, 2008.

"Zen." *Encyclopedia Britannica*, www.britannica.com/topic/Zen, accessed Sept. 17, 2018.

Zimmer, Carl. "A Blended Family: Her Mother Was Neanderthal, Her Father Something Else Entirely." *New York Times: Science*, Aug. 22, 2018, the actual study was published in *Nature* magazine.

___. "Unappetizing Experiment Explores Tools' Role in Humans' Bigger Brains." *New York Times: Science*, March 9, 2016.

___. "Down From the Trees, Humans Finally Got a Decent Night's Sleep." *New York Times: Science*, Dec. 17, 2015.

___. "Agriculture Linked to DNA Changes in Ancient Europe." *New York Times: Science*, Nov. 23, 2015.

___. "DNA Deciphers Roots of Modern Europeans." *New York Times: Science*, June 10, 2015.

Zimmer, Heinrich (edited and completed by Joseph Campbell). *Philosophies of India*. Princeton: Princeton University Press, 1969.

Zongpo, Tokmé. *Reflections on Silver River*. Trans. Ken McLeod, Los Angeles: Unfettered Mind Media, 2013.

Index

A

Abhidharma, 143.
Abraham/Abrahamic, 47, 69, 78, 84, 85, 87, 89, 90, 91, 92, 95-98.
Actor(s) or *agent(s)* (in cognitive science), 5, 26-30, 31, 36, 37, 39, 47, 51, 57.
Adam and Eve, 56, 83, 83n42, 86, 100.
Adorno, Theodor, xxiii.
Africa/African, xii, 7-10, 11, 13, 13n27, 81, 84, 268, 275.
Agency Detective Device (ADD), 30.
Ahīmsa (non-violence), 117, 118.
Ahriman, 80, 81.
Ahura Mazda, 81, 89.
Ajita, Kesakambali, 107, 109, 112, 113.
Ajīvika(s), Ajīvikism, xx, 103, 105, 113-118, 120, 121, 136, 140, 159.
Alexander, 128.
Algebra, xxii.
al-Ma'arrī, Abul 'Alā. 221, 222, 222n25, 255.
Alpha male, xxiv, 23, 40, 54.
Altruism, 38, 57, 201.
Aminrazavi, Mehdi, vii, 215n3, 233n40.
Amitābha Buddha, 151.
Ammon, (god of mystery), 89, 90.
An-ātman, 164, 180, 196.
Angels, 3, 31, 93-94, 222n25.
Anitya (impermanence), *nitya* (permanence)196, 197.

Anthropocentric/non-anthropocentric, ix, xxi, 28, 29, 30, 31, 41, 62, 134, 210, 227, 234, 240.
Anthropomorph/ized/ism/ization, xvi, 25, 30, 32, 84, 87, 90, 103, 262.
Apollo/Apollo-worship, 82, 83, 95, 100, 150.
Arberry, Arthur J., 223.
"arche-purpose", 60-61.
Artemis, 95.
Ārya (noble), 156, 175.
Ash'arites, 218.
Asoka, 117, 113n45, 142n6, 150.
Assmann, Jan, 47, 86.
Ataraxia, 123, 126, 127, 129, 130, 137, 170n82, 224n34.
Athens, 124.
Atīśa, 167.
Atom(a), xxii, 118, 121, 122, 131, 132, 134, 217, 218, 226, 228, 230, 231, 232, 235, 246-251, 255, 261, 263.
Atomism, xxii, 109, 114, 121-124, 131, 134, 135, 217, 218, 226, 248, 249, 250, 261, 263.
Atrahasis, 85.
'Attār (Persian poet), xiii, 219.
Australopithecus (Lucy), 7.
Avalokiteśvara, 152, 152n42.
Avery, Peter, 223.
Avicenna (Ibn Sīnā)/Avicennian, 218, 220, 233n40.
Avidyā (ignorance), 157.
Axial Age, 103, 103n1,121.
Az-Zamakhsharī, 222.

Aztecs, 43, 59.

B

Bahram – king, 248.
Bahubhati, 117.
Baily, Kent, 22.
Balcerowicz, Piotr, 114.
Balkh, 219, 220n17.
Basham, Arthur L., 114.
Batchelor, Stephen, vii, 144, 148, 149, 175.
Beck, Ulrich, 279n52.
Beckwith, Christopher, 128.
Bergson, Henri, 45.
Bible/Biblical, 81, 81n39, 83, 84, 85, 85n48, 86, 86n50, 92, 93, 263.
Bio-cognitive, 35, 49.
Biocultural, 33.
Biology of Religion, xix.
Bipedal/bipedality, 4, 8-9.
Black Stone (in *Ka'ba*), 92, 92n62.
Blumenberg, Hans, 77.
Bodhicharyāvatāra (The Way of the Bodhisattva) - Shāntideva, 200, 201n76.
Bodhidharma, 145, 195, 207, 211, 216.
Book of Exodus, 86.
Book of Genesis, 56, 83, 90, 92.
Book of Samuel, 86.
Boyer, Pascal, 48.
Bracciolini, Poggio, 131.
Bronze Age, xxiii, 79, 88, 94, 103, 121, 136.
Bouchard, Thomas, 53.
Brahman, 81, 89, 104.
Brahmanical/Brahmanism, 81, 104, 111, 112, 118, 120, 139-143, 149, 150n37, 155.
Buddha-nature, 151, 182, 193, 194, 198.

Buddha-worship, 142, 150, 151, 152.
Burkert, Walter, 94, 95.

C

Campbell, Joseph, 73, 99, 100.
Capture (David Kessler), 71.
carpe diem, 224, 225, 215n3.
Catholic, 257, 279.
Carthage, 96.
Çārvāka(s), vii, xx, 105, 106-113, 118, 120, 122-125, 127, 136, 137, 140, 143, 181, 203, 206, 216, 217, 218, 224n35, 255, 257, 268, 269, 272, 277.
Cassirer, Ernst, 75-76.
Central Asia/Asian, xxii, 7, 10, 82, 89, 128, 143, 219, 272, 272n46.
Central Asian Enlightenment, 272.
Chaldean, 122.
Charron, Pierre, 262n15.
Chernobyl disaster, 279n52.
Chimu civilization, 43.
China, 143, 145, 193, 196, 216n4.
Chinese, 14, 117, 144, 145, 149.
"Chosen People", 39, 83, 97.
Christian cosmology, ix.
Christian mythology, 91.
Christian, xxi, 56, 84, 91, 93, 96, 97, 98n75, 135, 219n13, 224, 257, 262n17, 263, 267.
Christianity, 47, 90, 90n59, 91.
Chuang Tzu, 272.
Church (Catholic), 135, 257, 258, 259, 260, 263, 264.
Cline, Eric, 85.
Closed Religions, 46-47.
Code of Hammurabi, 88, 88n54.
Cognitive dissonance, x, xxii, 44, 203.
Cognitive modules, 27-28, 36.

Index

Cognitive Science of Religion (CSR), 27, 28, 30.
Cohen, Hermann, 75.
Compassion (see also *karuṇā*), 159, 199-202, 213.
Conger, George P., 121.
Consciousness, xvi, xvii, 68, 71, 76, 81, 100, 105-106, 108, 118, 122, 137, 151, 180, 181, 183, 196, 209, 213, 225, 227, 230, 236, 247, 252, 253.
Cooper, William, 40, 41.
Copernican, 43.
Counterintuitive, xvii, 3, 23, 42, 44, 48, 75.
Crucifixion, 91.
"cult of the dead" (Egypt), 88.
Cultural DNA, 8.
Cuneiform tablets, 85.

D

DNA, ix-x, 3, 8, 10-11, 15, 17, 23.
Dahr (Universe, material world), 234, 237.
Dalai Lama, 279, 279n53.
David and Goliath, 86-87, 87n52.
Dawkins, Richard, 57, 60, 62n37, 62n38.
de La Mettrie, Julien, 258n2, 264, 265n29.
Declaration of Independence, 135, 265.
Deer Park-Śārnath, 171n84.
Deist/ deistic, 46.
Delusion/Delusional, 35-37, 134, 157, 158, 213.
Democritus, xxi, 109, 117, 117n58, 121, 122-123, 123n77, 124, 127, 128, 130, 131, 136, 217, 218, 226, 255, 265.
Demythification, 212.

Denisovan, ix, 3, 5, 8, 10, 13-15.
Dennett, Daniel, 60, 61.
Dependent Arising (see also *pratītyasamutpāda*), 153, 159, 163, 177, 183, 186, 187n132, 190, 199.
Determinism, xviii, 114, 116, 143, 182, 232.
Deuteronomy, 98.
Devil, x, 32, 81, 94, 100.
Dharma, 130, 139, 142, 146, 148n26, 149, 150, 152, 155, 162, 166, 167, 183, 193, 194, 208, 212.
Dharmakāya, 151n39, 163, 170.
Dharmakīrti, 111n32, 206.
Dialectical reductionism, 190, 225.
Diderot, Denis, 258n2, 263-264.
Dignāga, 206.
Dīnāvarī, 219.
Dionysus, 90.
Diphtheria, x.
Divan (Rumi), 275.
Dōgen, 146, 146n21, 172, 178, 183, 193, 194, 194n153, 195-198, 204, 207, 208, 255n48.
"don't-know mind", 193.
Dopamine, 26, 33, 34.
Dream Conversations (Muchū Mondō), 192.
Druid, 35.
Duḥkha (in Sanskrit, see also dukkha), 174.
Dukkha (in Pali), 155, 157, 159, 163, 164, 174-177, 179, 180, 196, 224n33.
Dukkha-dukkhatā, 176.
Durga, 95.
Düsseldorf, 10.
Dveśa (liking-disliking), 157, 168.

E

EEG, 18.
Egypt/ Egyptian, 69, 83, 86, 86n50, 88, 88n54, 89, 90, 97, 123.
Egyptian Book of the Dead, 87-88, 88n54.
Eightfold path, 156-157.
Eliade, Mircea, 73, 74, 74n17, 75, 99.
Emptiness (general), 60, 116, 134, 156, 163, 172, 198, 224, 225, 226, 246, 270.
Emptiness (philosophical - *śūnyatā*), 159, 160, 163, 173, 177, 178, 181, 182, 183-195, 200, 201, 210, 255n48, 271.
Enlightenment (Buddhist), 118, 146, 152n42, 154, 155, 157, 160, 161, 193, 195, 200, 202, 270.
Enlightenment (European), xxi, xxiv, 131, 135, 257-265, 266-268, 277.
Enlightenment (general), xiii, 167, 170, 213, 268, 269, 271, 272, 274, 276, 278.
Enlil, 90.
Epicurus, vii, xvii, xxi, 109, 121, 122-127, 129, 131, 135, 136, 170n82, 216, 217, 218, 224, 226, 255, 257, 258, 260, 263, 264-268, 272, 275, 280.
Epicurean/ Epicureanism, xxiv, 122, 124, 125n86, 126, 131, 134, 135, 137, 213n213, 218n10, 224n35, 258, 258n2, 260, 262, 262n17, 263, 264, 265, 265n29, 266, 267, 268, 269, 274, 277.
Epiphenomenon, 108, 132.
Eternal life, 87, 88, 89, 133.
Eternalist, 186, 190.
Ethiopia, 123.
Ethology/ Ethologist, 39, 41.
Evil, 5, 32, 80, 82, 83n42, 86, 89, 94, 98, 169, 212, 255.
Evolution (general), ix, x, xv, xviii, xix, xxiv, 3, 4, 7-9, 14-19, 21-23, 27, 29, 31, 32, 35, 40, 41, 44-45, 52, 57, 69, 82, 83, 89, 135, 140, 145, 153, 174, 188, 194, 236, 243, 274.
Evolutionary Biology, x, xxiv, 7, 27, 40, 187n130.
Evolutionary Anthropology, 11.
Eurasia, 14.
Europe/European, xxi, 7, 10, 11n14, 13, 14, 17, 21n35, 81, 82, 128n95, 135, 184n123, 257, 258, 260, 264, 265, 267, 269.
Exclusivist, 47, 206, 211, 275.

F

Faith, 35, 36, 38, 42, 55, 62, 86, 87, 94, 98, 147, 152, 153, 156, 205, 218, 275.
Fallen Angel, 3, 94.
Fear, irrational, xviii.
Fear, roots of, xv.
Feierman, Jay R., 39.
Fereydoun, 80-81.
Fetchenhauer Detlef, 41, 44.
Fire or flame, Buddha's allegory of, 155n56, 156.
FitzGerald, Edward, 218n10, 222-224.
Flintoff, Everard, 128-129.
Four Noble Truths, 119, 156, 157, 175, 216n4.
Frankl, Viktor, 38, 68.
Frey, Ulrich, 29, 30.
Friend, Tim, 53.
Fromm, Erich, 55, 55n16, 70.

Frontal lobe/cortex (brain), 26, 27, 34, 37, 49, 51.
Fuhlrott, Johann Carl, 9n10.

G

Gabriel (angel), 92.
Gagarin, Yuri, ix.
Galileo, 259-260.
Garden (school of Epicurus), 124-125, 125n86, 265.
Garden of Eden, 83, 86.
Genetic(s), ix, x, xv, xix, 3, 4, 5, 7, 9, 10, 11, 13-15, 17, 19, 22, 23, 35, 38, 76, 84.
Genital mutilation, 54, 278.
Genjokoan, 183.
Geocentric, ix, 43.
Ghazzāli-al, 120, 271.
Gilgamesh, 85-86.
Glasenapp, Helmut von, 153.
Glenn, John, ix.
Gelug, 190.
"god logic", 42.
"golden cage" of Paradise, 56.
Gombrich, Richard, 158.
Gośala, Makkali, 105, 114, 116, 117.
"gradual nirvana", 163, 164, 199.
Greco-Roman, xii, xxi, 92, 103, 121, 136.
Greek, see also Hellenic, xii, xxii, 46, 82, 83, 83n42, 89, 90, 116, 117, 117n58, 121, 122, 125, 129, 137, 216n6, 257, 265,
"Greek Buddhist" (Pyrrho), 127-128.
Greenblatt, Stephen, 56, 131, 134, 135.
Gymnosophists (naked sages), 117, 117n58, 128.

H

Hades, 82, 89.
Hajj (pilgrimage), 91-92, 92n63, 95.
Hansen, Gerhard A., x.
Heart Sūtra, 144, 180.
Heaven and hell, 106, 110, 149, 205, 211, 221, 221n23, 245, 254, 271.
Hebrew Bible, 263.
Hedāyat, Sādiq, 220, 224n35, 233n40.
Hédoné, 125, 137, 224n34, 225.
Hedonism, 109, 112, 125, 126, 215n3, 222, 223-224, 273.
Heidegger, Martin, 210, 215.
Heliocentric, 43.
Hell, 44, 88, 97, 106, 107, 109, 132, 148, 149, 150, 226, 235, 245, 254, 255, 262.
Hellenic (see also Greek), xx, xxi, 82, 109, 121-123, 127-129, 136, 170n82, 213n213, 218, 220, 229n38.
Helvétius, Claude Adrien, 258n2, 264.
Heraclitus, 272.
Herd (mentality), 20, 22, 23, 48, 57, 62, 111.
hīch (nothingness), 225-227, 230, 232, 251-255, 255n48.
Hindu, Hinduism, 89, 95, 141, 142, 150n36, 194.
Hölderlin, Friedrich, 216.
Holocaust, "whole burning", 96.
Homo erectus (Turkana), 4, 7, 16, 17.
Homo heidelbergensis, 16.
Homo naledi, 7.
Human Leukocyte Antigen (HLA), 12.

Hume, David, 258n2, 269.
Hunter-gatherers, xix, 5, 20, 21, 21n53, 35, 52n11, 69, 83.

I

Ibrāhīm ibn Adham, 219.
Ikkyū Sōjun, 191.
Illogic, illogical, 33, 42, 43, 44, 60, 164, 202, 203, 206.
Illusion, xxi, 29, 59, 126, 133, 134, 154, 178, 181, 182, 187n130, 189, 226, 227, 240, 249, 262.
Imitation (in religion), 48, 49, 57, 58-60, 62, 97.
Impermanency/Impermanence, 119, 157, 159, 160, 163, 166, 168, 172, 174, 176, 179, 180, 192, 195-199, 201, 202, 209, 213, 244, 255, 270, 273.
Inclusivist, 211.
India/Indian, xii, xx, xxii, 44n53, 47, 52n11, 81, 81n39, 88n55, 89, 95, 103, 104, 106, 107, 113, 117, 117n58, 121, 123, 127, 128, 128n97, 129, 140, 142, 143, 144, 147-150, 153, 167, 171n84, 177, 180, 201, 217, 220, 223, 229n38, 257, 268, 275, 279n53.
Indian philosophy, 104, 104n2, 109, 136, 218, 226.
Indra, 82.
Inference, 110-111, 127, 203, 204, 206.
Interbreeding, ix, xv, xvi, 3, 4, 10-15.
Iraj, 80.
Iran – Iranian, xii, xx, xxii, 80, 81, 89, 90, 122, 123, 128, 201, 215, 220, 233n40, 257, 272n45.
Iron Age, xxiii, xxiv, 5, 68, 70, 75, 79, 89, 94, 95, 103, 136.

Isaac, 96.
Ishmael, 92, 96.
Ishtar, 90.
Islam – Islamic, 47, 56, 84, 86, 87, 91, 92, 92n62, 93-96, 98, 120, 219, 219n13, 220, 220n18, 224, 234, 235, 272, 274n47, 275-276, 278n51.
Israelites, 86, 86n50, 87, 97, 98.
Isrāfīl (Archangel Raphael), 93.
Īśvara, 206.
Izrā'īl (angel of death), 94.
Izutsu, Toshihiko, 172, 197.

J

Jacob, 90, 92.
Jain, Jainism, xx, 104-106, 109, 110, 112, 113, 114, 116, 117-121, 128, 136, 140.
James, William, 71, 74, 272.
Jamshid (Avestan Yima), 80.
Japan/Japanese, 117, 144-146, 147n21, 193, 194n153, 216n4, 255n48.
Jasper, Karl, xi, 103n1.
Jātakas, 143, 149, 238n41.
Jefferson, Thomas, 135, 265.
Jerusalem, 93, 96.
Jesus, 56, 90, 91, 96, 97, 100, 279.
Jew/Jewish – Judaism, 91, 95, 96, 99n76, 219n13.
Jinns (genies), 94.
Job, 93, 98, 99n76.
Judaized Christians, 91.
Judeo-Christian, 56, 84, 93, 224, 263.
Jung, Carl, 73.
Jupiter (god), 92.
Jyotistoma (Vedic sacrifice), 112, 112n38.

Index

K

Ka'aba, 91, 92, 92n62.
Kāfir, 98, 275.
Kahneman, Daniel, 58.
Kālāma Sutta/Sūtra, 153, 154.
Kām(a) (pleasure), 112, 137, 217, 239, 240, 241, 242.
Kandaraka Sutta, 155.
Kant, Immanuel, 62n41, 258.
Kantian logic, 41.
Karma, 104, 114-115, 119, 124, 147-149, 154, 161, 176-177, 205, 206.
Karunā (see also compassion), 164, 199, 200.
Kessler, David, 71.
Keyumars. 81.
Khāk (dust), 230, 232, 248.
Khayyamian, 216n4, 225, 227-230, 233, 233n40, 237, 239, 240, 242, 247, 271, 272.
Kirāmān Kātibin (Islamic angels), 94.
Kleśas (poisonous tendencies), 157.
Kōans, 210.
Koch, Robert, x.
Kokushi (see Musō Soseki), 173.
Koran/Koranic, 79, 83, 84-86, 91, 92, 98, 221.
Krishna, 81.
Kuzeh-gar (pot-maker), 229, 237.
Kuzminski, Adrian, 128, 129.
Kyoto School, 177.

L

Lamrim (stages of the path), 167.
Language (Sacred), 76, 77.
Lao Tzu, 209n197, 216, 217, 272.
Leap forward, 18, 20, 23, 57, 76.
Leprosy, x.
Laertius, Diogenes, 117n58, 122, 124, 126, 128.
Leucippus, 109, 121, 123, 124.
Leviticus, 98.
Locke, John, 261, 269.
"logic of decision", 44.
Logic (inductive/deductive), 110, 154, 163, 189, 191, 202-205, 206, 259, 260, 266, 270, 273.
Logic (religious), 41-43.
Logic (static), 41.
Lokāyata (people's philosophy), 106n7, 107, 107n8, 141.
Lorenz, Konrad, xi, 22, 41, 74, 62n41, 135.
Lotus Sūtra, 144.
Love (Buddhism, Rumi), 201, 275, 276.
Lucretius, xxi, 121, 126, 131-136, 137, 216, 216n5, 217, 218, 224, 224n35, 226, 255, 257, 260, 261, 263, 264, 265, 267, 268, 272, 273.

M

Macroevolution, 3.
Madhyamika, 115, 129, 130, 185, 186, 188, 189, 190, 192, 196, 200, 200n173, 207, 208, 229n38.
Magian, 122, 128.
Maha-Parinirvana Sūtra, 160.
Mahāvira (Jain), 105, 107, 113n45, 114, 117, 118.
Mahayana, 140, 144, 151, 185, 187, 188n133, 189, 192, 196, 200, 216n4.
Mahayanist, 142, 151, 185, 189.
Mahdi (messiah), 93.
Maitreya (the last Buddha), 150, 152n42.
Majjhima Nikaya, 152, 188.

Maladaptive, 62, 62n37, 62n38.
Malāmatī, 218, 219.
Malebranche, Nicolas, 258n2, 262, 262n17.
Mani/Manichaean/Manichaeism, 91, 91n60, 219, 219n13.
Māra (diabolical temptations), 169.
Marduk, 90.
Margreiter, Reinhard, 75.
Marx, Karl, 107n10, 265, 266, 266n30.
Masnavi, 120, 275, 275n48.
Mauryan period/king, 113, 113n45, 150.
Max Planck Institute, 11.
Maya, 226, 227.
McEvilley, Thomas, 121, 122, 136.
Mecca, 91, 92, 92n62, 93, 100.
Mechanical Philosophy, 246, 247, 251, 261.
Mediterranean, 80, 90.
Melanesians, 14.
meme (imitating behavior), 57.
Merton, Thomas, 280.
Mesopotamia/n, 69, 83-85, 86n50, 88, 89, 90, 95.
Metaphor of "god", 42, 77.
Metaphorology, 77.
Meteorite, 91-92.
Microevolution, 9.
Middle Way (see also Madhyamika), 163, 185, 186, 189, 190, 229n38.
Milgram, Stanley, 55, 55n16.
Mind-Only School, 192.
Mini-Nirvanas, xxi, 139, 140, 161, 162, 164, 165, 213.
Miracle(s), 5, 67, 84, 86, 90n59, 152, 264.
Mithra/Mithras/Mithraistic, 90, 90n58, 90n59.

Modularity (cognitive or computational), 32.
Moha (delusion), 157, 171.
Mohammad, 87, 87n52, 92, 279.
Monotheism/monotheistic, 32, 46, 47, 75, 90, 245, 276.
Montagu, Ashley, 97.
Montaigne de, Michel, 262.
Montesquieu, 261.
Morris, Desmond, 40.
Moses, 86, 86n50, 88, 91, 279.
Mūlamadhyamakākārikā (Nāgārjuna), 144, 187, 190.
Muslim(s), 84n44, 87, 91, 92, 92n62, 95, 97-98, 220, 221, 275.
Musō, Soseki (Kokushi), 146, 173, 192, 193, 194, 194n153, 202, 208, 209n197, 210.
Mysticism, 45, 274n47, 276.
Myth-making, xv, xix, 5, 60, 63, 67-69, 77, 79, 80, 85, 89, 96, 99, 158.

N

Nāgārjuna, 127, 129, 144, 180, 184, 185, 187, 188, 188n133, 189-191, 193, 200, 204, 206, 209, 210.
Nakir and Munkir (Islamic angels), 94.
Naraka (hell), 149.
Nastikā Schools, xx, 103, 104, 105, 121, 131.
Native Americans, 35, 268.
natura naturans (Spinoza), 263.
Natural selection, 5, 9, 10, 17, 22, 32, 37, 40, 41-42.
Nature of Things, The (Lucretius), 126, 131, 135, 136, 216n5, 260.
Neanderthal, ix, xv, 3, 4, 7, 8, 10-15, 11n14.
Neander Valley, 10, 10n9.

Index

Near East/ern, 7, 10, 17, 80, 81, 87, 89, 94, 122.
Neishābur, 215, 218, 219, 219n13, 220.
Neolithic, xix, 3, 17, 18, 20, 21n52, 52, 68, 70.
"neo-purpose", 60.
Nepal/i, 95, 174.
Neurobiology, 32.
Neurocognitive science, 28.
Neuroplasticity, xvii.
Neurotheology, 32, 33, 33n24.
Newton, Isaac, 135, 260, 261.
Nietzsche, Friedrich, 127, 265, 266.
Nihilism, 184n123, 223, 224-226, 255.
Nixon, G. M., 76.
Nile (River), 88.
Nirmāna-kāya, 151.
Nirvana, ubiquitous.
Nishitani, Keiji, 60, 177, 198.
Noah, 81, 81n38, 84, 85, 91.
Noah's flood/Ark, 84, 92.
No-Mind school, 192.
Non-absolutist (views), 120, 131, 154.
Non-Euclidean geometry, xxii.
Non-modular/ity, 33.
Non-Muslims, 275.
Non-self, ubiquitous.
Non-Self Sermon (Buddha), 156.
Nontheism, 105, 106, 118, 121, 134, 143.
Nonviolence (see also *Ahīmsa*), 117, 118, 275, 277.
North Whitehead, Alfred, 229n38, 272.
Nothingness (see also *hīch*), xxii, 60, 115, 166, 184n123, 215, 217, 225-228, 230-232, 246, 251-255, 255n48.

Nowness, 22, 159, 164, 195-199, 225, 226, 228, 230-232, 239-246, 280.
Nyaya-Vaisesika, 109, 218.

O

Obedience (in religion), 48, 49, 53-61, 62, 99, 258.
Obsessive Compulsive Disorder (OCD), 33-34.
Old Testament, 88n54, 89, 96, 98.
Open Religion(s), 45-47.

P

Pääbo, Svante, 11.
Paleolithic, 12, 18, 21.
Paleopsychology, 22.
Paley, William, 28, 29, 29n10.
Pāli (language and Canons), 151n39, 174, 174n93, 188, 224n33.
Pancātantra, 117.
Papyrus of Ani, 87n53.
Paradise, 56, 83, 92, 150, 245.
Parināmanā, 168, 168n76, 199.
Parinirvana, 116, 143, 159, 160, 162, 181, 271.
Parkinson's Disease, 34.
Parshwānath, 118.
Pascal, Blaise, 44.
Pentateuch, 98.
Persian/Persianate, xiii, xxi, 84n44, 106, 121, 125, 125n86, 137, 174n94, 215, 216n4, 217, 217n7, 218n10, 222, 223, 223n32, 232, 233n39, 234, 236, 242n44, 243, 248, 254, 272, 274, 275.
Pharaohs, 69, 87n53, 88, 89.
Phoenicians, 96.
Piaget, Jean, 58.

Placebo, 37.
Plato, 121.
Pollan, Michael, 17n41, 72.
Polytheism/Polytheistic, 46, 89, 104, 118, 245.
Portugal, 11.
Poseidon, 82, 89, 95.
Post-Traumatic Stress Disorder (PTSD), 53.
Pragmatism (William James), 74.
Prajapati, 81.
Prajñā, 171, 182, 194.
Prajñāpāramitā (Sūtras), 144, 144n7, 145, 185, 188, 216n4.
Prakrit, 158, 174, 174n93.
Pramāna (epistemology), 109n25, 111n32, 163, 191, 202-207, 270.
Pramāna-vārttika (Dharmakīrti), 206, 206n191.
Prāsangika, 190-191.
Pratītyasamutpāda, 163, 183, 186, 187n132.
pre-linguistic, 197, 210.
pre-Socratic, 121, 216n5.
Principia Mathematica, 261.
Primate(s), ix, 3, 7,8, 16, 17, 19, 19n48, 22, 23, 39, 40, 53, 54, 57, 78, 78n33.
Process Philosophy, 229, 229n38, 272.
Prometheus, 61.
Psychedelic drugs, 72.
Ptolemy, ix, 43.
Purānas (Vedic anthologies), 81n39, 141.
Pyrrho of Elis, xxi, 117n58, 123, 127-131, 136, 170n82, 216, 217.
Pyrrhonism/ Pyrrhonist, 122, 127, 128, 128n95, 129.

Q

Quinn, Daniel, 62, 99n77.

R

Ra (the sun-god), 89.
Rāga (greed, desire), 157, 165.
Ram, 81.
Ramachandran, V. S., 17, 18.
Ramses (king), 90.
Rebellion (Buddha-Zen), 139, 140-143, 145-150, 155, 211.
Reformation, 257.
Reincarnation/ Rebirth, 38, 62, 87n53, 88, 88n55, 104, 106, 107, 108, 109, 124, 132, 133, 141, 142, 143, 147, 148, 149, 160, 161, 176, 205, 230, 247.
Renaissance, xxi, xxii, 131, 135, 257-260, 268, 274n47.
Revelation, 78, 79, 86, 123.
Rewiring (neural pathways), xiii, xviii, 3, 5, 26, 27.
Rinzai Zen school, 194, 194n53, 195.
Rishābha, 118.
Risikogesellschaft (risk society), 279n52.
Rizzolatti, Giacomo, 17, 18n45.
Roman, xii, xxi, 83n42, 90, 92, 103, 121, 125, 131, 136, 275.
Rousseau, 261.
Rubā'īyyāt (quatrains of Khayyam), xxi, 215, 216n4, 219, 221, 222, 223, 224, 232, 233, 242, 252.
Rumi, 120, 123n79, 217, 217n7, 257, 268, 274-277.

Index

S

Sacrifice, animal, human (religious), x, xx, xxii, 40, 43, 80, 94-96, 104, 111, 112, 112n38, 114, 136, 140, 141, 142, 201, 202.
Saint Augustine, 56.
Śakyamuni, 128.
Śamathā meditation, 164, 172.
Sambhoga-kāya, 151.
Samkhya School, 106n5, 107n8.
Samsara, 115, 143, 159-162, 170, 177-179, 182, 196, 199.
Samyutta Nikāya, 179.
Sangha, 152, 162.
Sankhāra-dukkhatā, 176.
Sapolsky, Robert, xviii.
Sargon (king), 86n50.
Sarvāstivādin, 188.
Satan, 86, 94.
Schaaffhausen, Hermann, 10n9.
Scholastic, 129, 130, 137, 139, 140, 144, 145, 148, 152, 219, 274.
Schopenhauer, Arthur, 217, 224n35.
Scott, James C., 62, 83.
Scripture(s), 21, 32, 35, 47, 68, 69, 78, 83n42, 105, 106, 107, 108, 110, 120, 139, 140, 142, 143-150, 153, 154, 160, 164, 176, 205, 207, 216n4, 262, 280.
Scythian, 128.
"Second" Enlightenment, 257, 267, 267n38, 268.
Secular – Secularization, xi, xxii, 4n1, 36, 47, 139, 213, 267, 268, 269, 270, 274, 274n47, 275, 277, 278, 280.
Selbstbestimmung (self-determination, Kant), 258.
Self-Rule (philosophical), ubiquitous.

"selfish gene", 57, 57n23.
Semitic languages, 81.
Seven Truths (Jain), 119.
Sextus Empiricus, 127, 128n95.
Shahnameh (Firdousi), 80.
Shahristānī (al-), 122, 124, 218.
Shamanism, 51.
Shams (Tabrizi), 274, 274n47, 276.
Shankara, 142.
Shāntideva, 200-202.
Sharāb (wine), 240.
Shi'ite, 87.
Shiva, 82, 100.
Shōbōgenzō (Dōgen), 147, 183, 194n153, 255n48.
Siberia (Neanderthals and Denisovans), 10, 14.
Siddhartha, 140.
Silk Route, 220.
Skandhas, 180, 180n116.
Skepticism/ Skeptics, xxi, 5, 127, 128, 128n95, 129, 130, 136, 154, 218n10, 221, 257, 264, 273.
Slavery, xix, 20, 98, 98n75.
Sogdian text, 149.
Son of God, 90.
Sōtō Zen school, 194, 194n153.
South Africa, 7.
South America/ns, 59, 268.
Spinoza, 262, 263, 263n20.
Substantialist, 186.
Sufism, 219, 271-2n45, 274n47, 275.
Sukkha/ sukkha (joy of existence), 159, 175, 224n33.
Suñña (empty), 187-188.
Śūnyatā (emptiness), 163, 178, 184, 187, 188, 255n48.
Sutta Pitaka, 149.
Sūtra(s), see specific sūtra.
Suzuki, D. T., 145.

Svātantrika, 190-191.
Syllogistic construction, 190.

T

"Take refuge in yourself", 182, 213.
Tanahashi, Kazuaki, 193.
Tantric (Buddhism), 140.
Tao Te Ching, 104, 170n82, 209n197, 216n5.
Tathāgata (the Buddha), 157, 158, 177, 202.
Tathāgatagarbha, 151, 157, 158, 164,
Tathāgatagarbha Sūtra, 151, 157.
Taxila, 123n77.
Ten Commandments, 88, 88n54.
Tetralemmas of Nāgārjuna, 190.
Thar (the god of the underworld), 89.
Theory of Mind Mechanism (ToMM), 30.
Theravada, 140, 142, 143, 151n39, 188n133.
Thomson, Anderson, 70.
Thor, 82.
Three poisons, 157-158, 163, 175, 200, 213.
Tibet/Tibetan, 144, 150, 167, 170, 190, 191, 206, 216n5, 279.
Tibetan Buddhism, vii, 88n55, 147.
Tigris and Euphrates, 83.
Toffler, Alvin, xii.
Tremlin, Todd, 30, 34.
Trikāya, 151, 152.
Tripitakas, 143.
Tṛṣṇā (thirst, craving), 165.
Truth-seeking, ubiquitous.
Tuberculosis, x.
Tushita (heaven), 150, 150n36.
Type I behavior (primate), 39, 40.
Type II behavior, 40.

U

Udāna (Discourses), 120, 169,
Umma, 98.
Upādāna (attachment), 165.
Upanishad/ Upanishadic, 81, 89, 104, 136, 142, 216n4, 217.
Utilitarian, 38, 42, 154, 264.
Utnapishtim, 85.

V

Vaas, Rüdiger, 35.
Valla, Lorenzo, 135.
Valley of the Kings (Egypt), 88.
Vasubandhu, 178, 179, 207.
Vedanta, 142, 219n13, 226.
Vedic, 81, 82, 112, 118, 140, 141, 142, 147, 149.
Vegetarian, 116, 117, 221.
Victorian era, 223.
Vinaya, 143.
Violence, 21n52, 40, 47, 83n42, 105, 168, 277.
Vipariṇāma dukkhatā, 176.
Vipassanā meditation, 164, 172.
Viśnu, 81, 141, 142, 150n37.
"vital nirvana", 163, 164.
Voland, Eckart, 38.
von Behring, Emil, x.
Voltaire, 224n35, 261.

W

"watchmaker" (metaphor), 28, 29, 29n8, 29n9.
West Semites, 96.
Wheel-model (for Khayyam), 228-233.
Wine, 109, 117, 125, 126.
Wine (metaphor-Khayyam), 215n3, 224, 225, 230, 236, 237,

240, 241, 243, 244-246, 248-250, 250n45, 251, 253, 254.
Wrangham, Richard, 16, 17.

Y

Yahweh, 90.
Yanā (vehicle, raft), 166.
Yogācara, 115, 178, 192, 200n173, 207.
Yogananda, 218n10, 223, 223n32.

Z

Zahak, 81.
Zanzibar (Rumi's metaphor for Africa), 275.
Zarreh (atom), 230, 232, 248, 250.
Zen, 140, 143, 145, 146, 154, 155, 167, 173, 187, 192, 193-197, 199, 202, 204, 207, 209, 210, 211, 215n5, 255n48, 274.
Zeus, 61, 82, 83, 89, 95, 100.
Ziusudra (king), 85.
Zoroastrian – Zoroastrianism, 80, 81, 219n13, 220.

www.ingramcontent.com/pod-product-compliance
Lightning Source LLC
Chambersburg PA
CBHW052146300426
44115CB00011B/1548